GROUND STUDIES FOR PILOTS

By the same authors:

AVIATION LAW FOR PILOTS

By H. A. Parmar:

NAVIGATION GENERAL AND
INSTRUMENTS (published
by H. & J. Parmar)

Ground Studies for Pilots

S. E. T. TAYLOR
Chief Ground Instructor
Malaysia Air Training
formerly BOAC and Chief Ground Instructor
London School of Flying

H. A. PARMAR
formerly Chief Ground Instructor
Malaysia Air Training
formerly RAF and Specialist Instructor
London School of Flying

CROSBY LOCKWOOD STAPLES
LONDON

Granada Publishing Limited

First published in Great Britain 1970 by Crosby Lockwood & Son Ltd
Reprinted 1972 by Crosby Lockwood Staples Frogmore St Albans Herts
and 3 Upper James Street London W1R 4BP

Second edition 1974, reprinted 1976

ISBN 0 258 96983 0

Contents

Preface

The prospective civilian pilot is faced at the outset of his professional career with two vital technical examinations; the first is for the Commercial Pilots' Licence (CPL) which is in the nature of a qualifier to operate at all; the second is for the Air Line Transport Pilots' Licence (ATPL), taken after some route experience, which carries certain privileges, usually an entitlement to be considered for command. In instructing students for these Licences, we have found a dearth of information available in handy form which this book seeks to remedy.

We have started from first principles and progressed to the more erudite matters, thus serving, adequately we hope, not only the ambitious youngster and the private pilot, but also the pilot actively operating on public transport aircraft.

In this volume, the Navigation subjects are covered. Aviation Law will follow separately, as it is restricted to the UK. But Meteorology is omitted entirely from our series, as 'Elementary Meteorology for Aircrew' and the 'Handbook of Aviation Meteorology', both from HMSO, are inexpensive and directed to the same purpose.

All the subjects in this book are thoroughly inter-related, and they cannot be studied in long discursive reading; frequent reference from one section to another will be needed, and occasionally simultaneous reading will help to clarify. Some exercises have been included for a preliminary application of the knowledge gleaned, but it must be stressed that speed of thought and action are very much an ingredient of the ground examinations. In an Appendix, we have noted where and how to obtain practice papers, as well as the necessary equipment.

With the prospect of the introduction of the metric system and the usage by some countries of a comma to represent the decimal point, whole numbers of 1 000 or more are written according to the latest accepted practice of a substituted space.

Finally, we should like to thank the Board of Trade, the Air Ministry, Messrs Decca, International Airadio, Smith's Instruments and Sperry for their assistance and advice when we were writing this book.

S.E.T. Taylor
H.A. Parmar

THE EARTH

1: Form of the Earth

The Earth

The Earth is not a true sphere but is flattened slightly at the poles. The more correct description of its shape may be an ellipsoid. Its Equatorial diameter of 6 884 nm exceeds its Polar diameter by about 23 nm. This flattening is known as Compression, which is merely the ratio of the difference between the two diameters to the larger diameter. Expressed in mathematical terms:

$$\text{Compression} = \frac{\text{equatorial diameter} - \text{polar diameter}}{\text{equatorial diameter}}$$

and its value approximates $\frac{1}{300}$. However, for our purposes, the Earth is a sphere.

Great Circle (G/C)

We all agree that a line which directly joins any two places on the Earth represents the shortest distance between them. Now, if we continue one end of this line in the same direction right round the Earth until it finally joins up at the other end, we find that the circle we have drawn just divides the Earth into two equal halves. Try it on an orange, keeping the knife blade at 90° to the skin. Putting the story in reverse we can state that the smaller arc of a great circle always represents the shortest distance between two places. This is all important from our point of view.

To define it, a Great Circle is a circle on the surface of the sphere whose centre is the centre of the Earth, whose radius is the radius of the Earth and which divides the Earth into two equal parts. Rather a lengthy one to learn, but know it and keep it in mind when dealing with Great Circle problems. The definition in fact tells us more about the nature of a great circle than just its contents:

(a) that only one Great Circle could be drawn through any two places – try again on an orange;

(b) but if those two places were diametrically opposite an infinite number of Great Circles could be drawn. Lines joining the two Poles are examples.

The Equator and all the lines of meridians (longitudes) are examples of Great Circles (although, technically, meridians are semi-great Circles).

Small Circle

A Small Circle stands in contrast to a Great Circle. By definition, any circle on the surface of the Earth whose centre and radius are not those of the sphere itself is a Small Circle. All latitudes (except the Equator) are Small Circles. They do not represent the shortest distance between two places.

Latitude and Longitude

A reference system in international use of which you have no doubt heard. First of all, a Great Circle is drawn round the Earth through the North and South Poles passing through Greenwich. That half of the Great Circle between the two Poles which passes through Greenwich is called the Prime or Greenwich Meridian. The other half is called the anti-Greenwich Meridian. The Greenwich meridian is labelled $0°$ and its anti-meridian, $180°$. Thus, with this E – W division established, more Great Circles in the form of meridians could be drawn, both to the east of Greenwich and to the west.

The next step is to have a datum point for N – S divisions. This is obtained by dividing the Earth by a Great Circle mid-way between the two Poles, all points on it being equidistant from the Poles. Such a Great Circle, to your surprise, is called the Equator, and labelled $0°$ Latitude. Small Circles are now drawn, parallel to the Equator, towards both poles – these are parallels of latitude.

Definition of Latitude : it is the arc of a meridian intercepted between the Equator and the reference point. It is measured in degrees, minutes and seconds, and is termed North or South according to whether the place is to the north or south of the Equator.

Definition of Longitude : longitude is the shorter arc of the Equator intercepted between the Greenwich meridian and the reference point. It is measured east or west of the Prime meridian in degrees, minutes and seconds.

It is the meridians themselves that indicate North – South direction : the parallels run East – West.

The whole network of Latitude and Longitude (also called parallels and meridians) imagined to cover the Earth is called a Graticule. Thus, on a complete graticule we would see meridians starting from Greenwich as $0°$ going right round to the East and West up to $179°59'59''$ E and $179°59'59''$ W. $180°$ is common. Similarly to N – S, we would have parallels right up to $90°$ N and S, the Poles. A degree is divided into 60 minutes, and each minute is divided into 60 seconds $(1° = 60' ; 1' = 60'')$.

And while on the subject of latitudes and longitudes, there are two more definitions you ought to be familiar with. They are : Change of Longitude and Change of Latitude.

Change of Longitude : it is the smaller arc of the Equator intercepted between the meridians of the reference points. It is named East or West according to the direction of the change.

Change of Latitude : it is the arc of the meridian intercepted between the parallels of the two places and is named North or South according to the direction of the change.

In the following sketch, if the flight was made from A to B, the ch long (change of longitude) is $2°$E; ch lat (change of latitude) is $5°$N. If the flight was from B to A, the ch long is $2°$W and ch lat $5°$S.

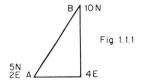

Fig. 1.1.1

Rhumb Line (R/L)

We established above that the shortest distance between any two places is along the Great Circle. This would be the ideal line (call it a "Track") to fly. However, there is this disadvantage: the Great Circle from one point to another will cross the converging meridians at different angles. Since the meridians form the basis of our track angle measurements, this would mean continuous alterations to the track angles as the flight progresses.

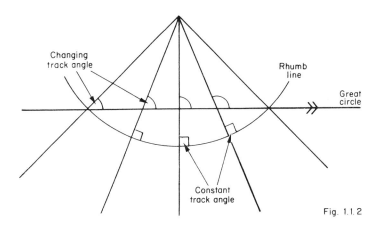

Fig. 1.1.2

Now, if a line joining the points was drawn such that it crossed each meridian at a constant angle, it must be a curve, not the shortest distance, but most convenient to follow, since alterations would not be forced on the aircraft simply to relate its direction to True North across the converging meridians on its route. Such a line is called a Rhumb Line. Definition : a Rhumb Line is a regularly curved line which cuts all the meridians at a constant angle.

Note these points :

(a)   An aircraft flying a constant track is following a Rhumb Line track. This means that it is not doing the shortest distance.

(b)   On the Earth, the meridians and the Equator are the only examples of Great Circles which are also Rhumb Lines.

(c)   Parallels of latitude are rhumb lines.

Distances on the Earth's Surface

There are three different standards of measurements – nautical mile (nm), statute mile (sm) and kilometre (km).

A nautical mile is the distance on the surface of the Earth which subtends an angle of one minute of arc at the centre of the Earth. One minute of latitude is one nautical mile, average distance of 6 080 feet, that is, when measured up a meridian. One minute of arc along a Great Circle is one nm, and therefore, one minute of longitude on the Equator is one nm. But a minute of longitude measured along any other parallel will not be a nautical mile, since parallels are Small Circles, and the meridians converge towards the Poles where they all meet absolutely.

A statute mile is 5 280 feet and is used by motorists and jockeys. A kilometre is $\frac{1}{10\,000}$ of the distance from either Pole to the Equator, 3 280 feet, and is becoming increasingly used world-wide for meteorological distances.

Finally, on this quick run over of the elementary stuff known to all except those who suffered from a classical education ("Caesar was 2 milia passuum from the cohorts of Balbus") the conversion from one to another is on the circular slide rule on the computer; and on a map or chart, a distance on the dividers taken to the latitude scale, up and down the meridians, will give the distance in nautical miles, with reservations. Apart from the above, the following are useful figures to remember :

$$
\begin{aligned}
100 \text{ nm} &= 185 \text{ km} \\
66 \text{ nm} &= 76 \text{ sm} \\
1 \text{ inch} &= 2\cdot54 \text{ cm}
\end{aligned}
$$

NAVIGATIONAL PLOTTING

1: Theory and Practice; Plotting on the Mercator Chart

If you wish to fly from one place to another, the first step is to join these places on the topographical map, marking this line with two arrows to show the direction of flight. This is your Track, and since it refers entirely to movement over the Earth's surface, the speed you go along a Track is not unnaturally called Ground Speed.

In flying, the wind speed, and the direction from which it blows, will affect the aircraft's movement: speed from a given direction being defined as velocity, the Wind Velocity will affect the aircraft's speed as well as Drift it from the direction which its nose is pointing to. Thus, if an aircraft has an Airspeed, and is set on a Heading, the W/V will act on it, resulting in a Track and Ground Speed.

Say your destination is due North of the departure point: the Track is 000° or 360°, angles always being measured from 000° all the way round to 000°, or 360° again; due East is 090°, due South 180°, and so on, always measured to the nearest degree. A wind from the West will clearly blow the aircraft off its Northerly Heading towards the East: so to keep on a Northerly Track would mean heading the aircraft to the West of North, the amount depending on the wind speed and the aircraft speed. This amount, measured from the Heading is called the Drift.

The exact solution of this triangle of Velocities:

Heading and Airspeed
Wind direction and Wind Speed
Track and Ground Speed

is of vital importance to the pilot. Knowing any four of the six ingredients, he can readily find the other two. We will do it from the basic triangle first, addressing ourselves to the problem as it faces a pilot preparing for a flight from:

NORTHAMPTON (SYWELL)   5218N 0047W
                to
CARLISLE (CROSBY)   5456N 0248W

Remark how place names are always in capitals, and the ° and ' signs are usually omitted when written by hand to avoid misinterpretation or ambiguity.

The Track is 335 True, True because we are referring to the True North Pole, and the protractor has been set on the chart with the True North arrow pointing precisely up the meridian through SYWELL. The Met man tells us that the W/V at the height we wish to fly is 270/40, i.e. the wind is blowing <u>from</u> due West at a speed of 40 knots (we always work in knots, nautical miles per hour). The aircraft we are using has a True Airspeed of 120 kt — more about the True bit later — irrespective of any forces acting on it, its speed through the air is 120 kt. We can now construct a Triangle of Velocities, to some suitable scale to find the two unknowns — the Heading of the aircraft, and its Ground Speed:

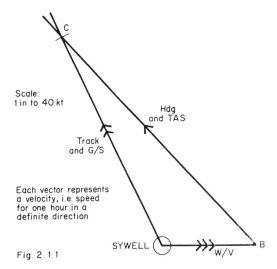

Fig. 2.1.1

Lay in the Track of 335. Lay in the Wind from 270, for 40 kt to B. With Centre B, and radius 120 kt, i.e. 3 inches strike an arc on the Track at C. Join BC.

BC is the Heading True of the aircraft – 318.

SYWELL to C measures 98 kt to scale – the G/S. All done – and note the arrows for Wind direction (3 of them) for Heading (1) and these two sets follow each other always.

That is the pre-flight case. Now consider a situation in flight, where the aircraft's heading is known, its True Airspeed is known, the W/V is known, and an idea of its Track and G/S is required: Heading 170(T), TAS 120 kt, W/V 220/20 – the terminology is self-explanatory.

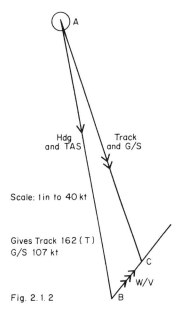

Fig. 2.1.2

Or another case, in flight, with the aircraft on a definite Heading at its TAS, finds its Track and G/S by the pilot's skilful map reading and facile calculations: Heading 083(T), TAS 120 kt, Track 098, G/S 130 kt, what's the W/V?

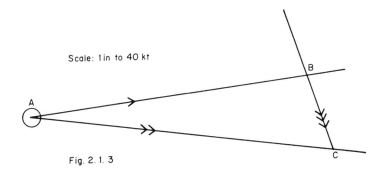

Scale: 1 in to 40 kt

Fig. 2.1.3

The W/V is 342/35, and the pilot now has an up to date W/V for immediate use.

All these problems are done to vector scale, and the solution to any problem can readily be found, e.g. for a given TAS and W/V, state and show by means of a diagram, whether the greater drift will be experienced when wind direction is at right angles to Track, or at right angles to Heading.

Assume:

(a) TAS 120 kt, W/V 240/40 Hdg 330(T)
(b) TAS 120 kt, W/V 240/40 Track 330(T)

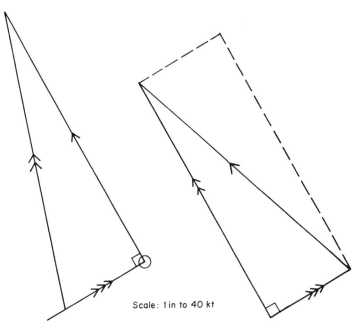

Scale: 1 in to 40 kt

(a) 18° Starboard drift, i.e. Track 348   (b) Drift 20 S, i.e. Heading 310

Fig. 2.1.4

The drift is to starboard (that is, to the right of Heading) in each case. Greater drift is experienced when the W/V is at right angles to Track. In this case, the aircraft has had to turn its nose into the wind in order to maintain the required Track; in so doing, the G/S is reduced, thereby contributing to an increased drift. But in the second case with the W/V at right angles to Heading, the aircraft is simply being blown on to a Track which is not necessarily the required one. The difference in drift between the two cases is quite small.

It is commonplace to compare G/S with TAS by referring to a Headwind or a Tailwind component, always applied to the TAS. In (a) above, TAS 120 kt, G/S 127 kt, the tailwind component is 7 kt. In (b) above, a G/S of 113 kt gives a Headwind comp of 7 kt.

A further example:

When flying along a Track of 090(T), the drift is 16°S, and the wind component (i.e. difference between TAS and G/S) is zero.

(a)   What is wind direction?

(b)   Estimate TAS if wind strength is 80 kt.

Proceed as follows:

Draw from a point A the Track 090(T)

Drift is 16S, Heading must be 074(T)

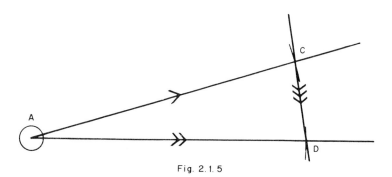

Fig. 2.1.5

With centre A and any convenient radius, strike off arcs C and D,

i.e. TAS = G/S = zero wind component.

Join CD and measure wind direction 350(T), and check the rules that Hdg and wind arrows follow each other.

Measure CD. That distance = 80 kt and say it is actually $\frac{7}{8}$ in. Return to vector scale. Measure AC, say $3\frac{1}{8}$ in. = TAS.

Thus, by simple arithmetic:

$$\frac{25}{8} \div \frac{7}{8} \times 80 = 286 \text{ kt} = \text{TAS}$$

Once you settle down to flying for an airline, it is highly unlikely you will ever consider the triangle of velocities again: the solution to all the problems associated with it is done rapidly on the navigational computer, on the reverse of which is a circular slide rule which copes at once with times, speeds, distances, conversions, TAS, altitudes. You've bought one — if not, get cracking now — and be sure you have the explanatory tables that go with it. And to start with, why not check the above examples on the computer now?

Chart Work

You can now proceed to navigate on a suitable chart: the hoary old favourite is the Mercator chart, on which latitude and longitude lines are straight lines at right angles to each other. So get out the GSGS 1938, all your navigational tools at the ready, and while it may be necessary within the confines of this slender volume to be repetitive, it will all help when delving deeper into map construction.

Briefly, unlike the meridians on the Earth, which are semi-great circles meeting at the Poles (a Great Circle is a circle on the Earth's surface whose plane passes through the Earth's centre), the meridians on the Mercator appear as straight lines parallel to, and equidistant from each other. Unlike the parallels on the Earth, which are Small Circles whose planes are parallel to the plane of the Equator, the parallels on the Mercator appear as straight lines, parallel to each other all right, but increasing in distance apart towards the Poles.

This is the penalty for trying to spread part of a spherical surface into a workable plane surface. The full story is in the section Navigation General, but for the creative activity you are about to embark on, mark the following important properties:

(i) A straight line drawn anywhere on the chart cuts all meridians at the same angle.

(ii) One minute (1') of latitude, up the side, represents one nautical mile in that area. Take your dividers, set them up the side or Latitude Scale between 5210N and 5240N. That represents 30 nm in the area roughly 5200N and 5300N. Keep that divider distance, and set one point on 5500N: up the scale it shows 28 nm. So you must always measure distance in the mean area of the line you are dealing with.

(iii) The longitude scale is constant, and measures longitude East or West of the Greenwich meridian and that's all.

So, if an aircraft is to go from WATTISHAM to MANCHESTER:

WATTISHAM   is Lat   5208N (of the Equator)
Long 0057E (of the Greenwich Meridian)
MANCHESTER is Lat   5320N
Long 0216W

Plot in the places carefully on the chart, using a protractor for precision: circle each point, the symbol for a Fix (a known position), and join them up, putting the two arrows on the line, about a third of the way along, to indicate the Track you wish to follow over the Earth's surface.

To measure the Track Angle

Slap the centre of the protractor exactly over the point of WATTISHAM, with the North pointer due North, and the grid of the protractor exactly lined up with the grid of the chart. The Track measures 302(T) and never try to read half degrees.

To measure the distance

The latitude scale will be used, at about the mid-part of the Track. A satisfactory span here would be from 5230N to 5300N, representing 30 nautical miles; having selected this, you must keep to it for the whole Track: do *not* try to be terribly clever and measure the odd bit over at say 5210N. Take the mean 30 nm span, move it over the Track from WATTISHAM to MANCHESTER – 4 times and a bit over: the bit measured at 5230N is 18 nm.

The distance then is 138 nm.

To find the Estimated Flight Time

On the circular slide rule, at a G/S of 330 kt, for example, the time to fly this distance (138 nm) would be 25 minutes. An elementary flight plan is on its way, but let's consolidate the fundamentals first. Plot the following positions, and in each case find the Track and distance.

 (i) Posn A 5220N 0531W to Posn B 5517N 0531W
       (Track is 360(T), and the distance can be a simple subtraction
       of 5220 from 5517 = 177 minutes of latitude = 177 nm)

 (ii) Posn C 5410N 0450W to Posn D 5410N 0210W
       (Track is 090(T), and the distance will be taken from a 40 nm
       span covering 20 nm each side of 5410N = 95 nm)
       You put in the Track arrows, I s'pose?

 (iii) Posn F 5451N 0502W to Posn G 5545N 0102E
       (Track is 075(T), distance 215 nm. Span here say 50 nm across
       the Track on the 0200W meridian)

Now to the circular slide rule: how long to fly each of these Tracks at a G/S of 280 kt? (38 minutes; 20 minutes; 46 minutes). And if in actual flight you did:

       A to B in 40 minutes
       C to D in 24 minutes
       F to G in 42 minutes

What was the actual G/S in each case? (265 kt, 237 kt, 306 kt).

The Tracks you have drawn are Rhumb lines, which cross each meridian at the same angle, easing the navigation of the trip. The shortest distance between any two points though is the Great circle, which appears on the Mercator chart as a curve concave to the Equator. We shall look into this matter fully ere long.

To find Heading and Ground Speed

Back to WATTISHAM – MANCHESTER, Track 302(T), distance 138 nm. Using a TAS of 240 kt, W/V 240/45, follow computer instructions to find the a/c's Heading and its G/S (292(T), 216 kt). The estimated flight time is solved as 38 minutes from the circular slide rule, and if one left WATTISHAM at 1215 hrs GMT (always work in GMT, even down under), the Estimated Time of Arrival, the ETA, is 1253 hrs.

Thus, the basic flight plan data for the trip is known, and we can soar into the air and navigate.

The Track is in already; at WATTISHAM, mark in the actual time of departure, the ATD, as 1217; plot in the a/c's True Heading 292(T), inserting the one arrow symbol. The Air Plot has been started, consisting of the Heading along which only TAS can be measured; the Air Plot, the Heading, can only be started from a Fix, the name given to a position known for sure. This we have done.

Flying this Heading, we pass over PETERBOROUGH (5235N 0015W) at 1230 hrs precisely. Plot the position, as a small circled dot; it is a Pinpoint, the name given to a Fix obtained by visual observation of the ground; append the time 1230 to the symbol.

Now a Fix is wasted unless it is used to find some current information for the purpose of the flight; the uses are various, such as to find the W/V, check the G/S, amend the ETA, restart the Air plot (i.e. plotting the Heading one is on <u>at that time</u> from the Fix so that all information found henceforth is up to date), alter Heading to keep to the required Track to destination, and so on.

We will proceed first to find the W/V; there are two methods.

Method 1: To find the W/V by Track and G/S

The Heading and TAS we know to be 292(T), 240 kt. The Track we have made good, the TMG, is still 302, i.e. the drift is still 10S.

The distance from WATTISHAM to PETERBOROUGH is 51 nm, and this has taken 13 minutes, giving a G/S of 235 kt. So from the computer with this information, the wind is:

213/42 (Tr and G/S)

The method of solution often put in brackets after the value, though it's in no way obligatory.

Method 2: To find the W/V by Air Plot

Measure along the Heading a distance of 52 nm flown in 13 minutes at a TAS of 240 kt, and mark with a '+' symbol for Air Position, with the time 1230.

Join the Air Position to the Fix for the same time 1230; this is the wind which has affected the a/c for the 13 minutes of flight.

Wind blows from air to ground in this horizontal relationship; this case measures 209(T), and the line is marked with 3 arrows pointing in the direction to which it is blowing. The distance is just over 9 nm, and since this effect has taken 13 minutes, the wind speed is 42 kt. We have then a W/V:

209/42 (Air Plot)

and the slight discrepancy from the previous solution arises from fractional differences; the protractor is not guaranteed accurate to $\frac{1}{2}°$, and a W/V found over a period of less than 20 minutes magnifies small errors.

Having found the W/V, the next step is to put it to good use. The Fix is nicely on Track, yet the W/V found is different from forecast, so the Heading, G/S and ETA must be checked as a matter of routine.

Restart the Air Plot from the 1230 Fix, in other words plot in the Heading of 292(T). While the pinpointing, plotting and wind finding was going on, so was the aircraft; it is customary to plan alterations of Heading and its associated G/S, distance, time and ETA adjustments 6, 9, 12 or 15 minutes ahead of the Fix, depending on the speed of work and the time some Fixes take to obtain. These time intervals allow calculations to be done mentally, as they are simple proportions of an hour. The sample we are working on is but a few moments' task, so 6 minutes will suffice.

From the 1230 Fix, along the Heading just drawn, mark the Air Position at 1236, i.e. 24 nm (6 minutes at TAS 240 kt) in the accepted fashion. From this Air Position, lay off 6 minutes of W/V 209/42, i.e. 209/04.

This is the Dead Reckoning position, short for Deduced Reckoning, a term used by the sailor boys, I think: referred to as the DR Position, and the precise dot of the position enclosed by a triangle: where you think you are, or hope you are at 1236.

Join this DR Position to MANCHESTER: this is the new Track required. It happens to be 302(T) still, and the distance is 62 nm (measured, of course, with a span of 20 nm across the 5300N parallel).

On the computer then:

    Track 302(T)
    TAS   240 kt
    W/V 209/42

We find the Heading to steer will be 292(T), G/S 239 kt and on the slide rule time $15\frac{1}{2}$ minutes, call it 16 minutes and ETA 1252. Check.

So although the G/S and ETA are the only changes, a comforting routine check of the progress of the trip has been made. Now plot in <u>from the 1236 Air Position</u> the Heading 292. From now on, the voyage is up to date as though it had all started <u>from the 1230 Fix.</u>

As a rider here, in actual flight, one would call this W/V 210/40. All winds are mean, they just do not blow for a period of time as a steady blast from a given direction.

Continuing our trip, tuning in to MANCHESTER on the Radio Compass, one can Home on without further worry. The *nose* of the aircraft on this instrument is 000, the tail 180, the exact starboard (right) beam 090, the exact port (left) beam 270, and so on. There is no reference to True North, or geographical direction, whatever, only a bearing relative to the aircraft's head. Thus, on MANCHESTER, nose 000, the 10° starboard drift we hope for will be proved by the needle pointing to 010 on the radio compass, steady, and all is well.

Your plot looks like this:

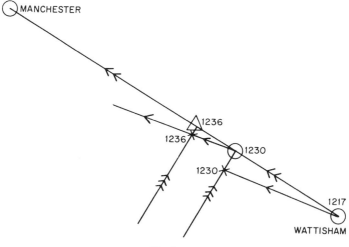

Fig. 2. 1. 6

Keeping an Air Plot going

Of course, one can fly a series of Headings, and keep a plot of them: the Air Plot must start or restart from a Fix, and all information required will relate in time from that Fix; all alterations of Heading will be from Air Positions.

Here's a practice run, the story on the right hand side: various accepted abbreviations are introduced, mostly self-evident, but all in the Glossary anyway.

0818 Posn A 5442N 0415W set Hdg 194(T)   20 min at 220 kt
     TAS 220 kt   = 73 nm
0838 A/H 230(T)   7 min at 220 kt
0845 A/H 175(T)   = 26 nm
0850 PP 5313N 0430W   5 min at 220 kt
                                          = 18 nm
                              Join Air Position
                                   to Fix
                              W/D is 240
                              W/E is 32 nm for
                                    32 min

(a) What mean W/V has been experienced?   ∴ (a) 240/60
                              Restart Air Plot at
                              0850 Fix

0901 A/H 088(T)   11 min along 175(T)
                              at 220 kt = 40 nm
0911 A/H for Posn B 5345N 0010E   At 0901, plot 088(T)
                              for 10 min at 220 kt
(b) What is DR Position at 0911?   = 37 nm
(c) Give Hdg(T) and ETA Posn B.   At 0911, lay off W/E
                              for 21 min = 240/21
                              ∴ (b) 5245N 0255W
It all looks like this: Join DR Posn to B.
                              Track required 061(T)
                              Distance 126 nm
                              So with W/V 240/60,
                              TAS 220 kt
                                (c) Hdg 061(T)
                              G/S 280 kt, time 27
                              min ∴ ETA 0938

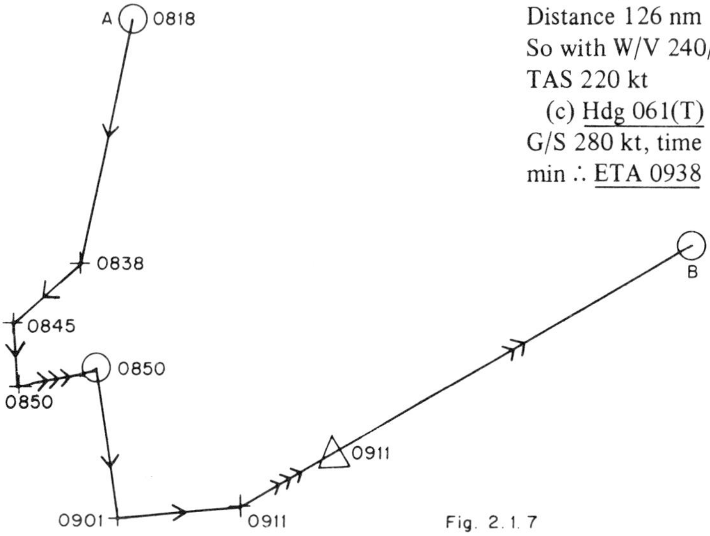

Fig. 2.1.7

Headings True, Magnetic and Compass

A fuller story of these cheerful differences is given in the appropriate chapter, but now consider them from a simple and practical viewpoint.

The True North Pole is a pointer for all plotting, the meridians of longitude converging there. The Magnetic Pole is some hundreds of miles from the True North, and it is the Magnetic North Pole which is of value to the airman, since a freely suspended magnet will point to it. This magnet is the compass needle, which is used in one form of another to indicate direction to the pilot in his aircraft, in the clear or cloud, by day or night.

To be brief, and to avoid the theory for the moment, at any spot on the Earth's surface, the Magnetic direction varies from the True, and this Variation is measured as a number of degrees E or W of the True North Pole, e.g., a perfect magnet, freely suspended, might point to a position 5°W of the True North Pole. On the chart in front of you, you will find that all places of equal magnetic variation are joined by lines called Isogonals, and the value of the variation printed on each. You will notice that a date is also given, for the Magnetic Pole adds to the confusion by moving round the True North Pole in a clockwise direction at the rate of about one cycle every 960 years. The annual amount of the change of value of local variation is noted on the Chart in the bottom left hand corner, 7'E. Thus, for a place where variation is "10W 1961", in 1970 the variation would be 9 x 7'E = 1°03'E, lessening the 10W variation by 1° to 9W for our purpose.

An additional complication for the pilot is the fact that he is using a sensitive compass needle housed in a metallic box of tricks called an aeroplane, chockful of electrical and radio gear, all of which affect his particular compass, and give it an error one side or the other of the Magnetic North. This error is called Deviation, and is labelled E or W of the <u>Magnetic</u> North Pole. Remember that it is the deviation of one particular compass in one particular aeroplane, and the deviation will have been found and recorded on a card beside the compass.

Examine Figs. 2.1.8 and 2.1.9, opposite.

And the rule:

Start at the compass, move towards Magnetic, thence to True, then W is minus, and E is plus.

The examples would read:

C	D	M	V	T
071	6W	065	15E	080
270	10W	260	20W	240

Cadbury's Dairy Milk Very Tasty. You fly Compass, you plot True.

True Airspeed (TAS), Rectified Airspeed (RAS), Indicated Airspeed (IAS)

The Airspeed on the dial of the instrument on the panel is the Indicated Airspeed: correct this for any error caused by the peculiarities of the aircraft or of the particular instrument itself (usually again from a card nearby, and the correction varies with speed), and we get the Rectified Airspeed.

Now the thing is ploughing through the air which is very very variable in density due to changing temperatures and pressures, and it cannot cope:

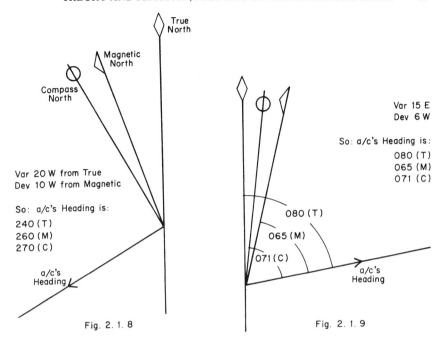

True North

Magnetic North

Compass North

Var 20 W from True
Dev 10 W from Magnetic

So: a/c's Heading is:

240 (T)
260 (M)
270 (C)

a/c's Heading

Fig. 2. 1. 8

Var 15 E
Dev 6 W

So: a/c's Heading is:

080 (T)
065 (M)
071 (C)

080 (T)

065 (M)

071 (C)

a/c's Heading

Fig. 2. 1. 9

so a correction must be made to allow as much as possible for the conditions the aircraft is flying in. This is done from a window in the circular slide rule or from a graph in many modern aeroplanes; this correction of height and temperature to RAS gives the TAS, the actual speed the a/c is making through the air, of vital significance in navigation plotting, to say nothing of cruise control. An example or two:

60 000 ft altitude, Temp $-60°C$, RAS 100 kt gives TAS 315 kt
10 000 ft altitude, Temp $-10°C$, RAS 100 kt gives TAS 114 kt

Navigation on the Climb

Actually, this is mainly of academic interest: the pilot keeps an eye on the radio instruments as a check, but the first real Fix is wanted on levelling-off, check the level TAS, find after a little time the W/V, find out how the forecast wind compares and so on. BUT, the wind blowing at expected levelling altitude will be different from the mean W/V experienced on the climb, so the Heading to hold to keep to Track must be flight-planned, and the first Fix obtained either on the way up or on levelling off is of value only for checking position in relation to the Track required. A found W/V would be very mean indeed, and pretty futile for navigational use. So keep the Air Plot going, always, until good level fixes are obtained, and useful indicative W/Vs can be found for use in the next leg, or part of a leg. And don't forget, however sophisticated one's departure from an aerodrome using radio aids, though you may be keeping to Track, constant checking is vital.

The method is not at all difficult, and can be used before and in flight. As an example, a climb from 1 000 ft to 17 000 ft gives a mean altitude of 9 000 ft; this is found by adding the lower altitude to the upper and then dividing by 2, though there's nothing to prevent the rational way of 17 000 − 1 000 = 16 000, divide by 2 = 8 000, and as the climb began at 1 000 ft, then the mean is 9 000 ft. Taking this mean altitude, where the Temp is say −10°C, and offering a constant climb RAS of 180 kt, the mean climb TAS is readily solved as 202 kt. This is quite adequate for the flight plan, and in flight too if required.

Try a plot question on the Mercator to clinch the deal, step by step:

0900 Posn 5217N 0528W S/H 013(T), 1 000 ft, climbing

Forecast 2 000 ft W/V 250/35 Temp + 5°C

5 000 ft W/V 265/50 Temp −1°C

10 000 ft W/V 270/60 Temp −11°C

15 000 ft W/V 285/60 Temp −21°C

RAS 167 kt for the climb

0936 Level 13 000 ft, RAS 190 kt

Give DR position at 0951.

The mean altitude is 7 000 ft, and the Temp at 7 000 ft is −5°C by interpolation; climb TAS is therefore 182 kt. Plot the Hdg 013(T) for 36 min at this TAS = 109 nm, and mark this Air position with symbol and time as usual. Solve the level TAS, 13 000 ft, RAS 190 kt, Temp −17°C = 227 kt

From the 0936 Air position, continue the Hdg 013(T) for 15 min at 227 kt = 57 nm, and mark it as 0951.

The W/Vs experienced so far are:

36 min of climb W/V meaned at 7 000 ft 267/54

15 min of level W/V at 13 000 ft   279/60

So at the 0951 Air position, plot the W/E for the climb 267/32 and from the end of this line, add the W/E for the period of level flight 279/15.

This is the DR position 5458N 0305W and the plot looks like this:

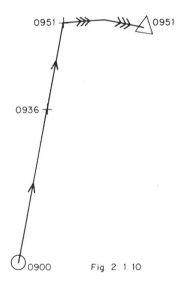

Fig. 2.1.10

Being of an enquiring mind, you will have asked yourself why not work out climb Track at climb G/S for 36 min, and level Track at level G/S for 15 min and arrive at once at the DR position. In a simple case like this, the answer will be correct, but the Air Plot hasn't kept going, breaking the fundamental rule of plotting the known factors of Hdg and TAS at all times.

As you're in the mood, try this:

1230 Position A 5210N 0550W, Heading 350(T), 3 000 ft Temp −3°C
        climbing to 17 000 ft at a constant RAS 148 kt, mean W/V 320/30
1248 Level 17 000 ft, Temp −29°C, RAS 180 kt, W/V 290/45 A/H 050 (T)
1308 A/H to return to Posn A
    (a) Give the DR position at 1308
    (b) What is Hdg(T) and ETA posn A?
Answer: (a) 5336N 0355W
             (b) 230(T), ETA 1340

Position Lines

Having mastered the elementary rules of plotting, it is necessary now to address ourselves to the problem of how to get a Fix. So far, we have been served only by Pinpoints, picked up by identifying a spot on the ground and transferring its Lat and Long to the chart.

A Position Line is the line on the chart, straight or curved, on which the aircraft is known to be, or to have been, at a particular time. Should an a/c cross a railway line, then its ground position is somewhere along the railway at the time of crossing; another bearing from some other location at the precise time of crossing would fix the a/c's position at the point of intersection of the two position lines.

The commonest way of obtaining a position line (P/L) is by radio compass. Bearing in mind that the nose of the a/c is 360°, an a/c tuned in to a radio station might read an angle of 283°, say, and this angle is relative to the a/c's Heading. If the relative bearing is added to the a/c's Heading, then the bearing from True North is found; the reciprocal, or 180° different, can be plotted from the station, whose position is of course known. Here's an example, with the face of the radio compass enlarged:

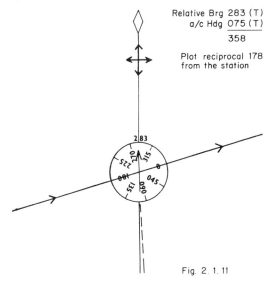

Relative Brg 283 (T)
a/c Hdg 075 (T)
358
Plot reciprocal 178
from the station

Fig. 2. 1. 11

Consider the case of an a/c passing North of a radio station on a Heading 270(T), making good or hoping to make good a Track of 260(T).

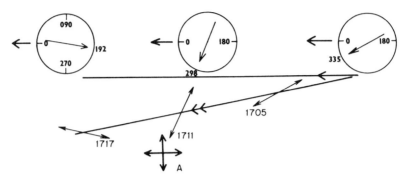

Fig. 2. 1. 12

1705 Bearing Relative of A 335
1711 Bearing Relative of A 298
1717 Bearing Relative of A 192

The bearings are relative to the nose of the aircraft, i.e. its Heading(T), and the working looks like this:

	1705	1711	1717	
Brg Rel	335	298	192	You can always
Hdg(T)	270	270	270	subtract 360–
	605	568	462	you are only
	−360	−360	−360	going round the
Brg(T)	245	208	102	clock again.
Plot	065	Plot 028	Plot 282	

Imagine now that the radio station moves in the same direction at the same speed for the same time as the aircraft, i.e. at its Track and G/S, then the first two P/Ls could be placed at 1717, and the P/Ls would be <u>transferred</u> as though the station had stayed with the aircraft. Thus, the P/Ls are transferred along the Track to produce what is strangely enough called a Running Fix, with the P/Ls emanating from the same station abeam of the Track.

The example above would be calculated as follows for a G/S of say 200 kt
the 1705 P/L could be transferred for 12 minutes – 40 nm
the 1711 P/L could be transferred for 6 minutes – 20 nm
along the track. Where they all cross will give a Fix, and despite any incorrect assumptions about the track and G/S, the Fix will be reasonable if not perfect.
Thus

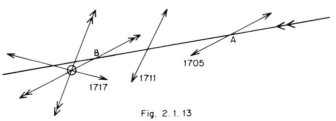

Fig. 2. 1. 13

A transferred P/L is symbolised by double-arrowed ends, and is untimed: the distance A 1705 to B 1717, the transfer point, is the 40 miles referred to, and the 1705 P/L is simply paralleled through this point with the protractor. The Fix at 1717 may not be so clear cut, and could have the following appearance.

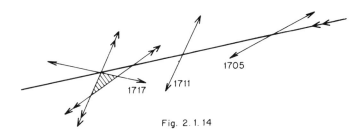

Fig. 2.1.14

The shaded area is called a Cocked Hat, and while it would cause some dubiety about its accuracy, it's better, far better, than no Fix at all. The centre of the cocked hat is taken as the Fix: theoretically bisect each angle of the triangle, and the intersection of the bisectors gives the Fix. In practice, point the Fix visually, but if it's a large cocked hat, don't call it a Fix but an MPP, a Most Probable Position, so that when a reliable accurate Fix does come along you know to what extent to pin your faith on W/V and G/S found.

A P/L that cuts Track at right angles, or very nearly so, can be used to check G/S, and that G/S used for the transfer of P/Ls at the time: you would have to be well off the Track you thought you were making good to have a really appreciable error.

A P/L that is parallel to the required Track indicates the distance off; and should you know the distance flown from the last Fix, the Track Made Good (TMG), can be fairly established.

A steady back-bearing from a departure point, or from a station which the aircraft has recently passed overhead, will indicate TMG, and in fact that is a common method of departure from aerodromes

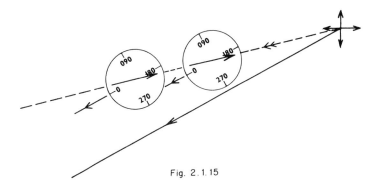

Fig. 2.1.15

All straightforward practical stuff. A P/L can be circular, such as the distance from a station registered on the Distance Measuring Equipment (DME) dial on the panel. To transfer one of these, transfer the origin at the same Track angle at the same G/S for the required time, and replot the P/L from the new centre viz:

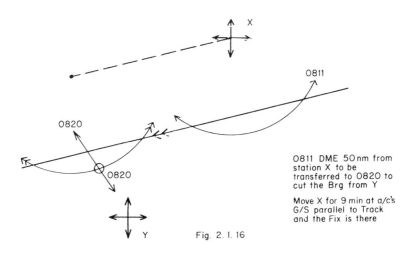

0811 DME 50 nm from station X to be transferred to 0820 to cut the Brg from Y

Move X for 9 min at a/c's G/S parallel to Track and the Fix is there

Fig. 2. 1. 16

Conditions will arise when a decision may have to be taken as to which part of the arc is the correct one; invariably the DR G/S will give the clue.

Transferred P/Ls along the Air Plot

P/Ls can be transferred along the Air Plot when one does not know the Track or is highly suspicious of it, making the G/S a matter of guesswork. The topic is of academic interest, but sufficiently simple to be worth knowing. The odds against using it in the air are enormous.

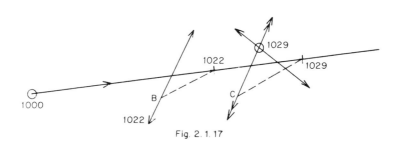

Fig. 2. 1. 17

Join 1022 Air Position to any point B to give a convenient vector of 22 units, the minutes flown since the last Fix. At Air Position 1029, parallel this line for 29 units to a point C. Transfer the P/L through C.

It matters not at all which direction the 1022 vector is taken; the parallel at C to scale will give the correct transfer.

Radio Position Lines

This type is in constant use. They are often plotted on special charts which already have numbered series overlaid, so that having obtained a reading on a particular aid, it can be plotted at once by visual interpolation near the Track. Here for the moment we will concern ourselves with the simple types to be plotted on the Mercator chart before us.

Yet another problem now rears its head; all radio waves follow the shortest route over the Earth's surface, that is, they are Great Circles, and would appear on the Mercator as curves, impossible to plot. A G/C must be converted in consequence into a R/L, using a well-worn factor called the Conversion Angle.

Consider this example:

An a/c on Hdg 330(T) obtains a relative bearing of station A of 268. The measuring is done in the aircraft.

Brg Rel	268	
Hdg(T)	330	
	598	
	−360	
Brg(T)	238	G/C see diagram
CA	− 2	for example
Brg(T)	236	R/L
Plot	056	reciprocal from the station

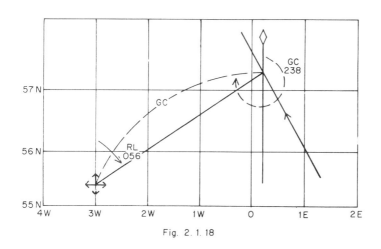

Fig. 2. 1. 18

It can be seen that:

    (i)   The work of measuring has been done in the a/c, the angle 268 relative, G/C.

    (ii)   The Rhumb Line bearing from True North must be less than the Great Circle bearing from True North.

    (iii)   The conversion angle depends on the change of longitude between the a/c and the station at the time of taking the bearing.

½° are ignored, and the CA can be read off the ABAC scale in the top corner of the chart.

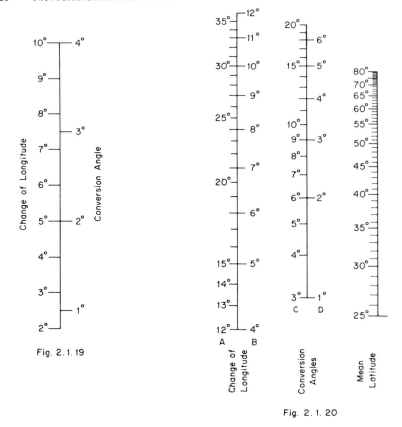

Fig. 2.1.19

Fig. 2.1.20

Fig.19 shows the very basic type on the Mercator GSGS1938 as used in the CPL examination. Fig. 20 gives the operational ABAC scale as used in flying practice; if scale A is used for change of longitude, read off CA on scale C; if scale B is used ditto read off CA on scale D. A ruler is placed across. The ABAC scale solves graphically the formula for conversion angle

CA = ½ ch long x sin mean lat

We've never known anyone carry log tables in the air, nor have we ever known an airman who can roll off the sine of any angle from memory; it was different on ships, perhaps, but on aeroplanes the time is rather short in which to work out the stuff.

A ch long of 0 will give a CA of 0, since the a/c is on the same meridian or so as the station, and a meridian is both a G/C and a R/L.

Consider now an a/c taking a bearing on a station on the a/c's Easterly side:

Brg Rel	123	
Hdg(T)	330	
	453	
	−360	
Brg(T)	093	G/C
CA	+ 2	for example
Brg(T)	095	R/L
Plot	275	from the station

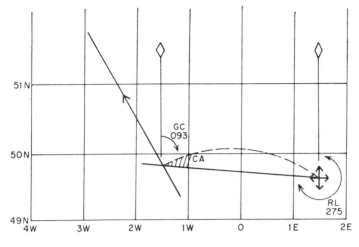

Fig. 2. 1. 21

The CA in this case is added; the rule is apply the CA towards 180, that is if the bearing is more than 180, subtract CA, add if less. The diagram will help in clarifying the rule, but always ask yourself who is doing the work and apply the CA to the angle measured. In the example, the angle of 093 was measured in the a/c, and this is the figure to convert; thence proceed to plot from the known station.

This is the rule in the Northern hemisphere. In the Southern, apply away from 180, subtracting if less than 180, adding if more.

Here is the same example down South, CA now −2, illustrated as follows:

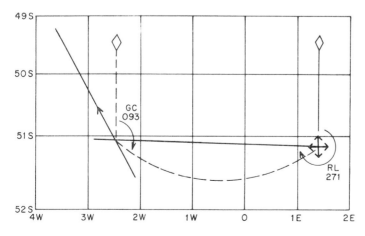

Fig. 2. 1. 22

Plotting radio bearings given by a station

A radio station can give you:

> QTE "your bearing True from me is ...."
> QDM "your Hdg(M) to reach me with zero wind is ...."
> QDR "your bearing(M) from me is .... "

These are the commonest ones, and the station can give them to an a/c either verbally on the R/T, or the signal can be picked up automatically and read off a dial on the panel. Remember though that the station has sent out the signal, and all the work of measurement has been done on the ground; no part of the work has been done in the a/c. So we must concern ourselves only with the station and the signal or bearing that emanated therefrom. To get the R/L bearing, we must get to the station first, get rid of the Variation, if applicable, which is noted there, and apply the CA to the G/C bearing from it.

For example: VOR gives QDM   244

Var	10W	at the station
G/C	234(T)	received in the a/c
	180	
G/C	054	station sent out
CA	+ 2	say
R/L	056	which plot

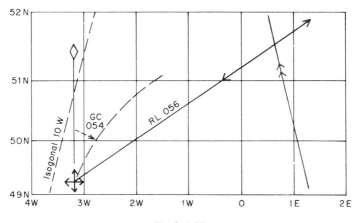

Fig. 2. 1. 23

It's the station that's done the work. The same rules about the application of CA towards 180 in the Northern hemisphere, away from 180 in the Southern, hold good, but get what the station measured True first.

Try this little exercise:

0316 DR Position 5340N 0140W, Hdg 334(T), RAS 130 kt, flight level 8 500 ft, Temp −10°C, W/V 030/40

0326 NDB in position 5430N 0040E bears 101 relative

0331 VOR in position 5500N 0500W QDM 307

0337 NDB in position 5540N 0210W bears 043 relative

Give the a/c's position at 0337.

Check your working, and flagellate yourself if you fell into any of the traps like setting Hdg from a DR position, like not reading drift at once off your computer to find the Track from a given Heading, with no fiddling.

TAS 200 kt, Track 324(T), G/S 180 kt

0326		0331		0337	
Brg Rel	101	QDM	307	Brg Rel	043
Hdg(T)	334	Var	11W at the stn	Hdg(T)	334
	435		296(T)		377
	−360	Recip	116		−360
Brg(T)	075 G/C	CA	+ 1	Brg(T)	017 G/C
CA	+ 1	Plot	117	CA	0
Brg(T)	076 R/L			Brg(T)	017 R/L
Plot	256			Plot	197

Transfer 0326 P/L for 11 min at G/S 180 = 33 nm
Transfer 0331 P/L for 6 min at G/S 180 = 18 nm
The Fix at the crossing of the three P/Ls is 5432N 0246W

This method of setting out helps to check the point of application of CA; the first and last bearings were actually measured in the aircraft, while the middle one was a dial reading of a particular signal lined up at the station.

That's about it for plotting on the Mercator; here is a paper to work through to consolidate the essentials.

Chart GSGS 1938, and use variation for the year of the chart.

Question 1
0910 Position A 5310N 0550W S/H 025(T), RAS 165 kt, F/L 12 000 ft,
       Temp −15°C. Forecast W/V 340/35. The following bearings are
       obtained from a station in position 5540N 0420W
                     0955 QTE 151
                     1003 QTE 123
                     1011 QTE 095
       (a) Give the position at 1011.
       (b) What mean W/V has been experienced since 0910?
1017 A/H for Position B 5600N 0300E
       (c) What is DR position at 1017?
       (d) Give Hdg(M) and ETA position B. (Use mean Variation)

Question 2
1120 DR position 5450N 0220W, Hdg 026(T), TAS 180 kt,
       forecast W/V 320/45.
1123 NDB at position C 5330N 0100W bears 138 relative by radio compass.
1129 NDB in position B 5531N 0000 bears 047 relative by radio compass
       Give the position at 1129.
Question 3
1210 VOR position C 5330N 0100W S/H 005(T), TAS 180 kt. Subsequently
       VOR equipment tuned to C indicates a steady QDM 204
1240 VOR position D 5457N 0040E QDM 114
       What is W/V?

Question 4

1325 Position D 5457N 0040E S/H 160(M), 1 500 ft climbing to 11 500 ft at RAS 145 kt, mean Temp for climb 0°C, mean W/V for climb 230/25.

1345 Level 11 500 ft, Temp −11°C, RAS 160 kt, W/V 255/40 A/H 180(M)
     Give the DR position at 1405.

Question 5

1500 Position E 5200N 0100E S/H 290(M), TAS 180 kt, forecast W/V 050/30

1528 A/H 335(M)

1550 A/H 240(M)
     What is DR position at 1612?

Question 6

     Hdg 295(C), deviation 2W, variation 6E, RAS 150 kt, flight level 12 500 ft, Temp −10°C.

     The aircraft flies a distance of 260 km in 43 min making good a Track of 292(T).

     What is the W/V?

Answers

  1 TAS 194 kt, Track 034(T), G/S 170 kt.
     Plot QTEs direct from station, CA 0 in each case.
     Transfer 0955 P/L for 16 min at G/S 170 kt = 45 nm.
     Transfer 1003 P/L for 8 min at G/S 170 kt = 22 nm
     (a) Fix 5536N 0255W
     TMG 035 ∴ drift 10S
     178 nm in 61 min = G/S 175 kt
     (b) 330/38 (Tr and G/S)
     Plot Hdg 025(T) from Fix for 6 min at TAS 194 kt = 19 nm
     Plot W/E 330/04
     (c) DR position 5550N 0238W
     Track required 087(T), distance 194 nm to B
     Hdg 077(T) = Hdg 085(M). G/S 208 kt, time 56 min
     (d) 085(M) ETA 1113

  2 Track 041(T) G/S 167 kt

1123 Brg Rel 138		1129 Brg Rel 047	
Hdg(T)	026	Hdg(T)	026
Brg(T)	164	Brg(T)	073
CA	0	CA	0
	164		073
Plot	344	Plot	253

     Position at 1129 5517N 0125W

  3 QDM 204 = 195(T) Plot 015(T) = TMG
     1240 QDM 114 = 106(T) Plot 286
     Drift 10S, distance gone 99 nm, G/S 198 kt
     W/V 252/39 (Tr and G/S)

  4 Mean height on climb 6 500 ft, mean Temp 0°C gives climb TAS 158 kt
     20 min on Hdg 152(T) = 53 nm
     Level TAS 187 kt for 20 min on Hdg 173(T) = 62 nm
     Lay off climb W/E 230/08

From end of climb wind, lay off level W/E 255/13
   DR position at 1405 <u>5316N 0206E</u>

5 Airplot   Hdg   282(T) for 84 nm
              Hdg   326(T) for 66 nm
              Hdg   230(T) for 66 nm
   W/E for 1 h 12 min = 050/36
   DR position at 1612 <u>5209N 0427W</u>

6 295(C) = 293(M) = 299(T)
   TAS 180 kt, 260 km = 140 nm in 43 min = G/S 195 kt
   TMG 292(T) gives drift 7P
      W/V <u>060/28</u> (Tr and G/S)

2: Plotting on the Lambert Conformal

This chart is often used in the air, and of course has its virtues balanced by consequent drawbacks; these are fully dealt with in the Navigation General section; here we will use it practically.

Radio bearings are G/Cs, and straight lines drawn on a Lambert are G/Cs for all practical purposes, so we're on easy street at once. A G/C Track can be flown, and it's the shortest distance between two points. The snag is the meridians converge towards the nearer Pole, so that an angle measured at one meridian will be different from that angle measured at another for the same straight line by the amount the meridians converge. The value of this convergence is found from the formula:

Convergence = ch long x n

where n is the sine of that parallel of latitude on which the chart is constructed to make convergency constant over that particular sheet. This is noted in a corner of the chart as an actual figure. On the plotting charts specially prepared for the CPL examination, n is taken as ·8, being the sine of the mid-parallel 52N, quite accurate enough to one place of decimals.

Before discussing the methods of allowing for convergence, examine the implications of the following diagram:

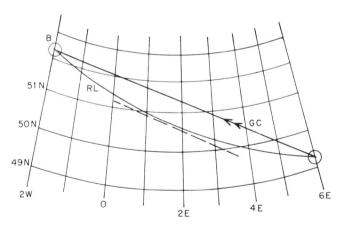

Fig. 2. 2. 1

1. The mean G/C Track would be measured at meridian 0200E.
2. As the R/L is concave to the nearer Pole, the tangent to this curve measured at 0200E would be the R/L Track.

3.   The initial G/C Track would be measured at 0600E. On a long drag, clearly this would be required for a start, and if regular fixes are obtained at shortish intervals, new Tracks would be progressively measured at new meridians; adjust yourself to the mean meridian over the next leg to be covered.
4.   Distance is measured on the latitude scale as usual. The scale of the chart is sufficiently correct for all practical purposes, so any part of the latitude scale will do.

To plot radio bearings
As always with radio bearings, ask yourself the question "who is doing the work"? Such bearings as QDM, QDR, QTE present no problem; they are sent out from a station whose position is known, whose meridian is known, and it is there that the measuring is being done, so convergence is no factor in their plotting. But where the working and measuring are done in the aircraft at the aircraft's meridian, and the plotting must then be done from the station's meridian, then convergence is in with a bang; it must be applied.
      The simple case first:

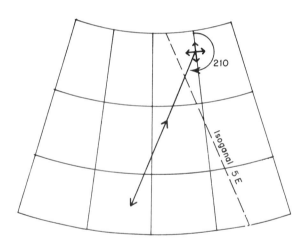

Fig. 2. 2. 2

Station gives QDM 025
                    Var   5E at the station
                    G/C   030(T)
      Plot 210 from the station, using his meridian.
And that's all.
      Now to measure a bearing in the aircraft and plot it from the station; the convergence between the aircraft's DR position and the station must be considered. There are two methods, and the first is the safer, easier and more practical. This is to transfer your meridian to the station and measure from that.
      For example, an aircraft on Hdg 325(T) measures a relative bearing 100 from a radio station. Proceed as follows:

Brg Rel 100
Hdg(T) 325
        ‾‾‾
        425

        −360
        ‾‾‾‾
Brg(T) 065 G/C
Plot   245 from the transferred meridian

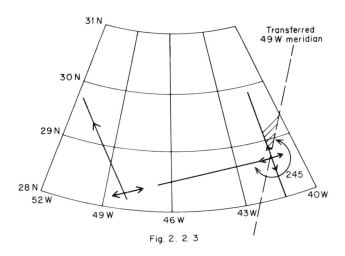

Fig. 2. 2. 3

The alternative method is to use the convergence formula

Convergence = ch long x n

In the above case 8 x ·5 as n will be about sin 30
The working is:

Brg Rel 100
Hdg(T) 325
        ‾‾‾
        425

        −360
        ‾‾‾‾
        065

Converg + 4
          ‾‾‾
          069

Plot   249 from the station's meridian

The shaded angle on the diagram has been mathematically taken care of. The rule for application is the same as for conversion angle on the Mercator, towards 180, and throw it in before you extract the reciprocal to plot.

Here is an exercise, using Lambert Misc 325, the CPL exam chart:

1100 Position C 5545N 0213E S/H 188(T), TAS 195 kt
1125 VOR C gives QDM 008
    (a) What mean drift has been experienced since 1100?
1135 NDB in position 5400N 0200W bears 092 relative by radio compass
    (b) Give the position at 1135
    (c) What mean W/V has been experienced since 1100?

Answer
1125 QDM 008

    Var   7W at C
          ‾‾‾‾‾
          001(T)

    Plot   181(T) direct = TMG which gives <u>drift 7P</u>   (a)

1135 Brg Rel 092

    Hdg(T) <u>188</u>

    Brg(T)   280 G/C

    Plot   100 from the meridian 02E transferred to the station

    Alternatively   Brg Rel 092

                    Hdg(T) <u>188</u>

                    Brg(T)   <u>280</u>

                    Converg − 3
                            ‾‾‾‾
                             277

            Plot   097 direct from the station

    The convergence being 4 x ·8 = 3°

                    Fix <u>5338N 0209E</u>   (b)

    Distance run on TMG in 35 min = 128 nm = G/S 219 kt

                    W/V <u>320/34</u> (Tr and G/S)   (c)

Southern hemisphere

The application of convergence in the Southern hemisphere follows the rules
again; it is added if the bearing True is more than 180, subtracted if less.

    While you are fairly with this topic and its complexities, it may be opportune
to have a look at the chapter in the Navigation General section.

3: Sundry Comments on Navigational Plotting

Most of the methods of obtaining fixes have been mentioned as far as the plotting of them is concerned: straight pinpoints, Loran or Gee fixes are only slung into an examination plot mainly to get all the plotters to the same place for ease of marking: the activity is centered normally round position lines, demanding a Track and G/S, if only DR, for their transference. And the P/Ls are usually radio, as they are in flight, and thus G/Cs: we've done the routine methods of plotting them, converting them to R/Ls if using a Mercator, nothing is plotted that is not True (confusing QDR, QDM, forgetting to apply variation at the station are common errors brought on entirely by examination twitch) and so on. A Fix from DME and QDM shows up occasionally, very easy, as it is meant to be: and don't forget an RMI reading is just a QDM.

Another type of P/L is the Consol Bearing, the theoretical breakdown of which is in the Radio Section. This is an aural radio aid, long range (a good 1 000 miles day or night). The listener counts a series of dots/dashes from a starting signal which includes the call sign: the dot/dashes or dashes/dots, merge during each burst into a equisignal and the signals must add up to 60 before the next burst begins: one could finish a count with say, 41 dots 15 dashes, which means 4 signals have been lost in the equisignal: the reading is meaned to give 43 dots, 17 dashes, and this count would be referred to as 43 dots for plotting purposes. A dozen or less G/C bearings are available for such a count from the station tuned in, and the appropriate one must be chosen. These bearings are often printed on charts as ·20, ·30, ·40 and so on, and the interpolated P/L readily plotted, as the appropriate sector is quickly discernible near to DR Track. The more primitive extraction of the P/L is done from CAP 59, and this is used in the exam. As a sample, 43 dots on STAVANGER gives True bearings from it of 011·9, 038·8, 059·8, 079·9, and so on (love those decimals of a degree). The DR position at the time of taking the count must be known more or less to select the appropriate bearing. They are G/Cs, and can be plotted direct on a chart where the G/C is a straight line; if using a Mercator, Appendix III gives, for each station, the conversion angle per change longitude <u>and</u> instructions on how to apply it as if you didn't know: interpolation is simple, or, if change longitude 5° for example, read off for 50 and divide by 10.

The Charts generally used in the ATPL Exam are Mercator, scale 1:3,000,000 at some quoted latitude: they are biggish sheets, clear to work on, with some facilities and coastlines shown: precision in plotting is called for, though, so keep your pencil sharpened. For practice exercises, from ATPL papers previously set (published regularly by HMSO for a few shillings), the charts are available from International Aeradio Ltd, Hayes Road, Southall, Middlesex, or Edward Stanford,

12-14 Long Acre, London WC2: the chart sheet is always given at the beginning of the plot question paper.

A Handy Reference Check for Plotting
Nothing is ever plotted that is not <u>True</u>.
Every line <u>must</u> have its proper arrows.
A symbol <u>must</u> have a time.

<u>Heading and TAS</u>
      Refer to <u>Air</u>

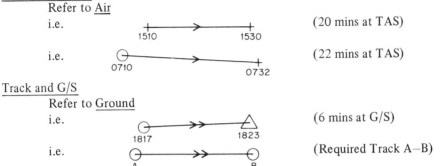

      i.e.   (20 mins at TAS)

      i.e.   (22 mins at TAS)

<u>Track and G/S</u>
      Refer to <u>Ground</u>

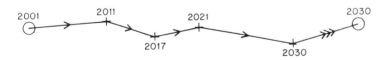

      i.e.   (6 mins at G/S)

      i.e.   (Required Track A—B)

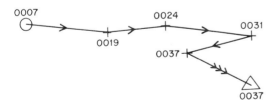

      i.e.   (Required Track from
                                                      DR position to F)

<u>Wind Velocity</u>
      Wind speed from a definite direction.
      Wind blows from air position to Fix or to DR position.
      Wind effect is wind for the time since the last Fix.
      i.e. wind effect for 29 mins:

      i.e. using wind effect for 30 mins:

<u>Fix</u>
      Where you <u>know</u> you are.
<u>DR Position</u>
      Where you <u>hope</u> you are.
      It can only be on a Track, never on a Heading.

Air Plot

A plot of Headings flown, the time of each at TAS.

It can only be started from a Fix.

It must be re-started from a Fix.

It can be carried on from an Air Position.

And it can be carried on for ever, knowing Heading & TAS.

Conversion Angle

Converts a Great Circle to a Rhumb Line, or vice-versa.

All radio bearings are Great Circles.

On Mercator, all straight lines are Rhumb Lines.

CA = ½ ch Long x sin mean Lat or use the ABAC scale.

1. Relative bearing measured in the aircraft + Hdg(T) ± CA then plot reciprocal from the station.

2. QDM, QDR, QTE.

Get to True.

Deduce bearing from the station.

Apply CA then plot from the station.

Convergence

Allows for the convergence of the meridians on Lamberts where G/Cs are straight lines; must be considered when the a/c's Hdg is part of a plotting calculation.

Convergence = Ch long x n

or

Transfer the a/c's meridian to the station if measurement has taken place at that meridian.

If a station gives a bearing, plot what he measured True direct from the station.

4: Grid Navigation

Here we will touch only on the practical plotting on a Grid chart, as the theory of the system is discussed fully in the Navigation General section. The use of the Grid chart for air navigation is the easiest thing in the world, overprinted on any chart with converging meridians.

A reference meridian is paralleled across the chart in an outstanding colour, and this Grid Line is used to measure angles, ignoring the meridians, to obtain, for example, a Track (G). Also dotted across the chart are the Grid Variation isogonals, called lines of Grivation. Before you mutter any imprecations, the happy word is that:

Track (G) ± Grivation = Track (M) and the sign of Grivation is treated as for Variation. Similarly for a Heading, of course, so that you at once have the Heading (M) to steer, and all problems of angular measurement on a chart with converging meridians are avoided.

A Heading (G) will in fact differ from the Heading (T) at any meridian by the convergence between that meridian and the reference meridian. This convergence has been applied algebraically to the Variation to give Grivation so that:

Heading (G) ± Grivation = Heading (T) ± Variation.
When working on the Chart, then, all angles (including W/V) can be used quite satisfactorily in Grid.

Have a check on the following run down, on a bit of the gridded Lambert Chart, N. Atlantic (see Fig. 2.4.1 overleaf): the reference meridian on this one is in fact the Greenwich meridian, and n for the sheet is given as ·748819, another way of saying ·75. Convergence thus becomes for the N. Atlantic Lambert:

ch long x ·75

A 5000N 4000W to B 5500N 5000W
    (i) Measured from the 45W meridian: Mean G/C Track 310
                                    R/L Track 310

Convergence = ch long x n
              = 10 x ·75
              = 8°
This gives the initial G/C Track of 314 (R/L 310 + ½ Convergence)
           and final G/C Track of 306 (R/L 310 − ½ Convergence)
    (ii) Now the mean G/C Track of 310, keeping to the 45W meridian, would be 340 (M).
          The Grid Track there is 344 (G)
             Grivation there is 4E
          giving a Track of 340 (M), no different from the basic solution. The Grid can be used overall, holding the a/c on the mean G/C, avoiding

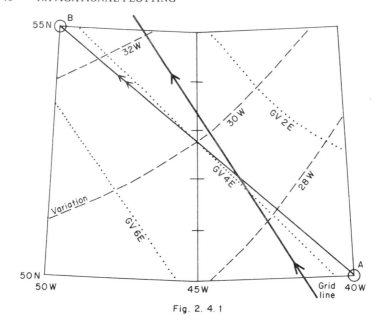

Fig. 2. 4. 1

the complications of the converging meridians.

There must be no mixing, of course; all the information in Grid will evolve the correct navigational information. Take this example, on the computer:

Conventionally: Mean G/C Track 310 (T), TAS 300 kt
                  W/V 250/40
                  ∴ Hdg 303(T), Var 30W
                  = Hdg 333(M) and G/S 280 kt
Grid: Track 344(G), TAS 300 kt
                  W/V 284/40(G)
                  ∴ Hdg 337(G), Griv 4E
                  = Hdg 333(M) and G/S 280 kt

The relationship between Track(T) and Track(G) is the value of the convergence of the reference meridian or Grid line and the longitude in question; in this case, just a straight 45 x ·75 = 34°, as the Grid line is the Greenwich meridian.

5: Radio Navigation Charts

These are commonly called Aerad Charts, and are available for nearly all areas of the world where navigation can be carried out by the use of radio whether from the ground or from within the aircraft, with no real plotting required. Skilful use of all radio aids plus adept handling of the computer are sufficient for position finding and accurate ETAs: additionally, complete reporting to the appropriate authority is essential so that the aircraft's position and height are known at any moment in flight. A definite route between reporting points must be followed. It is usual on a trip of this nature to prepare two Flight Plans, one the Fuel Flight Plan such as we shall shortly be much exercised with, using Mean Tracks; the other the Airways Flight Plan, detailing each leg with Tracks(M), Hdgs(M), distances and times, together with details of communications frequencies, and of frequencies of the aids to be used.

Nowadays, every aircraft in flight is under strict ground control and reports must be made at specified points on Track: an ocean crossing cannot be made on Airways, though Track must be adhered to within tight laid-down limits and neither height nor Track can be amended in flight without the Controller's permission. An airway may be laid-down over the desert with not quite the same tightness of control, but the distances between reporting points are often great (and the range of the radio aids often leaves much to be desired too), so that pure navigation is called for. Over most land areas, however, the main trouble is the multiplicity of radio aids and only experience will teach the pilot which to use, ignore or doubt. The Airways coverage means less and less navigation, but plenty of hard work in the cockpit: a guarantee of safety if the rules are obeyed exactly, the radio aids used skilfully and the Controller's instructions carried out ably. Rules of communications are established prohibiting chatter of an idle nature — there's no time anyway.

The Airspace left uncoloured on these charts is Controlled Airspace, and can only be used by any old pilot in VFR as laid down in the Air Pilot RAC 11. At night, and by day unless the strict VFR requirements can be met, then IFR flight, and the pilot must hold an Instrument Rating, have his aircraft equipped with the necessary radio equipment and frequencies, know the procedures, have had his Flight Plan cleared, and agree to carry out Control instructions: the Instrument Rating, therefore, is only granted after a stiff practical test.

The charts are all Lambert projection, or in process of conversion to Lambert, and are loaded with information which is constantly changing, causing a need for frequent reprints. About 18 of these charts cover Europe, and many other areas are charted too. In USA, another type is produced, also with wide coverage.

A Legend card is available for the interpretation of the numerous symbols, but a different Legend for different areas; the number of the card for a particular chart is noted on the chart's left hand bottom; in practice, this is not as frightful as it sounds. Take EUR 1/2 with Legend card No. 1, the UK cover, and let us consider the salient points.

1. All Tracks noted are Magnetic, and the white spacing on each side of Track represents the maximum tolerence permitted, actually 5 nm either side of the centre line. The isogonals are lightly started and ended only at top and bottom of the chart, the date and annual change noted in the box at bottom left.

2. Distances are given between compulsory or on-request reporting points, the solid or blank triangles; sometimes between intersection or turning points marked with a cross, so watch it, though this symbol is rapidly going out of use.

3. The most compulsory reporting point on any route is crossing a boundary from one Information Region to another, marked with a symbol or not. The parallel of latitude 5230N from 0246E to 0530W is marked with a definitive line indicating such a boundary, and on it the name of the region on the appropriate side, London and Preston. A report must be made to each on crossing. There are three boundaries meeting on the 10W meridian at 5430N, for example, Easy to recognise here; wait till you get near Brussels, where a twisting river provides the boundary.

4. A report is made only to the Air Traffic Control Centre (ATCC) of the Flight Information Region (FIR) in which the aircraft is flying; thus, a report in the London FIR is to London Airways.

5. The reporting centre and its frequency are noted along each Track. Further useful frequencies for Flight Information Services (FIS), Met, and so on, are given on a margin fold under the heading Area VHF Communication Frequencies.

6. The message content is crisp and its form invariable, once communication has been established (Preston Airways, this is Golf Alpha Sierra Tango, on 125·9, do you read?). "Preston Airways, this is Golf Alpha Sierra Tango, Lichfield 27, Flight level 80, estimate Oldham 39, over". That's all. Who you are, where you are, your Flight level, ETA next point, over.
   A listening watch must be kept on the appropriate frequency in case the Controller wants to give instructions, but the pilot only initiates reports at the proper points.

7. Now height to fly. Flight level(FL) as usual means the altimeter set to 1013·2 mb, and the last two noughts are omitted; FL 250 means 25 000 ft on 1013·2. On Airways, FL is always flown, unless instructed otherwise by ATCC. However, QNH safety minimum altitudes, shown by the full representation 5 000 for 5 000 ft on QNH for example, are often noted on Tracks; all of them in Ireland, in fact. In these circumstances, a FL in thousands of feet must be flown which will give the minimum altitude at least. The lowest forecast regional QNH, or the QNH from ATCC, might be say 1003 mb, so FL 50 would mean flying a QNH altitude 4 700 ft and the rules would be broken; FL 70 would be selected, the a/c would be 6 700 ft amsl give or take a few feet, the vital minimum is well below the a/c, and the rule of 'odd' or 'even' on the

Airway has been obeyed, for these refer to thousands of feet FL.
On the Aerad chart in the UK, pecked lines separate Altimer Setting Regions (ASR).
No reporting as such is required, but a pilot will request from ATCC the lowest
forecast regional QNH for the sector he is entering; this will be set on the second
altimeter as an immediate check for safe clearance over high ground. This QNH is
valid for one hour, and is amended hourly; the lowest forecast ensures full safety
over the whole region. The pilot in command is still flying a FL.

A further method of ensuring safety is the insertion on Tracks of a Terrain
Clearance Height, 2·5 meaning 2 500 ft amsl. This includes a specific allowance for
clearance above the highest known ground within 30 nm range of the Track and at
each end too.

The top and bottom limits of an Airway are shown by a fraction which is
self-evident; some leeway is built in for safety, usually 500 ft at the bottom to keep
out unqualified intruders.

Consider the route BROOKMANS PARK 5145N 0006W to PRESTWICK
5529N 0436W via Amber 2 and Amber 1.(The details which follow are correct at
the time of going to press).
BROOKMANS PARK is a compulsory reporting point with an NDB call sign (c/s)
BPK frequency 328 kHz. FL is 'even', so suggest FL 80; instructions in
conjunction with the filed Flight Plan would be given by London Airways.
The next reporting point is on request only, and if Control demanded, the aircraft
would report passing through the 347 radial from Bovingdon.
DAVENTRY is compulsory reporting point, Track unaltered, distance 18 nm.
VOR facility c/s DTY, frequency 115·0 MHz.
All reports of the a/c's position are passed to London Airways on 135·25 as noted
along the Track; for a considerable area around the busy capital you will see that
London Airways is precisely called London Control.
Airway A1 actually starts from DAVENTRY NDB c/s DTY, frequency 249 kHz, but
the distance along the airway is measured from the DTY VOR facility.
The next compulsory reporting point from DAVENTRY to LICHFIELD is
crossing the FIR boundary to sign off with London Airways and be taken over by
Preston Airways. The Track is 335(M), and the distance must be measured, 23 nm.
A scale line is placed at the top of the chart to avoid cluttering the meridians which
are deliberately faint anyway. Check any change in FL; the bottom of the Airway
changes, but our FL 80 is still OK. The report is made to both FIRs in the usual
accepted form, so ETA LICHFIELD must be to hand, on the same Track, 17 nm
to go.

LICHFIELD has NDB, c/s LIC, frequency 543·5 kHz.
OLDHAM compulsory, NDB c/s OLD, frequency 344. That intervening
MILLBROOK is for a/c on B1 only, so not applicable to us on A1.
The Track to OLDHAM is 355(M), distance 50 nm, minimum FL for us
60, and Terrain Clearance 3 500 ft amsl for 30 nm range from the centre
line and OLDHAM itself.
POLEHILL VOR, c/s POL, frequency 112·1, Track to it 355(M), distance 11 nm.
DME is available here on Channel 58, and this will give a distance presen-
tation in suitably equipped aircraft simply by tuning in the VOR frequency
given in brackets; where the Channel is given without a frequency, it can be

found listed against Tacan channels in the supplement to the Aerad Flight Guide carried in the aircraft.

DEAN CROSS again compulsory, VOR, c/s DCS, frequency 115·2 MHz, Track to it 332(M), distance 73 nm, our FL 80 OK. DME is available on Channel 99 as just this moment explained.

NEW GALLOWAY Track to it 326(M), distance 39 nm, but a position report is mandatory at the FIR boundary, measured as 23 nm from DEAN CROSS. Check FL obeys the rules; all is well as the base of the Airway in Scottish FIR is 4 000 ft on the QNH, but as we approach the destination airfield, we must be ready for instructions.

PRESTWICK has VOR c/s PWK, frequency 117·5 MHz, DME on Channel 122, NDB also c/s PWK frequency 355 kHz. Unless instructed, FL would be maintained, but round about NEW GALLOWAY we enter a large area shown in white and labelled 'Scottish TMA'. As a landing is intended, communication with the TMA is made as soon as permissible, the frequency given on the margin fold. Instructions will now flow in. The dotted line surrounding PRESTWICK and GLASGOW is Scottish Zone, the Transition Altitude is given, the frequency is the same as the TMA, and the purpose is to control departing and arriving aircraft over these two aerodromes only.

A larger scale area chart is available over busy areas shown on the chart as a double lined rectangle; Scotland, Belfast, Manchester are examples. Also, each airfield has its Approach charts giving all the facilities and facts, with separate sheets for ILS letdowns, ADF, overshoot, holding, noise abatement procedures and the lot.

Danger Areas should be checked before flight; this chart shows a permanent Danger Area as a continuous brown line, a temporary one as a dotted, whereas on most other charts in the Aerad series, there is a definite distinction by using heavy or light lines between up to above 10 000 ft or below 10 000 ft. The possible hazardous ones on the trip are D304 halfway to Oldham and D303 near Oldham. The details are given on the margin fold, and if you can read them, you've no worries about eyesight tests on your next medical. Many of the Danger areas are notified in 'Notams' when they are active; others are active at specified times. HJ means daylight hours to prove the mapmakers deep knowledge of the French tongue, HN night; these are measured from half an hour before Sunrise to or from half an hour after Sunset. Most countries calculate HJ and HN from straight S/R and S/S, except UK, France, Germany, Malta and Czechoslovakia.

There are a few differences of a minor nature usually on different charts, and for sure you will come across an occasional inexplicable detail; small brown flags refer to the direction of Magnetic North from an NDB, and have nothing to do with local golf courses. Another old favourite was PPO for prior permission only printed in such a way about the facility as to look like 'odd', giving a certain trauma to a pilot in a congested area that he's flying the wrong FL.

In tracing an interesting trip from somewhere like Brecon to Shannon, it is well worth while asking yourself what would the twin VORs and twin ADFs be tuned to at any given point; what would they read on a particular Hdg(M); what would the position reports contain, who would you be reporting to, and on what frequency; where would you contact TMA, get Met information, and other such very practical questions.

Before leaving the topic, it is convenient to run over Transition Altitude, Transition Level and Transition Layer. The Spaniards have their own solution which is tabulated on the chart, but the accepted way is mainly held to internationally. On take-off and landing, climb and descent, they are quite distinct.

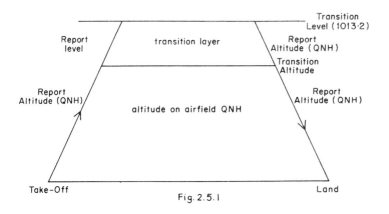

Fig. 2.5.1

The airfield QNH is given. Transition Altitude is always specified; it must be at least 1 500 ft above the aerodrome, and it is usually 4 000 ft in Controlled Airspace, 3 000 ft outside. The Transition Level is the lowest FL available for use above the Transition Altitude. The depth of the Transition Layer can cause some confusion; the idea is to make this as thin as possible. Take an airfield QNH of 1003 mb, Transition Altitude 4 000 ft, Transition Level 50; the moment the Transition Altitude is passed on the climb, the altimeter is set to 1013 mb which will make it register 4 300 ft; thus, the Transition Layer is 700 ft thick. The Transition Level merely refers to a FL in any direction, and there is no involvement with the FL the a/c is finally going to settle at. A QNH of 1013 mb could give the ideal, no Transition Layer at all, while a QNH higher than 1013 mb would deepen the Transition Layer.

The Aerad charts are of course constantly being brought up to date, and the operational use of the very latest issue is imperative.

Section 3

FLIGHT PLANNING

STAGE		Press height ft × 1000	RAS kt	Temp °C	TAS kt	W/V	Tr (T)	Hdg (T)	Var	Hdg (M)	Dist nm	G/S kt	Time min	ETA	Fuel flow kg/hr	Fuel kg
From	To															
ALICE SPRINGS	Abm OODNA	31	258	−45	423	270/60	149	156	5E	151	237	450	32	0447	3900	2080
Abm OODNA	LEIGH	31	258	−46	423	260/60	149	156	6E	150	231	442	31	0518	3860	2000

1: Principles of Flight Planning

Introduction

Before flight in the commercial business of carrying passengers or cargo for hire or reward, a very comprehensive Flight Plan must be made, giving the Headings Magnetic to steer, the time on each leg, the fuel to be consumed, the height to fly, the alternates available, and any other detail useful for the trip. It is a plan, a guide, and its main purpose is safety, ensuring primarily that sufficient fuel is uplifted plus a bit extra for mother. In the air, amendments to Headings and times will be made, with a continuous check on fuel consumption and weather ahead, by actual navigation.

The first pre-requisite on arrival at the field is a visit to the Met Office to get a briefing on the forecast weather for the route, and for all the aerodromes likely to be used; forecast Wind Velocities and temperatures at pertinent heights will be given, and from these, the Flight Plan can be filled in. This done, adequate fuel can be ordered and other matters such as range, point of no return can be duly entered. The complete plan will be reported to Air Traffic Control, so that in the air a full surveillance of the aircraft's progress will be kept.

A couple of lines of a Flight Plan might look like the example opposite.

Having gaped at that lot for a moment or two (and perhaps checked the TAS, times, Headings on your computer), you will appreciate that here is most of the information required for the trip and on the trip; but of course, temperatures, Wind Velocities are forecast, fuel consumption may not go according to the book, ETAs will invariably change, but the Plan is there.

You will have remarked that fuel consumption has decreased slightly on the second leg: as the weight of the aircraft decreases with fuel being burned off, so there is less weight to heave through the air, and consumption will be reduced. This is a very broad statement: there's more to it than that, for the power can be reduced to conserve fuel thereby dropping the airspeed, for example; cruise control techniques are various, but experience has cut them down to two basics:

1. **Constant Power.** Keeping the power constant will result in the airspeed increasing as the weight decreases with fuel consumption reasonably constant.

2. **Long Range Cruise.** Power is decreased as the weight reduces to conserve fuel with a TAS reasonably constant.

The refinements of these types are numerous, and airlines and aeroplanes usually have some rule of thumb starters to help the pilot decide in the light of all conditions the safest and most suitable control to select. For quick trips of an internal nature, a short-range cruise control is possible in order to adjust TAS to give a suitable G/S to maintain a tight schedule, with fuel consumption a minor consideration. But generally the two types above are the main ones and a pilot can switch in flight when he likes: with good terminal weather forecast, and ahead of Flight Plan at his en route check points, he will reject any further need to conserve fuel, and switch from Long Range Cruise to Constant Power. Or, if terminal weather is forecast poor, with a possibility of a diversion or a long hold in the stack, he will chuck out Constant Power and switch to Long Range Cruise for safety, as the priority is no longer to arrive on time but to be prepared for exigencies.

The Principles of Flight Planning

In the very first place, with the information available before flight, the problem is one of work with the computer to resolve this information into the essentials for the flight itself. After this, as the pilot considers fuel, it is aircraft weight which is the governing factor; this weight decreases dramatically as the trip progresses with the high rate of fuel consumption, and a mean consumption or a mean TAS *per sector* must be deduced. Aircraft manufacturers set out this data in the aircraft manual, and for a "weight at start" of a leg will, for the altitude and temperature, proffer a consumption for the next hour, or even for only the next half-hour, as we shall see. Such data sheets are used in the ATPL exam, but in CPL the knowledge of principles is introduced, and the averages of consumption or TAS must be calculated.

Let us consider first a Flight Plan for a voyage where the TAS is reasonably constant, or in other words, is given, but the fuel consumption varies as the aircraft's weight reduces.

A snippet from the data:

Consumption (kg/hr) at varying weights (kg)			
70 000	65 000	60 000	55 000
4 200	4 000	3 900	3 800

Take-off wt: 68 500 kg

Climb: Mean TAS 340 kt, time 38 min,
           fuel used 3 900 kg

The body of the flight plan — RAS, G/S, times, distance covered on the climb and descent, ETAs, can be completed straight off. The weight at start is 68 500 kg, so at the top of climb, having used 3 900 kg, it will be 64 600 kg for the commencement of level flight. We need the mean weight on the next leg in order to estimate as closely as possible the average consumption on it. Assume for ease of example that the leg will take one hour; from the table above, after half an hour, about 2 000 kg will have been burnt off, giving a weight in mid-leg of 62 600 kg; using this figure to enter the table, a mean consumption will be extracted of 3 950 kg, rounded off to avoid pedantic digits.

To proceed, the weight at start of the next leg is 60 650 kg (having flown for one hour at a consumption of 3 950 kg/hr from a start of 64 600 kg): say the leg will take 40 min. After 20 min at 3 910 kg/hr — and do not strain here, visual and mental calculation is enough − 1 300 kg will be burnt off and the mean weight may be taken to be 59 350 kg. This weight from the tables gives a consumption of 3 890 kg/hr, which is entered on the plan, and in 40 min will use 2 590 kg, giving a weight at start of the next sector of 58 060 kg. And so on.

A Flight Plan with a constant consumption but varying TAS is somewhat more involved; the plan must be done line by line, and the estimation of weights to find a mean TAS has its hazards, since no times on the legs are available.

A snippet from the data :

Consumption	Mean Weight (kg) v. TAS (kt)			
kg/hr 2 400	79 000 300	77 000 308	74 000 319	72 000 326

Weight at commencement of climb: 81 000 kg
Climb: Mean TAS 235 kt, time 48 min, fuel used 2 250 kg

The climb leg can be solved for G/S, time, distance and the rest, and the weight at start of level flight is 78 750 kg.

Without a G/S or time for the next leg, one can only look at the distance, glance at the data, and extract visually a likely TAS; obtain from this TAS and the forecast W/V a rough G/S; with this G/S, get an approximate time for the leg; halve it, and suggest a fuel used by mid-leg; and thereby calculate a mean weight.

Thus:

Weight at start 78 750 kg, next leg 190 nm
W/V 140/35, Track 210(T).
Try TAS 305 kt; this gives G/S 290 kt.

Total suggested time: 39 min therefore

Mid-time   =   20 min
20 min at 2 400 kg/hr = 800 kg
∴ Mean weight   = 77 950 kg

Use this weight to extract the TAS from the table = 304 kt and complete the leg of the Flight Plan. The actual fuel used will be 1 560 kg. Check. The weight at start of next leg is 77 190 kg, whence to continue the exercise.

On finishing the final line to destination, the fuel used from departure to destination can be totted up (Item A), as well as the weight over the destination field at some specified altitude; this weight, less any fuel used for descent and landing, will give the anticipated landing weight.

In calculating the fuel or TAS for the alternate from the data given, it is sufficient to use the weight at start of descent as a leader into the requirements for the leg.

The fuel to destination plus alternate fuel plus contingency fuel plus taxi, take-off, circuit, landing plus any other reserves or percentages will give the total fuel required for the trip; from this figure, the payload can be worked out, and this is what keeps us in business.

All this, the type of Flight Plan in qualifying exams for pilot licences, may have astounded you in its vagaries and guesswork; have no fear, it is but a presentation of the <u>principles</u> of the stuff to the student pilot: the manuals are of course much more precise, full of information garnered from tests and checks carried out with care and accuracy, but still on mean weights as shown, though for a specified period of time. We will move on to this practical matter at once.

Presentation of Data

Every aircraft type produces a cruise control manual, wherein all information at all heights at all temperatures for each specific purpose is shown, either graphically or tabulated, the latter by far the more popular. Climb, short range diversion, level cruise by appropriate methods, 4-engines, 3-engines, 2-engines, level cruise; in fact anything that the pilot requires for his aircraft for his route, presented succinctly, for rapid production of the Flight Plan with the station manager breathing down his neck to get him away, the fuel wallah palpitating for the fuel requirements, the load people agitating for pay load particulars. You won't get the aircraft type on your licence till you've mastered the manual, but for examination purposes, the Civil Aviation Authority has produced some Data Sheets set out along the accepted lines. Data Sheets 33 are part of your equipment, so we'll refer to them constantly and work out a Flight Plan sample.

First, though, an understanding of a primary problem is necessary. A pilot is mainly required to fly at a Pressure Altitude, simply an altitude with 1013·2 mb set on the sub-scale, but the aircraft's performance is vitally affected by the density of the atmosphere it is flying in, the TAS increasing for a given power as the density decreases: thus, density altitude is the operative altitude, — <u>the pressure altitude corrected for temperature.</u>

In the tables, you will see that in the right hand top corner of each sheet is the temperature square covered by that particular table, noted in relation to standard; the standard of +15°C at mean sea level, pressure 1013·2 mb, decreasing at 1·98°C per 1 000 feet, and the rest. This square contains the temperature deviation. To avoid undue strain on the pilot's grey matter, on page 33F, the standard temperatures at all pressure altitudes to 42 000 ft are set out. The relation of the forecast temperature at required altitude to standard can thus readily be obtained, and the appropriate sheet used for the Flight Plan.

Let us now plough gently through the following Flight Plan, assisted by Data Sheets 33: remember the penalties are heavy for violent arithmetical inaccuracies in the exam as well as in the air: — you would feel a real charley to find in mid trip that you'd uplifted 1 000 kg too little fuel.

Information is as follows:

A flight is to be made from ROME TO ACCRA. LAGOS is the terminal alternate. Route details are given on the pro forma.

Loading:	Weight at start of take-off is 130 000 kg.
Climb:	Climb on track from 1 000 ft over ROME to flight level 340. (Table 33A).
Cruise:	Cruise at the levels given in the Flight Plan (Table 33C).
Descent:	Descend on Track to arrive over ACCRA at 1 000 ft. (Table 33E).
Alternate:	Use Table 33G. Assume diversion is commenced 1 000 ft over ACCRA and ends at 1 000 ft over LAGOS.
Fuel: (i)	Sufficient for take-off and climb to 1 000 ft over ROME, plus:

STAGE		Flight Level	Temp. Dev. °C	WIND		Track °(T)	Drift	Heading °(T)	T.A.S. kt.	Wind comp. kt.	G/S kt.	Distance n.m.	Time min.	Fuel flow kg./hr.	Wt. at start Kg.	Fuel required Kg.
From	To			Direction	Speed kt.											
TAKE OFF FUEL																
ROME	Top of climb		− 3	040	20	170						244				
Top of climb	PALERMO	340	+ 2	340	50	170								—		
PALERMO	IDRIS	350	+ 4	290	70	180						331				
IDRIS	GHAT	350	+ 4	310	50	198						490				
GHAT	NIAMY	350	+ 8	280	80	213						824				
NIAMY	Top of descent	350	+12	210	15	197					—	487		—		
Top of descent	ACCRA		—	200	10	197										
ACCRA	LAGOS		—	200	20	075			—		—	217		—		

FLIGHT PLAN

| STAGE | | Flight Level | Temp. Dev. °C | WIND | | Track °(T) | Drift | Heading °(T) | T.A.S. kt | Wind comp. kt | G/S kt | Distance n.m. | Time min. | Fuel flow kg./hr. | Wt. at start 130000 Kg. | Fuel required Kg. |
From	To			Direction	Speed kt.											
TAKE OFF FUEL		↕											02	→	←	1000
ROME	Top of climb	↗	−3	040	20	170	2S	168	379	+14	393	131	20	—	129000	4400
Top of climb	PALERMO	340	+2	340	50	170	1P	171	488	+49	537	244 / 113	12¼	7050	124600	1470
PALERMO	IDRIS	350	+4	290	70	180	8P	188	486	+20	506	331	39¼	6900	123130	4600
IDRIS	GHAT	350	+4	310	50	198	6P	204	486	+17	503	490	58¼	6710	118530	6550
GHAT	NIAMY	350	+8	280	80	213	9P	222	486	−36	450	824	1.50	6430	111980	1179
NIAMY	Top of descent	350	+12	210	15	197	0	197	494	−15	479	394	49¼	6115	100190	5055
Top of descent	ACCRA	↗	—	200	10	197	0	197	569	−10	559	487 / 93	15¼	—	95140	700
															94440	
												Item A				5560
ACCRA	LAGOS	↗	—	200	20	075	2P	077	—	+12	—	217	35	—		5730

(ii)   Sufficient for flight from ROME to ACCRA and to alternate LAGOS, plus:

(iii)   800 kg for circuit and landing, plus:

(iv)   9 000 kg reserve

    (a)   Complete the Flight Plan.

    (b)   What weight of fuel is required?

Before starting, note that computer work is reduced by Drift and Wind Component Tables, pages 24 and 25 of the Data Sheet leaflet. The TAS is regarded broadly to give sufficient accuracy for flight planning purposes: a set is provided for each aircraft, with its mean cruising speed, mean climb and mean diversion speed. Here we have two tables, 480 kt and 380 kt; the wind speed is set out across the top, with the angle between wind direction and Track down the side. Thus, a drift and wind component can be read off, though the port or starboard bit must be determined. Thus, Track 180(T), W/V 290/70, your expected TAS 486 kt — angle is 110° down the side, against wind speed 70, drift is 8, component +20; use G/S 506 kt, and with a southerly Track with rough westerly wind, drift is clearly port. The appropriate table can be used to press on with the Flight Plan.

Wrinkle number 1 is to put your weight at start of take-off, 130 000 kg, on top of the column. On Table 33A, four engined climb, on the sheet labelled "Standard −5°C to −1° C" in the right hand corner, −3 being the temp dev from standard, mean for the climb. The notes on the bottom are very pertinent; so take-off fuel to 1 000 ft is 1 000 kg, time 2 min, which can be filled in on the Flight Plan: the weight at the start of the next leg is thus 129 000 kg, but this is filled in on the 'Take-off fuel' line.

Climb

To make it easier the actual TOW is along the top, the pressure height at the side. Along the height 34 000 to climb to, read off TAS 379 kt, and continue along to the 130 000 kg TOW column, read off fuel consumed 4 400 kg, time 20 min, and enter in: weight at start of next leg, now 124 600, and the line can be completed, including a distance of 131 nm, leaving 113 nm to go from top of climb to PALERMO. Check.

Level

All the time the temp dev and FL must be watched: there is absolutely no reason why one shouldn't move from one page to another. And as an obiter dictum; Flight Level is the same thing as Pressure Height. Here we go to Table 33C, Standard 0 to +9°C. The top line is separated into individual hours of cruise, and the side has again pressure height and mean TAS: if you started at 137 000 kg, at 34 000 ft and flew at that pressure height, providing the temperature did not go outside the limits for the table, one could go steadily along the line. In this case, our weight at start is 124 600 kg, at 34 000 ft, TAS is straight 488 kt, but we must interpolate for fuel flow between the column:

$$129 \ : \ 7 \ 300 \ \text{and} \ 122 \ : \ 6 \ 900$$

The columnar weight difference is 7 000 kg for a consumption difference of 400 kg

So: 124 600 − 122 000 =   2 600

$$\frac{2\,600}{7\,000} \times 400 \text{ gives } 150 \text{ kg to the nearest } 10 \text{ kg}$$

∴ consumption for 124 600 kg initial weight
is 6 900 + 150   =   7 050 kg

which enter, and complete the PALERMO line, and be careful where you enter the fuel required of 1 470 kg (that's what you made it, I hope). The biggest boobs in Flight Planning are invariably arithmetical, cocking up a thousand with a hundred digit.

Proceed now with a start weight of 123 130 kg to IDRIS, checking the temp dev, O.K., keep the same page: but the pressure height is now 35 000 ft. From the notes on page 2 of the Data Sheets, an en route climb of 4 000 ft is ignored for time, but add 200 kg to fuel used: to be perfect then, we need to chuck in 50 kg to the fuel required on the IDRIS leg for a 1 000 ft climb. From Table 33C, TAS 486 kt, and 6 900 kg is accurate enough for 123 130 kg weight at start. Complete the line, and you'll find 39½ min gives you 4 550 kg required, + 50 kg, a round 4 600. Weight at start for GHAT 118 530 kg. Into the Tables again, check the temp dev, O.K. Interpolate as before, between 123 : 6 900 kg and 116 : 6 600 kg for a consumption at 118 500 kg aircraft weight.

$$\frac{2\,500}{7\,000} \quad \times \quad 300 \quad = \quad \frac{750}{7} \quad = \quad 110 \text{ kg}$$

to be added to the 116 000 weight consumption = 6 710 kg, and the TAS is still 486 kt.

Complete the GHAT and NIAMY lines. We now must deal with the descent line to find time and distance covered before we can find out how far along the Track NIAMY – ACCRA to fly before commencing the descent. This is Table 33E, and is as plain as a pikestaff : as we're leaving 35 000 ft, TAS is 369 kt, fuel used 700 kg, time 15½ min. Complete the descent line, enter distances for the level and descent bits, and now to finish off NIAMY – TOD: the temp dev is +12°C, so with a weight at start of 100 190 kg on the table marked "Standard + 10°C to + 14°C", enter at 35 000 ft, TAS 494 kt, interpolate for 100 000 kg between 103 : 6 200 and 96 : 6 000, giving 115 kg to add to 6 000, giving 6 115 kg consumption. Finish off so far: add the fuel requirements from departure to destination, usually known as Item A, and above all check that your weight at ACCRA + this figure = 130 000 kg.

The alternate must now be dealt with, Table 33G. The explanatory notes are reasonably clear: enter the tables for your conditions, and then make corrections. We're at 1 000 ft, will climb to 35 000 ft and descend to arrive over LAGOS at 1 000 ft. From drift and wind component table for TAS 380 kt, extract drift 2P, wind component +12, enter 33G and with a spot of visual interpolation: 35 min, 3 620 kg. Corrections are: none for height, weight is 94 440 kg ∴ add 3%, 108 kg say 110, used 3 730 kg. The corrections are all straightforward, and they are set out for you: no need to learn them by heart; it is automatic to check them, though, in every Flight Plan.

All that needs be done now is to tot up the Fuel on Board requirements, as demanded by the question, or by the Station Officer on the route. It is wise to set it out as on a fuel chit.

Item A	35 560
Alternate	3 730
Circuit & Landing	800
Reserve	9 000
FOB	49 090 kg

This makes it easy to deduce the landing weight at ACCRA, for example: you will use the 800 kg for circuit and landing, but still have alternate and reserve fuel in the tanks.

Divers problems in Flight Planning (Data Sheets 33)
The quite practical type of problem that involves a trip of a certain distance, part at low altitude (29 000 ft or below), part at high, hold and descend, is straight forward once you know your way around the Data Sheets. The information presented to you in an examination or in the Briefing Room must be complete enough for an answer to be arrived at, and there should be no difficulty, for example, in working out a descent before solving the time and fuel for cruise: there's nothing new in that. Table 33E for descent couldn't really be easier. I'm not trying to offend your intelligence in reminding you that a hold is a hold, where a ground speed is unnecessary: in the artifical atmosphere of the exam room, it is easy to start hunting for the absurd like "how far have I gone on the hold leg".

Table 33D gives the Low Level Cruise information, and do, oh do, notice the footnote about the mean weight of 100 000 kg. A mean weight of 135 000 kg increases the consumption at 15 000 ft at ISA +7, by 705 kg/hr. The table other-wise is self explanatory, calling for only the simplest interpolation.

A climb from 15 000 ft to 34 000 ft in Table 33A demands a simple subtraction of fuel at 15 000 ft for the weight at start of climb from the fuel at 34 000 ft, but a visual interpolation is required at bottom and top for intermediate weights. Keeping ISA +7, with a weight of 133 840 kg at 15 000 ft to start the climb to 34 000 ft, the table says —

Press Height	Mean TAS	135 000 kg		130 000 kg	
		Fuel kg	Time min	Fuel kg	Time min
34 000	387	5 800	31	5 300	28
15 000	324	2 100	9	2 000	9

Fuel at 15 000 ft for 133 840 kg aircraft weight is 2 080 kg
Fuel at 34 000 ft for 133 840 kg aircraft weight is 5 700 kg
Fuel used for this climb, then, is 3 620 kg, and such a round-off figure is quite adequate, as is the similarly subtractive time of 22 min.

The mean TAS for this climb demands an entry into the graph labelled for the exercise as Table 33B: enter with top of climb height across to the appropriate start of climb height curve, drop to the Reference line, and then parallel up or down as far as the temp dev axis, and read off the mean TAS. Our example above gives 418 kt. Interpolation of the bottom of climb curve is visually done. Don't make a large theoretical chore of any of this: the table, anyway, gives an example, which is worth a moment's study.

Descent is plain sailing (Table 33E) just read off TAS, fuel used and time taken from altitude to 1 000 ft: if the bottom of descent is not 1 000 ft, subtract one fuel from t'other, ditto time; add the two TAS and subtract 290. Hold is taken at the altitude on Table 33D, and the fuel calculated for the time of hold.

Try this, using Data Sheets No. 33

An aircraft is to fly from A to B, a distance of 950 nm on a Track of 250(T). Take-off weight is 140 000 kg, and the aircraft will successively:

(i)   Climb from 1 000 ft to 15 000 ft, and then cruise at this level for 25 min.

(ii) Climb from 15 000 ft to 34 000 ft and cruise at this level until a descent is made to arrive over B at 6 000 ft.

(iii) Hold at 6 000 ft over B for 30 min (Table 33D) and then descend over B to 1 000 ft.

Details of these stages, temp dev and W/V are given below.

Complete the Flight Plan, giving the total fuel required and the total time.

STAGE Press Alt	Temp Dev	W/V	TAS	Wind Component	G/S	Dist	Time min	Fuel Flow kg/hr	Start Weight kg	Fuel kg
T/O & climb to 1 000 ft	–	–	–	–	–	–		–		
1 000 – 15 000 ft	+3	200/40						–		
Level 15 000 ft	+6	240/50					25			
15 000 – 34 000 ft	+6	260/60						–		
Level 34 000 ft	+8	290/70								
34 000 – 6 000 ft	–	230/50						–		
Hold at 6 000 ft	+6	–		–	–	–	30			
6 000 – 1 000 ft	–	–		–	–	–		–		
						950				

Answer: 24 000 kg; 3 h 02 m.

The following problem is really an exercise in figure manipulation and logical method, but it has a very practical role, for often the weight of the aircraft at destination is the limiting factor.

Using Data Sheets No. 33, a flight is to be made from A to B, distance 1 150 nm, to arrive over B at 6 000 ft at weight 98 000 kg

Climb   On Track from 1 000 ft over A to FL 340 (Temp dev +6, head wind component 30 kt)

Cruise   Four-engine level cruise at 0.86 Mach at FL 340 (Temp dev +6, head wind component 55 kt)

Descent On Track to arrive over B at 6 000 ft (head wind component 25 kt)

Give the time and fuel required for:

(i)   Climb from 1 000 ft

(ii)   Cruise

(iii) Descent

Descent first, from Table 33E:

TAS (367 + 300) − 290 = 377 kt:

∴ G/S is 352 kt. Time given 12 min, so distance 70 nm:

                  Fuel given 600 kg:

Weight at start of descent is therefore 98 600 kg.

Level next, Table 33C, temp dev +6°C:

TAS 488 kt ∴ G/S 433 kt.

The aircraft's weight is going to finish the cruise sector at 98 600 kg; in the Table, from 102 000 to 98 600 kg gives:

                  Fuel 3 400 kg.

At noted consumption of 6 200 kg/hr, this takes 33 min:

            33 min at G/S 433 kt gives distance 238 nm

The next hour uses 6 400 kg and distance 433 nm

A mental check indicates that there may be little cruise distance left, so take a summary:

After the climb and an undetermined period of cruise, the all-up-weight is:

        98 000 + 600 + 3 400 + 6 400   =   108 400 kg

Similarily, the distance gone is:

          1 150 - (70 + 238 + 433)   =   409 nm

To enter the climb table, the TOW is required, so this must at this stage be estimated as accurately as possible. A glance at the appropriate page of Table 33A suggests a 22 min climb at a TOW of 115 000 kg, fuel used 4 300 kg; the climb G/S 357 kt for this time means 131 nm will be covered on the climb, and 278 nm is left for the very first cruise bit. Continuing with this procedure, enter the level cruise Table, read off the consumption 6 700 kg/hr, calculate the time to do 278 nm at G/S 433 kt; thus, 38½ min and fuel used 4 300 kg. The approximate TOW is:

        108 400 + 4 300 + 4 300   =   117 000 kg,

and although the climb table gives fuel and time from 1 000 ft which is just what the question demands, the top line is classified as TOW and 1 000 kg must be included in the TOW figure for the initial take-off climb. Entering the table then with 118 000 kg:

    Climb takes 23 min, uses 4 500 kg, distance 137 nm. Level flight starts at 112 500 kg all-up-weight (the initial climb fuel of 1 000 kg being allowed for), and so this portion will take 38 min to fly the 272 nm at G/S 433 kt, at fuel consumption 6 600 kg/hr = 4 200 kg. There is an element of meaning-off the extracted figures from the entered figures in the tables for intermediate weights, but there is no need for pedantic precision.

The answers are:

              (i)   Climb: 23 min, fuel 4 500 kg
              (ii)   Cruise: 2h 11m, fuel 14 000 kg
              (iii)   Descent: 12 min, fuel 600 kg

Diversion and Hold

Another practical problem in this paper is a diversion arranged for you somewhere in the closing stages of a trip. As the examiner wants to know if you are really familiar with the tables, he will divert you half way down the descent, and give you a hold. At one fell swoop, he's got you in every table in the book, and a good thing too. Since a diversion is assumed to be demanded after a shot at landing which has proved out of the question, diversion tables have overshoot, climb to a suitable level, reserve fuel all included in the figures; to peel off on the way down and head for the alternate field must require suitable corrections to these figures. In Data sheets 33 these corrections are clearly shown, but in sheets 34 they are not, and circumstances will decide which of the more thumbed tables are appropriate in the latter case, not forgetting the Low Level Cruise set.

Perhaps it's opportune to take a look at Data sheets 34; these are geared for heavier aircraft, but are similar in format, and mainly self-explanatory, though watch the footnotes as before. Interpolations for fuel consumption between stated weights are definitely only to the nearest 100 kg, and the Low Level cruise table is the one to use if holding.

An aircraft cruising at 0.83 indicated Mach at 34 000 ft pressure height is on Track to destination B which is 640 nm distant. Aircraft weight is 238 500 kg, temp dev $+7°C$, headwind component 40 kt.

Later, descent on Track is commenced, headwind component 20 kt.

(a) Give the time and fuel required for:
   (i)   Cruise
   (ii) Descent

The aircraft arrives at B, but diverts after an overshoot to D, 156 nm distant, tailwind component 30 kt, temp dev $+8°C$.

(b) Give the aircraft weight at commencement of diversion.

(c) Determine time, flight level, and fuel required for diversion.

The aircraft holds over D at FL 160 for 17 min, temp dev +14 (Table 34D).

(d) Give the fuel required for holding.

Descent   14½ min, 2 000 kg, TAS 372 kt, from Table 34E
           ∴ G/S 352 kt, distance run 85 nm.

Cruise   which will be for 555 nm
           TAS 486 kt, ∴ G/S 446 kt, time 1 hr 14½ min

AUW 238 500 kg
           so in Table 43C, temp dev $+7°C$, interpolate for weight and height to give fuel flow 9 700 kg/hr for the first hour, and 9 500 kg/hr for the second.

                Cruise fuel : 1 hr   9 700
                              14½ min 2 300
                              Total 12 000 kg

Answer (a) (i)   1 hr 14½ min, 12 000 kg
             (ii) 14½ min, 2 000 kg

Now for the diversion; fuel used to B is 14 000 kg, and the aircraft weight after overshoot is 238 500 − 14 000 = 224 500 kg.

Entering Table 34B, interpolate for 156 nm and a 30 kt tailwind, read fuel 13 900 kg, FL 220, time 31 min. The start of diversion weight is 30 500 kg less than tabulated, so footnote correction (a) must be applied; this is 6% of 13 900, subtractive, 800 kg, = 13 100 kg.

Answer (b) 224 500 kg
        (c) 31 min, FL 220, 13 100 kg.

For the hold, TAS 434 kt is extracted from the Table 34D, but the fuel flow must be checked against aircraft weight as per the footnote. Diversion started at 224 500 kg AUW, and 13 100 kg was to be used; this figure contains 7 500 kg reserve, and the aircraft has descended only to FL 160. Of the actual fuel required, 5 600 kg (13 100 − 7 500), the amount unused at the hold point would be the descent from FL 160 to landing, a figure of 1 800 kg from the descent table. A round estimate of what fuel has in fact been burnt off would be 3 800 kg, and the AUW at holding 220 700 kg. Thus, the noted consumption of 12 500 kg in the Table is satisfactory, and the correction element is not applicable.

<u>Answer</u> (d) 17 min at 12 500 kg/hr = 3 550 kg.

This example has put you into the diversion table, but if the descent had been broken off, say, at FL 180, whence to proceed direct to the alternate, then the calculations must be made from the descent, climb and cruise tables, starting from the AUW at the time of break off; since the diversion table showed that FL 220 would be climbed to, then from FL 180 a climb to around FL 340 would be possible and advisable.

Just to make sure you're not betting on avoiding a question on 3-engine operation, take a schufti at Table 34G in Data sheets 34 for such a problem as the following.

An aircraft en route to K goes on 3 engines at 1307.

Descent will be made on Track. Details are:

Distance	926 nm
Track	123(T)
Mean W/V	180/60
FL	310
Temp dev	+8°C
Aircraft weight at 1307 is 235 700 kg	
Fuel in tanks at 1307 is 41 300 kg	
(a) Give ETA K	
(b) How much fuel remaining on landing?	

<u>Descent first</u>:   TAS 358 kt, fuel 1 900 kg, time 14 min
∴ G/S 322 kt, distance 75 nm, and cruise
distance is then 851 nm.

AUW 235 700 kg, mean TAS 451 kt, 9 700 kg/hr at first, from the appropriate section of Table 34G.

∴ G/S 418 kt, time 2 hr 02 min

<u>Fuel</u>	first hour	9 700 kg	
	second hour	9 200 kg	
	02 min	300 kg,	this calculated at 9 000 kg/hr to be precise, but it becomes pedantic in this case
	Cruise fuel	19 200 kg	
	+ Descent fuel	1 900 kg	
	Total used	21 100 kg	

This total subtracted from fuel available at 1307 gives 20 200 kg left on landing.

ETA 1307 + 2 hr 02 cruise + 14 min descent = 1523 hrs

<u>Answer</u> (a) ETA K 1523
          (b) 20 200 kg.

Quite straightforward, providing you have familiarity. As a rider, the 3-engine cruise in our favourite Data Sheets 33, Table 33H, is set out page by page for temp dev from standard, giving TAS at height and consumption per hour for a given weight at start: descent would call for normal descent Table 33E. Take a look at it right now or you'll be sorry.

To sum up for the Flight Plan itself, and such matters just discussed, you will need to do some of the published exam papers to get up some reasonable speed with accuracy: there is no need to be pedantic about fuel consumption. For instance, the tables themselves are not precise to a couple of hundred kilos – a weight of 101 000 kg gives a consumption 6 400 kg/hr and the following hour the AUW at start is 95 000 kg. There is a lot of averaging out, and though precision is always to be aimed for, it must be reasonable. You will find too the Drift and Wind Component table at the end of the book helps speed things along, using the appropriate table for the climb or level: all that computer work is avoided. The failing point in Flight Planning is pure arithmetical error, frequently induced by examination neurosis.

2: Choice of route

On an Airline running schedule services, it would appear at first sight that the Captain has precious little say: certainly the majority of local trips around the UK to the European continent are fixed on an airways route at pre-arranged altitudes, and fortunately for pilot morale, however much they may appear to resemble a taxi service, the vagaries of weather and the need to practise all types of let-downs are ever present. On long routes, despite the firm establishment of various different tracks across the water or desert, the Captain must study the overall weather picture at selected heights and pick the best route for speed, the best height for his particular aircraft under the conditions, never forgetting passenger comfort (or animal comfort if he's carrying a load of monkeys), viewing the whole thing with an eye on fuel consumption and safety at all times. This takes some expertise to do briskly and surely, and while there is nothing worse than the type who hums and ha's muttering 'ye canna be too careful', it is positively better than the impulsive one who decides too quickly and pours his 100 ton flying cigar into turbulent weather away from operating navigation aids.

The scheduled services are but a part of the Airline picture: any number of firms specialise in charter operations, and the majority are prepared to do charters, hiring aircraft if necessary from their competitors. Immediately, the profit motive could incite the Captain to take undue risks, especially if he is recently promoted to command and is anxious to make a name for himself as a good company man. Happily, by the time he is ready for such elevation, he has learnt more sense, apart from the legislative exercises he has had to undergo.

In such operations, the route and height are his decision: he will have in good time pondered the variables, and be ready at the Met briefing with a selection of possible routes from which to make a quick and safe choice; in fact, he may already have decided from his bed side after a chat with the met man and the operations chap, so that on arrival at the field the Flight Plan is prepared and he needs only to check and corroborate that the latest information confirms his previous telephone briefing.

The procedure hardly varies; knowing his aircraft's heights for optimum operation, power-and fuel-wise, he will view a route first which will give him the best time track, examine it for trappy forecasts of turbulence or icing; for nav aids en route; for active danger areas notified for the time on the Notams; for Air Traffic Control restrictions and requirements; for safe clearance of topographical obstacles. Can he get over the highest mountains en route at the weight he will be at the time he gets there? Not only over them, but well over them? The broad decision now taken, he must at once examine the forecast weather at destination and departure field and at suitable alternates; not only alternates at his destination, but at the departure point, in case of return. Is there an en route aerodrome available for landing if the destination clamps, thereby avoiding a possible diversion to some destination alternate when fuel is getting low, and the destination alternate is suffering from the same foul weather as the destination itself? Is a chosen alternate not only far enough away from the clamped destination to be reached comfortably with the fuel aboard, forecast OK for weather, but also politically OK for the passengers and crew to be allowed through immigration in the case of a long wait? Is the required type of fuel available there? Are the take-off and landing conditions restrictive? Are the necessary services available there at the possible arrival time? The world is scattered with airfields which do not fill all these requirements, only useful in case of force majeure.

The next check is on TOW and landing conditions: at expected TOW will the met conditions allow a safe unstick? With that TOW, less the expected fuel con-sumption from departure to destination (Item A + oil and water used, + extra required for climb, taxi, T/O, circuit and landing), is the maximum landing weight greater than the maximum allowed for the aircraft or by the airfield itself? If so, will the fuel uplift be reduced to allow a safe operation? Or shall the payload be reduced?

He can now address himself to cruise control and fuel: long range cruise, or constant power, depending on whether fuel conservation is more important than speed, or whether speed is possible with no fuel problems. All aircraft manufacturers produce their tables, and a little experience of their operation makes the decision more or less immediate. With the Item A + fuel required for alternate (latter usually at Long Range Cruise) he now considers his reserves, bearing in mind all the previous factors mentioned. A Route Contingency reserve is usually laid down by the Company, a percentage of Item A, with a maximum amount: this allows for the hard trip when actual winds are more adverse than forecast or for any of those happenings which are part of the flying game, such as being ordered to fly at an unsatisfactory altitude for the aircraft, or to move off Flight Planned Track for any reason, weather or traffic. The amount of contingency fuel is normally determined by the route: over country plentifully supplied with good airfields, the percentage of Item A would not be so large as that over the oceans or deserts. A similar percentage is usually applied to the alternate fuel, and for the same reasons. An emergency reserve is frequently added for Mother, + a goodly quantity for stand off, climb out, and taxi, the amount depending on the aircraft, and the complexity of the traffic at destination. It is almost normal in dodgy weather to have a stack of 20 aircraft at a place like NEW YORK, and plaintive cries from pilots that fuel is low and precedence is required are viewed very palely indeed from the other poor devils holding at precise altitudes for hours on end.

The only likely major difference to this type of routine will be if the destination is an island set solitary-like in the silver sea, a hearty distance from another aerodrome. Then, once having passed the Point of No Return, or the latest time to divert to a suitable field on the beam of Track, and a landing at destination becomes obligatory, an Island Reserve is substituted for alternate fuel, reserve fuel, and stand off fuel, to permit a long hold.

Add the lot up, and that's the Load Sheet Fuel: an Endurance is worked out from this from a graph or a rule of thumb average to give the maximum time the aircraft can be airborne.

Sundry wrinkles will become apparent, nearly all allowed for in the Aircraft Type Manual. The total fuel on board may include a quantity of unusable fuel in the tanks: the only interest in this for the operation is that it's part of the weight. Climb, taxi, take-off fuel will be laid down in the Manual, and included on the Flight Plan; en route climb and allowances for it will be considered in the body of the Flight Plan from an appropriate table or graph; fuel for heaters, de-icers and so on are similarly allowed for. One pretty point often overlooked especially on shortish sectors is to jug up to the gills with fuel where the price is cheap, or to take the minimum consonant with safety where it is high: this will endear you to the commercial side of the company, for the savings can be appreciable.

3: Weight calculation

Being in an international business the pilot is constantly plagued with units different from the ones he's been brought up on, and despite efforts to bring them all to one acceptable type world-wide, there's always the nation which won't confer or won't agree. In general, kilograms are becoming the accepted weight unit, though the pilot will find pounds aplenty on the trips. Volume should thus be in litres, and this comes hard to many, used to Imperial gallons. The U.S. gallon is only about 4/5 of the Imperial gallon, so there's another snag. It is quite unnecessary to memorise the conversion units, they're all on the computer anyway or in the Flight Manual, but when dealing with large figures, you should have an approximate idea of the relationship in order to get the number of noughts correct.

    1 kilogram is 2.2 lb
    1 litre is about 1/5th Imperial gallon
    1 litre is about 1/3rd of a US gallon

    The weight of fuel varies with temperature and air density, as it will according to its octane value: the conversion from volume occupied (i.e. litres or gallons) to weight (kg or lb) is found by knowing the fuel's specific gravity at the time of loading. An engineer will have used his hygrometer to find this, and the sum is simple. It must of course be entered on the Load Sheet; on the Flight Plan, weight is the only concern.

    The specific gravity is simply the relation of the weight of fuel at the time for a given volume to the weight of water for the same volume.

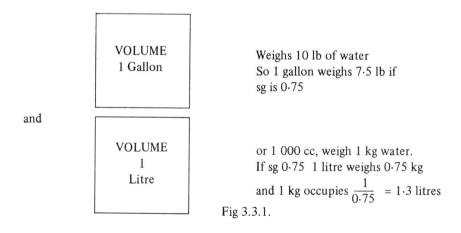

and

Fig 3.3.1.

The circular slide rule works all this out for you, and you will see that kg to lb is straight forward, but you cannot convert litres to kg, galls to lb, or any variant of these without knowing the sg — the errors can be considerable, and there must be no guesswork at all.

The precautions to be observed with respect to maximum TOW and maximum landing weight after obtaining total fuel requirements have already been mentioned; the fuel requirements, although calculated with precision, are the minimum requirements for safe operation, for there would be no point in lugging excess fuel around; thence, the payload carried must be such that these maxima are not exceeded, and off-loading passengers or freight is a serious decision in a commercial concern. But just as maxima are laid down for aircraft weight, so for each flight there must be a maximum payload that can be carried.

Consider the following example:

Maximum TOW 250 000 kg
Maximum Landing Weight 190 000 kg
Weight without Fuel or Payload 170 000 kg
Fuel on Board 23 535 kg
Fuel required from departure to destination 16 535 kg

The point to start with is Max Ldg Wt 190 000 kg. The only difference between this imperative maximum and the actual TOW is the fuel used up from departure to destination, the "burn-off".

So 190 000 kg
<u>   16 535</u>
    206 535   is the TOW

This is well below the maximum TOW, but dare not be exceeded, for if it was, the aircraft would be above maximum landing weight at the destination and would be forced to chunter around simply to use fuel and get the weight down.

The weight without fuel or payload, 170 000 kg, may now be added to the total fuel on board to give 193 535 kg, the weight without payload. Then 206 535 − 193 535 = 13 000 kg payload, pretty poor for such a heavy aircraft, but when going to spots like Iceland, calling for much fuel for an alternate in Scotland, such a case can frequently happen.

One more then:

Maximum TOW 47 300 kg
Weight less fuel and payload 33 400 kg
Fuel required from departure to destination 9 775 kg
Reserve fuel (assume unused) 1 985 kg

What is maximum payload that can be carried?
47 300 − 33 400 = 13 900 kg = fuel + payload.
FOB is 9 775 + 1 985 = 11 760 kg
∴ Payload is 2 140 kg

All the problems boil down to either of these types, and in practice the Station Duty Officer has a simple form to resolve them. The "burn-off" will usually include not only the fuel used from departure to destination but also oil and water.

Regulated landing weight	52 618	kg	Max TOW under forecast
Burn-off	18 240		conditions 72 575
	70 858	kg	
RTOW	70 858	kg	
Estimated weight, no fuel			
(Empty Tank weight)	42 628		
Max Fuel Available	28 230	kg	
Flight Plan Fuel	28 230	kg	
Excess Available	NIL		
Loadsheet Fuel	28 230	kg	
+ Taxi and etc.	500		

This is the fuel in your tanks   28 730 kg   TOW 70 858 kg

And you will see that the restricting factor on this trip was landing weight, and the fuel uplifted exactly the Flight Plan requirements.

4: Point of No Return

PNR is the point beyond which an aircraft cannot go and still return to its departure field within its endurance.

This is entirely a fuel problem, and some reserve for holding or diversion should always be allowed for before setting about the calculation. A PNR is scarcely pertinent on trips over land well served with airfields, though a pilot will often prefer, if his destination and destination alternates are forecast en route to be below limits for his ETA, to return home rather than lob into an airfield where conditions for waiting with a crowd of passengers are miserable, expensive or politically troublesome. But over the oceans and deserts, a PNR is a must; the time to it is noted on the Flight Plan, and the ETA thereat put in on departure: it can be amended on the way if forecast winds are diabolically different from actual, or the flight is conducted at a different height or power than planned.

The solution of the problem is invariably found by formula, simply solved on the computer. The distance to the PNR is the distance to be covered back if the aircraft returns, i.e. distance Out = distance Home. The time for this distance at Ground Speed Out plus the time for this distance at Ground Speed Home will equal your endurance time excluding reserves.

If E = total endurance in hours (excluding reserve)

T = Time to PNR in hours

O = G/S Out.

H = G/S Home

R = Distance to the PNR.

Then:

$$E = \frac{R}{O} + \frac{R}{H}$$

$$EOH = R(O + H)$$

$$R = \frac{EOH}{O+H}$$

and since $T = \frac{R}{O}$

$$OT = \frac{EOH}{O+H}$$

$$T = \frac{EH}{O+H}$$

Work in minutes, if you like, as the computer work is eased; and beware of assuming that a wind component Out of +20 must give a Wind Component Home of −20; at lower G/S, drift is greater, so check the G/S out and home against Track out and home. Having obtained the Time to PNR, the distance can be readily found at

G/S out, e.g. endurance 4 hours, excluding 45 min reserve, Track 300(T), W/V 270/40, TAS 200 kt

$\therefore$ G/S Out 164 kt   G/S Home 234 kt

$$T = \frac{240 \times 234}{164 + 234}$$

$$= 141 \text{ min}$$

and 2h 21m at 164 kt = 386 nm

All straightforward and the accuracy of the result can be checked − 2h 21m out + 386 nm at G/S 234 kt or 1h 39m = 4h endurance.

Point of No Return on two or more legs

Weather systems and Traffic Control systems seldom permit a long drag on a Single Track nowadays, and finding the PNR on a route where one or more changes of Track are involved is quite simple, and rational.

Example

Following are route details: ignore climb and descent:-

	Track(T)	Distance	W/V
TAIPEH − KAGOSHIMA	042	606	260/110
KAGOSHIMA − SHIZUOKA	064	417	280/80
SHIZUOKA − TOKYO	011	61	290/50

ATD TAIPEH 1020 GMT
TAS 410 kt
Fuel Consumption 3 000 kg/hr
Reserve (assume unused) 45 min
Fuel on Board 15 000 kg
    Give ETA PNR.
Endurance first for the calculation:
    15 000 kg = 5hr
Less reserve 45 min
    4h 15m
Now essential Ground Speeds:

	G/S Out	G/S Home
TAIPEH − KAGOSHIMA	491	318
KAGOSHIMA − SHIZUOKA	470	344
SHIZUOKA − TOKYO	396	415

To get rid of the TAIPEH − KAGOSHIMA leg
    at G/S Out 491 kt takes 1h 14m
and if return to TAIPEH from KAGOSHIMA
    at G/S Home 318 kt takes 1h 55m
    $\therefore$ 3h 09m would be required for KAGOSHIMA and back

So endurance from KAGOSHIMA is 1h 06m, and clearly the
PNR is on the SHIZUOKA leg.

$$T = \frac{EH}{O+H} = \frac{66 \times 344}{470 + 344} = 28 \text{ min}$$

∴ from TAIPEH, time to PNR is 1h 14m + 28 min = 1h 42m
and ETA is 1202 GMT.
And check:

Out to KAGOSHIMA	1h 14m
plus KAGOSHIMA to PNR	28m
Out	1h 42m

Home 28 min at G/S Out 470 = 220 nm	
220 nm Home to KAGOSHIMA at G/S Home 344 kt	38 min
KAGOSHIMA — TAIPEH	1h 55 min
Home	2h 33 m

Total 4h 15m = endurance, leaving 45 min reserve.

The method out and back on Leg 1 could be repeated on further legs until the
endurance remaining clearly must resolve the leg on which the PNR is placed.

It is commonplace when a situation arises that an aircraft turns back or
diverts, to adjust the power and height, if permissible, in order to economise on fuel;
the consumption outwards might be high and carefree but having turned back for
any reason at all, it will be very cautious. The PNR in this case becomes a
matter of simple algebra, based on the essential knowledge that endurance is known.

e.g.   G/S Out 180 kt, G/S Home 240 kt, consumption out 2 400
        kg/hr, consumption home 2 000 kg/hr, fuel available for this calculation
        12 500 kg.

Remembering that the distance to the PNR = distance from PNR back home
= X nm

$$\text{Then } \left(\frac{X}{180} \times 2\,400\right) + \left(\frac{X}{240} \times 2\,000\right) = 12\,500 \text{ kg}$$

a case of time against consumption out and back.

X, the distance to PNR = 576 nm
and the time to it at G/S Out 180 kt = 3h 12m

A problem of this sort on various legs would be tackled as before, arriving at a
turning point with the new fuel remaining, after calculating out and back on
previous sectors.

Graphical Solution

Much against our will, we'll put this into the story: it will become part of the Flight
Progress graph, another quite unnecessary sheet on any flight, as it presupposes that
all aircrew are incapable of understanding anything unless presented to them in
pictorial form. It's included in the syllabus in case you find yourself flying for a firm
of graph maniacs.

Given: FOB 750 gal, TAS 180 kt, Consumption 95 gal/hr
          Headwind component 25 kt
          Find the PNR, leaving 50 gal in reserve.

Steps: (i)   Endurance for 700 gal at 95 gal/hr = 442 min
          (ii)   Distance OUT for 442 min   = 442 min at G/S 155 kt
                                                     = 1 142 nm
          (iii) Distance HOME for 442 min   = 442 min at G/S 205 kt
                                                     = 1 505 nm
          (iv)   With coordinates fuel and distance, plot these curves.

The point of intersection is the PNR

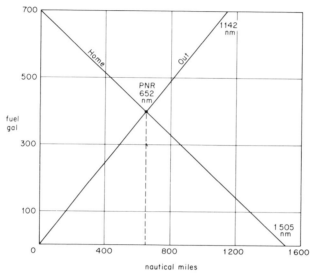

Fig. 3. 4. 1

This can be checked correct with the formulae. On the graph, as large a scale as possible should be chosen to ensure an accurate result.

This simple method is of no avail if climb, cruise, descent are involved, or TAS or consumption are variable factors: this lot is part of any decent trip in a decent aeroplane, and the solution by graph becomes quite a sweat.
Proceed as follows:
          (i)   Complete the Flight Plan.
          (ii)   Plot the Fuel/distance Out, starting with TOC and ending with TOD, reading the stages off the Flight Plan. This is in fact the chart to be used for the Flight progress; as the turning or reporting points are reached, the fuel used so far is entered on the graph, and a comparison with fuel planned is at once visually apparent.
          (iii) Draw a line across the graph to represent the fuel available for PNR calculation; where this line meets the fuel coordinate may now be deemed the 'departure point' whither the aircraft is returning having used the PNR fuel.
          (iv)   From this point, work <u>backwards</u> to TOD and thenceforth in fuel used per sector, until the curves cross. Fig. 2.
This is all very clever (apart from being very tedious) as an academic exercise:

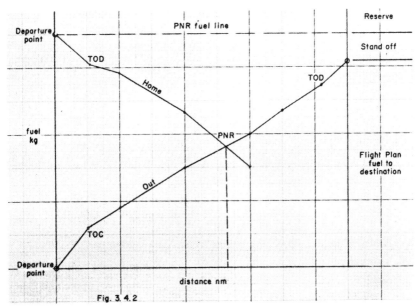

Fig. 3. 4. 2

in practice, fuel consumption varies as AUW decreases, or ditto TAS. To do the
reverse Flight Plan, the aircraft's weight must be known overhead departure point
on return to it: this is found by subtracting the fuel available for PNR from the
original TOW, and as the flight home progresses backwards, and the details
plotted, a reasonable assumption can be made for the AUW over the obvious PNR
leg.

The PNR is usually solved, however, by straightforward methods, and here's
a sample to work through, and you should check every figure so that wrinkles can
be spotted, and the method acquired.

Using CAP 159, for a flight from A to B assume:

(i)   Distance 1 870 nm

(ii) TOW 67 000 kg

(iii) Outward: Climb on Track from 1 000 ft at A to 33 000 ft pressure
               altitude. Temp dev − 3°C, wind component + 20.
               Cruise at 0.75 M_{ind} at 33 000 ft Temp dev +1°C, wind
               component + 45.

(iv) Homeward: Cruise at 0.75 M_{ind} at 32 000 ft Temp dev - 1°C, wind
               component - 40. Use subsidiary table to allow for
               descent to 1 000 ft over A.

(v)   Fuel available, excluding reserves: 19 800 kg.

Determine the flight time and distance to the PNR.

Here goes!

(i)   Climb Table 31A - 3°C Temp dev
         To 33 000 ft for TOW 67 000 kg

                 Fuel 2 550 kg   Time 21 min
                 +   500   +   2 min (T/O to 1 000 ft)
                    ───────   ───────
                    3 050 kg   23 min   footnote

         TAS 338 kt, G/S 358 kt for 21 min   =   126 nm

(ii)   Cruise Table 31D +1°C Temp dev
AUW at start of cruise 67 000 kg − 3 050 used on climb
= 63 950 kg
and fuel remaining   = 16 750 kg (total PNR fuel 19 800
− 3050 climb)
Extract TAS 432 kt   ∴ G/S 477 kt
From 63 950 kg to 58 300 kg AUW
Consumption is 4 000 kg/hr
= 5 650 kg to use, takes 1h 25m = 678 nm

We've done just over 800 nm, and used nearly 9 000 kg of fuel, and some watch must be kept on consumption outward and homeward.
The next 2 hours on the table we're in gives a consumption of 3 800 kg/hr, but only 1½ hr on the homebound table of Temp dev −1°C at 32 000 ft
So 1h 30m at 3 800 kg/hr = 5 700 kg
and all is correct whichever way we're going, out or home.

Fuel used so far: Climb   3 050
Level   5 650
5 700
_____
14 400   kg, leaving 5 400 kg in tanks

This must be homeward, and AUW by then is
67 000 − 14 400 = 52 600 kg
Extract from the −1°C table at 32 000 ft, 3 600 kg/hr and the remaining
5 400 kg will go in 1h 30m
From TOC, the endurance is therefore 4h 25m but in this figure we must balance the 126 nm flown on the climb, and give a thought to the ultimate descent.
From the Temp dev −1°C Table, TAS is 429 kt
∴ G/S 389 kt and 126 nm takes 19 min
AUW over A on return will be 67 000 kg − 19 800 kg
= 47 200 kg
From table, consumption at the end is 3 600 kg/hr
so 19 min   = 1 140 kg
The footnote for descent gives 300 kg and 9 min, the fuel being a subtractive element.
Thus, the outward climb distance has been balanced on return by 840 kg (1 140 − 300), 19 min of time; the extra time on descent being as it were non-fuel consuming. The cruise endurance is 4h 06m, and the balancing act of that 126 nm can be omitted from the solution by formula viz:

$$\frac{T}{E} = \frac{H}{O+H} \quad \frac{T}{246} = \frac{389}{477 + 389} = \frac{246 \times 389}{866}$$
$$= 1h\ 50m$$

Add on the 23 min of climb and the time to the PNR from T/O is 2h 13m resolving itself into a distance from A of 126 + 878 = 1 004 nm.
A Check of this could now be made from the start, and an answer within 200 or 300 kg of the original FOB of 19 800 kg would be satisfactory, as one does avoid half minutes and fuels are rounded off to the 50s.
A question like this at first sight looks best solved graphically; do try it and see.

5: Critical Point

Critical point is the point from which it would take equal time to continue to destination as to return to departure field.

This is not a function of fuel at all whatever: there is a critical point when crossing the road or swimming a river: distance and related G/S are the factors to consider and it is important to bear in mind that it is a Flight Plan problem initially, to prepare for some eventuality like an engine failure when an instant decision must be taken to proceed or return, the quicker being the choice as there is some concern among those present.

Again, the solution is done by simple formula, and the ETA CP entered on the Flight Plan; the same arguments hold as previously as to the trips on which a CP is vital.

Take a straightforward case first

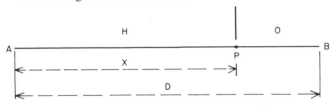

Fig. 3. 5. 1

Where D is total distance
        P the Critical Point
        X Distance to CP in nautical miles
        O Ground Speed Out in knots
        H Ground Speed Home in knots
Then by definition:
        P to A at G/S Home = P to B at G/S Out.

i.e. $\dfrac{X}{H} = \dfrac{D-X}{O}$

$OX = H(D-X)$

$OX = HD-HX$

$OX + HX = HD$

$\therefore \quad \dfrac{DH}{O+H} = X$, the distance to the CP.

Now the CP is bursting with importance when the aircraft is acting up, usually an engine out, not in itself an emergency, but leading towards it if something else happens: an aircraft on 3 engines will not go as fast as on 4, strangely enough, especially when fuel conservation is high priority. An operator, therefore, lays down in the manual an average 3-engined and 2-engined TAS at specified heights; thus, the CP data must be worked using the reduced TAS so that the equal times home and away from the CP are appropriate to the conditions should the exigency occur. In the air, once the CP is passed (and the ETA to it will be calculated at normal G/S, just like a reporting point), the pilot will proceed to his destination. A separate CP at full TAS can be calculated readily, to cope with serious situations like a loose panther in the hold, or a berserk and frothing passenger which affect the safety of the aircraft and its occupants, but not its power. But in a pressurisation failure, for instance, while the power is unaffected, the CP is dependent on a TAS at a new enforced height with implications very similar to the engine failure cases. This, too, calls for a separate CP, not an arduous calculation since the action for the pressurisation failure will be laid down and the optimum height with the appropriate data is set out in the aircraft manual.

There are several pertinent possibilities, then; and bear in mind that they are just that. One or more CPs are noted on the Flight Plan to be referred to as though they are turning points, with their ETA. Once a CP is passed, the pilot's action is clear: if a near-emergency arises, he will aim for the destination airfield. The CP is but a preparation in case of emergency, and if that emergency happens, he has the facts before him at once.

Some samples:
1.   Track 240(T), W/V 310/35, TAS 260 kt Distance 530 nm
$\therefore$ G/S out = 245 kt   G/S home = 270 kt

$$\text{Distance to CP} = \frac{DH}{O + H}$$

$$= \frac{530 \times 270}{245 + 270}$$

$$= 278 \text{ nm}$$

and time to CP   = 278 at G/S out 245 kt = 1h 08m
Check
278 at G/S home 270 kt   =   1h 02m
(530 − 278) at G/S out 245 kt   =   1h 02m

2.   What is distance to CP en route from DARWIN and MELBOURNE distance
1 728 nm, cruise TAS 425 kt, 3-engine TAS 400 kt, headwind component from CP to MELBOURNE 5 kt, headwind component CP to DARWIN 20 kt?
$\therefore$ for the CP calculation: G/S out   =   395 kt,
                                     G/S home   =   380 kt,

$$\text{Distance to CP} = \frac{DH}{O + H}$$

$$= \frac{1\ 728 \times 380}{395 + 380}$$

$$= 847 \text{ nm}$$

You check.

The ETA CP can then be found simply from the normal Flight Plan after departure; this type of problem is most frequently used in practice and, despite finding the wind components by inspection, is proved reasonably accurate: with a long trip going fairly to plan until an engine drops out, a pilot who turns back because it happens 5 minutes before the CP cannot be criticised for being dogmatically correct, but his employers and passengers might think him rather lacking in dash and élan.

3.   Now for the several Track CP.

TAS 200 kt Engine failure TAS 160 kt

Route

BAGHDAD–BASRA	Track 115(T), Dist 170 nm W/V 180/20
BASRA–KUWAIT	Track 178(T), Dist 110 nm W/V 230/30
KUWAIT–BAHRAIN	Track 129(T), Dist 147 nm W/V 250/15

Find ETA CP if ATD BAGHDAD is 1115.

Draw a freehand diagram, and set in the G/S out and home at reduced TAS.

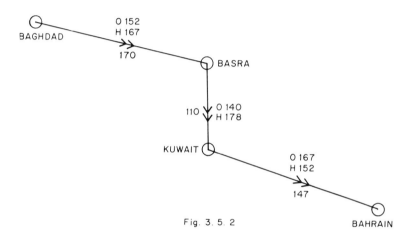

Fig. 3. 5. 2

Remember we are concerned in the air, with an engine out, with equal time home and on: we have to get the CP placed on a single leg, balancing the time home with time out.

On BASRA home to BAGHDAD 170 nm at 167 kt gives 1h 01m

Now balance that 1h 01m out on the KUWAIT–BAHRAIN leg,

    147 nm at G/S out 167 kt takes 53 min

There are still 8 min out to take care of, and that will be used up on BASRA–KUWAIT leg.

    8 min at G/S out 140 kt   =   19 nm

Thus 1h 01m home balances 1h 01m out, and the CP is on the BASRA–KUWAIT leg, the total distance to be considered

    110–19   =   91 nm from BASRA

$$\frac{DH}{O+H} = \frac{91 \times 178}{140 + 178} = 51 \text{ nm from BASRA}$$

ETA CP BAGHDAD–BASRA 170 nm at cruise G/S 192 kt = 53 min

    BASRA – CP 51 nm at cruise G/S 180 kt   = 17 min

    Total time at normal cruise 1h 10m

    ∴ ETA 1225

You check, that if engine fails at 1225, the time back to BAGHDAD is equal to the time on to BAHRAIN.

Graphical Solution

Critical Point problems may be solved graphically by plotting two curves, one for the flight out and the other for the flight home on a distance/time axis graph. The intersection of the two curves indicates CP for the flight, time and distance being read off the appropriate graph axes.

Example: Speed OUT is less than speed HOME.

A – B 750 nm wind component – 15 kt

TAS : 180 kt Full

140 kt Reduced

Find CP for both speeds

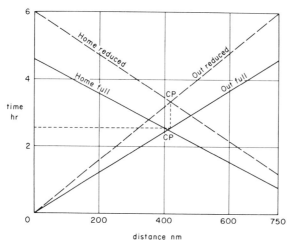

Fig. 3. 5. 3

Solution: Full Speed

G/S Out 165 kt dist 750 nm Time 273 min

G/S Home 195 kt dist 750 nm Time 231 min

Plot the coordinates distance/time. See Fig. 3. CP occurs at distance of 406 nm, time 2h 28m.

Reduced Speed

G/S Out 125 kt dist 750 nm time 360 min

G/S Home 155 kt dist 750 nm time 290 min

Plot the coordinates distance/time. CP occurs at distance 415 nm. To find the time to CP, draw in a line from the point of intersection to the Full Speed out line at a distance of 415 nm and read off the time on the vertical axis of the graph. The time is 2h 31m.

The above solutions may be checked by use of formula.

The accuracy of the result depends on the graph scale.

Example: Speed OUT is more than speed HOME. In this case, the time Home will be greater than time Out. The best way to approach this situation is to find the time out normally, and then, work out the distance that would be travelled HOMEWARD in that time. Say the ground speed Out is 195 kt, the ground speed Home is 165 kt, the time taken Out is 231 min and in that time the distance covered on Homeward flight will be 634 nm.

Plot the two curves now and point of intersection is the CP.

AIRCRAFT INSTRUMENTS

1: Airspeed Indicator (ASI)

The principle of an Air Speed Indicator (ASI) is the measurement of two pressures called Static and Pitot pressures.

If you move an open ended tube through the air, pressure will be exerted at the closed end of the tube. This pressure is composed of two components: that pressure which would be present at the closed end of the tube irrespective of whether the tube is stationary or moving. This is due to the atmospheric pressure and is called "static" pressure. The other component is the additional pressure entirely due to the tube's movement through the air. The faster the tube is moved, greater the pressure that is exerted. This pressure is known as "dynamic" pressure. The sum total of the two components is known as "pitot" pressure. That "additional" or dynamic pressure mentioned above is the one representative of the air speed of the tube and the one we are interested in. But the pressure produced at the closed end of the tube is pitot pressure. Thus, to have an indication of the air speed it is merely the question of extracting dynamic from pitot pressure.

Pitot pressure, P, equals dynamic pressure, D, plus static pressure, S:

$$\text{or,} \quad P = D + S$$
$$\therefore \quad \underline{D = P - S}$$

An ASI measures the dynamic pressure by solving the above formula, that is, by subtracting static pressure from pitot pressure continuously through the flight and presenting the information in terms of the aircraft's air speed.

Construction

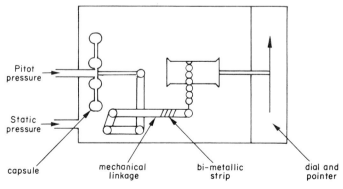

Pitot pressure

Static pressure

| capsule | mechanical linkage | bi-metallic strip | dial and pointer |

Fig. 4.1.1

The construction of an ASI is shown in fig 1 above. In place of an open ended tube, the ASI uses an open ended capsule, fixed inside an air tight case. The open end of the capsule is connected to a tube installed in the aircraft's nose or on one of its wings, and facing the air flow. This tube is called a pitot tube or sometimes, pressure head. Thus, the pressure produced inside the capsule is the pitot pressure and the other face of the capsule will expand or contract in response to the variations in this pressure. Inside the case (but not inside the capsule) static pressure is fed. The result of the presence of this static surrounding the capsule is to check the expansion of the capsule since the face of the capsule expanding under pitot pressure must overcome the opposition due to this static. The resultant expansion will, therefore, be equal to the value of P – S which is dynamic pressure.

All that remains to be done now is to transmit this capsule face movement (expansion and contraction) to a pointer. This is done by means of a suitable mechanical linkage. We are not interested in the details of the interior mechanism except that somewhere in the mechanical linkage a bi-metallic strip is introduced to compensate for expansion/contraction of the linkage due to temperature variations.

Calibration

This is a problem, where, having constructed an ASI one asks oneself, "Where, on the face of the dial, am I going to mark off 60 kt and 100 kt and the rest of the speed range?" The problem is not a simple one since here we are dealing with atmospheric pressures. You may, for example, take the ASI for calibration in a car. Run the car up to 60 kt, and where the pointer reaches at that speed, mark off 60 kt. But the question is, will the pointer reach the same position when the car is doing 60 kt the following day? Or, for that matter, the following hour? The answer would be "no", for the pressures vary from hour to hour and day to day. It is, therefore, necessary first to adopt some standard in calibrating the ASI and then make allowance for known departure from that standard. The standard adopted is the International Standard Atmosphere (ISA) air density at sea level. This is that density which is produced when the pressure is 1013.2 mb and the temperature is +15°C. The calibration formula is :

$$P = \tfrac{1}{2}\rho V^2 \left(1 + \frac{V^2}{4C^2}\right) \quad \text{where} \quad \begin{aligned} P &= \text{pitot pressure} \\ \rho &= \text{air density under ISA} \\ V &= \text{indicated air speed} \\ C &= \text{speed of sound} \end{aligned}$$

Errors

An ASI suffers from the following four errors:
1.   Instrument Error. This is due to small manufacturing imperfections and the fact that a very minute movement of the capsule is expanded to give a reasonable movement of the pointer. The extent of this error can be determined by comparing the readings at various air speeds against a standard ASI. The errors so found are recorded on a card. The reading you take from the Air Speed Indicator is known as "Indicated Air Speed" (IAS).
2.   Pressure Error. This error is also known as "Position Error." The pressures presented inside the capsule and inside the case must be correct pressures if correct speed is to be measured. As far as the pitot tube is concerned to a large extent it gives correct values. Static is the main source of the error since to be correct it must

be entirely free from any air flow under pressure or from other
disturbances caused by aerodynamic surfaces. If the static tube is combined with
the pitot head, an arrangement shown in fig 2, it will be seen that the static tube
will be surrounded by disturbed air flow and some dynamic pressure will enter it

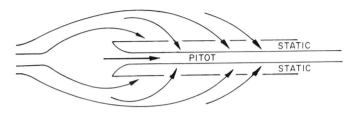

Fig. 4. 1. 2

giving erroneous results. These errors can be minimised if the static source is
completely divorced from the pitot head. Under this arrangement it takes the form of
a "static vent" (as against static head). It consists of a small copper plate with a hole
drilled radially through the centre. The air under static pressure enters a tube
through this hole and is conveyed to the inside of the instrument case at the other
end of the tube. An ideal position is found for installation of the static vent where
the disturbance is minimum and to improve the results further the plate is fixed
flush with the fuselage skin to avoid encouraging local disturbances. Approximately
95% of the pressure error is reduced by using this arrangement.

There are two distinct types of pressure errors.

Position Error. This is the error entirely due to the location of the pitot head
and static vent, and the magnitude of the error depends on this. As we saw above
the static is the main source of the error and no matter how ideal a position for
static vent is found there is bound to be some disturbance present around it. The
magnitude of the error also depends on the aircraft speed, since, generally, higher
the speed greater the disturbance. This error, like instrument error, is a known factor
and can be determined throughout the ASI's speed range. In practice both instrument and position errors are combined together on a single card, called "Pressure
Error" (PE) Card. The reading taken directly from the instrument is called
Indicated Air Speed (IAS). PE is applied to the IAS to give Rectified Air Speed
(RAS).

Manoeuvre-Induced Error. This error occurs when the pitot head is not directly
facing the air flow, for example, when an aircraft is in a climb or descent. The error
also occurs when extraneous disturbance is caused by the pilot's actions such as
lowering of the undercarriage or manipulating flaps. The aircraft is then no longer
aerodynamically 'clean' and the static will be affected. The situation is aggravated
by the fact that short term pressure fluctuations are present during rapidly
changing manoeuvres and that some time, however small, must elapse between
arrival of the pressure at one end of the tube and its delivery at the instrument end
of the tube. Thus you may have an indication which was true a few moments ago.
These errors are random and therefore cannot be pre-determined for recording on
a card.

To summarise, the magnitude of pressure errors depend on:

(a) the position of the static vent;

(b) aircraft speed;

(c) angle of attack and type of manoeuvre;

(d) aerodynamic state, e.g. whether flaps down etc.

3. Density Error. This error occurs due to the calibration of the ASI. An Air Speed Indicator reads correct air speed only when flying in an air mass of such density as would be produced if the prevailing pressure was 1013.2 mb and the temperature was +15°C. These data describe the ISA density at the sea level but the conditions may prevail above the surface in its near vicinity. By "near vicinity" we mean a few hundred feet rather than a few thousand feet. At 5 000 ft for example for this density to exist the temperature required is approximately −32°C and at 10 000 ft it is −73°C. Thus, it is most unlikely that an ASI would read correct air speed at 10 000 ft.

As for the nature of the error, as the height is gained the atmosphere becomes rarer and density decreases. Therefore, the dynamic pressure falls and the indicator gives a reading which is too low for a given air speed. The rectified air speed must therefore be corrected for density error to give the true indication of the speed and you will have noticed from above that in the majority of the cases it will be an additive correction. The correction is made on the computer by setting pressure altitude against temperature in the 'air speed' window and reading off True Air Speed (TAS) on the outer scale against rectified air speed on the inside scale.

To summarise:

IAS ± PE   = RAS;

RAS : Density Error   = TAS

TAS is the air speed the aircraft is actually doing through the air.

From the foregoing it will be appreciated that an aircraft flying straight and level from warmer air mass into colder air mass or vice versa will experience changes in the air speed indications. For example: an aircraft is flying at 10 000 ft and the temperature is −5°C, its RAS is 130 kt. The TAS for this pressure altitude, temperature and RAS is 150 kt. Later the same aircraft enters an air mass having temperature of, say, −15°C. This air mass is relatively colder and therefore denser, so the new dynamic pressure will be higher and the indications will change. On the computer, to maintain a TAS of 150 kt as before but under the new set of conditions, the RAS will show an increased reading of 133 kt − a higher indication. Alternatively if you are maintaining an RAS of 130 throughout the new TAS is reduced to 147 kt.

In absence of a computer, density error may be estimated from the following formula:

TAS = RAS + (1.75% of RAS per 1 000 ft of altitude)

For example, RAS is 130 and height 10 000 ft:

TAS = 130 + 1.75% of 130 per 1 000 ft x 10

    = 130 + 17.5% of 130

    = 130 + 22

TAS = 152 which compares with above illustration.

4. Compressibility Error. This error generally applies to high speed aircraft doing a TAS of 300 kt or over. At such speeds air compresses when brought to rest in

front of the pitot head and consequently enters the tube under higher pressure, giving an overread of IAS. Thus, compressibility error is corrected as a subtractive factor. Air nearer the Earth's surface is not easily compressed since it is already dense and the compressibility error near surface levels is negligible. The error increases with altitude. For a given altitude an increase in air speed increases the error. That portion of the calibration formula given in the brackets is known as the Compressibility Factor. It confirms the above two statements. The correction for this error is made on the computer. Frequently graphs for a particular aircraft are available which correct for this as well as pressure error in one operation. The corrected speed so found is known as Equivalent Air Speed (EAS).

Blockages
Blocked Pitot. If the pitot tube gets blocked by ice or other obstruction before take-off there will be no reaction at all and the instrument will read zero. In level flight should the pitot get blocked the dial will hold the reading unless pressure leaks away in which case the pointer will return to zero. During a descent a blocked pitot will give an underread as the increasing static will put up increasing opposition to constant value pitot pressure trapped inside the tube.

If the pitot tube develops a leak the ASI underreads.

Blocked Static. Should the static become blocked during take-off the instrument will underread (high value static is trapped in). During level flight the instrument continues to give the same reading. During a descent it will overread and a dangerous situation can readily be envisaged when the aircraft could stall at an air speed indicated as being well above the stalling speed.

Serviceability Checks
As far as the instrument itself is concerned there is nothing a pilot can check except that the pointer is not stuck on the dial. A pilot must check that the pitot head cover and the static vent pins are removed, that the pitot head is not bent, cracked, misaligned with the airflow or otherwise damaged in any way.

2: Altimeters

Pressure Altimeter

The atmosphere has weight and this weight exerts pressure. An ordinary household barometer measures this pressure and indicates the weather. If we took this barometer to the top of a tall building it would be noticed that for the same weather conditions the pressure indication is less. This is because the atmosphere remaining above the barometer at height is less than at ground level. If we knew the rate of the fall of pressure with height, we could graduate that barometer to read in terms of height instead of reading the pressure. An aircraft altimeter is simply an aneroid barometer adapted for use in aircraft on the basis that 1 millibar of pressure change takes place for a change of height of approximately 27 feet. In the above illustration, if the barometer reads 1010 mb at ground level and 1008 mb at height, the top of the building is approximately 60 feet (30 ft to a millibar is a good figure to use unless the examination question gives a specific figure).

Construction and Operation

Two or three capsules each having vacuum or partial vacuum in them are used to achieve sensitivity. They are stacked together with one face fastened down to the base permitting movement due to pressure changes at the other end.
Fig 1.

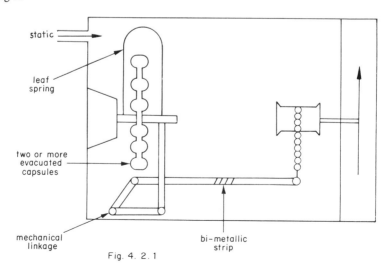

Fig. 4. 2. 1

To prevent the capsules from collapsing (because of the vacuum in them) a spring called the leaf spring is used to hold up the moveable face. The movement of the capsules in response to change in height is transmitted to the pointers, usually three pointers, through a suitable mechanical linkage. Somewhere in the linkage a bi-metallic bar or other similar device is inserted to compensate for temperature variations. The whole assembly is encased in a container, having an inlet for the static pressure but otherwise airtight.

As the aircraft gains height the value of static decreases and the capsule expands under the tension of the spring.
Fig. 2.

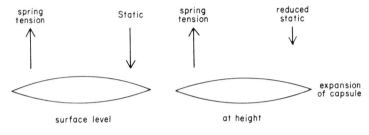

Fig. 4. 2. 2

Similarly, as the aircraft descends, static increases and the capsule contracts. These movements are magnified sufficiently to give reasonable pointer displacement, which move around a dial calibrated in feet.

Calibration

Like the ASI we are here dealing with constantly varying atmospheric pressures which show up so vividly on a household barometer. Therefore, a standard for calibration must be adopted and this standard is the International Standard Atmosphere as follows:
1. The sea level pressure is presumed to be 1013.2 mbs.
2. Sea level temperature +15°C.
3. The temperature falls with height at the rate of 1.98°C per thousand feet up to a height of 36 090 ft. Above this height the temperature remains almost constant at −56.5°C. Note that this item is not included in calibration of an ASI, and that this is not the complete definition of International Standard Atmosphere.

Errors

The instrument suffers from five different errors as follows.
1.   Instrument Error. This error is similar to that in an ASI except that one more factor must be considered. That is the presumption that the rate of fall of pressure with change in height is a constant value. In actual circumstances, as the atmosphere becomes rarer that rate of fall must decrease with height. To this extent the altimeter becomes unreliable when flying at high altitudes.
2.   Pressure Error. This error occurs for reasons similar to an ASI and both its components, position and manoeuvre induced errors, are present. As regards the

error due to the position of the static vent a PE card is available for correction to the readings taken from the instrument.

3.   Barometric Error. A household barometer again comes in handy to show that if it was calibrated to give 0 ft reading whc.e the pointer stood one day, the next day the pointer would suggest that the house had gained or lost height. As for altimeters, any variations from the standard calibration conditions will give an error. This is known as barometric error, known in the early days as Pressure Error. It is most important that the altimeter hands are set to read height above the ground or mean sea level before taking off, thus correcting for pressure difference from 1013.2 mb. This is done by setting the appropriate pressure on what is called the 'millibar sub-scale', the sub-scale being visible through a window on the instrument. A knob is provided on the instrument to set the desired pressure. When it is turned the whole mechanism inside the instrument turns, turning the pointers with it. Various pressure settings available are considered later in the chapter.

4.   Temperature Error. The instrument presumes each pressure to be assoc-iated with a temperature and a fall in the temperature at ISA rate ($1.98°C/1\ 000$ ft.) Where there is any departure from this value an error will occur. Generally no allow-ance is made for this error in flight but there is a facility on the computer to calculate it.

5.   Time Lag Error. This error occurs due to the time that the pressures take, however small, to travel from one end of the tube to the other. (Pressures travel at approximately 1 100 ft/sec and on a modern aircraft the distance to travel may quite easily be of the order of 50 ft.) This error is most noticeable during steep climbs or descents. During a climb, higher pressure is present at any given instant and the altimeter underreads. Similarly during a descent, time lag causes an altimeter to overread. Masked time lag errors are also present during other manoeuvres.

Blockage

Should the static vent become blocked through ice or other obstruction old static will remain trapped and height changes will not be indicated.

Pressure Settings

Due to the nature of calibration and various other factors an aircraft altimeter rarely reads correct height. With this limitation in mind we are ready to familiarise ourselves with various settings available. At the outset it must be emphasised that when a specific pressure is set on the sub-scale that pressure becomes the datum from which the difference in pressures between it and the actual pressure experienced at aircraft level is measured. It is this difference which positions the pointers.

Let us take an illustration. The datum set is 1 000 mb and, say, the pressure upon the aircraft altimeter is 700 mb. The difference of 300 mb between the datum and actual pressures resolves into a pointer displacement of 300 x 30 = approximately 9 000 ft. If the datum set was 1020 in the same circumstances the difference would be 320 mb and the pointer displacement of 320 x 30 = approx. 9 600 ft. From the illustration we conclude that if pressure setting is increased, the height reading is increased, and vice versa.

Various settings available are given names in Q code. These are:

QFE: the barometric pressure at the level of the aerodrome. When set the altimeter indicates height of the aircraft above the highest point on the manœuvring area on the aerodrome. This setting is generally used for take off, landing and particularly when carrying out radar approaches.

QFF: the barometric pressure at aerodrome level, reduced to mean sea level. This reduction is made using the values of actual pressure and temperature conditions prevailing at the time and not the ISA values. This setting is mostly used by meteorological offices for plotting synoptic charts.

QNH: the barometric pressure at aerodrome level, reduced to mean sea level using ISA formula. When set, an altimeter calibrated in ISA reads height of the altimeter above mean sea level. This height is called Altitude. Two types of QNH values are available – spot QNH and Regional QNH. Spot QNH is only valid for the spot (aerodrome) where the pressure reading took place. This may be used when taking off or landing as an alternative to QFE. The law requires a pilot taking off in controlled airspace to have at least one altimeter set to aerodrome QNH value.

Regional pressure setting (i.e. QNH) in contrast to spot or aerodrome QNH is applicable throughout the region for which it is given. For the purpose of providing this service UK is divided in 13 regions known as Altimeter Setting Regions (ASRs). Each region produces, on the hour, a forecast of the lowest values in the area, and such forecast QNH is valid for one hour. Being the lowest forecast value, the setting is used for the purpose of maintaining adequate terrain clearance. When a lower value is set a lower indication results, and maximum safety is assured. The indication may not be a correct indication of the altitude but the error is in favour of safety. We said it may not be correct, because, first of all, it is a forecast value and secondly, the value chosen is true for only a small area in the region where lowest values were recorded. Elsewhere in the region, higher pressures may be expected.

Standard Setting: strictly, this is the altimeter reading on the ground with 1013.2 mb set on the sub-scale, but is commonly taken to be 1013.2 mb setting, used for flight separation between aircraft flying under IFR. With this setting the altitude indicated is called pressure altitude and the level at which an aircraft flies is called flight level. For example, if 10 000 feet of pressure altitude is indicated, the aircraft's flight level is 100. It will be appreciated that the aircraft's altitude and pressure altitude will be the same only when the QNH value is also 1013.2 mb. At all other times the indication will be in error on a 1013.2 setting. However as between two aircraft flying close to each other and therefore in the same air mass, both will have similar error in indication. The separation can therefore be maintained accurately*.

Pressure – Altimeter Relationship

From the above it will be apparent that once an aircraft departs from a place with correct setting, the indication will remain correct (disregarding limitations of QNH mentioned above) only as long as the datum pressure continues to prevail. When new pressures are encountered, the indication becomes erroneous. For the sense of the error, the rule is: when flying from an area of high pressure to an area of low

*For fuller discussion on this topic the student is advised to consult Ch. 3 of the companion volume "Aviation Law for the Pilot".

pressure the altimeter overreads. The rule may more easily be remembered from the phrase — "high – low – high." The reverse is also true. This is illustrated in fig 3. The pressure at position A is 1 000 mb:

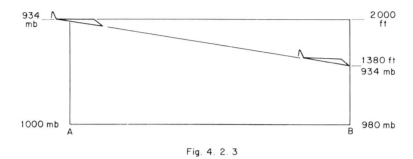

Fig. 4. 2. 3

and an aircraft is flying with this setting, its indication being 2 000 ft. The pressure upon the altimeter

$$= \frac{2\,000}{30} = \ 66 \text{ mb less than } 1\,000$$

$$= \ 934 \text{ mb}$$

In order to maintain an indication of 2 000 ft the aircraft must fly in the airspace where the pressure on the altimeter is 934 mb. Let us assume that the pressure at B is 980 mb. At B, the height at which pressure of 934 will occur   = 980 – 934

= 46 mb

= 1 380 ft

Thus, the aircraft will actually be at 1 380 ft although the indication is 2 000 ft. The aircraft flew from an area of high pressure to an area of low pressure and high – low – high rule applied.

Temperature – Altimeter Relationship

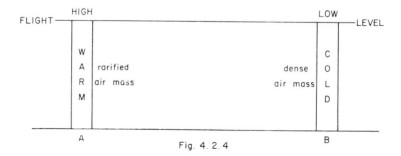

Fig. 4. 2. 4

In fig 4 above, the area around A is warmer than area around B. Therefore, at given level, the altimeter will experience higher pressure above it when over A than over B. Thus, flying from A to B without altering the datum will amount to flying from high pressure to low pressure: high–low–high: and the altimeter will overread. The reverse is also true.

Drift — Altimeter Relationship

From the following diagram it will be observed that if an aircraft (aircraft A in fig 5) experiences persistent starboard drift in the northern hemisphere, that aircraft is approaching a low pressure area and the pilot must anticipate that his altimeter will read too high. Aircraft B with port drift is approaching an area of high pressure and the altimeter will underread. Reverse results are obtained in southern hemisphere.

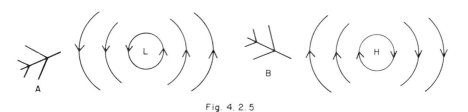

Fig. 4. 2. 5

Indicator

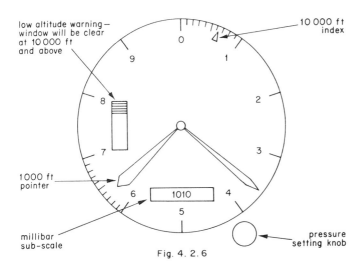

Fig. 4. 2. 6

Density Altitude

This is defined as the height in ISA at which prevailing density will occur. Density altitude is mainly used in ascertaining the performance data of aircraft. It is the same as pressure altitude when local temperature is ISA temperature. If the local temperature is lower than ISA the density altitude is lower than the pressure altitude, and vice versa. 1°C difference of temperature causes density altitude to separate from pressure altitude by approximately 119 ft.

Servo Altimeters

These are second generation altimeters designed to overcome generally some of the serious limitations of the conventional altimeters and to improve overall performance.

Capsules are still retained – generally two of them and evacuated of air – which expand and contract with changes in pressure. The rest of the mechanical linkage is replaced by a servo-assisted transmission system. The altimeters operate as follows.

The mechanism consists of a two bar (called E and I bars) induction pick-off, a servo and a cam. During a straight and level flight through a uniform air mass the system is in balance and the pointer remains steady.

When a pressure change is met the movement of the capsules is transmitted mechanically (this being the only unassisted mechanical link in the whole system) to one of the two bars of the pick-off, moving the bar in response (Fig 7). This movement throws it out of balance and an error signal is raised in the pick-off. This signal is amplified and fed to the motor. As the motor turns it drives the cam which, in its turn, moves the other bar of the pick-off. When this bar has sufficiently moved to regain balance, the error signal disappears, movement of the motor, cam and the other bar stops and the system comes to rest.

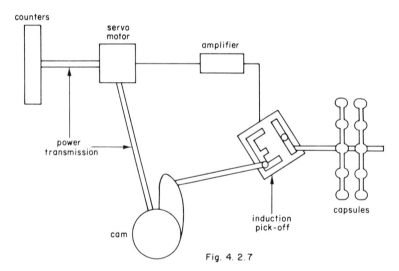

Fig. 4. 2. 7

As the motor turns, it also turns the height counters and the instrument's single pointer simultaneously with the cam. Thus, the transmission of information from capsules to counters can be said to be almost instantaneous.

Servo altimeters have the following advantages over conventional altimeters:
1.   At high altitudes very little pressure change takes place for a given change of altitude with the result that the capsule movement is considerably less than for the same change of altitude at lower levels. This factor makes ordinary altimeters inefficient at higher levels whereas the servo mechanism will pick up a capsule movement as little as 0.0002 inches per thousand feet.
2.   Power transmission gives better accuracy.
3.   There is practically no time lag between arrival of new pressure and placing of the counters.

4.   Being an electrical system, correction for pressure error could be made and an Altitude Alerting device may be incorporated.

The appearance of a typical indicator is shown in Fig 8 below.

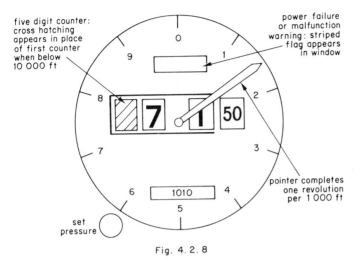

five digit counter: cross hatching appears in place of first counter when below 10 000 ft

power failure or malfunction warning: striped flag appears in window

pointer completes one revolution per 1 000 ft

set pressure

1010

Fig. 4. 2. 8

3: Vertical Speed Indicator (VSI)

Vertical Speed Indicator (VSI) is a pressure gauge which utilises the principle of differential pressure to indicate an aircraft's rate of climb or descent.

Construction and Operation

In construction, the VSI consists of a capsule held in an airtight case and fed with outside static pressure. Outside static is also fed to the inside of the case (that is, outside the capsule) but in this case it has to pass through a carefully calibrated restrictive device called the metering unit. The effect of the metering unit is to present static inside the case after a calibrated delay.

Thus, as the outside pressure alters, as it will when an aircraft commences to climb or descend, the capsule will be affected by the change almost immediately, whereas the change will reach inside the case only after a slight delay. This lag will occur every time the aircraft climbs or descends. Therefore as long as the aircraft maintains climb/descent attitude a differential will exist between the two (inside the case and inside the capsule). This differential will result in expansion or

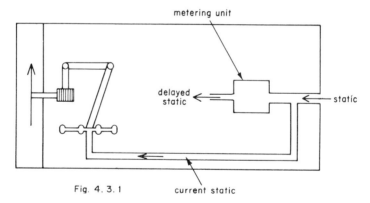

Fig. 4. 3. 1

contraction of the face of the capsule depending on whether the pressure in the case is lower or higher than the pressure inside the capsule. For example, during a climb, denser pressure (appropriate to lower altitudes) will be present in the case and less dense (or current) pressure inside the capsule. The capsule will contract.

This expansion/contraction of the capsule is transmitted to the pointer system through a suitable mechanical link. The movement of the capsule being proportionate to the rate of change of pressure, the pointer indicates the rate of change of altitude. See Fig. 1.

In level flight both pressures will be equal and the pointer will indicate 0 position.

In order to ensure the correct rate of flow through the metering unit in varying density conditions, a mechanical temperature/pressure compensatory device is generally introduced in the metering unit. Thus, correct flow is maintained during climb and descent.

Errors
1.   Time Lag Error. During sudden changes in pitch attitude, a certain time must elapse before the new pressures reach the instrument and the differential is established.
2.   Pressure Error. Error due to the position of the static vent, as well as due to manœuvre, affect the instrument. Errors due to manœuvre can cause any pressure instrument to misread for up to 3 seconds at low altitude and up to 10 seconds at 30 000 ft. The times for a VSI are even longer than these (ref. B.O.T. Circular 86/1966). Thus, during any manœuvres involving change of attitude or aerodynamic configuration, absolute reliance should not be placed on VSI.

The Indicator
Straight and level position is indicated by the pointer at 9 o'clock position.

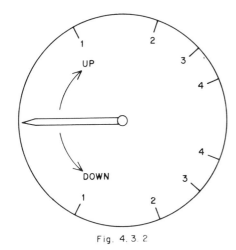

Fig. 4. 3. 2

The pointer travels through the top portion of the indicator (Fig 2) to indicate rate of climb up to 4 000 ft per minute. Similarly, it travels through the bottom portion of the indicator to indicate rate of descent up to 4 000 ft per minute. The maximum points are separated by an intervening space to prevent any chance of confusion as to which way the pointer movement took place. On some indicators the calibration is based on logarithmic scale (Fig 2), the largest pointer movement occurring near the zero position. This enables small variations from straight and level flight to be shown up.

4: Machmeter

Mach Number (MN)

A Machmeter indicates an aircraft's mach number. A mach number is defined as the ratio of its true airspeed to the speed of sound in the airspace in which it is flying.

Expressed in a formula:

$$M = \frac{V}{C} \quad \text{where} \quad \begin{aligned} M &= \text{Mach number,} \\ V &= \text{TAS} \\ C &= \text{Local Speed of Sound} \end{aligned}$$

Thus, a machmeter in fact gives the pilot a continuous indication of the ratio of TAS to the local speed of sound.

It may be asked why this indication is necessary. This knowledge is of vital importance to the aircraft flying in the vicinity of the speed of sound. As the flight approaches these speeds it is found that the behaviour of the aircraft changes. The aircraft becomes less stable, buffeting and vibrations start to occur. This happens

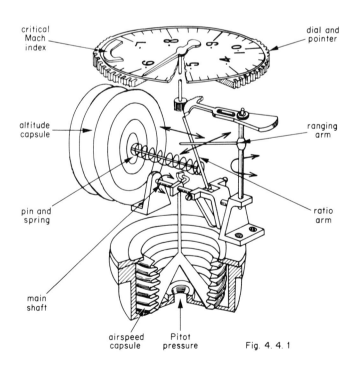

critical Mach index

dial and pointer

altitude capsule

ranging arm

pin and spring

ratio arm

main shaft

airspeed capsule

Pitot pressure

Fig. 4. 4. 1

for any particular aircraft when the aircraft's speed is a constant proportion of the speed of sound (which is the mach number)irrespective of its height and ambient temperatures. This mach number, when the aircraft begins to lose stability, etc, is called its *Critical Mach Number* and its value depends on the type of aircraft and the design of the aerodynamic surfaces. In other words, every type of aircraft that flies in these speed ranges has a Critical Mach Number which, if passed, would impose heavy stresses on the airframe.

Principle of Construction

We require the ratio of two elements — TAS and Local Speed of Sound. Now, TAS is the function of dynamic pressure, P — S, and the density. Speed of sound is the function of static pressure, S, and the density. Density being a factor to both sides of the fraction, the equation may be re-written as :

$$\text{Mach No} = \frac{P - S}{S}$$

P — S suggests ASI, or more appropriately an airspeed capsule. Similarly, S suggests altimeter capsule. Therefore, if we had two capsules, one responsive to airspeed and the other to altitude, placed 90° apart to give a ratio, by interlinking their movement to the pointer we could read off mach number. That is precisely what is done in a Machmeter. Fig. 1.

Operation

Expansion/contraction of the airspeed capsule is transmitted through main shaft to the ratio arm. Similarly, expansion/contraction of altitude capsule is transmitted to the ratio arm through a pin which is kept in position by tension of a spring.

The airspeed capsule causes movement of the ratio arm in one plane, whereas altitude capsule causes movement of the ratio arm in another plane. The two planes of movement are 90° apart.

The movement of the ratio arm is transmitted through the ranging arm to the pointer. The movement of the various arms is linked to the pointer in such a way that for an increased altitude or airspeed, a higher mach number is indicated.

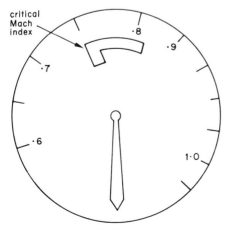

Fig. 4. 4. 2

Mach numbers are printed on the face of the instrument (Fig 2.) An adjustable lubber mark is fitted over the dial as shown, to indicate critical mach number.

Errors

This instrument only suffers from Instrument and Pressure errors, and these are similar to other pressure instruments.

Density Error. Machmeter does not suffer from this error since, as we saw above density is a factor applicable to both sides of the equation and thus, its effect is eliminated.

Temperature Error. This again causes no error as it is eliminated with the density.

Compressibility Error. Since compressibility depends on $\dfrac{\text{dynamic}}{\text{static}}$ and the instrument is calibrated for this ratio, there is no compressibility error.

Therefore, since instrument and pressure errors are relatively small in value as compared with the TAS of the aircraft we can say that indicated mach number equals true mach number. In practice, mach number is always spoken of as indicated mach number and no distinction is made between Indicated, Rectified and True Mach Numbers.

Mach Number – TAS – Speed of Sound Relationship

This relationship as we noted at the beginning is given in the formula MN $= \dfrac{V}{C}$

In order to understand its implication, it is important to understand how TAS and the speed of sound vary with altitude.

TAS

1. In International Standard Atmosphere, RAS = TAS at mean sea level.
2. As the height increases, for a given RAS, TAS increases and vice versa.
3. RAS – TAS conversions may be made on the computer using the ISA rate of fall of temperature with height of $2°$ per thousand feet.

Speed of Sound

1. In the standard conditions the speed of sound is 661 kt at sea level and 573 kt at 36 090 ft and above.
2. Thus, the speed of sound decreases as altitude is gained. The speed may be calculated from formula $C = 39 \sqrt{T}$ where T is Absolute temperature. It may also be directly read off the computer: set MN index against corrected air temperature, and read off speed of sound on outer scale against 1 on the inner scale, or it may be interpolated – speed falling at 2.5 kt per thousand feet.

You should now appreciate, for example, what your RAS would do if you were climbing at constant MN. You may work this out directly from application of the formula: $M = \dfrac{V}{C}$. Since you are climbing, C is a decreasing value. Therefore, V must decrease in order to maintain a constant mach number. If V has to be decreased, RAS must decrease.

Alternatively, you can show this by putting figures in the formula, say, at sea level, RAS = TAS = 300 and you are climbing to 30 000 ft at constant mach number.

$$\text{MN at SL} = \frac{300}{661} = .45$$

$$\text{At 30 000 ft MN of } .45 = \frac{V}{590}$$

∴ V = 590 x .45
   = 266 kt.
ISA temp at 30 000 ft = −45°C. For this temperature on the computer RAS = 166 kt.

Serviceability Checks
On the ground : check that the pointer is not resting at any place other than at 0 position.
    In flight : a rough check may be made by noting a reading of .5 mach against IAS of 330 kt near sea level.

Accuracy
± 0.01 mach, except at limit of the range where it falls to ± 0.02 M.

5: Gyroscope

Try balancing a stationary bicycle wheel and see how hard the task is. Now give it a gentle tap at the rear and make it roll. You will notice that while it is rolling at reasonable speed it does not fall down. The explanation is contained in the gyroscopic properties of the rolling wheel. A gyroscope may be described simply — any wheel that spins on its axis is a gyroscope. A spinning top, motor car wheels, aircraft propellers — these are just a few examples.

When a wheel spins on its axis it acquires two properties called Rigidity in Space and Precession.

Rigidity is the reluctance of a gyroscope to change the direction of its spin axis. This property is acquired in obedience to the Newton's First Law of Motion which states that a body continues to remain in state of rest or uniform motion unless an external force is applied to change that state.

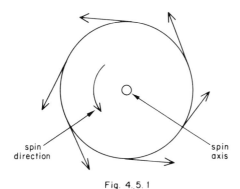

spin direction   spin axis

Fig. 4.5.1

In Fig. 1 the gyro axis is in the horizontal plane and the wheel is spinning in the vertical plane. As the wheel spins, each particle of the wheel tends to continue in its instantaneous direction as shown in the figure. This is to be expected, according to Newton. The fact that the particles do not fly off the wheel due to the tensile strength of the metal does not in any way affect this directional characteristic acquired by the moving particles. Any attempt to change the direction of the spin axis in any plane will therefore be met with opposition. This is the property of rigidity: once spinning, the gyro axis will remain pointing in the same direction in space. For the bicycle wheel to fall down while rolling, the spin axis must change its direction by 90° and unless external force is applied, it will not do so as long as it has a reasonable speed. The magnitude of rigidity is directly proportional to the speed of the wheel. The faster it spins, the greater the rigidity it acquires. It is also proportional to the moment of inertia of the wheel. To improve moment of inertia, the gyro wheel is given as large a radius as the design factors would permit and the bulk of its weight is concentrated at the rim. If you think back to the magnetic compass you will notice that this is just the opposite of what you did in that compass to achieve aperiodicity. Finally, rigidity is inversely proportional to the external force applied. To put this in mathematics,

$$R \propto \frac{SI}{F}$$

where R = rigidity
S = speed of the wheel
I = moment of inertia and
F = External Force

Precession

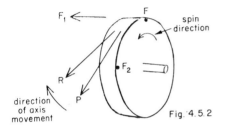

Fig. 4.5.2

In Fig. 2, P is the instantaneous direction of travel of a moving particle in a wheel spinning with its axis horizontal. F is a force applied at top of the wheel, resulting in force vector, F_1. If the wheel was stationary the effect of F_1 would be to topple the gyro, since vector P is absent. In the case of a spinning wheel, however, the two vectors will resolve into a resultant direction, R, and the axis will move clockwise from P to R. This is like saying that force was applied at point F_2 on a stationary wheel. This is precession.

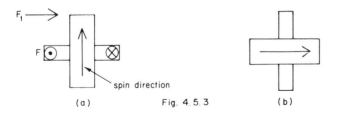

(a)   Fig. 4.5.3   (b)

In Fig. 3(a) force F is applied so as to rotate the axis anti-clockwise in the horizontal plane, as viewed from above. (Force F is applied at the paper, coming out towards us). That force will travel through 90° and act at point F_1 and the gyro will topple – Fig. 3(b). This is again precession. Precession can, therefore, be described as follows: when a force is applied to a spinning wheel, that force does not act at the point of application, but acts at a point which is 90° removed from it in the direction of the spin. Going back to the bicycle wheel, if you wish to turn the direction, you tap the appropriate side of the wheel at the top. A stationary wheel would have fallen down with this tap. In a moving wheel this force travels forward through 90° and acts. Thus, say the tap was from left to right. This left to right force acts at the forwardmost point (90° removed in the direction of the spin) of the wheel and turns the wheel to the right.

In order to precess a gyro we must overcome its rigidity. The higher the speed, greater the force required to precess it. Similarly, the larger the moment of inertia the greater the force required. Mathematically, therefore:

$$\text{Precession} \propto \frac{\text{F}}{\text{SI}}$$

These two expressions reveal that rigidity and precession are opposing terms, which is quite true. Rigidity is the reluctance to move; precession is the tendency to move.

Types of Gyroscope

The basic classification of gyroscopes is as follows:

Space Gyro. A gyroscope having freedom in all three planes is called a space gyro. The three planes relate to the three axes of aircraft, i.e. fore-and-aft axis, athwartships axis and vertical axis. There is no means of any external control over a space gyro, a feature which distinguishes it from tied gyro and earth gyro.

Tied Gyro. This is a space gyro which has a means of external control. Being basically a space gyro a tied gyro has freedom in all three planes. An uncontrolled space gyro would be of no practical use in an aircraft instrument where the gyro is required to be set up and maintained in a certain direction. We will learn the control systems with individual instruments later.

Earth Gyro. This is, again, a space gyro but controlled by the gravity of the Earth.

Rate Gyro. This is a gyro having one plane of freedom only, the plane of freedom being 90° removed from the plane of rotation. It is utilised to measure rate of turn and we will learn more about it later.

Gyro Wander.

Any deviation of the gyro axis from its set direction is termed as gyro wander. It is of two types.

Real Wander. Any physical deviation of the gyro axis is called real wander. A gyro axis ought not to wander away but various forces do effectively act on the gyro and cause it to precess. For example, some friction is always present at the spin axis. If this friction is symmetrical it merely slows down the rotor; if it is asymmetric, a force will arise which will have a precessing effect on the gyro. Similarly, friction in the gimbal rings (rings that hold the rotor and allow it movement in various planes) will precess the gyro. Another instance is the shift of the centre of gravity of the gyroscope from its dead centre position. This usually occurs as a result of wear on the gyro. When flying through turbulent air, turbulent vectors acting on the gyro will resolve in an ultimate direction and a precessing force will result. These errors are not constant; they vary with time and therefore no calibration cards are produced.

Apparent Wander. As the term suggests the gyro axis in this case does not physically wander away and yet to an observer it appears to have changed its direction. The reason for this is quite simple: the gyro maintains its direction with reference to a fixed point in space whereas we, on the Earth, rotate with the rotating Earth. Thus, since we ourselves do not maintain a fixed direction in space, the gyro must appear to us with the passage of time to have altered direction. We will study the affects due to the Earth's rotation on a horizontal axis gyro and a vertical axis gyro separately.

Horizontal Axis Gyro

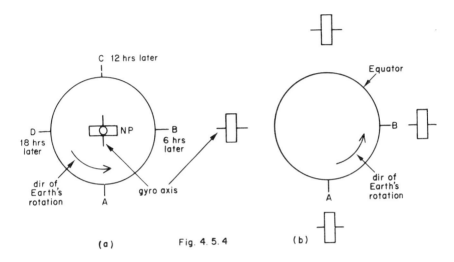

(a)   Fig. 4. 5. 4   (b)

In Fig. 4(a) we have a horizontal axis gyro at the North Pole. An observer at A sets the gyro so that its axis is aligned with him, as shown in the figure. Six hours later the Earth will have rotated through 90° and the observer will be viewing the same gyro from position B. To the observer who does not appreciate his own velocity, the gyro axis appears to have moved clockwise in the horizontal plane through 90°. Twelve hours later he will be observing the gyro along its axis but from the opposite end. Eighteen hours later he will be at position D and the axis will appear to have rotated through 270°. Finally, twenty-four hours later he will be again at Position A and view the axis just as he had initially set it.

This is an example of apparent wander. Apparent wander in the horizontal plane as we discussed above is known as gyro drift, and since at the Poles there is a drift of 360° in 24 hours, we can say that the drift experienced at the poles is the maximum possible value (that is, rate of drift is the same as the angular velocity of the Earth). To be more precise the rate of drift is 15·04° per hour.

In the above discussion, you would notice that with the horizontal axis gyro all the apparent movement occurs only in the horizontal plane. In other words, the gyro does not show up any movement in the vertical plane in terms of its axis rising or falling. Any movement of the gyro axis in the vertical plane is called gyro topple, and in this case there is no topple.

In Fig. 4(b) the gyro is a horizontal axis gyro and is placed at the Equator. Here, its axis may be aligned in the north-south direction, that is along the observer's meridian or it may be aligned in the east-west direction, that is along the Equator. At the Equator all meridians are parallel to each other and a gyro axis aligned with a meridian will remain with that meridian throughout the period of twenty-four hours. This means that there will be no drift and no topple. If the axis is aligned with the Equator as in the figure it will be noticed that six hours later the horizontal axis gyro will appear to be a vertical axis gyro (position B). This is an apparent change in the vertical plane and therefore, a topple. Further, the axis appeared to move through 90° in six hours, which means the rate of topple at the Equator is the maximum possible (15·04° per hour). The axis otherwise does not appear to move in the horizontal plane and thus there is no drift. To summarise:—

Horizontal axis gyro: at Poles   :   maximum drift; no topple;

at Equator :   no drift; maximum topple.

Vertical Axis Gyro

In Fig. 5(a) an observer at the North Pole sets up a gyro with its axis vertical. It will be apparent that the Earth will rotate beneath the axis, and the gyro axis will neither appear to topple nor drift.

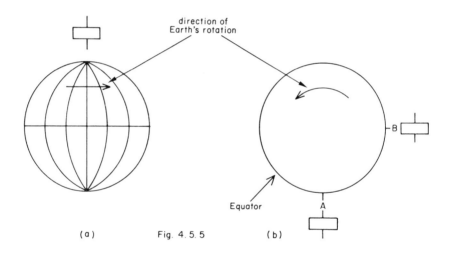

(a)   Fig. 4. 5. 5   (b)

In Fig. 5(b) the observer is shown at the Equator at position A with gyro axis vertical. The effect is similar to the horizontal gyro in Fig. 4(b). Six hours later when in position B the gyro axis will appear to have spun through 90° in the vertical plane to become apparently a horizontal axis gyro. To summarise:—

Vertical axis gyro: at Poles   :   no drift; no topple;

at Equator: no drift; maximum topple.

Combining the two we may summarise that drift at the Poles is 15·04° per hour and 0 at the Equator. Topple is 0 at the Poles and 15·04° per hour at the Equator. From this, drift and topple at intermediate latitudes bear the following relationship:

Drift   = 15·04° x sine of the latitude per hour, and

Topple = 15·04° x cosine of the latitude per hour.

Let us take an example to clarify the discussion. Say we set up a horizontal axis gyro, the axis facing east-west direction at 30°N. We want to know what will be the attitude of the axis after four hours. Since it is a horizontal axis gyro at an intermediate latitude facing east-west, it will both drift and topple.

$$\text{Drift} = 4 \times 15 \cdot 04 \sin 30$$
$$= 30 \cdot 08°$$

From Fig. 4(a) we note that the gyro axis drifts clockwise in the northern hemisphere (and therefore anti-clockwise in the southern hemisphere). Thus, the axis is now aligned with $090 + 30 \cdot 08 = 120 \cdot 08°/300 \cdot 08°$ direction.

$$\text{Topple} = 4 \times 15 \cdot 04 \cos 30$$
$$= 52 \cdot 1°$$

As the Earth travels from west to east and the axis remains pointing in the same direction in space, the eastern end of the axis will appear to have risen by $52 \cdot 1°$ and the western end similarly depressed.

6: Directional Gyro (DGI)

Directional Gyro Indicator (DGI) employs a horizontal axis gyro and utilises the principle of rigidity to indicate aircraft's heading. A spinning rotor, as we saw in the previous chapter, has the property of rigidity in space. Thus once the DGI rotor attains its full speed and its axis is manually aligned with a datum (true or magnetic north) it will continue to point in that direction in space during the rest of the flight. When the aircraft alters its heading it does so relative to the gyro axis, that is, the aircraft and the gyro case turn about the gyro axis. Changes in headings are thus indicated instantaneously.

It also utilises the property of precession for two purposes:
(a) to provide gyro control and (b) to compensate for apparent wander.

Construction

The DGI rotor is mounted in two rings called the inner gimbal and outer gimbal. Each gimbal has movement independent of the other. The rotor is mounted in the inner gimbal, the gimbal itself lies in the horizontal plane and the rotor which it holds spins in the vertical plane. The inner gimbal is mounted in the outer gimbal pivoted at two points on the inner gimbal which are 90° removed from the rotor axis. See Fig. 1. This allows the rotor to move about the horizontal

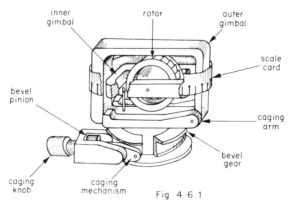

Fig. 4. 6. 1

axis. This movement, however, is restricted to 110°, that is, 55° either side of the rotor's vertical plane. This limits the aircraft's manœuvres in pitch and roll and if the limits are exceeded the inner gimbal will come in contact with a mechanical stop and the gyro will precess. The restriction is necessary in order to prevent the inner gimbal from coming in contact with the outer gimbal and damaging the instrument.

The outer gimbal is mounted in the case of the instrument and pivots about the vertical plane. This ring has freedom of 360° and carries the scale card. The rotor is driven by a jet of air from a nozzle, air entering the rotor case through a hole in the periphery of the case. Air impinges on small buckets carved out on the rim and spins the rotor at about 12 000 rpm.

The initial setting of the heading and subsequent resettings during the flight are carried out by use of the gyro caging control. The caging knob on the instrument is depressed and turned until the required heading appears in the window. When the knob is so depressed a bevel pinion engages a system of bevel gear, part of the outer gimbal. Thus, by turning the knob, the outer gimbal carrying the scale card is turned. The knob, when depressed, also locks the inner gimbal by means of a caging arm. This prevents the rotor from toppling while the force is being exerted on the outer gimbal. (Set the heading when the aircraft is flying straight and level as otherwise a small error may occur in the reading.)

The gyro should be caged during violent manœuvres or manœuvres likely to exceed the limits. The caging control is also used to erect the gyro should it inadvertently topple. This is because the caging arm rights the rotor before it locks it.

Finally it is important to remember that the gyro must be uncaged and resynchronised before the DGI is used again.

Gyro Control

When an aircraft alters its heading it turns about its vertical axis. Thus, the heading measurements will only be correct when measured with reference to that axis. This means that the rotor attitude must be controlled so that during banked turns it remains spinning in the aircraft's vertical plane (and not true vertical). This is achieved as follows. In Fig. 2(a) the aircraft is straight and level,

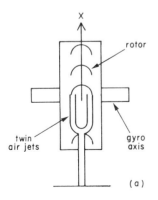
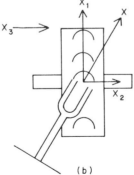

Fig. 4. 6. 2

the rotor is in the aircraft's vertical plane and the air jets driving force, X, is fully utilised to drive the rotor. In Fig. 2(b) the aircraft is in right bank. It will be seen that the driving force is not fully utilised to drive the buckets. Therefore, this force, X, must break down in two components, X_1 and X_2 at 90° to each other. X_1 acts along the rotor, now driving it at reduced speed. X_2 acts on the rim of the rotor. This component will precess through 90° in accordance with the precession rule in the direction of spin and act at X_3 in the direction shown. The effect of this force is to precess the rotor until it is aligned once again with the air jets as illustrated in Fig. 2(a). The rotor is then in the aircraft's vertical axis.

Gyro Drift

All horizontal axis gyroscopes are subject to drift as explained in the previous chapter, and the DGI is no exception. The drift occurs due to both real and apparent wander and the DGI should be reset at regular intervals during the flight. An instrument in good condition should not precess more than 4° every 15 minutes.

The real wander occurs due to friction, static unbalance (e.g. shift of the centre of gravity) and air turbulence. There is no means of predicting these errors to enable us to allow for them since wear and tear alter the values. The apparent wander occurs at the rate of approximately 15·04° sin lat per hour. The effect of this on heading indications is discussed in the following paragraphs.

We will take the northern hemisphere for illustration and study the effect on the heading reading in four situations, that is, effect when aircraft is stationary, aircraft on easterly track, aircraft on westerly track and finally, aircraft on northerly-southerly track.

In Fig. 3(a) below let us say that we lined up the DGI with the local meridian at position A. The heading indicated is 090°. Consider the effect one hour later, the

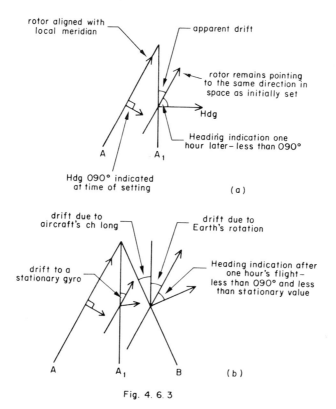

Fig. 4. 6. 3

gyro remaining stationary. The local meridian will have changed its direction in space due to the Earth's rotation and let us say that it arrives at position A_1. Now, the gyro rotor remains aligned with the local meridian direction one hour ago (assuming that there is no real drift) and this phenomenon must cause a discrepancy between the two gyro readings, that is the initial reading of $090°$ and the reading one hour later. The error occurs at the rate of $15·04$ sin lat/hr and the readings, as will be seen from the diagram, decrease.

Suppose the aircraft took off from A on an easterly track. One hour later, when the Earth's meridian A has reached A_1, the aircraft will have travelled to a new meridian, B. At B the heading will be in error due to two causes: Earth's rotation and the aircraft's change of longitude (again assuming no real wander) and the reading will be still less, Fig. 3(b).

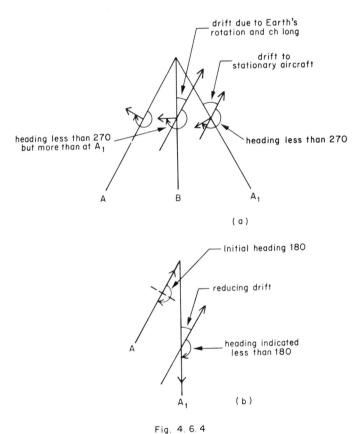

Fig. 4. 6. 4

In Fig. 4(a) the gyro is shown with its axis aligned with local meridian A and the aircraft is on a track of $270°$. In one hour's time meridian A will have changed direction to A_1 and if the aircraft was stationary an error of $15·04$ sin lat would be recorded, the readings reducing. However, the aircraft flying on westerly track will arrive at longitude B in one hour's time. The reading at B will still be less than $270°$ but more than what would be indicated if it remained stationary. The aircraft in the illustration is presumed to have its speed less than the speed of the Earth at the local parallel. It will be appreciated that if an aircraft is flying at the same speed as the speed of the Earth but on a westerly track it would negative the Earth's easterly velocity. In that case it would reach position A in the same time that original A displaced itself to A_1 and the gyro would give no error.

In Fig. 4(b) the aircraft having aligned its gyro to the local meridian sets off from A on a southerly track and arrives at A_1 after one hour. The aircraft is flying down the same meridian; the deviation to A_1 is due to the Earth's rotation. The reading here is less than 180, and it should be noticed that the magnitude of the error is a continuously decreasing value as the aircraft travels southward (sine of Equator is 0). Similarly on northerly track the readings decrease but the rate of decrease quickens as the flight progresses northward.

To summarise

Stationary gyroscope: drift = $15.04°$ sin lat/hr. Aircraft on easterly track, drift is more than stationary value; on westerly track, less than stationary value; on southerly track, stationary value at start, the value decreasing and on northerly track, stationary value, the value increasing.

In all cases in the northern hemisphere (on assumptions stipulated in the above discussion) the readings decrease.

Mathematically, drift may be expressed in the following equation:

$$\text{Drift} = {+ \text{ East} \atop - \text{ West}} \text{ ch long/hr} \times \text{sin lat/hr}.$$

Southern Hemisphere. The results are opposite to NH in that the readings increase. One example is sufficient to show this. In Fig. 5 an aircraft on longitude A sets up its gyro with the local meridian and the reading is $090°$. If the aircraft

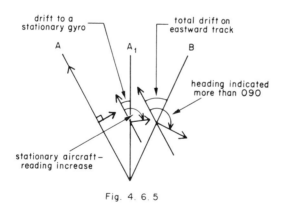

Fig. 4. 6. 5

remains stationary, in one hour's time meridian A will change direction to A_1. The indicator reading as can be seen in the figure has increased, the rate of increment still being $15.04°$ sin lat. If the aircraft was flying on an easterly track it will arrive at B in one hour and the heading indicated will have increased still further.

Compensation for Apparent Wander

Where an aircraft operates in the vicinity of a given latitude the gyroscope may be mechanically precessed equally and in the opposite direction to the drift experienced at that latitude, thus compensating for the apparent wander. The mechanism involved is a nut called the latitude nut which is screwed on the horizontal axis of the gyroscope. A balance weight at the opposite end of the axis balances the weight of the nut when the nut is riding in the central position. The latitude nut is then screwed inward or outward as required to produce a force in the vertical plane which precesses the rotor in the horizontal plane. In Fig. 6:

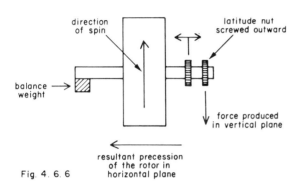

Fig. 4. 6. 6

the nut is screwed outward to compensate for drift in the southern hemisphere. It should, however, be appreciated that it only compensates for that latitude for which it is corrected, as long as the gyro remains stationary. Errors will arise on all tracks, and in assessing these errors the effect of the compensating device will have to be considered. A latitude balanced gyro will give errors as follows:

on easterly track   —   readings decrease in the NH;
on westerly track   —   readings increase in the NH;
on southerly track —   readings increase in the NH and
on northerly track —   readings decrease in the NH.

Opposite results are found in the southern hemisphere when on east/west tracks.

Gimballing Errors
These are minor errors which occur due to the geometry of the gimballing system. They occur when the aircraft is banked, in a climb or a descent. They disappear as soon as straight and level flight is resumed.

Type of Gyro
Gyro used in DGI is a tied gyro, having freedom in three planes. The axis of the gyroscope is aligned with the 000 – 180 indication. Being a horizontal axis gyro the forces imposed on the axis during a turn result in the movement of the rotor in the vertical plane. Any such movement has no effect on the heading indication and therefore, a DGI does not suffer from conventional turn and acceleration errors.

Typical Problems

1. A gyro is compensated for 50°N. What will be the rate of drift when at 50°S?

$$\text{Drift at } 50°N = -15.04 \sin 50° \text{ (readings in NH decrease and therefore}$$
the drift is given a minus sign; plus in
the SH)

$$= -11.52°/\text{hr.}$$

∴ Compensation applied = + 11.52°/hr.

At 50°S, drift = + 15.04 sin 50°
$$= + 11.52°/\text{hr}$$

∴ Total drift at 50°S = + 11.52
+ 11.52
─────
23.04° per hour.

2. A stationary gyro at 50°N gives a drift of −4°/hr. Where would the drift be zero?

Apparent drift at 50°N = −15.04 sin 50°
$$= -11.52$$

Actual drift   = − 4
Real drift   = + 7.52°
                     ─────

For zero drift, neutralise the real drift by going to a latitude where the apparent drift is, in this case, − 7.52°.

Drift = 15.04 sin lat

or, $\sin \text{lat} = \dfrac{7.52}{15.04}$

No.	log
7.52	0.8762
15.04	1.1772

$$= 30°N \qquad \overline{1}.6990 = 30°N$$

Practice Problem

An aircraft is travelling along 30°N at G/S 240 kt, Tr 090°. What is the rate of change of drift if the gyro is free from real wander?

Answer: 9.8°/hr.

7: Artificial Horizon

Principle
An artificial horizon employs a vertical axis Earth gyro having freedom in all three planes and indicates the aircraft's attitude in pitch and roll. The gyro axis is maintained vertical with reference to the centre of the Earth so that a bar across and at 90° to the rotor axis indicates the horizon. In flight an aircraft rolls and pitches about the gyro axis which remains rigid and the indications are instantaneous.

Construction
The rotor of the gyro is encased in a sealed case which acts as inner gimbal. Air is let into the case under pressure, the pressure either created by a pressure pump or by creating suction inside the case. The suction required is 4″ of mercury. The rotor spins under air pressure at the rate of approximately 15 000 rpm. Having spun the rotor, the air escapes from the case through four exhaust ports in a pendulous unit mounted at the base of the gyro. Electrically driven gyros require a supply of 115V 3 phase 400 cycles AC and produce a spin rate of approximately 22 500 rpm.

The inner gimbal is mounted in the outer gimbal with its axis athwartships. The outer gimbal is mounted in the case with pivot points in the fore and aft axis of the aircraft. The inner gimbal having its movement about the athwartships axis controls the indications in pitch attitude. It has the freedom of movement of 55° either side of the central position. The outer gimbal controls the indications in the rolling plane (bank) and has freedom of about 90° from its central position. Later

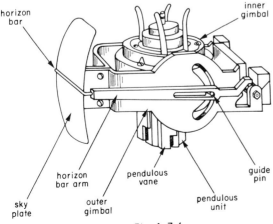

Fig. 4. 7. 1

models of electrical gyros have complete freedom in roll and 85° in pitch. With such gyros it is possible to do a complete loop without affecting the gyro rotor. Fig. 1.

Operation

Any movement relative to the inner gimbal is transmitted to the horizon bar arm through a guide pin on the inner gimbal. The guide pin engages the horizon bar arm through a curved slot in the outer gimbal – Fig 1. During level flight the aircraft's vertical axis is parallel to the rotor axis and the guide pin is in the centre of the slot. Horizon bar arm is in the centre, and its extension across the face of the dial is in the centre of the dial behind the miniature aircraft. When the aircraft climbs or descends the rotor case (that is, the inner gimbal) remains rigid whereas the outer gimbal and the instrument case move with the aircraft. Due to the movement relative to the inner gimbal the guide pin gets displaced in the slot taking the horizon bar arm with it. Thus an indication of climb or descent results. Fig 2(a) represents the relative positions of the miniature aircraft and the

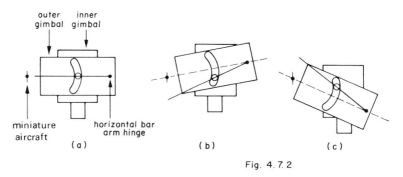

Fig. 4. 7. 2

inner and outer gimbals in straight and level flight. Fig 2(b) and 2(c) represent the relative positions in climb and descent respectively.

The bank indication is given by an index on the sky plate which is directly connected to the outer gimbal. The index reads against a scale printed on the glass face of the instrument. When an aircraft banks, the rotor, inner gimbal and outer gimbal remain rigid in level position and the instrument case together with the printed scale moves with the aircraft. Thus, the position of the index on the sky plate indicates the bank angle against the scale.

Gyro Control

The erection mechanism of a pressure driven artificial horizon consists of a pendulous unit with its four exhaust ports, two in the fore-and-aft axis and two in the athwartships axis of the aircraft. Pivoted on top of the ports are four vanes, each covering half the port in straight and level flight. In this condition the air escapes equally from all four ports and the system is in equilibrium.

If the rotor axis departs from the vertical, the pivoted vanes will still remain in the true vertical with the result that one pair of ports will be out of balance (one port will be more than half open; its opposite port similarly closed). In fig 3(a) the rotor axis is shown as vertical, air escaping equally through all four ports. In fig 3(b) the rotor axis is shown tilted. The vane on one port has fully uncovered the port

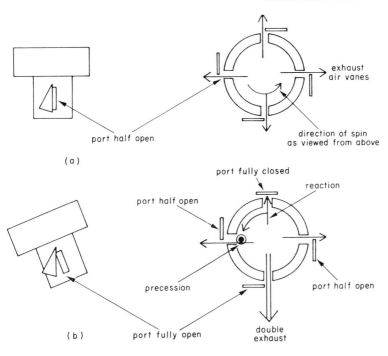

exhaust
air vanes

port half open

direction of spin
as viewed from above

(a)

port fully closed

reaction

port half open

precession

port half open

(b)   port fully open

double
exhaust

Fig. 4. 7. 3

and the vane directly opposite to it has fully covered up the port. Unbalanced airflow will take place as a result, setting up reaction in the direction of the closed port.
This reaction force will precess through 90° in the direction of the spin and erect
the gyro. The resulting rate of precession is deliberately kept low so that the rotor
will not precess when the vanes are being thrown about in turbulent flight
conditions.

Electrically driven rotors are controlled and kept in the vertical by means of a pair
of torque motors and level switches. The torque motor correcting in the roll axis is
mounted on the starboard side and the one correcting in the pitch axis at the rear
of the instrument. Two level switches contain mercury liquid as a contact agent and
the switches are placed at the base of the inner gimbal. When the gyro is level,
the mercury is held in the centre of the trough, no contact is made at either of the
two electrodes at the sides of the trough and the torque motor is switched off. When
the gyro is not level, mercury rolls down to the lower sides and completes the
circuit at one of the contacts. This energises the appropriate torque motor which
applies a torque to the rotor in the correct direction and erects the gyro. Fig 4.

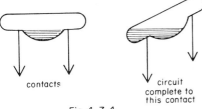

contacts

circuit
complete to
this contact

Fig. 4. 7. 4

Errors

Unlike the DGI an artificial horizon suffers from both acceleration and turning errors. In the following discussion the rotor of the artificial horizon is assumed to turn anti-clockwise as viewed from above.

Acceleration Errors. These are also known as 'take-off' errors since they are most noticeable during this phase of the flight. There are two elements which introduce the errors: the pendulous unit and the vanes.

The pendulous unit makes the rotor bottom heavy. Thus when an aircraft accelerates a force due to the unit's inertia is felt at the bottom, acting towards the pilot. This force precesses through 90° in an anti-clockwise direction and lifts up the right hand side of the outer gimbal. The skyplate attached to the outer gimbal rotates anti-clockwise, the bank index indicating a false starboard turn.

Also during acceleration both port and starboard side vanes are thrown back with the result that the starboard side port opens up fully and the port side closes down fully. The reaction occurs on the port side, precesses through 90°, and lifts up the inner gimbal from the point nearest to the pilot to indicate a false climb.

Turning Errors. During a turn the fore and aft vanes will be displaced due to the centrifugal force in a direction away from the centre of the turn. Thus, one port will be open and its opposite one closed. The reaction will be set up in the fore and aft axis of the aircraft which will precess through 90° to lift up the outer gimbal at the port or starboard side. This results in indication of false bank. The sense of the indication depends on the direction of the turn. This particular error is also known as erection error.

Centrifugal force also acts on the pendulous unit, the force acting from starboard to port or vice versa, depending on the direction of the turn. This force affects the inner gimbal, giving a false indication of climb or descent. This error is also known as pendulosity error.

The combined effect of the two is to displace the gyro rotor in two planes. If a turn is made through 360° the error reaches maximum at 180° and then starts reducing until the turn is complete when the error will have reduced to zero. In modern gyroscopes, the rotor axis is displaced from the true vertical to counteract these errors. But the correction is only valid for a given rate of turn and a given speed. For example, a pressure driven gyro, offset 2½° forward and 1¾° to port corrects for a rate one turn at 190 kt. The tilt does not affect straight and level indications as the scales are similarly offset.

Operational Limits

If the gyro limits are exceeded the gyro will topple. Therefore, where the facility is available, the gyro should be caged before entering severe manœuvres. An electrically driven gyro with 85° freedom in pitch may be taken through a loop without affecting the rotor. As the loop angle progresses between 80° and 100°, the horizon bar smartly travels across the face of the instrument from the bottom to the top. The skyplate bank index will similarly appear at the top. To the pilot who is inverted the indications will look correct. (What is the normal top is the bottom when looking at it upside down if you see what we mean). A similar change in the opposite direction takes place when the loop is going through the 260° – 280° zone.

Indications

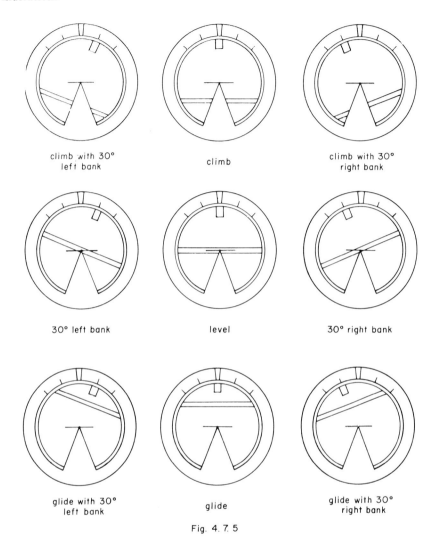

Fig. 4. 7. 5

8: Turn and Slip Indicator

These two instruments are generally combined, with two pointers giving two types of information read in conjunction with each other.

TURN INDICATOR
This part of the instrument indicates the rate of turn and utilises the principle of gyro precession to do so.

Construction
The instrument employs a horizontal axis gyro, the rotor being mounted in a horizontal ring in the athwartships axis. This ring itself is mounted in the fore-and-aft axis of the aircraft in the instrument case. Thus, the gyro has freedom of movement about one plane only, that is, about the fore-and-aft axis. The rotor is driven by an air jet which impinges upon the buckets on the rotor rim and spins it at an approximate rate of 9 000 rpm. This speed is considerably lower than DGI or Artificial Horizon speed, for the reasons that the Turn indicator utilises the principle of precession for its operation and that the instrument incorporates two springs which hold the gyro axis horizontal in level flight. The rotor spins away from the pilot.

Operation
During straight and level flight the springs hold the gyro axis horizontal preventing unwanted precession, and the pointer attached to the vertical rotor indicates central or zero position on the instrument against the printed scale. Fig. 1.

As the aircraft enters into a turn, say a turn to the left, the gyro axis being rigid, opposes the turn and a force is experienced on the axis, as shown in Fig 2 (a). On the left hand axis the force is coming out of the paper. Let us call this force 1.

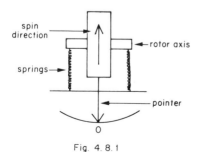

Fig. 4. 8. 1

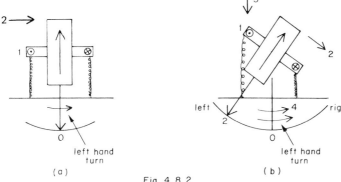

Fig. 4. 8. 2

This force will precess through 90° and act at the top of the rotor, force 2, causing the rotor to tilt. This tilt is called primary precession. If no springs were attached to the rotor axis, the rotor would continue to tilt until it is spinning in the horizontal plane, with its axis vertical. This attitude would give no indication of the rate of the turn. However, having the springs, as the rotor starts to tilt, one spring stretches and the other contracts. In a left hand turn, as shown in Fig 2 (b) the left hand spring is stretched. This produces a pulling down force on the left hand axis or a pushing up force on the right hand axis – force 3. This vertical force on the axis will precess the rotor in the horizontal plane in the direction shown – force 4. This is called secondary precession. If you notice, force 4 acts in the same direction as the direction of the turn. As the rate of turn is established, force 1 becomes a constant value. When force 4 reaches the value of force 1, we have a situation where two forces of equal value are acting for opposite purposes (force 1 is due to rigidity of the axis; force 4 is precession force). At this stage, the gyro cannot tilt any further. Whatever tilt has duly occurred is entirely due to force 1, which in its turn, is due to the rate of turn. Therefore, the gyro tilt together with the pointer displacement represent the rate of turn.

If the instrument case is not airtight, air will be drawn in from leaking points due to suction inside the case and loss of efficiency will result. If the rotor speed is less than the rated speed, the pointer will indicate a lesser rate of turn; similarly, if the speed is too high, it will indicate a higher rate of turn.

The spring tension is adjusted for a given rate of turn, usually rate one, and at all other rates the indication will be progressively in error.

Movement in the looping plane theoretically will have no effect on the gyro since the aircraft loops about the gyro axis and not against it as it does when it enters into a turn.

SLIP INDICATOR

This part of the instrument is entirely mechanical and depends on the forces acting on a pendulous weight for its indications. In straight and level flight the pendulous weight is acted upon by the force of gravity which keeps it in the true vertical. The pointer attached to the system indicates the central position, that is, no slip or skid.

During a turn the weight is acted upon by two forces : gravitational force acting downwards and centrifugal force acting away from the centre of the turn. The pendulum takes up the position which is the resultant of the two.

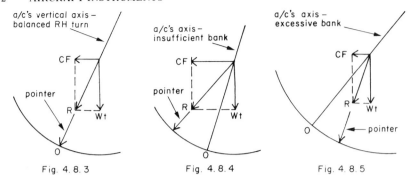

Fig. 4.8.3   Fig. 4.8.4   Fig. 4.8.5

If the turn is a balanced turn, the two vectors must be of such dimensions as to shift the weight from the true vertical to the aircraft's vertical. This is so, because in a balanced turn weight opposes lift, and the lift acts at 90° to the wings, that is, in the aircraft's vertical axis. Therefore, weight must lie in the vertical axis. Fig. 3.

In Fig. 4, aircraft is shown in a RH turn with insufficient bank. The aircraft skids outwards from the centre of the turn. The pointer is displaced in the opposite direction to the direction of the turn.

In Fig. 5 aircraft is in RH turn, having an excessive bank. The aircraft slips inwards, the pointer is displaced to the right of the zero, that is, in the same direction as the direction of the turn.

Some models employ a ball in the tube arrangement in place of a pendulum. The ball itself has weight (it is not a bubble) and thus, it is affected by the aircraft's relevant manoeuvres in exactly the same way as the pendulum weight and the resulting indications are alike, except that the ball itself indicates slip or skid instead of a pointer.

From the above, the rule of interpretation is that if the rate of turn pointer and slip pointer (or the ball) are displaced in the same direction, the aircraft is slipping inwards towards the centre of the turn. If the two are displaced in the opposite direction, the aircraft is skidding outward. If the turn is indicated but the slip pointer is at zero position, it is a balanced turn.

Serviceability Check
While standing on level ground both pointers should indicate zero position. While taxying, check indications by a slight turn. The turn should be indicated in the correct direction and slip pointer should indicate a skid (insufficient bank!).

Electrical and Pressure driven gyros
Electrically driven gyros have some distinct advantages over air driven gyros, the main advantage being that it is possible to run electrical rotors at higher speeds. As we saw earlier, higher speeds impart greater rigidity and therefore greater accuracy where rigidity is utilised as the operating principle of the instrument. From the designing angle, electrical gyros yield neater designs since air passage tubing and filtration devices are no longer required. This permits gimbal designs giving greater operational limits. Further, since air no longer enters the rotor unit, there is freedom from filtration troubles and moisture corrosion. Finally electrical rotors are not affected by rarer atmosphere at high altitudes.

Indications

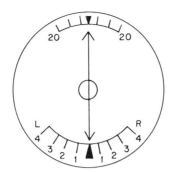

straight and level

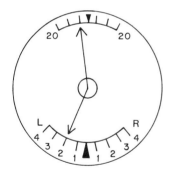

correctly balanced —
left turn rate 2

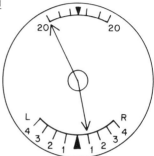

rate 1 right turn – skid

rate 2 left turn – slip

straight and level

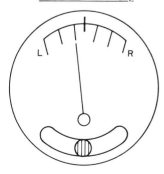

rate 1 left turn – balanced

Fig. 4. 8. 6

rate 1 left turn – slip

MAGNETISM AND COMPASSES

1: Magnetism: General and Terrestrial

Magnetism: General and Terrestrial.
This is an interesting study, and of great importance: at last the divorce from the boatmen has been accomplished, though the decree nisi was long enough, Heaven knows. The student pilot need no longer learn about Kelvin's balls, but about air-borne compasses which are now highly accurate and trouble free. Yet a simple magnetic compass must always be aboard just in case. So off we go from the fundamentals of magnetism.

A magnet has the following properties:

1. It attracts iron filings, and more strongly at the poles. The attraction can be exerted at a distance, the effect decreasing with increasing distance.
2. When a magnet is freely suspended, one end tends to point in a Northerly direction and is called the North-seeking or RED Pole.
3. With two magnets near each other, the red pole will tend to attract the blue pole of the other, while like poles repel each other.
4. The amount of possible magnetism is limited by the mass of magnetic material in the magnet. When a magnet can no longer by any means be made more powerful, it is said to be saturated.
5. No magnet can exist with only one pole: even if broken into pieces, each piece would become a complete magnet with poles of equal strength.

The Molecular Theory supports this: any old piece of iron consists of molecules, each of which is a magnet but exerting its magnetism haphazardly giving no resultant magnetism to the iron bar. On magnetisation, however, each molecule is lined up so that all of them exert their magnetism in the same direction; with every one lined up, the bar is now a magnet, and magnetically saturated, at its maximum magnetic strength.

The sphere of influence of a magnet is called its magnetic field, composed of its magnetic lines of force. These are the lines the direction of each being the path in which an isolated red pole free to move would travel. They are quite definite, and never cross, since they depend on their position with regard to the attracting blue pole, the repelling red pole. Thus, a magnet lying across the magnetic field of another magnet would tend to take up the direction of the line of force running through it with the opposite poles nearer to each other.

Hard and soft iron

Any metal which can be magnetised at all comes under one of these headings: soft iron can be easily magnetised and will just as readily lose its magnetism when the magnetising influence is removed. Hard iron is difficult to magnetise, but once done tends to remain permanently so. Hard iron magnetism is called 'permanent' while soft iron is called 'temporary' or 'induced'.

The Coercive Force is the power which hard iron has of resisting magnetisation, or if already magnetised, of resisting de-magnetisation.

Terrestrial Magnetism

The Earth itself is a magnet, with its own magnetic field, with a blue pole in the vicinity of the True North Pole: thus a freely suspended compass needle will line itself up with its red pole pointing to the Earth's Magnetic North Pole.

The Magnetic Poles are areas on the Earth's surface where a freely suspended compass needle, influenced only by the Earth's magnetic field will stand vertical.

The Angle of Dip in this case is $90°$; the Angle of Dip is defined as the angle between the horizontal and a freely suspended compass needle influenced only by the Earth's magnetic field. Thus the Magnetic Equator is an imaginary line on the Earth's surface joining all points where the Angle of Dip is Nil, and can be said to be the dividing line between the Earth's blue and red polarity.

The Earth's line of total force at any particular place is the line of force in which a freely suspended compass needle lies in the Earth's magnetic field when influenced only by the Earth's magnetic field. It follows that only at the Magnetic Equator will the needle be horizontal, only at the Pole will it be vertical. The Directive Force is that component of the Earth's total force which acts in a horizontal plane, known as "H"; likewise the Vertical force in the vertical plane, known as Z. The Magnetic Meridian is simply the direction in a horizontal plane of the freely suspended compass needle influenced only by the Earth's magnetic field, i.e. the direction of the directive force. Thus, we have a triangle of forces depending on the position of the compass needle in the Earth's magnetic field which solves the actual horizontal direction and angle from the horizontal which it will actually take up along the line of the Earth's total force.

A change of magnetic latitude will thus affect the freely suspended needle: the nearer to the Pole, the greater Z, and the less H: conversely, near to the magnetic equator, Z is small, H is high. The triangle thus:

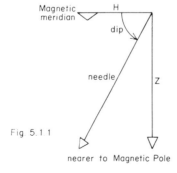

Fig 5.1.1

nearer to Magnetic Pole

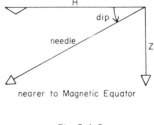

nearer to Magnetic Equator

Fig. 5.1.2

Changes in the Earth's Magnetic Field

There are several causes:

1. <u>Secular</u>: The Magnetic North Pole, situated broadly about 17° from the True North, moves round the True North in a clockwise direction making a complete cycle in about 960 years.
    This is reasonably predictable.
2. <u>Annual</u>: A slight oscillation of the magnetic poles, only a matter of 4' or 5' of arc, which has something to do with the position of the Earth in its orbit round the Sun.
3. <u>Daily</u>: A quite irregular change of up to 12' of arc due to Sunspots.
4. <u>Magnetic Storms</u>: These can for short periods cause some slight change: they are connected with an eleven year cycle of sunspot activity; the aurora borealis, the primary cause of which is the movement of charged particles in the atmosphere deflected by the Earth's magnetic field, can be contributory.
5. <u>Local Effects</u>: These can be considerable due to deposits of magnetic material causing local deviation. The effect decreases with height – Greenland for instance is a tidy magnet in its own right, and there is a small area in mid-Atlantic, a few miles in diameter, too.

The regular changes can be allowed for when the isogonals are plotted for an area – those lines joining places of equal magnetic variation, and the amount of annual change of variation forecast: in the UK, the total change is about 7'E, and is hardly likely to be of significance to the pilot until he uses a chart more than 5 years old. Remember the definition of variation? The angular difference between the true and magnetic meridian at a point measured in degrees East or West of True. A line joining places of nil variation is the agonic line. And isoclinals are lines joining all places of equal magnetic dip.

To redefine deviation, the angular difference between the magnetic meridian and the direction taken up by a particular compass needle, measured E or W of the magnetic meridian. Aircraft are full of disturbing magnetic influences, and considerable thought is given by constructors and designers to reduce them. A diagram to illustrate, and refresh your memory.

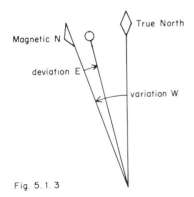

Fig. 5. 1. 3

2: Aircraft Magnetism

An aircraft contains both hard and soft iron giving rise to permanent and temporary magnetism.

Permanent magnetism in aircraft arises chiefly from hammering whilst under construction and the effect of the Earth's line of total force running through it during building. The molecules in the hard iron tend to line up in the direction of the Earth's line of total force giving red polarity at the north-pointing end. The nature of this permanent magnetism depends on:

1. Magnetic heading during construction.
2. The Angle of Dip at the place of construction.
3. Amount of coercive force of the metals used.
4. And of course the amount of hammering, battering and rivetting.

Some permanent magnetism can also be set up by the introduction of electro-magnetic material, radio and radar equipment, electric currents. A demagnetising effort called 'de-gaussing' is made before an a/c is sent from the workshop, but there is always some residual magnetism.

This permanent magnetism and its effect on the magnetic compass can be measured per aircraft, and a suitable correction card placed nearby. The 'Induced' or temporary magnetism in soft iron components of the structure (brought about by the Earth's field, giving these components a changing magnetic value depending on the variable strength of H and Z as the aircraft goes about its business) is not so readily taken care of.

In order to analyse the effect of permanent magnetism, we imagine it to be due to 3 components, acting respectively in the fore and aft, athwartships and vertical line of the a/c.

P is the parameter (or component) acting in the fore and aft line of the compass named + when the blue pole is forward of the compass.

Q is the parameter acting in the athwartships line of the compass, named + when the blue pole is starboard of the compass.

P and Q are horizontal hard iron, then, in the horizontal line of the compass needle itself.

R is the parameter acting in the vertical line of the compass, named + when the blue pole is beneath it. Its effect on the compass in straight and level flight may be taken as negligible.

Analysis of + P

Imagine the a/c on 8 headings, with a blue pole in the nose, red pole abaft the compass, pardon the expression.

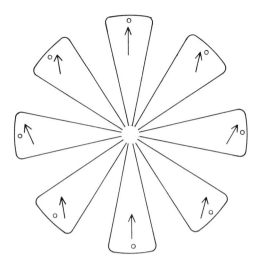

Fig. 5.2.1

Drawing up a table of deviations, and a graph of them:

Hdg(M)	Deviation
N	No deviation; directive force increased
NE	Easterly deviation
E	Max Easterly deviation
SE	Easterly deviation
S	No deviation; directive force decreased
SW	Westerly deviation
W	Max Westerly deviation
NW	Westerly deviation

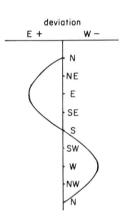

Fig. 5.2.2

and we have a sine curve; on the quadrantal Headings Magnetic the deviation will therefore be ·7P. A parameter of negative value, −P, would give a Westerly deviation on Easterly Headings Magnetic. We can summarise then by saying that the deviation due to P is proportional to the sine of the aircraft's Heading Magnetic, or

Deviation = P sin Hdg(M)

and P is positive or negative depending on Easterly or Westerly deviation with the aircraft on Headings Magnetic between North and East.

Analysis of −Q

The red pole is to starboard of the compass. You draw it out and agree the following graph:

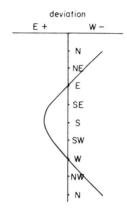

Fig. 5. 2. 3

This is a cosine curve, and the sign of Q is determined by the sign of the deviation obtained on aircraft Hdgs(M) from North to East.

Q is proportional to cos Hdg(M), therefore:

Deviation = Q cos Hdg(M)

and again the deviation on the quadrantals is ·7 of the parameter, in this case ·7Q.

P and Q are horizontal hard iron, permanent: we can conveniently co-relate with them certain soft iron components which act in the same manner on the compass; these induced effects are dependent on the strength of the Earth's magnetic field at the place, and of course on the coercive force of the soft iron itself.

These parameters are 'c' and 'f' ("little c and little f")

'c', a pair of vertical soft iron rods one before the compass, one behind, each with a pole in the horizontal plane of the compass needle. In the Northern Hemisphere, the bottom pole would be induced with a red magnetism, and we assume the forward vertical rod to have its blue pole level with the needle, the rear rod its red pole, then we have effective poles acting on the compass like + P.

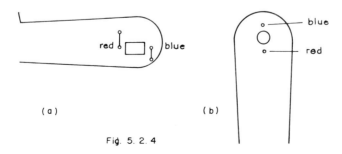

(a)   (b)

Fig. 5. 2. 4

Similarly for 'f', this time athwart the compass.

Vertical soft iron will not change its polarity with change of heading; thus, we consider P + c and Q + f at the same time for this analysis.

Proceeding to find a method of correction of the deviations obtained to render the compass as extensively serviceable as possible, the value of the deviations caused by P + c is resolved into Coefficient B, in degrees of deviation.

Coefficient B = P + c

which has maximum deviation on Easterly and Westerly Headings: thus, the Coefficient can be rendered as a numerical number of degrees by

$$\text{Coefficient B} = \frac{\text{Deviation on E} - \text{Deviation on W}}{2}$$

for the deviation on Westerly Heading is expected to be of opposite sign to that on Easterly, and we wish to remove the mean maximum deviation. The sign of the deviation is ready for correction on East Magnetic. Similarly,

Coefficient C = Q + f

and is calculated by:

$$\text{Coefficient C} = \frac{\text{Deviation on North} - \text{Deviation on South}}{2}$$

The value is given a sign ready for correction on a North Heading (M). Thus, while not expecting complete perfection of compass reading, we can eradicate the effect of fore/aft and athwartship hard iron magnetism, and vertical soft iron magnetism present.

Once found, coefficients B and C can be to some extent neutralised by setting up a local magnetic field: this correcting device is called the micro-adjuster, and is placed directly under the compass as an integral part of the instrument. Two pairs of magnets, one pair fore and aft, the other pair athwartships; the magnets of each pair can be opened like scissors from the null position to form effective poles at right angles to the original line of the magnets. A key is inserted to operate either pair of corrector magnets, and the rule is to use the key hole which lies at right angles to the compass needle.

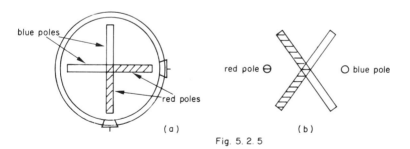

Fig. 5. 2. 5

Fig. 5(b) illustrates the opening of the fore and aft pair to give an effective blue pole to starboard, which would correct a negative Coefficient C (Q + f).

Coefficient A

This is caused by deviations which are the same on all headings, and nearly always is due to incorrect mounting of the lubber line. The rear of the compass bracket is screwed in against a span of $10°$ either side of centre, and the mounting of $0°$ may not be in the fore and aft axis of the aircraft: this would lead to a constant deviation on all headings: a Heading of 000(M) giving a compass reading of 010(C) entirely due to incorrect mounting would give a deviation of -10, which would be repeated on all headings, since the lubber line is displaced to starboard. This is called Apparent A, due to mechanical error. Real A, due to Horizontal soft iron, giving a constant graph of deviation too, is fortunately not part of our study.

Coefficient A is deduced by the deviations on 8 headings, adding them algebraically, and dividing by 8.

Thus, the deviation on any Heading Magnetic due to the three coefficients discussed is:

A + B sin Hdg + C cos Hdg and the sign of the deviation will take care of itself.

e.g. A + 3, B + 2, C − 10

What deviation would be expected, (a) on 222(M), (b) on 146(M)?

(a) $+ 3 + (+2 \sin 222) + (-10 \cos 222)$
    $= +3 + (2 \sin -42) - (10 \cos -42)$
    $= + 3 -2 \sin 42 + 10 \cos 42$
    $= +3 -1.3382 + 7.431$
    $= 9°$ Easterly

(b) $+ 3 + (+2 \sin 146) + (-10 \cos 146)$
    $= + 3 + 2 \sin 34 + (-10 \cos -34)$
    $= + 3 + 1.11838 + 8.2904$
    $= +12°$ or $12°$East

Now to swing a compass: the methods are legion, and the usual method is to have a bod with a landing compass mounted accurately on a tripod well in front of the a/c so that he can sight down the fore and aft line: not as difficult as it sounds, since the tail unit can be sighted as a thin line in the viewer of the landing compass. This ineffably tedious job is now entirely in the hands of a trained Compass Adjuster, and the pilot only gets nobbled to drive occasionally. The procedure is as follows:

1. Check compass for serviceability (details of this under the title 'P type' compasses).
2. Ensure all equipment not carried in flight is removed.
3. Ensure all equipment carried in flight is correctly stowed.
4. Take the a/c to a suitable site, at least 50 yards from other aircraft, 100 yards from the hangar. Most airfields have a favourite and magnetically clean area for compass swinging.
5. Ensure that all flying controls are in normal flying position, engines on, radios and electrical circuits on.
6. Place a/c on Hdg South (M) and note deviation.
7. Place a/c on Hdg West (M) and note deviation.
8. Place a/c on Hdg North (M) and note deviation.
9. Calculate Coefficient C, apply it direct to the compass reading, and set the required corrected reading on the grid ring.
10. Place the Key across the needle and turn the Key until red is on red. (The Key is turned anti clockwise for + deviation).

11. Remove the Key.
12. Place a/c on Hdg East, note deviation
13. Calculate Coefficient B, and correct as before. (Key would be placed in fore and aft position).
    The correcting swing is complete.
14. Carry out a check swing on 8 headings, starting with SE.
15. Calculate Coefficient A. Loosen retaining screw on rear bracket of compass, and turn the Instrument clockwise if A is + ve, by the quantity found.
    An example:

Correcting Swing

	Landing Compass	P4	Deviation	Corrected Reading
S	184	183	+ 1	180
W	272	268	+ 4	270
N	000	353	+ 7	356
E	088	088	0	086

Coefficient C $\dfrac{+7-1}{2}$ = + 3

Coefficient B $\dfrac{0-4}{2}$ = −2

and the corrected readings after these coefficients have been eliminated are as in the end column.

Check Swing

L/C	P4	Devn	Residual Devn after Correction	
134	129	+ 5	+ 1	
181	177	+ 4	0	
225	222	+ 3	− 1	
272	270	+ 2	− 2	Coefficient A
314	308	+ 6	+ 2	$\dfrac{+31}{8}$ = + 4
357	353	+ 4	0	
048	044	+ 4	0	
094	091	+ 3	− 1	

Now a deviation card is filled in to be placed next to the compass, so that who ever takes the aeroplane can fly as accurately as possible the required Hdg(M).

FOR	STEER
000	000
045	045
090	091
135	134
180	180
225	226
270	272
315	313

It is necessary in flight to check the compass by astronomical means, especially on freighters, when unusual loads may be carried: and we've already seen that soft iron magnetism does change with change of magnetic latitude.

Occasions when a compass should be swung
1. New compass fitted.
2. Every three months.
3. After a major inspection.
4. With any change of magnetic material in the aircraft.
5. If transferred to another base involving a large change of latitude.
6. After a lightning strike or after flying in static.
7. After standing on one heading for more than 4 weeks.
8. At any time when the compass or recorded deviation is suspect.

Change of Latitude and its effect on Compass Deviation
The conclusions arrived at so far are that the deviations leading to the resolution of Coefficients B and C are horizontal hard iron P and Q, and vertical soft iron c and f.

Horizontal Hard Iron (HHI)
By definition, the deviating force is constant as measured, but with a change of strength of the Earth's horizontal component H, the effect of this deviating force will vary as the directive force on the compass needle varies. As H increases in strength, so the effect of a constant HHI deviating component will decrease, and vice versa. The deviation of the compass will be doubled if H is halved. This can be stated as

$$\text{Deviation due to HHI is proportional to } \frac{1}{H}$$

The value of H anywhere in the world is known, measured in Gauss, and the directive force on the needle of ·25 Gauss is resisting a deviating force more strongly than of ·15 Gauss. The deviation can be resolved then at a new magnetic latitude by the formula:

$$\frac{\text{New deviation}}{\text{Old deviation}} = \frac{\text{Old H}}{\text{New H}}$$

Vertical Soft Iron (VSI)
Once again, deviation must vary inversely as H, the ability of the needle itself to resist any deviating force. Additionally, the magnetism induced into vertical

soft iron will vary as the vertical component of the Earth's magnetic field varies, i.e. it varies as Dip. At the Poles, then, maximum deviation will be caused by VSI where maximum Dip induces maximum magnetism: at the Magnetic Equator, where Z is nil, the value of induced magnetism in VSI will be nil.

Deviation due to VSI is proportional to Z and inversely proportional to H

∴ Deviation due to VSI is proportional to $\dfrac{Z}{H}$ or tan Dip

Dip, too, is known world wide, as an angular measurement from the horizontal; while Z is measured in Gauss, and Z changes its sign as it crosses the Magnetic Equator.

The new deviation due to VSI with change of magnetic latitude can be found from the formula.

$$\frac{\text{New Devn}}{\text{Old Devn}} = \frac{\text{New Tan Dip}}{\text{Old Tan Dip}}$$

Providing clarity is preserved between the two formula, a new deviation can be readily found when magnetic latitude has been changed.

At BERKER, where H = ·15 gauss, deviation due to P is + 3, and due to c −4; Dip is 48°, what is total deviation due to P + c at POOTLE where H = ·6, dip 32°?

HHI
$$\frac{\text{New Devn}}{\text{Old Devn}} = \frac{\text{Old H}}{\text{New H}}$$
$$\frac{x}{+3} = \frac{·15}{·6}$$
$$= +·75$$

VSI
$$\frac{\text{New Devn}}{\text{Old Devn}} = \frac{\text{New Tan Dip}}{\text{Old Tan Dip}}$$
$$\frac{x}{-4} = \frac{\text{Tan }32}{\text{Tan }48}$$
$$= -4 \tan 32 \cot 48$$
$$= -2·27$$

Total devn due to P + c = −1·52 at POOTLE

Component R

This is vertical hard iron assumed for analysis to be situated above or below the compass. In level flight, its effect on the compass is nil, but tail down or up, the hypothetical magnet is resolved into two parts, one of which introduces a fore and aft effect, as it were a false component P.

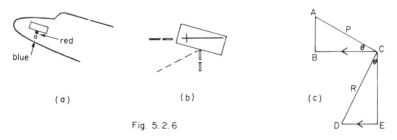

Fig. 5.2.6

In Fig. 6(c) components P and R are shown (we can assume the inclusion of 'c') where AC = P and CD = R, $\angle\theta$ = the angle of tail down: the needle remains in the horizontal plane by construction.

Then BC = deviating effect due to P = P cos θ

DE = deviating effect due to R = R sin θ

$\therefore$ Total deviating effect = P cos θ + R sin θ; the action in the horizontal plane of component R introducing an additional effect like B (or P).

R is termed + with a blue pole beneath the compass and its deviative value depends on the angular distance of the a/c from the horizontal. It can be readily proved that the actual position of the applied force will change from fore to aft of the needle with change of a/c attitude from climb to descent.

e.g.   In the air, B is $-$ 7; on the ground, 15° tail down, B is $-$ 4. What is the deviation on a Westerly heading climbing at 20°?

Total deviating force = B cos θ + R sin θ

$-4 = -7$ cos 15 + R sin 15

R = + 11

In the air,

Deviation = -7 cos 20 + 11 sin 20

= -3, and this will be on East.

$\therefore$ +3° on Westerly Heading.

And another:

Climbing at 10° on East, the deviation due to P and R is + 10°, whereas climbing on the same Heading at 20°, the deviation due to P and R is + 3°. What is the deviation due to P on Hdg 315(M) in level flight?

Total deviation = P cos θ + R sin θ

10 = P cos 10 + R sin 10

and 3 = P cos 20 + R sin 20

$\therefore$ 10 = ·98P + ·17R

3 = ·94P + ·34R

which solves into

P = + 17

In level flight, on a Hdg(M) of 315, with R inoperative, the deviation due to P will be ·7 of $-$ 17, or to put it another way, + 17 sin 315, an answer of $-$ 12°.

Finally, if the aircraft is banked, there will be a resolved component due to R appropriate to the rules of Coefficient C; but the manœuvre is not sufficiently prolonged or directionally important enough to be worth considering, especially if account is taken of the larger effects of turning errors on the basic magnetic compass.

Sundry tips and reminders

First, are you a bit shaky on how to find cos 324? sin 179? tan 139? Whatever the angle, apply it to 360 or 180 to get below 90: then for the quadrant it falls in, the rule is:

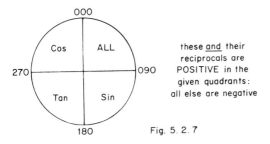

these *and* their
reciprocals are
POSITIVE in the
given quadrants:
all else are negative

Fig. 5. 2. 7

For example:

cos 324 = cos 036 and it's positive
sin 179 = sin 001 and it's positive
tan 139 = tan 041 and it's negative

Mathematics and so on

1. Know the formula; $B = \dfrac{E - W}{2}$ and $C = \dfrac{N - S}{2}$

2. If the value of B is known, the deviation on any other Heading is found from:
    Deviation = B sin Heading
    Similarly, Deviation due to C = C cos Heading

3. If the deviation on a Heading is given, B and C are calculated thus:
    $$B = \frac{\text{Deviation}}{\text{sin Hdg}} \qquad C = \frac{\text{Deviation}}{\text{cos Hdg}}$$
    and these can be re-written:
    B = Deviation cosecant Heading
    C = Deviation secant Heading

4. If the values of B and C are given and it is required to calculate the deviation on a given Heading, the problem is best solved in two parts: First, calculate the deviation due to B on the Heading given; then calculate the deviation due to C. The algebraic sum of the two is the deviation on that Heading due to the combined effect of both B and C.
    Deviation = B sin Hdg + C cos Hdg.

5. Maximum deviation
    Values of B and C are given, and it is required to find the Heading on which maximum deviation will occur, together with its value.
    The formula to be used is:
    $$\text{Tan Heading} = \frac{B}{C}$$

This will give a Heading between 0 and 90 degrees. It will then be necessary to ascertain the quadrant in which the maximum value occurs and from knowledge of the quadrant, the Heading is converted into that quadrant. The quadrants are easily found from the following diagrams:

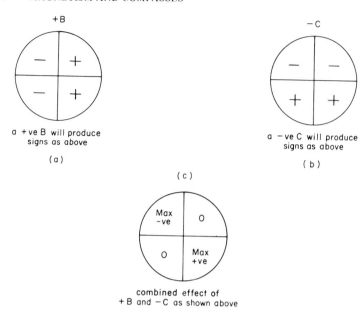

a +ve B will produce
signs as above

(a)

a −ve C will produce
signs as above

(b)

(c)

combined effect of
+ B and −C as shown above

Fig. 5. 2. 8

Example: Given B = +4, C = −3, find the Heading on which the deviation will be maximum.

From the diagrams above, it is seen that the maximum Westerly deviation will occur between 270 and 360, and maximum Easterly deviation between 090 and 180.

$$\text{Tan Heading} = \frac{B}{C} = \frac{4}{3} = 1.333, \text{ which is the Tan of } 53° \text{ from the tables.}$$

∴ Max westerly devn = 360 − 53 = 307

Max easterly devn = 307 − 180 = 127 (this must be the reciprocal of the Hdg which gave maximum deviation of opposite sign)

Once the Heading is known, the value of the deviation may be found from the normal formula, e.g. on Hdg 307

Total deviation = B sin Hdg + C cos Hdg
= 4 (−sin 53) + (−3 cos 53)
= −4 x ·7986 + (−3 x ·6018)
= −3·1944 − 1·8054
= 4·999 Westerly

The value may also be found by Pythagoras, since B and C act at right angles to each other and we are interested in their resultant. In the above example:

$$(\text{Maximum value})^2 = 4^2 + 3^2$$
$$= 25$$

∴ max value = 5, and give the sign according to the quadrant.

The whole problem could be solved by scale drawing, and such a method is sometimes called for in the ALTP examination. But its real virtue lies in the fact that by learning this method, a firmer grasp of aircraft deviations is acquired. We'll do the same problem this way. It looks like this:

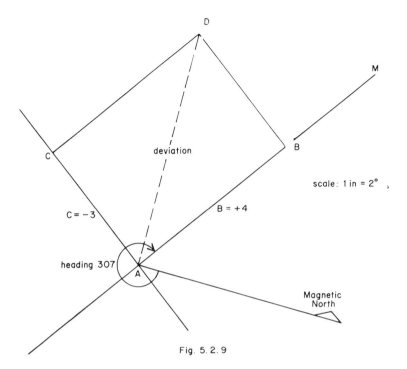

Fig. 5. 2. 9

Construction
(i)   From a convenient point A, draw AM to represent any Heading of the aircraft.
(ii)   Along the Heading AM, let AB represent to scale the value of B, in this case +4. If it had been a −ve B, it would have been plotted towards the tail from A.
(iii) At A and at right angles to AM draw AC to represent to scale the value of C, in this case −3. Being negative, C acts to the port of the aircraft.
(iv)   Complete the parallelogram ABDC. AD then represents the maximum deviation, and measures about 5°.
(v)   To find the Heading on which this will occur, draw in the magnetic meridian from A, so that it is at right angles to AD, since maximum deviation occurs when the deviating force acts at 90° to the needle.
(vi)   Measure the Heading; it is 307.
(vii) The maximum Easterly deviation will occur on the reciprocal, 127.
5a.   Maximum Deviation
       Another case is when the maximum value and the Heading on which it occurs are given, and it is required to separate B and C. You will recognise this as a problem in reverse of the previous one. It is best solved by scale diagram.

Example: Given that the maximum deviation is +5 on a Heading of 127°, find the value of Coefficients B and C.

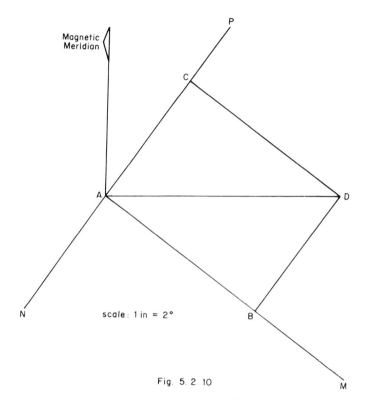

Fig. 5. 2. 10

In the figure, AM is the given Heading from the Magnetic datum, and NAP is the aircraft's athwartships axis.

AD is plotted to scale along the East-West line, and being given as +ve, in an Easterly direction therefore. The maximum value has in fact been plotted at 90° to the needle.

From D, drop two perpendiculars DB and DC to AM and AP respectively. Measure AB, 4°, and it is +ve since it acts towards the nose of the aircraft. Measure AC, 3°, and it is −ve since it acts towards the port. The same values for B and C would have been found if the given maximum deviation was −5 on a Hdg of 307; it's worth the effort of drawing out as a check.

6. Zero Deviation

   If the values of B and C are given, the Heading of zero deviation is found from the formula:

$$\text{Tan Heading} = \frac{C}{B}$$

and its derivation is as follows:

   Deviation = B sin Hdg + C cos Hdg = 0

   ∴ B sin Hdg = C cos Hdg

$$\frac{B}{C} = \frac{\cos \text{Hdg}}{\sin \text{Hdg}} \quad \text{or} \quad \frac{C}{B} = \text{Tan Hdg}$$

In the problem, tan Hdg = ¾ = ·75 = 037° or 217°, the Headings where zero deviation occurs.

Of course, it will be appreciated that once the Heading of maximum deviation is found, the Heading of zero deviation is 90° removed from it. Occasionally, illustrations of zero deviation conditions are called for by means of a scale diagram.

Example: B is —ve and is half the value of C which is +ve. Draw a diagram to illustrate the heading on which these two forces will cause zero deviation.

The solution is similar to that for finding maximum deviation, except that the magnetic meridian is placed along the resultant and not at right angles to it.

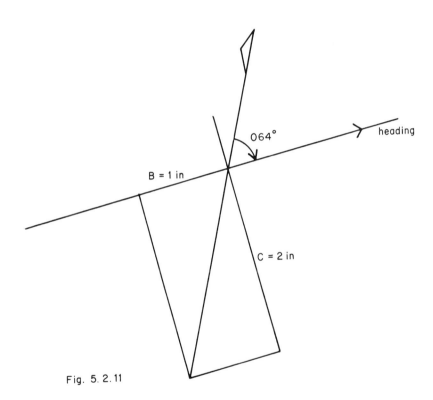

Fig. 5. 2. 11

Construction
(i)   Draw in any straight line to represent the aircraft's Heading.
(ii)   At a convenient point on that straight line, draw in another straight line at right angles to it to represent the aircraft's athwartships axis.
(iii) From this point plot B and C. B is —ve, so is plotted toward the tail. C is +ve, so is plotted to the starboard.
(iv)   Complete the parallelogram and extend the resultant as shown in the diagram to represent the Magnetic meridian.
(v)   Measure off the Headings of zero deviation. They are 064° and 244°.

3: P type compass; E2 compass

The basic compass, simply a needle which points to the North, adapted for aerial use. It is mandatory to carry in civil transport aircraft a compass which does just this, so that if the splendidly refined direction-indicating gear goes for a burton, you are down to basics. The 'P' type is rather bulky and is seldom selected nowadays by sophisticated operators, but it is in constant use world-wide nevertheless, and is beloved of examiners.

A freely suspended magnet would settle along the Earth's line of total force, providing it were clear of other magnetic influences, which means it would point to Magnetic North in the horizontal plane, and dip from the horizontal in the vertical plane (66° in the U.K.): the latter effect must be got rid of somehow, for we are interested only in the Earth's horizontal force H.

For the compass to function efficiently it must:
1. Lie horizontal
2. Be sensitive
3. Be aperiodic or dead-beat.

The first requirement is obtained by making the magnet system pendulous. Four magnets are used in fact, and they are mounted close together below the pivot, so that when tilted by the Earth's vertical force Z, the centre of gravity moves out from below the point of suspension bringing a righting force into action: the magnet will take up a position which is the resultant of the two equal and opposite forces, the tilting of the needle due to Z being counteracted by the weight of the magnet system acting through the C of G. The final inclination of the compass to the horizontal is actually about 2°/3°, but it will increase with increased Z until 70N or S where H is so weak and Z so strong as to render the instrument useless.

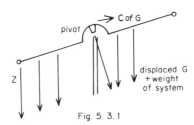

Fig. 5. 3. 1

In the N. Hemisphere, the C of G would be considered to be southwards of the point of suspension, since the correcting force must be away from the north seeking end which is trying to dip: it must be stressed right now that this displacement of the C of G is a factor brought into play by the system's pendulosity: there is not, repeat not, some built-in mechanical adjustment to the pivotting of the needle which would render such a compass useless in the other Hemisphere. The C of G is displaced automatically from beneath the pivot to correct for dip whichever end of the needle does the dipping.

The second requirement of sensitivity can only be done by increasing the pole strengths of the magnets used so that the needle stays firmly fixed along the magnetic meridian. This is helped by keeping pivot friction to a minimum by using iridium for the pivot which is suspended in what is laughingly called a sapphire cup: it's made of corundum actually. All this is suspended in liquid which reduces the effective weight of the system and lubricates the pivot.

The third requirement of aperiodicity is a trifle more complex. If a suspended magnet be deflected from its position of equilibrium and released, it oscillates between positions on either side of the equilibrium position for some time before coming to rest. Period of oscillation is the time taken in seconds to travel from one extreme position to the other and back again. A period is undesirable in a compass, and the ideal compass would stop without oscillation, when it could be said to be 'aperiodic'. In the air, the compass needle is readily moved from its alignment with the magnetic meridian by accelerations and turns. Aperiodicity is attained in a/c compasses by the following means:

1. The bowl is filled with methyl alcohol, and damping filaments are fitted to the magnet system.
2. Several short powerful magnets are used instead of one large one, thereby increasing the righting force, and reducing the moment of inertia.
3. The apparent weight of the system is reduced by the buoyancy of the liquid, and that weight is concentrated near the centre, by mounting close to the pivot. The moment of inertia is even further reduced.

The liquid is actually methyl alcohol, double deaerated; ideally it should be transparent — it is; have wide temperature range — it has, $-50°$ to $+50°C$; low coefficient of expansion — it hasn't, it's about 12% over the full temperature range; low viscosity and low specific gravity — not too bad; non-corrosive — not so important with plastic bowls, but it can eventually get at the rubber gasket of the verge ring. Since the liquid will change in volume with temperature variations, some expansion device is necessary. At the bowl base, an expansion chamber is fitted in the larger types or a sylphon tube in the smaller, of thin corrugated metal.

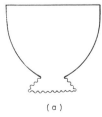

(a)

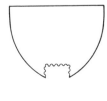

(b)

Fig. 5. 3. 2

One disadvantage to the use of liquid is that in a prolonged turn it will turn with the aircraft, taking the magnet system with it tending to affect indicated readings on completion. This is offset to some extent by keeping a good clearance between the damping wires and the wall of the bowl; the effect is small, since the viscosity of the liquid used is low, too, but liquid swirl does prevent an immediate settling down on a new heading compass.

The Magnet System

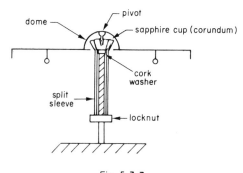

Fig. 5.3.3

The split sleeve overlaps the ledge surrounding the dome and prevents the whole works falling apart when the compass is inverted.

The Bowl
The lubber line on the bowl is fixed on the a/c's fore and aft axis precisely, and we have already seen the effect of any displacement of it, as well as the ease of correction. The suspension of the bowl and its expansion device is such that vibration which would harm the pivot is reduced to a minimum: it stands on 4 bronze helical springs which are attached to the outer case spaced at 90° apart, and a floating ring, to which friction springs are attached, supports the bowl in slots to prevent azimuth movement.

The grid ring fits over the verge ring which seals the liquid in the bowl, and has direction marked every 10° graduated in 2° divisions, luminous. Additionally, the North point is a red triangle, hence the expression "red on red", and parallel lines are marked across the plate, to be lined up with the needle precisely: the locking device is put to 'lock' once the desired heading is set against the lubber line, and the a/c turned till "red is on red". The North pointer of the needle is crossed to prevent error.

Serviceability Checks
1. Check liquid is free from bubbles, discoloration, sediment.
2. Examine all parts for luminosity.
3. Ensure that grid ring rotates freely through 360°, and that locking device functions positively.
4. Test suspension of bowl by moving gently in all directions and that there is no metal to metal feeling.

5. Test for pivot friction: deflect the magnet system through
    10—15° each way, and note the reading on return: each should
    be within 2° of the other.
6. Test for damping: deflect system through 90°, hold for 30 seconds to
    allow liquid to settle and time its return through 85°. The maximum
    and minimum times are laid down in the manufacturer's Instrument
    Manual, usually about 6·5 seconds to 8·5 seconds.

The E2 Compass

A small compass, vertical reading, which is the favourite as a standby compass:
invariably fitted between the two pilots above the windscreen, it is not expected
to be precise, but as a rough check on the main compass. It has correctors
built in for Coefficients B and C and R (there is another model, the E2A, which
omits the R corrector), on top of the bowl.

The bowl is of transparent plastic, and the lubber line is simply a luminous
line in the window: the magnet is a steel circle, domed, and from the dome a
pivot is dropped which rests in a sapphire cup on a stem fixed to the base of the
bowl. Thus dip is minimised as in the P type. The bowl is filled with a silicone
fluid, non corrosive, low viscosity, and low coefficient of expansion — but there
is a sylphon tube at the rear of the compass bowl.

The compass card is a light metal ring, marked off every 30°, graduated in
10°, attached to the circular magnet, and the dome of the bowl prevents the
system falling off when inverted. The E2 suffers from turning and acceleration
errors, and could in extreme climb or dive positions be not free to rotate.

4: Turning and Acceleration Errors

We're still on about compasses where a magnet system is fitted pendulously to counteract the effect of Dip: the residual angle from the horizontal is around 3° in U.K. latitudes, and in the reduction from 66° to 3° the C of G has been displaced from below the pivot to South of the pivot to pull the dipping North-seeking end up towards the horizontal. This displacement will vary with Z, and clearly in the S. Hemisphere the displacement will be of opposite sign, i.e. the C of G will displace itself to the North of the pivot to counterbalance the dipping South seeking compass pole.

This displacement, however, has a marked effect on the compass needle in turns, accelerations and decelerations, except at the Magnetic equator where Z is nil, and a fine old song and dance is made about these errors to pilots on their way up.

Acceleration Errors

On a Westerly heading, if speed is increased, the pivot and the magnet system will move forward with the a/c: there will also be an equal and opposite force acting on the centre of gravity, which in the horizontal plane is South of the Pivot: the resultant of this horizontal couple will rotate the needle in an anticlockwise direction, i.e. the North seeking end will be moved to the west. Additionally since the C of G is placed below the pivot in the vertical plane, the pivot assembly going forward while the C of G lags behind will cause a vertical tilt to the needle, since the needle, the pivot and the C of G are no longer in line with the magnetic meridian: the counteracting C of G against dip will thus be lost to some extent and the North end of the needle will be under some influence from Z, causing further rotation of the North seeking end in the direction of the acceleration. In fact, it is this part of the deal which contributes the major amount of the total error.

Fig. 5. 4. 1

Accelerating on an Easterly Hdg., with similar resultant forces, the needle would turn clockwise, showing an apparent turn to port, i.e., to the North. In all changes of speed, where the a/c's heading is across the needle there will be a compass error until constant speed is regained.

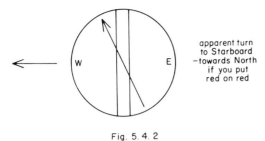

apparent turn
to Starboard
—towards North
if you put
red on red

Fig. 5. 4. 2

Summary of Acceleration and Deceleration Errors

HDG	SPEED	NEEDLE TURNS	EFFECT
E	Increase	Clockwise	Apparent Turn to N.
W	Increase	Anticlockwise	Apparent Turn to N.
E	Decrease	Anticlockwise	Apparent Turn to S.
W	Decrease	Clockwise	Apparent Turn to S.

N.B.
1. In Southern Hemisphere, above errors are opposite
2. No errors on Nly and Sly headings as the force acts along the needle.
3. They can occur in bumpy conditions.
4. No errors on the Magnetic Equator, as the pivot and the C of G are coincident.

Turning errors
These are maximum on N and S headings, and are important within 35° of these headings.

Consider a turn through N to starboard: the centripetal force acting on the pivot directed inwards towards the centre of the turn should balance the centrifugal force acting outwards: but the centrifugal force acts on the centre of gravity, which we know in the N. Hemisphere to be displaced south of the pivot. Thus the needle will be pulled outwards from its centre of gravity, turning the needle in the direction of turn, Easterly: and the compass will indicate less than the turn actually accomplished. Additionally, the unbalanced centrifugal/centripetal forces will set up a vertical pull on the slightly tilted North-seeking pole, accentuated by the fact that the needle has left the magnetic meridian; this vertical pull in the turn will manifest itself as a rotation of the magnet system in the direction of the turn, to the East: again, this is the major contribution to the error.

In turn we are considering, the needle can turn at the same rate as the a/c, and indicate no turn at all: it can turn slower than the a/c, indicating a smaller turn than actually accomplished: it can, in high rates of turn, move quicker than the a/c and indicate a turn in the wrong direction. In turns through South (we're in the N.

Hemisphere) the reverse will take place, and the compass will rotate in the opposite direction to the a/c, indicating a greater turn than that actually made: but as the needle turns as it were to meet the a/c, the result always is an overreading, and always in the right direction.

No fixed figure can be laid down to any of these errors, as so many variables are involved: but errors of up to 60° are not unusual in a prolonged turn, and only experience of a particular a/c with its particular compass type can avoid the fiddling and twiddling to get settled down on the precise compass heading required as soon as possible.

In the Southern Hemisphere, with the C of G displaced to the North of the pivot, the reverse results will be obtained. The swirl of the liquid which tends to turn in the same direction as the aircraft will, in the Northern Hemisphere, be additive to the error in turns through North, and subtractive in turns through South.

To summarise:

TURN	NEEDLE	EFFECT	LIQUID SWIRL	CORRECTION
Through North	Same as a/c	Under Indication	Adds to Error	Turn less than needle shows
Through South	Opp. to a/c	Over Indication	Reduces Error	Turn more than needle shows

N.B.
1. In Southern Hemisphere, above errors are of opposite value.
2. In turns about East and West, no errors to speak of, since forces act along the needle.
3. Northerly turning error is greater than Southerly, since liquid swirl is additive.
4. For accurate turns, use the DGI. How about that? All dynamic errors last only for the period of speed changes or turns: once a constant speed or level flight is resumed the compass needle finds North again.

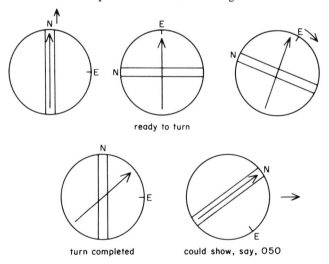

ready to turn

turn completed   could show, say, 050

Fig. 5. 4. 3

Check these pictures, for a turn to starboard from North, where the needle turns slower than the a/c. Repeat them for a variety of turns through N and S, in both hemispheres.

And for a rule of thumb:

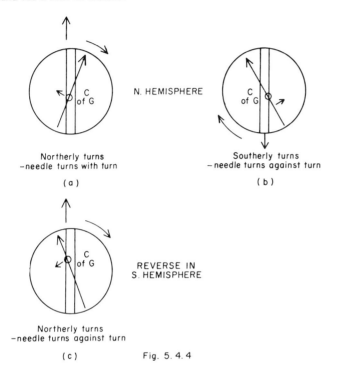

N. HEMISPHERE

Northerly turns
−needle turns with turn

(a)

Southerly turns
−needle turns against turn

(b)

REVERSE IN
S. HEMISPHERE

Northerly turns
−needle turns against turn

(c)   Fig. 5. 4. 4

5: Sperry's CL2 compass

The CL2 is a remote indicating compass and combines the use of a gyro with the Earth's magnetic lines of force, thus giving the best of both DGI and P type compasses. As for the magnetic part the system does not align itself with the meridian; it senses it, as we shall soon see. Since it is a remote indicating compass, the detector unit which senses the meridian can be placed outside the cockpit. In fact it is usually tucked away in the wing tip or other remote part of the fuselage where the magnetic interference is the least. This gives it a high accuracy of ±½°. The compass incorporates a facility to set variation, thus giving true headings, if required. Finally, the heading information may be transferred to a number of repeaters in the cockpit.

Principle of Direction Sensing
If you expose a highly permeable magnetic bar to the Earth's field the bar will acquire magnetic flux. The amount of flux thus produced will depend on two factors: latitude which governs the strength of the Earth's component H (assuming the bar is horizontal) and the direction of the bar relative to the direction of the component H. This second part is the key to the heading sensing.

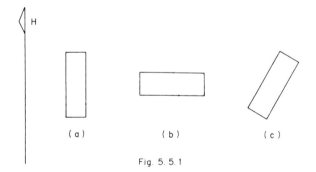

H

(a)   (b)   (c)

Fig. 5. 5. 1

In Fig 1 (a) above a bar is placed having its axis directly in line with the magnetic meridian as defined by the direction H. Since H goes right through the length of the bar the flux produced is maximum. If this bar was fixed in the fore-and-aft axis of the aircraft, maximum flux will result when the aircraft is on heading 000(M). In Fig 1 (b) the aircraft carrying the bar is on heading 090(M). Since component H acts at 90° to the axis of the bar, no flux will be induced. This is a cosine relationship. If the aircraft was on heading 030(M), the flux intensity would be H cos 30°. Now, on heading 150(M) the flux intensity will be the same as on

030(M) but the direction of the flux flow will have reversed (cosine of 150° is negative).

This, therefore, gives us a basic principle which may be adapted to give direction measurements. The flux intensity is the measure of the heading. The problem is to convert flux into electrical voltage and current. Now, this is an easy matter if the flux so produced was "changing" flux,for, according to Faraday, "Whenever there is change of flux linked with a circuit an EMF is induced in the circuit". It will be appreciated that in an aircraft at any given position the flux produced will be a steady, constant quantity. If this steady flux could be converted to changing flux, a current representing heading would flow. This is what we want, a current representing aircraft's heading.

Flux Valve. This is achieved in the CL2 by a device called the Flux Valve. It consists of two bars of highly permeable magnetic material – bars A and B in Fig 2

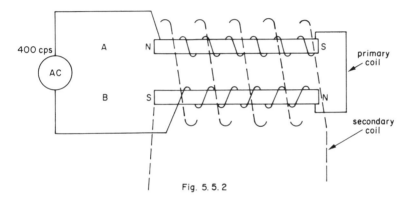

Fig. 5. 5. 2

above. Both the bars are wound with a coil and connected to an AC source in series. The coil is called the Primary Coil. Over the primary coil and going round both the bars is a pick-up coil, called the Secondary Coil. The effect of passing AC through these wirings is shown in Fig 3 below. The AC passed is of such strength that at the

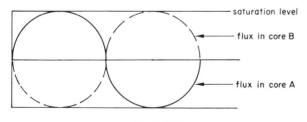

Fig. 5. 5. 3

peak it saturates both the coils, as seen in the figure. However, the flux produced in the above diagram will have no effect on the secondary coil since at any given instant two bars produce flux of equal intensity and opposite polarity. But in practice this situation does not arise, since a bar placed horizontally on the Earth's surface or at an altitude (as in an aircraft) has always present in it the Earth's component H (unless the aircraft is flying in the close vicinity of either Pole). This component H produces a static flux in both the bars which is shown in Fig 4.

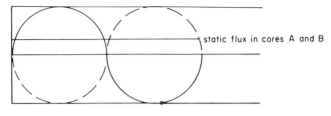

static flux in cores A and B

Fig. 5.5.4

The effect of this static flux is to saturate the cores before AC reaches the peak, as seen in Fig 5. The coils are saturated and AC is still rising. The effect will

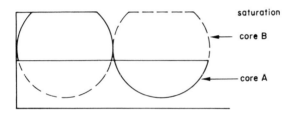

saturation

core B

core A

Fig. 5.5.5

be that from now on, as the saturation occurs, the intake of the Earth's flux will start reducing and on a combined figure it will appear as a curve – a changing flux. Fig. 6.

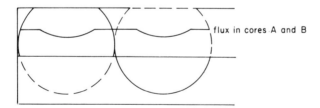

flux in cores A and B

Fig. 5.5.6

This changing flux will now produce voltage and current will flow in the secondary coil.

Basic Components of the Compass

CL2 comprises five basic units as follows:
1.   Detector Unit
2.   Master Indicator
3.   Amplifier
4.   The Gyro Unit
5.   Control Panel

Detector Unit

This is a very small unit in size and contains the sensing element. A simple flux valve as explained above would do as a sensing element but there are two disadvantages to its use. First, at varying latitudes, varying current will flow; second, an ambiguity exists. With relation to figure 1 above we said that the flux on headings 030(M) and 150(M) will be of the same intensity but of opposite polarity. That's OK, then, we can differentiate. On heading 330(M), however, as the cosine of 330 is also positive, the flux will be of the same intensity and polarity as on heading 030(M).

These disadvantages are overcome by the use of three simple flux valves instead of just one. They are placed 120° apart and all six cores (or bars) are excited by a common primary coil. To improve sensitivity six curved collector horns are attached to the outer ends of the bars. They collect the flux and feed into their respective spokes. Fig 7.

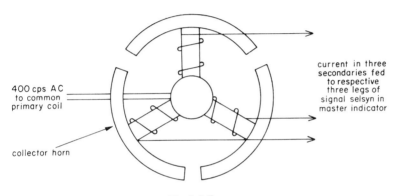

current in three
secondaries fed
to respective
three legs of
signal selsyn in
master indicator

400 cps AC
to common
primary coil

collector horn

Fig. 5.5.7

Signal Selsyn

This unit, located in the master indicator, receives the current from the detector unit. The selsyn unit consists of three legs similar to the spokes of the detector unit and a moveable coil, called the rotor, at the centre. The stators having received signals from the respective three secondary coils resolve the field produced in a final resultant direction. Detector unit and signal selsyn are shown in the following figure.

stator

rotor

to precession
amplifier

detector
unit

signal
selsyn

Fig. 5.5.8

Operation

Follow the operation with reference to Fig 9.

1.   On switching on, the detector unit will produce voltages in three secondary coils. These voltages are a direct measure of the heading.

2.   These voltages are fed to three respective stators of the signal selsyn. The stators resolve these voltages into a resultant field.

3.   That resultant field is a definite direction. If the pointer of the master indicator is indicating that very heading at this time the rotor of the signal selsyn will be at "null" position, that is, it will be lying at 90° to the direction of the resultant field. In this state no voltage is induced in the rotor.

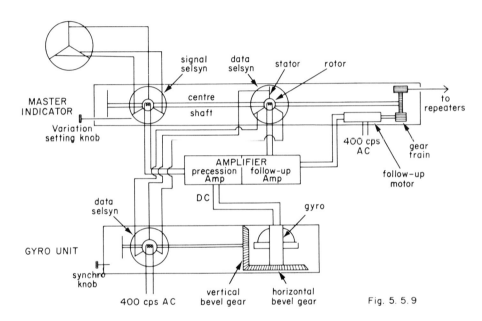

Fig. 5. 5. 9

4.   If the heading is not synchronised, the rotor will not be at null and voltage will be induced in the rotor.

5.   This voltage is fed to the precession amplifier where –
     a.   it will be phase detected
     b.   rectified (i.e. converted from AC to DC) and
     c.   amplified

6.   This DC signal is then passed to the precession coil in the Gyro Unit where the precession of the gyro takes place in the horizontal plane and in correct direction due to arrival of this signal. How this is done is explained later.

7.   As gyro turns, the horizontal bevel gear turns, turning the vertical bevel gear with it. The vertical bevel gear carries a shaft on which are mounted the gyro unit pointer (this is the pilot's indicator) and the rotor of the gyro unit data selsyn. Therefore, as the vertical gear and the shaft rotate, the pointer and the rotor of the data selsyn must rotate too.

8.   This data selsyn rotor of the gyro unit is continuously energised by AC and

therefore, has a standing field in it affecting its stators. When the rotor rotates, this field must rotate producing new signals in its stators.

9.   These new signals are passed to the respective stators of the data selsyn in the master indicator, altering the field in them.

10. This new field in the stators will affect the rotor and an AC will be induced in it.

11. This AC or error signal is passed to the follow-up amplifier where it is amplified and then sent out to a two-phase follow-up motor.

12. This will energise the motor and it will start turning the central shaft in the MI (Master Indicator) via the gear train. Mounted on this shaft are the rotors of the two selsyns. They will continue to rotate until the rotor of the signal selsyn is at null position to the resultant field in that selsyn.

13. At this instant, signal selsyn rotor will stop sending error signals to the amplifier and to the rest of the system. The gyro is now aligned with the magnetic meridian, both the pointers are similarly synchronised with the meridian, and the system comes to rest.

Let's go over the whole thing again, this time taking some figures. Say, on switching on, the nose of the aircraft is pointing to 060(M). This is the field the detector unit will produce and the stators of the signal selsyn will resolve. Say, at this time the pointers of the two indicators are indicating 050(M).

Field in the stators – 060; pointers are not indicating this heading, therefore signal selsyn rotor is not at null. It sends off an error signal to the precession amplifier where three things noted above happen. The signal is then passed on to the precession mechanism of the gyro.

This turns the gyro, horizontal and vertical bevel gears. The shaft in the gyro unit rotates, rotating with it the rotor of the gyro unit data selsyn. This rotor was initially aligned with 050 indication. Now, say, at a given instant it has rotated to be aligned with 058 (in the course of its turn in the direction of 060). This turning will cause a new field in its stators which will be repeated in the stators of the data selsyn in the master indicator.

This rotor was aligned to indicate 050; now the field in its stators equals 058. A signal will be raised in the rotor, amplified and passed to the motor. The motor turns, turning the shaft and the rotors with it. Signal selsyn rotor turns to align with 058 – all rotors are in synchronism but the signal selsyn rotor has not gained the null position: it still has two degrees to go and therefore, it continues to send out error signals.

When all three rotors are aligned with 060 no more error signals are raised, and the compasses are synchronised.

Manual Synchronising

In above illustration the pointer will take exactly 5 minutes to move round from 050 to 060 since the rate of precession of the gyro is limited to $2°$ per minute. This slow rate of precession is quite adequate to keep the gyro in the magnetic meridian throughout the flight – i.e. check the gyro's apparent wander. But where a large discrepancy between the nose of the aircraft and the indicated heading is present,,e.g. on initial switching on, the pointers are synchronised manually. This is done by use of the "synchronising knob" on the Gyro Unit. Fig 10.

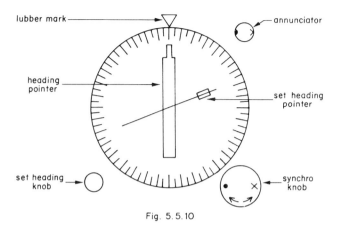

Fig. 5.5.10

The fact that the pointers are not indicating synchronised heading will be brought to your attention by the presence of a dot or a cross in the middle of the annunciator window on both the gyro unit indicator and the master indicator (which is the navigator's indicator). This indication is removed by depressing the synchro knob on the gyro unit and turning it in the direction shown by the arrow. When it is so depressed the gyro itself is disconnected and only the shaft and the pointers are turned.

Behaviour of CL2 in a Turn

Earlier, we said that the normal precession operation is adequate to take care of the gyro wander etc. This might give an impression that the pointers would get desynchronised during a turn. This is not so, because during a turn the gyro, due to its rigidity, drives the pointers and keeps them aligned with the instantaneous heading. This is what takes place.

The aircraft, and therefore the gyro case, rotates about the horizontal bevel wheel and the gyro. Thus, the vertical bevel gear goes round the horizontal bevel gear, and the shaft in the gyro unit rotates. Error signals raised in the stators of the gyro unit data selsyn are repeated in the stators of the master indicator data selsyn. The rotor in that data selsyn raises an error signal, the motor turns and the shaft in the master indicator turns. This keeps the rotors of the signal selsyn and data selsyn in synchronism with the instantaneous heading during a turn.

During all this time the detector unit is also turning with the aircraft. Therefore the field in the signal selsyn stators is also rotating. Both this field and the rotor rotate at the same speed and in the same direction. Therefore, continuous synchronism is maintained.

In a steep and prolonged turn a slight desynchronisation may be expected. This is due to the fact that the detector unit is no longer horizontal and a small component of Z will enter in it, giving rise to a false field. However, on coming out of the turn, the needle will be brought to correct reading by the normal precession process. Apart from this small error there are no turn and acceleration errors.

Variation Setting

The system incorporates a facility for setting variation on the compass so that true headings may be flown. This is done by turning the stators of the signal selsyn which has the effect of rotating the field in the stators by an equivalent amount. The facility for setting variation is located on the master indicator and as the knob is turned a scale in the variation window rotates behind a lubber line to indicate the amount of variation being set.

Precession Mechanism

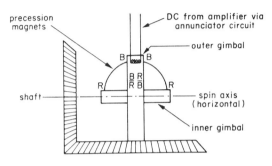

Fig. 5.5.11

The precession mechanism consists of a coil, called the precession coil, mounted in the outer gimbal, and a pair of horn shaped permanent magnets mounted on the inner gimbal. See Fig 11. The polarity of the permanent magnets is as shown in the figure. When desynchronisation occurs, a DC is passed from the amplifier via the annunciator circuit to the precession coil. (As a matter of interest AC models are also available). Depending on the direction of the current, two ends of the precession coil will acquire magnetic polarity. At one end this polarity will be in attraction and at the other end in repulsion to the polarity of the permanent magnet. This attraction and repulsion will apply a torque on the inner gimbal in the vertical plane and the gyro will precess in the horizontal plane, that is, the horizontal bevel gear will turn.

Erection Mechanism

It will be appreciated that, as with the DGI, the gyro in CL2 must be maintained horizontal. Erection mechanism ensures this. It consists of a two-phase torque motor with its stators mounted on the outer gimbal and a levelling switch mounted on the inner gimbal — see Fig.12.

The levelling switch is made up of a commutator split in two segments by an insulating strip. When the gyro axis is horizontal the stators rest on the insulated strip and the switch to the motor is off — Fig. 12(a). When the axis is tilted the stator will come in contact with the commutator and the circuit to the torque motor is complete. The direction of the current to the torque will depend on the direction of the tilt, as is seen in Fig. 12(b). The direction of the current decides the direction the torque will be applied, that is, clockwise or anti-clockwise. The torque so applied about the vertical axis will precess the gyro axis until it is once

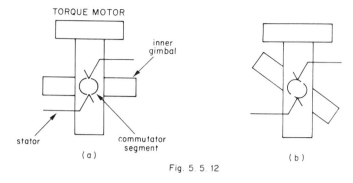

TORQUE MOTOR

inner
gimbal

stator

commutator
segment

(a)

(b)

Fig. 5. 5. 12

again horizontal when the stator will slip off the commutator and rest on the
insulated strip, switching off the motor.

The Annunciator

This unit gives the indication of synchronisation state, and consists of a pivoted arm
carrying a flag marked with dot and cross at one end and a permanent magnet at
the other. The magnet is held between two annunciator coils connected in series.
When the pointers are desynchronised from the magnetic meridian DC flows from

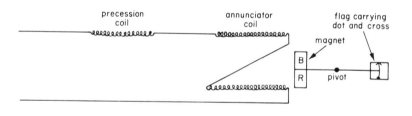

precession
coil

annunciator
coil

flag carrying
dot and cross

magnet

B

R

pivot

Fig. 5. 5. 13

precession amplifier to the precession coil. Use is made of this current flow which
passes through the annunciator circuit. As it passes through the two annunciator
coils (connected in series) the two ends nearest to the permanent magnet will
acquire opposite polarity, one end attracting the magnet and the other end
repelling. As the magnet is drawn towards one end of the coil the flag arm will
turn about its pivot, the flag will be displaced from the centre and one of its ends,
carrying either a dot or a cross, will appear in the window. Whether the dot or a
cross will appear in the centre of the window depends on which end of the
magnet is drawn towards the coils, which in its turn depends on the direction of
the DC.

Control Panel

With CL2 system there are two gyro units, one for each pilot, together with the
master indicator installed at the navigator's position. But as we saw above only
one gyro unit could be run together with the detector unit. In Fig. 9 we have no
accommodation for two gyro units. Therefore, the other gyro must run as a DGI.

On the control panel there is a three-position switch on which you may select gyro off, gyro on port, or gyro on the starboard side. In the off position, both gyros operate as a DGI, that is, unmonitored by the detector unit.

Adjustment and Calibration

Having done a normal swing and calculated coefficients A, B and C, proceed as follows to correct for them.

Equipment Required. A centre reading voltmeter (CRV). This is plugged in at the jack socket in the amplifier. This then by-passes the annunciator circuit; the CRV acts as a more sensitive annunciator. If no current flows through the CRV the system is synchronised. You also require a stable DC supply of 24 – 28V and a Compass Corrector Key.

Correction for B and C.

1. Having worked out the heading you want the compass to read, press the manual synchro knob on the gyro unit, turn it and give the required reading to the pointer.

2. Keep the knob depressed. If the knob is released the pointer will be precessed back to the original reading.

3. The CRV needle is now displaced from its zero position to one side or the other.

4. On the corrector box there is a two-position switch. In one position corrections up to 3° may be made; in the other, corrections over 3° may be made. If your correction does not exceed 3° place the switch to 3° position, otherwise on to 15° position.

5. Insert the compass corrector key in B or C socket as appropriate and turn the key until CRV reads 0.

6. Correction is complete; release the synchro knob.

Coefficient A over 2°

1. Steps 1, 2 and 3 are as per B and C above.

2. Turn the detector unit physically until CRV reads O.

3. Release the synchro knob.

Coefficient A – 2° and below

This is simply taken out on the Variation scale on the master indicator as follows:

1. Set the value of the coefficient A on the VSC as if you are setting variation. If A is positive set easterly variation of equivalent amount. If it is negative set westerly variation. For example you wish to correct for A, value −1. Set 1° westerly variation.

2. Insert compass corrector key in the groove on the side of the master indicator (approximately at the 8 o'clock position) and turn the key until the lubber line of the VSC moves and covers 0 variation. The lubber line was displaced by you when you carried out step 1 above.

Advantages of a Gyrosyn Compass

The advantages of a gyrosyn compass over a DGI are these:

1. DGI suffers from slow drift and has to be reset frequently in a flight. Further, when resetting, the aircraft must be flown straight and level to be able to take reading of a magnetic compass. CL2 does away with this, since its indicators are monitored by a detector unit.

2. The detector unit can be installed in a remote part of the aircraft where

influences due to aircraft magnetism are least. This gives a better accuracy to CL2 whereas a magnetic compass from which the DGI is reset is exposed to these influences.

3.   The flux valve used in the detector unit "senses" the meridian instead of "seeking" it. This avoids northerly turning errors.

4.   The compass can be detached from the detector unit by a flick of a switch and the gyro then works as normal DGI. This entirely does away with the requirement of a pure DGI in the cockpit. (CL2 is used as a DGI when flying in extreme northerly/southerly latitudes where H is very feeble.)

NAVIGATION GENERAL

1: Maps and Charts

The cartographer works from a model globe (the Earth reduced in size to required scale), marked out with the graticule, originally with a light source at some given point within the globe which projects the graticule on to a paper. The paper may be wrapped round the globe like a cylinder, or it may sit on the globe in form of a cone or it might be just a plane surface, tangential to the globe at a given parallel. Thus the term projection, and such a projection is simply a basic one. The aim is to transfer a certain portion of the Earth on to a flat piece of paper, without causing distortions yet preserving the properties required for air navigation. This is done by mathematical adjustment of the basic projection, discarding one property to achieve another. Ideally, we would like a chart with the following properties, all on one sheet:

1. The shapes to be represented correctly. This one property, however, can never be achieved on a flat surface. But this is only a technical distinction; in practice, shapes very close to true shapes are produced on certain projections.

2. The scale of our chart to be correct and constant. We want it to be correct because we need to measure correct distances; constant for the sake of convenience of measurement. Here again, we cannot have a chart with a scale which is both, constant and correct, but by mathematical manipulation a chart could be produced having its scale as good as constant.

3. Bearing measurements to be correct all over the chart. This property is. known as orthomorphism or conformality.

4. If a straight line drawn on the plotting chart represented a great circle, the navigator's task would become.much easier when plotting radio position lines. A radio wave travels along a great circle path over the surface of the Earth.

5. Adjacent sheets of the chart to fit properly, so that we could change over from one sheet to the next one when necessary.

When studying various projections we will be keeping these ideal properties in mind, but for the moment we will deal with one of them which is outstanding from the rest, i.e. orthomorphism.

Orthomorphism

A chart may be made so that the angle measured on the Earth's surface between a meridian and any line cutting it will be exactly the same as the angle between the corresponding meridian on the map projection. In other words, the angles measured on the chart are correct angles. It is quite immaterial whether the lines making these angles are straight or curved. This property is orthomorphism and a chart which has this property is called an orthomorphic chart.

In order to achieve orthomorphism, the projection must comply with two basic requirements:

1.   The meridians and parallels on the chart must cut each other at 90° just as they do on the Earth.

2.   At any given point on the chart the scale variation must be equal in all directions. The following diagrams illustrate the effect on bearing measurements due to unequal scale variation.

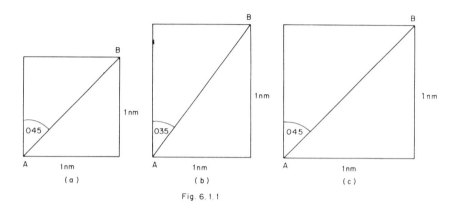

Fig. 6. 1. 1

In Fig. 1(a) the scale from point A represents 1 nm in all directions, and the bearing of B from A is 045°.

In Fig. 1(b) the scale in E–W direction is different from that in the N–S direction, and a wrong bearing is measured.

In Fig. 1(c) the scale in E–W direction is adjusted to equal the scale in N–S direction, and we once again measure a true bearing.

Scale

The model globe is true to scale everywhere, so $\dfrac{r}{R}$ = scale, where r = radius of the Earth in inches (250 000 000) and R is the radius of the model Globe. For example, if the radius of the model Globe was 500 in, the scale would be:

$$\frac{250\ 000\ 000}{500} = 500\ 000$$

This would mean that 1 inch of the model Globe would equal 500 000 inches on the Earth. This formula is often manipulated to solve for R when the scale is given. That should be simple enough.

When, however, the projection takes place on the paper outside the globe, the chart scale is correct only where the paper touches the globe. The scale on any chart is simply the ratio between the chart length, CL, and the ground distance, GD (also called Earth distance, ED), expressed in the same units. As a formula: Scale $= \dfrac{CL}{GD}$ and when solving this contrive (and you must) to have the figure 1 at the top (numerator) and a string of figures at the bottom (denominator). The scale is then said to be expressed as a *Representative Fraction*, e.g. $\dfrac{1}{1\,000\,000}$. This may also be written in another form, 1 : 1 000 000. In either case the scale tells us that a distance of 1 inch on the chart represents a distance of 1 000 000 inches on the ground. It also tells us that 1 cm on the chart equals 1 000 000 cm on the Earth. In other words the scale expressed as above has no inherent unit of its own; you provide a convenient unit and the result will be the same provided the same unit is used in denominator as in numerator.

Another point we need to note is that since we are dealing with a fraction of 1 the larger the figure in the denominator the smaller the scale we will have. 1 : 250 000 is a larger scale chart than one with a scale of 1 : 500 000. On a large scale chart, more ground details will be present since less ground distance is covered in unit distance on the chart.

Although this is the usual method of giving a chart scale in our business there are other methods of expressing the scale.

A Graduated Scale Line. This shows the actual lengths on the map corresponding to various distances on the Earth. It will be appreciated that such a scale can only be printed on constant scale charts.

Statement in Words. This expression is generally used on Ordnance Survey Maps and takes a form such as "One inch to the Mile". It is worthy of mention that one in quarter million scale (1 : 250 000) is approximately ¼ inch to the mile, or 1 cm to 2·5 km.

Worked Examples

1. How many nm to an inch are represented by a scale of 1 : 2 500 000?

$$1 \text{ inch represents } 2\,500\,000 \text{ inches or } \frac{2\,500\,000}{6\,080 \times 12} \text{ nm}$$

$$= 34 \cdot 26 \text{ nm}$$

2. You have a chart, scale 4 inches to 1 statute mile. Express this as a representative fraction.

$$\text{Scale} = \frac{CL}{ED} = \frac{4 \text{ inches}}{1 \times 5\,280 \times 12}$$

$$= 1 : 15\,840$$

3. If 100 nm are represented by a line 7·9 inches long on a chart what is the length of a line representing 50 km?

$$7 \cdot 9 \text{ in} = 100 \text{ nm} = 185 \text{ km}$$

$$\therefore 50 \text{ km} = \frac{50 \times 7 \cdot 9}{185}$$

$$= 2 \cdot 14 \text{ inches}$$

4. If the scale is 1 : 250 000 what is the distance on the chart between 32°11′N 06°47′E and 30°33′N 06°47′E?

Since both positions are situated on the same meridian the distance between the two in nautical miles is the arc of the meridian in number of minutes (1° = 60 minutes) intercepted between the two, viz, change of latitude in minutes.

Thus the distance in nm =

$$\begin{array}{r} 32°11' \\ - 30°33' \\ \hline 1°38' \text{ or } 98'. \end{array}$$

Now we proceed to solve the problem in the usual way — 1 in on the chart represents 250 000 in on the Earth, or

$$\frac{250\ 000}{6\ 080 \times 12} \text{ nm on the Earth}$$

$\therefore$ 98 nm will be represented by $\dfrac{98 \times 6\ 080 \times 12}{250\ 000}$ inches

$$= 28\cdot6 \text{ inches}$$

Practice Problems

1. How many kilometres are represented by a line 8·3 inches long if the scale of the chart is 1 : 250 000?

Answer: 52·70 km

2. What is the distance in inches on a chart representing 20 nm if the scale is 1 : 500 000?

Answer: 2·918 inches

3. 123 sm are represented on a chart by a line 22 in long. How many km will be represented by a line 10·8 in long?(41 sm = 61 km).

Answer: 97·2 km

4. If a line 12 in long represents 250 nm what is the length of a line on the chart in cm representing 560 km?

Answer: 38·9 cm

Chart symbols and relief

You learn all this from the maps and charts you come across in your flying activities from the word go: Civil Aviation Department Aeronautical Information Circular entitled Aeronautical Charts provides comprehensive information on various maps and charts available and the ICAO approved symbols. On Radio Navigation charts, the legend is available. Many maps print the key on the side of the map. Thus, as the psychologists say, this sort of knowledge is acquired "by use and wont". The only word of warning is spot heights: these are indicated by a dot with a figure by the side. Before using any chart, look around the margin to check if spot heights are given in feet or metres. 123 metres, for example, is 404 feet about — quite a difference. Relief on the topographic charts is usually shown by contours with a spot height. The nearer the contours the steeper the hills. Layer tinting is another method of showing relief. The depth of the colour as keyed at the side of the map indicates the gradient, again with a spot height to show the highest spot in the area. This boy scout stuff — which just comes naturally after the initial reading and use of various charts — should not be taken lightly, but armchair leisurely browsing at first.

Convergency

We have already seen (several times in fact) that a great circle cuts successive meridians at different angles because the meridians converge towards each other to the Poles. This inclination between any two meridians is called

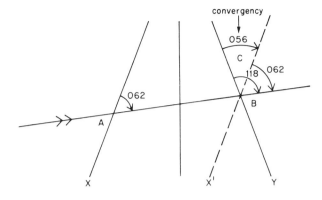

Fig. 6. 1. 2

convergency, and it equals the angular difference between the measurements of the great circle at each meridian.

The inclination of the meridians or convergency between two meridians X and Y (in Fig. 2 above) may be found by various methods, as follows:

1. By transferring on the chart the meridian X to X^1 (or the other way round) to pass through position B, and measuring the angle formed by the two meridians Y and X^1 at B (marked convergency angle in the figure).

2. By measuring the angle that the straight line joining A and B makes at positions A and B and calculating the difference. In above figure, $\angle C = 118 - 062 = 056°$.

3. By mathematical calculation, using formula

Convergency = ch long x sine lat.

The formula is derived from the reasoning that the meridians cut the Equator at 90° and therefore, they are parallel to each other and the angle of inclination between them is 0. At each pole every meridian on the face of the Earth meets in a point. The convergency or inclination of any two meridians here therefore amounts to the change of longitude between them. For example, two meridians 1° apart will make an angle of 1° at the Poles. Therefore, at any intermediate latitude, the convergency must equal change of longitude x sine of the latitude.

This formula is correct only when two places A and B are on the same latitude. If A and B are at different latitudes, the sine of mid-latitude between them may be used in the formula, giving sufficiently accurate results for our purpose.

Great Circle – Rhumb Line Relationship

A straight line drawn on the Earth or on a chart having correct convergency (that is, chart meridians inclining at the same angle as the meridians at the same place on the Earth) will be a great circle. The associated rhumb line will appear as a curve. (An important point is illustrated here also: the rhumb line, or to be precise the tangent to it, at the central meridian is parallel to the great circle; when using charts with converging meridians in practice, the Rhumb Line Track is the same as the mean Great Circle Track, measured at the central meridian between leaving and arriving meridians).

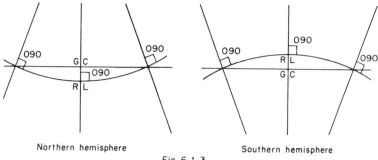

Northern hemisphere   Southern hemisphere

Fig. 6.1.3

However, on a chart which projects meridians as straight lines parallel to each other, a straight line will be a rhumb line and not a great circle (since it will cut all the meridians at the same angle). The example is the Mercator's projection, and on such charts the great circles must appear as curves. Fig. 4.

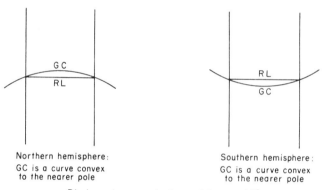

Northern hemisphere: Southern hemisphere:
GC is a curve convex   GC is a curve convex
to the nearer pole   to the nearer pole

RL in each case cuts the meridians at 90°

Fig. 6.1.4

If you observe figures 3 and 4 you will notice that in either hemisphere the rhumb line, as regards the great circle, always appears towards the equator, a point useful to remember when plotting radio position lines.

The angular difference between the great circle and the rhumb line is called Conversion Angle (see earlier chapter on plotting) and its value is half the value of the convergency.

To prove that Conversion Angle (CA) = ½ C (convergency)

AB and CD are two meridians (Fig. 5) and the straight line EF is a great circle.

$\angle$FEG is Conversion Angle and = $\angle$EFH

= $\angle$JFK

Transfer AB to $A_1 B_1$ to pass through position F. Then $\angle CFA_1$ is Convergency angle.

A rhumb line makes the same angle at each meridian,

$\therefore \angle$AEF + $\angle$FEG = $\angle CFA_1$ + $\angle A_1$FK $- \angle$JFK

But $\angle AEF = \angle A_1 FK$

and transferring $\angle JFK$ to the left hand side of the equation,

$\angle FEG + \angle JFK = \angle CFA_1$

or $CA + CA = C$

that is, $2CA = C$ or Conversion angle = half the convergency.

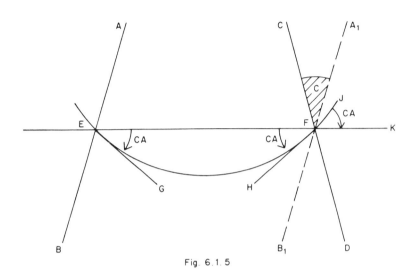

Fig. 6.1.5

Great Circle and Rhumb Line Bearings

Problems of the following nature are solved by application of the above theory.

1.   A bears 055° RL from B. What is the RL bearing of B from A? Since here we are only dealing with rhumb line bearings, B's bearing from A must be reciprocal of A's bearing from B. Therefore the answer is 235°.

2.   A bears 090° GC from B. Convergency = 4°. What is the GC bearing of B from A in the Northern and Southern hemispheres?

It is always advisable to draw up a simple sketch as shown below:

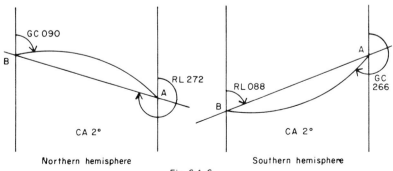

Fig. 6.1.6

Convergency given is $4°$; therefore CA = $2°$
A's RL bearing from B = 092; and B's RL bearing from A = $272°$
    ∴ B's GC bearing from A = $274°$
Southern Hemisphere: CA = $2°$; A's RL brg = $088°$; B's RL brg. from A = $268°$
    ∴ B's GC bearing from A = $266°$
3.   GC bearing of B from A is $095°$; RL bearing of A from B is $273°$.
    (a) What is the CA?
    (b) In which hemisphere are we?
    (c) What is the GC bearing of A from B?

Solution

    (a) CA is the angular difference between GC and RL
            ∴ CA = 095 + 180 = 275–273
                    = $2°$

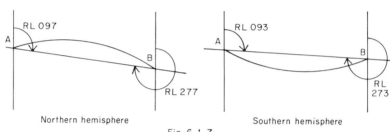

Northern hemisphere   Southern hemisphere

Fig. 6. 1. 7

    (b) In Fig. 7 above, for the Northern Hemisphere, the RL bearing of A
        from B = 095 + 2 + 180
                = $277°$
        and therefore the aircraft cannot be in the Northern hemisphere. The
        sketch for the Southern hemisphere illustrates the facts as given.
    (c) Since the RL bearing of A from B is 273, the GC bearing
            = 273 – 2 (CA)
            = $271°$

Practice Problems

1.   B bears $050°$ GC from A, CA $3°$. What is the RL bearing of A from B,
     both in Northern and Southern hemispheres?
     Answer: NH $233°$; SH $227°$.
2.   B bears $110°$ GC from A. A bears $298°$ GC from B in the Northern
     hemisphere. What is the convergency?   -
     Answer: $8°$
3.   A bears $070°$ GC from B. B bears $244°$ GC from A.
         a. Which hemisphere?   Answer: SH
         b. What is the convergency? $6°$
4.   A bears $272°$ GC from B. B bears $100°$ GC from A.
         a. Which hemisphere?   Answer: SH
         b. What is the convergency? $8°$

5. A bears 068° GC from B. B bears 254° GC from A.
    a. Which hemisphere?   Answer: NH
    b. What is RL bearing of A from B?   071°
    c. What is RL bearing of B from A?   251°
A further illustration:
    Calculate the convergency between A (48°30'N 28°12'E) and B
(55°00'N 10°00'E). If the Rhumb line Track between A and B is 300°,
what is the initial Great Circle Track?
Solution
              Convergency = ch long x sin mean lat
                           = 18°12' x sin 51°45'
                           = 18·2° x ·7853
                           = 14·3°

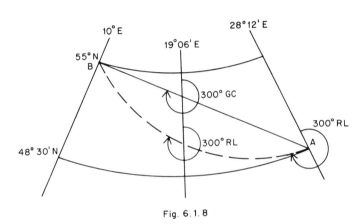

Fig. 6.1.8

    The GC and RL Tracks are the same at the mid-meridian, that is, in
this problem, at 19°06'E.
    The total convergency between A and B is 14°, therefore the
convergency between the mid-meridian and the meridian of A must be 7°; with
the RL Track of 300°, the GC Track from A is 300° + 7° = 307°, and the simple
sketch clarifies the solution.
Try this one:
    Position A (60°S 10°W) : Position B (55°S 10°E). If the initial GC Track
from A to B is 095°, what is the RL Track?
Answer: 086½°.

Change of longitude, distance along a parallel, departure
Because the meridians converge, it is clear that change of longitude is only a
measure of distance on the Equator, the only parallel which is a Great Circle. The
change of longitude on the Equator from 15°W to 20°W, say, is 300 nm but a
similar change of longitude at 70°N is nothing like that distance. But there is a
very definite relationship.

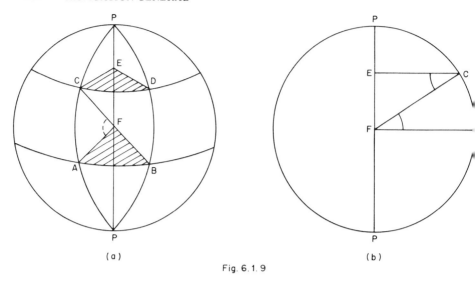

Fig. 6.1.9

In Fig. 9(a) AB is the arc of the Equator = change of longitude.

CD is the arc of parallel, of which the distance is required.

(It will be noticed that the distance CD becomes progressively smaller nearer to the Pole, but the change of longitude does not alter).

F is the centre of the Earth; PP the Earth's axis.

$\angle$AFC is the angle of the latitude CD

∵ Triangles ECD and ABF are parallel and equiangular

$$\frac{CD}{AB} = \frac{CE}{AF} \quad \cdots \cdots \cdots \cdots \cdots \cdots \cdots \quad (1)$$

In Fig. (b)

$$\frac{CE}{CF} = \text{Cos latitude}$$

$$\therefore CE = CF \cos \text{Lat}$$

$$= AF \cos \text{Lat (CF and AF being radii of the Earth} \ldots \ldots (2)$$

Substituting (2) in (1)

$$\frac{CD}{AB} = \frac{AF \cos \text{lat}}{AF}$$

or, CD = AB cos lat

Thus, distance CD = change of longitude x cosine latitude

The distance made good along a parallel (that is, in an East/West direction) is called <u>Departure</u>.

If the distance and latitude are given, by rearranging the formula Departure = Ch long x Cos lat, we can find the change of longitude.

Dep = Ch long x cos lat

$$\therefore \text{Ch long} = \frac{\text{Dep}}{\text{Cos lat}}$$

$$= \text{Dep x sec lat}$$

Or, given dep and ch long, latitude could be found:

$$\text{Cos lat} = \frac{\text{Dep}}{\text{Ch long}}$$

Above three variations of the formula are summarised below for convenience:

Departure = Ch long x Cos lat . . . . (1)

Ch long = Dep x sec lat   . . . . (2)

$$\text{Cos Lat} = \frac{\text{Dep}}{\text{Ch long}} \qquad \text{. . . . . (3)}$$

Examples

1. What is the rhumb line distance between A (53°23′N 01°19′W) and B (53°23′N 07°47′W)?

Departure = Ch long x cos lat
= 06°28′ x cos 53°23′
= 388′ x cos 53°23′
= 231·4nm

No.	Log
388	2·5888
Log cos 53°23′	$\overline{1}$·7756
	2·3644
Antilog =	231·4

2. An aircraft takes off from 40°20′N 178°38′E and flies a RL track of 090°. What is its longitude after it has travelled 219 nm?

Ch long = Dep x sec lat
= 219 x sec 40°20′
= 287·3′
= 4°47′
∴ new longitude = 176°35′W

No.	Log
219	2·3404
Log Sec 40°20′	0·1179
	2·4583
Antilog =	287·3

3. After flying 448 nm along a parallel of latitude an aircraft changes its longitude by 8°21′. What is the latitude?

$$\text{Cos lat} = \frac{\text{Dep}}{\text{Ch long (in minutes)}}$$
$$= \frac{448}{501}$$
$$= 26°35′ \text{ N or S}$$

No.	Log.
448	2·6513
501	2·6998
	$\overline{1}$·9515 = 26°35′ from
	log cosine tables.

Practice Problems

1. Rhumb line distance between two positions A and B in the same latitude of 52°S is 650 nm. What is the rhumb line distance between positions C and D which are respectively 420 nm north of A and B?

Answer: 746·6 nms

2. If a flight of 2220 Km is made along parallel 48°N what is the change of longitude?

Answer: 29°54′

3.   Given position X 50°S 179°W; Y 50°S 173°23′E.
       (a) What is the convergency between X and Y?
       (b) What is the rhumb line distance between X and Y?
       (c) What is the approximate GC bearing of X from Y?
Answer: (a) 5·83° (call it 6°)
       (b) 293·8 nm
       (c) 093°

4.   An aircraft, following a rhumb line track of 270° and doing a ground speed of 570 kt completes the trip round the world in 6 hr 35 min. At what latitude is he flying?
Answer: 80° N or S.

2: Mercator's Projection

Gerhard Kramer, a Fleming, was 57 years old when he published his projection in 1569. It was modish to have a Latin surname to be distinguished from the unscholarly plebs, hence Mercator. The chart was originally made for the sailors and it is now in common use by sailors as well as airmen. But before handing all credit to Gerhard Kramer, it was not until 1599 that the true principles on the method of computation and construction of the projection were made known by Edward Wright of Cambridge in a publication entitled Certaine Errors in Navigation.

Prior to Mercator, a simple, cylindrical chart was used by the sailors. Such a projection is formed when a paper cylinder is placed around the equator of the model Earth and a light source placed at the centre casts shadows of the graticule. On such a projection all meridians appear as straight lines equidistant from each other and the pole is projected into infinity. Parallels of latitude also appear as straight lines, but the distance between them progressively increases as the latitude increases. So far so good: the rectangular graticule will produce rhumb lines as straight lines and it will be possible to fly constant tracks. But on a projection such as this the variation of the scale from a chosen point in different directions does not occur in the same proportion, thus missing one of the two basic requirements of orthomorphism. In fact, the longitude scale expands as secant of the latitude while the latitude scale varies as secant^2 latitude. Thus, the projection is not orthomorphic.

Mercator modified this projection mathematically. As the converging meridians open up to appear as parallel lines on the chart the scale expansion takes place in E–W direction. Mercator increased the distance between each successive line of latitude in the same ratio as E–W expansion, that is, secant of the latitude. The expansion in E–W direction thus compensated, the scale variation from a given point is the same in all directions and the chart is orthomorphic.

The Properties of the Mercator
1. It is orthomorphic by construction.
2. Rhumb lines are straight lines.
3. Great circles on the Earth cut meridians at different angles. These must be curves on this chart where the meridians are parallel to each other. They curve concave to the Equator. However, the Equator and all the meridians together with their anti-meridians are great circles by definition, and appear as straight lines. They are rhumb lines as well.
4. Scale is not constant but increases as the distance from the Equator increases. A given chart length at 30°N will represent a larger distance there than at 60°N,

and the representative fraction at 60°N will have a smaller denominator, signifying a larger scale. Read that again.

5.   It follows that areas will not be correctly represented – an area with a long north-south coverage will appear elongated towards the north in the northern hemisphere.

6.   Convergency is <u>constant</u> on the chart (meridians are parallel to each other and therefore, the angle of inclination between any two meridians is a constant value of 0° anywhere on the chart). Because the convergency is constant, it cannot be correct anywhere on the chart except at the Equator (where the Earth convergency is also 0°).

7.   The Poles cannot be projected. The distance between parallels increases rapidly as higher latitudes are reached and the scale in these regions becomes unusable. Accordingly, the projection cannot be used above 70°N or 70°S.

Measurement of distances

Since the scale on the chart varies from place to place, care must be exercised in taking distance measurements. Always use the latitude scale (up a meridian) using a convenient section which straddles the middle of the line you are measuring. Keep that section for the whole of the line. For large distances, say in excess of 300 nm, section out the line to be measured and take a mean latitude cover for each section. Then measure each section separately and add up for total distance. Short distances readily spanned by the divider can be measured in one attempt over the mid-latitude of the line concerned.

Disadvantages of the Mercator

1.   The major one we have already met – radio bearings are great circle bearings which must be converted to rhumb lines before plotting.

2.   On a long drag, the rhumb line can add appreciably to the distance. It is then usual to plot the latitude and longitude of a series of points which constitute the great circle and join these points by rhumb lines forming a Composite RL track. This was common over the Atlantic and Pacific; nowadays, there is no such thing as a long drag with increasing aircraft speeds and the Lambert's projection can be used giving distances very close to great circle distances.

3.   The chart cannot be used in polar regions.

To form a local graticule

A local graticule of the Mercator can be constructed as follows:
    Say you wish to produce a graticule covering 55°N to 57°N, 100°W to 105°W.

Steps

1.   Choose a scale for longitude, say 1 in = 1° longitude.

2.   Draw a base line AB and mark off longitudes at a distance of 1 in per degree.

3.   Construct the meridians as parallel lines perpendicular to the base line.

4.   From the point of origin A draw an angle <u>from the base line</u> equal to the mean of the required parallels (see Fig. 1 above), and let this intersect the adjacent meridian at C.

5.   From A, with radius AC, draw an arc AD.

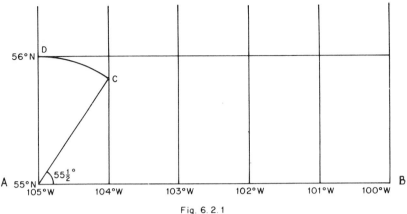

Fig. 6. 2. 1

6. At D, draw the line of latitude, parallel to the base line.
7. Repeat the process as required.
    The points to watch are that the angle is from the base line and not from North on the protractor; and relate the degrees of longitude to the degrees of latitude – one degree spacing in our sketch, but such a scale for 5° spacing of longitude for example must refer to a similar 5° spacing of latitude.

Plotting radio position lines

As all radio bearings are great circles, they must be converted to rhumb lines before plotting on a Mercator. This is readily done by applying conversion angle either from the formula CA = ½ ch long x sin mean lat, or from the abac scale printed and explained in the left hand corner of the chart, and demonstrated in the Navigation Plotting chapter of this book. Apply to the nearest whole degree, and bear in mind that the RL always appears towards the Equator. A thumbnail sketch is always useful.

Conversion angle is applied <u>where the work is done.</u>

Example

You are in DR position 30°N 20°W and receive a QTE from a station in 35°N 23°W of 123°.

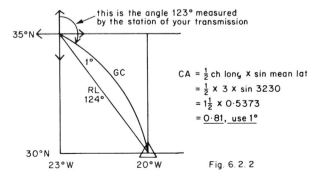

$$CA = \tfrac{1}{2} \text{ ch long} \times \sin \text{ mean lat}$$
$$= \tfrac{1}{2} \times 3 \times \sin 3230$$
$$= 1\tfrac{1}{2} \times 0.5373$$
$$= 0.81, \underline{\text{use } 1°}$$

Fig. 6. 2. 2

The work of measurement has been done at the station; the conversion angle must then be applied to this measurement: the GC bearing is 123°, add CA of 1°, and plot this RL of 124° from the station.

Now if the circumstances had been similar to the one quoted above, but you decided to measure the bearing of the station yourself from the aircraft, then what <u>you</u> measured is the subject for conversion; in other words, you have done the work. Say your Heading is 350°(T), and you took a relative bearing of the station on the radio compass of 315°.

$$
\begin{array}{lr}
\text{Relative bearing} & 315 \text{ GC} \\
\text{Add Heading True} & \underline{350} \\
& 665 \\
& \underline{-360} \\
\text{True bearing} & 305 \text{ GC – this is the work done} \\
\text{Conversion angle} & -\ \ 1 \text{ to bring it nearer to Equator} \\
\text{True bearing} & \overline{304} \text{ RL} \\
& \underline{-180} \text{ to get to the station for plot} \\
\text{Plot} & 124° \\
\end{array}
$$

Consider this example in the Southern hemisphere. QDM is 050°, variation at the station 5°E, CA = 4°.

Apply the station's variation to the QDM to give a Heading to steer with zero wind of 055°(T)

$$
\begin{array}{lr}
& 055 \\
& \underline{+180} \text{ to get to the station} \\
& 235 \text{ the actual work done} \\
\text{CA} + & \underline{\ \ 4} \text{ to bring nearer to Equator} \\
\text{Plot} & \overline{239°} \\
\end{array}
$$

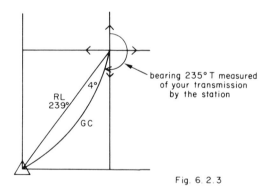

bearing 235° T measured of your transmission by the station

Fig. 6. 2. 3

Practice paper: Mercator North

Note: use CA throughout as 1° when its value is 0·5 or more.

Construct a Mercator graticule from 20°N to 25°N, 10°W to 15°W using the scale of 1 in = 1° longitude. Then answer the following questions based on it:

1.   Estimate RL track angle and distance from A (20°N 14°W) to B (24° 30′N 10°30′W).

2. Would RL track angle from 25°N 14°W to 29°30'N 10°30'W be more, same or less than answer in 1 above? Why?
3. What is the scale of your chart at the Equator?
4. What is GC bearing of (i) A from B; (ii) B from A?
5. Is convergency of the chart correct?
6. Is convergency of the chart constant?
7. Where is convergency of a Mercator chart constant?
8. Where is convergency of a Mercator chart correct?
9. Why is Mercator chart of little or no navigational value in high latitudes?
10. Give the track from F (22°30'N 15°W) to K (22°30'N 10°W) which will give the shortest distance.
11. Is your chart orthomorphic? Why?
12. Measure on your chart the GC bearing of M (25°N 13°W) from N (20°N 13°W).
13. Aircraft in DR position 20°20'N 14°50'W on heading 050° (T) obtains a relative bearing of 355° from station at 23°12'N 10°W. What would you plot?
14. Aircraft in DR position 24°30'N 15°W gets QDM 126° from station at 20°N 10°W. Station variation 9°E. What would you plot?

Answers:
1. 036°; 329 nm.
2. Less – expanding scale (meridians converge on the Earth).
3. 1 in = 60 nm at the Equator; therefore scale = 1 : 4 377 600.
4. (i) 217°; (ii) 035°.
5. No.
6. Yes.
7. All over the chart.
8. At the Equator.
9. Scale expansion.
10. Shortest distance is along GC track which is 089° (initial) 090° (mean) and 091° (final).
11. Yes, two basic requirements of orthomorphism are met.
12. 000°.
13. 226°.
14. 314°.

Practice paper: Mercator South
Note: use CA to the nearest whole degree.
    Construct a Mercator graticule from 20°S to 50°S, 30°E to 60°E (showing the meridians and parallels at 5° intervals) using scale 1 in = 5° longitude, and answer the following questions.
1. Two lines are drawn from 35°E to 55°E, the first at 22°S, the second at 47°S.
        (i)   Which represents the longer distance?
        (ii) Which has the smaller scale?
        (iii) What is the scale of this chart at the Equator?
2. How many Km are expressed by 1 cm at the Equator?
3. Point A is at 50°S 60°E; point B is at 25°S 35°E.
        (i)   What is RL track and distance from A to B?

     (ii)   Would RL track angle from 75°S 60°E to 50°S 35°E be greater or lesser than (1) above? Give a reason.

     (iii) What is the initial GC track from (a) A to B; (b) B to A?

     (iv) What is the mean GC track from A to B?

4. What track to nearest degree will give the shortest distance between (i) 47°S 30°E and 47°S 55°E? (ii) 47°S 30°E and 20°S 30°E?

5. Express the scale of this chart as a representative fraction.

6. Aircraft in DR position 40°S 55°E receives QDM 321°, (station variation 18°W) from X (30°S 30°E). What would you plot?

7. · Aircraft in DR position 49°S 46°E on Heading 090°(T) gets radio compass bearing (relative) of 268°, QC 0, from station at 25°S 45°E. What would you plot?

Answers

1. (i)   Line drawn at 22°S.
     (ii) 22°S.
     (iii) 1 : 21 888 000.

2. 218·9 Km.

3. (i)   322°; 1 950 nm.
     (ii) Greater – expanding latitude scale.
     (iii) (a) 314°; (b) 150°.
     (iv) 322° – GC and RL are same at mid-meridian.

4. (i)   Initial 099°; mean 090°; final 081°.
     (ii) 000°.

5. 1 : 17 929 000. The scale is found in two ways – (i) measure the distance at mid position on the chart (along a meridian) by dividers open one inch. Convert this distance as representative fraction. (ii) By calculation. The latter method is more accurate and is explained in the following pages.

6. 116°

7. 178°

Scale problems on Mercator

In tackling any problems on Mercator in which scale is involved we have only to remember that the scale varies as secant of latitude.

Problems

1. If the scale at Equator is 1 : 608 776 what is the scale at 56°N?

    The scale expands at the rate of secant of latitude, therefore Scale at 56°N = Scale at Equator x sec 56°

$$= \frac{1}{608\ 776} \times \sec 56°$$

As the numerator of the RF must be 1, the equation is rewritten:

$$= \frac{1}{608\ 776 \times \cos 56}$$

$$= 1 : 340\ 427$$

It is noted here, by the way, that the denominator at 56°N is a smaller figure than at the Equator. This indicates scale expansion; 1 inch at 56°N will measure lesser Earth distance.

2.   Scale at 56°N is 1 : 1 000 000. What is the scale at 46°N?

$$\text{Scale at Equator} \ = \ \frac{1 \times \cos 56°}{1\,000\,000}$$

$$= \ \frac{1}{1\,000\,000 \times \sec 56}$$

$$\therefore \text{Scale at } 46°\text{N} \ = \ \frac{1}{1\,000\,000 \times \sec 56 \times \cos 46}$$

$$= \ 1 : 1\,242\,250.$$

3.   Scale at 50°N is 1 : 608 000. What is the scale at 60N?

$$\text{Scale at } 60°\text{N} \ = \ \frac{1}{608\,000 \times \sec 50 \times \cos 60}$$

$$= \ 1 : 472\,930$$

4.   An aircraft flies from CLINTON, 43°37'N 81°30'W to NIAGARA, 43°07'N 79°00'W. The distance between the meridians of CLINTON and NIAGARA on a Mercator chart is 15 in. What is the scale of the chart at 45°N?

Change of longitude = 2°30' represented by 15 in on the chart.

$$\therefore 1° \text{ ch long} \qquad = 6 \text{ in}$$

and since the meridians on a Mercator are straight lines parallel to each other

1° at the Equator   = 6 in; or,

60 nm at the Equator = 6 in

∴ 10 nm at Equator   = 1 in and at

$$45°\text{N} = \frac{1}{10 \times 6\,080 \times 12 \times \cos 45}$$

$$= 1 : 515\,900$$

Practice Problems

1.   If meridians are spaced so that 1 in = 1° what is the scale at 35°N?

Answer: 1 : 3 585 800.

2.   If the spacing between meridians 1° apart is 3·576 cm what is the scale at 44°N? (1 in = 2.54 cm)

Answer: 1 : 2 237 000

3.   If the scale at 30°N is 1 : 1 000 000 what is the scale at 40°N?

Answer: 1 : 884 700

By applying above principles if the scale is given for a particular parallel the spacing between two meridians can be calculated. Here's an example.

What is the distance between two meridians, 1° apart on a chart whose scale is 1 : 5000 000 at 50°N?

Chart length = scale x ground distance;

Ground distance between two meridians one degree apart at Equator is 60 nm or 60 x 72 960 in.

Ground distance at 50°N, therefore, equals 60 x 72 960 cos 50° (distance between meridians reduces at the rate of cosine of the latitude). Now putting these figures in the equation:

$$\text{CL} = \frac{1}{500\,000} \times 60 \times 72\,960 \cos 50°$$

$$= 5·628 \text{ inches. (If the answer is required in cm, multiply this by 2·54)}$$

An alternative, perhaps even preferable method of solution is to reduce the scale to the Equator:

$$\frac{1}{500\ 000 \text{ x sec } 50^{\circ}}$$

arriving at the denominator which represents the Earth inches at the Equator per one inch on the chart; and as 1° of longitude at the Equator represents 60 nm, all that is left to do is to divide 60 x 72 960 by the figure found above.

A few more sums to round off

4.   On a chart, the spacing between two parallels of latitude 1° apart is 2·4 in. What is the scale in the area as an RF?

Answer: 1 : 1 824 000

5.   On a Mercator the spacing between meridians 1° apart is 2·71 cm. What is the scale at 47°N?

Answer: 1 : 2 798 100

6.   On a Mercator the scale at 40°N is 1 : 2 500 000. What is the distance apart in inches of the meridians spaced at 1° intervals?

Answer: 1·342 in.

7.   On a Mercator the spacing between two meridians one degree apart is 3·408 cm. Where will the scale be 1 : 2 500 000?

Answer: 40°N or 40°S.

8.   What change of longitude is represented by a line 15·24 cm in length drawn on a parallel on a Mercator whose scale is 1 : 2 330 000 at 50°N?

Answer: $4^{\circ}59'$

3: Lambert's Conformal

This is also referred to as Lambert's Second Conformal Conic and was developed by Johannes Lambert from the Simple Conic. Besides being orthomorphic, straight lines drawn on the chart are very nearly great circles, and the scale almost constant. On large scale charts (say 1 : 1 000 000) for all practical purposes straight lines may be taken to be great circles and the scale considered to be constant.

The simple conic is a projection reflected on to a cone whose apex is above the pole, the paper resting on a parallel of latitude of the model globe. Such a projection is of no practical use — it is neither orthomorphic, nor is the scale correct at any place other than at the Standard Parallel, that is, the parallel at which the cone is tangential to the model globe. But like the basic cylindrical, it provides a basis for further development.

The first matter for study is the shape of the cone when unwrapped from its position over the model globe, appearing as in Fig. 1.

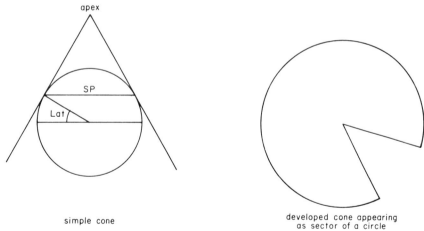

simple cone

developed cone appearing
as sector of a circle

Fig. 6.3.1

From above figure it will be seen that as a cone, it covered 360° round the model earth, but the cone itself is not 360° when it is laid flat. It is, in fact, a sector of a complete circle. In other words, in an area of less than 360° we projected 360° of the Earth. The ratio of the size of the sector to the size of the circle of the same radius is called the "constant of the cone", and is of great importance in calculating the convergence on the chart. The relationship is given in the following formula:

Convergence = change of longitude x factor n

where "n" is the sine of the standard parallel.

The next step in the development is to examine a conic projection where the cone cuts the model earth at two parallels. See Fig. 2.

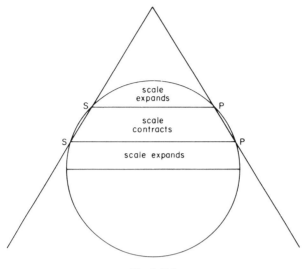

Fig. 6.3.2

The graticule produced as above is not orthomorphic. The scale contracts between the standard parallels (more Earth distance produced on a smaller size of paper) and expands outside the standard parallels. But the reason it is not orthomorphic is that at any given point the scale variation is not the same in all directions. Otherwise, the meridians appear as straight lines converging to the pole and parallels are concentric circles, cutting meridians at 90°; thus this requirement of orthomorphism is met.

Lambert modified the above graticule mathematically and produced orthomorphism. This was done by adjusting the radii of parallels (therefore adjusting the scale so that the scale variation is the same along meridians as along parallels) by use of orthomorphic formula. Thus, it is entirely a mathematical construction, and the completed graticule appears as shown in Fig. 3.

As in conic with two standard parallels, the meridians on a Lambert's are straight lines, radiating from the pole. Parallels are concentric circles around the pole. The standard parallels are placed $\frac{1}{6}$th and $\frac{5}{6}$th of the total N–S coverage in order to produce a near constant scale.

Properties

1. <u>Orthomorphism</u>. The projection is orthomorphic by construction.
2. <u>Scale</u>. Scale is correct along the two standard parallels. It contracts in between the standard parallels and expands outside the standard parallels. Thus, a span of say 1 in on the dividers measuring 5 nm along a standard parallel, will measure more than 5 nm inside the two parallels, maximum distance being measured along parallel of origin. Similarly, outside the two parallels (e.g. at

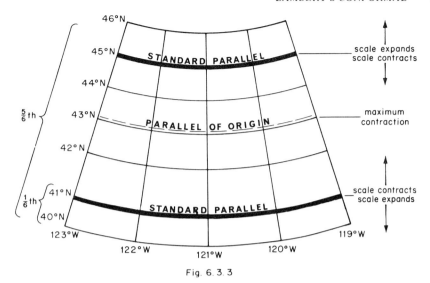

Fig. 6. 3. 3

46°N in above figure) it will measure less than 5 nm. In terms of representative fractions, if the scale was given as, say, 1 : 250 000, this is true for the two standard parallels. The denominator will be greater than 250 000 inside the two standard parallels and smaller to the outside.

Outside the standard parallels, the expansion towards the poles is not in the same proportion as towards the Equator. Rate of expansion towards poles is slightly higher than towards the Equator. For all practical purposes, the scale is considered to be correct on a given chart, and indeed, on some charts a constant scale graduated line is printed, which emphasises the point.

3.   Convergence. On Lambert's the value of convergence between two given meridians is given in formula:

Convergence = n x ch long

where n is the sine of the parallel of origin. Parallel of origin, or n, is a factor in the orthomorphic formula upon which the mathematical adjustment is based. Parallel of origin occurs in a position slightly displaced towards the pole from the parallel mid-way between two standard parallels. Its position is shown in Fig. 3 above. Value of n, however, is printed on the chart, but in the absence of this information, as pointed out above, the sine of the mid latitude of the two standard parallels may be used for calculation of convergence.

Example: Find convergence on a Lambert's projection between 119°W and 123°W at 43°N, given 43°N is the parallel of origin (Fig. 3)

C = Ch long x n
   = 4 x ·6820
   = 2·7280°

Referring back to Fig. 3, it will be noticed that the convergence between the same two meridians, that is 119°W and 123°W at any other latitude, say, 40°N will still be the same value – 2·7280°. In other words, on a Lambert's, Convergence is constant, its value depending on the value of n.

Next question is, is convergence correct? Well, if convergence is constant, it cannot be correct, because the Earth's convergency varies as sine of the latitude. In the above example at parallel of origin (43°N) the Earth convergency is

$$C = \text{Ch long} \times \text{sine lat}$$
$$= 4 \times \cdot 6820$$
$$= 2 \cdot 7280$$

which is the same value as on Lambert's. The reason is, on a Lambert's the convergence is shown correct only at the parallel of origin. At 40°N the Earth convergency:

$$C = \text{Ch long} \times \text{sine } 40°$$
$$= 4 \times \cdot 6428$$
$$= 2 \cdot 5712$$

whereas on Lambert's the convergence at 40°N is still 2·7280, which is too high. Similarly, towards the pole from the parallel of origin, the chart convergence is too low.

To summarise, the chart convergence is constant but not correct. Towards the Equator, the chart convergence is too high; towards the poles it is too low.

Great Circles

Say, a straight line is drawn on the Earth, joining position A (43°N 123°W) to position B (43°N 119°W). The convergency between A and B on the Earth is $4 \times \cdot 6820 = 2 \cdot 6°$. On a chart, if a straight line is to be a great circle, the two positions must produce the same chart convergence as on the Earth. Thus, a line joining A and B on the chart will be a great circle. Elsewhere on the chart, the convergence between any two places will be different from that on the Earth and such a straight line will not be a Great Circle. A great circle, away from the parallel of origin appears as a curve, concave to the parallel of origin. As the difference between Earth convergency and chart convergence increases with distance from the parallel of origin, so must the deviation between straight line and great circle. However, for practical purposes, a straight line drawn on a Lambert may be considered to be a great circle. See Fig. 4.

Further, since the convergence on the chart is different from that on the Earth (except at the parallel of origin) a radio wave travelling a great circle path will make different angles on the Earth and on the chart at a given meridian. Let's take an example. A radio wave leaves position 43°15′N 07°30′W on a bearing of 078° and crosses 10°E at 44°36′N.

The angle made by the radio wave at 10°E on the Earth =

$$C = \text{Ch long} \times \text{sin mean lat.}$$
$$= 17 \cdot 5° \times \sin 4355\tfrac{1}{2}$$
$$= 17 \cdot 5 \times \cdot 6936$$
$$= 12 \cdot 14°$$
$$\therefore \text{Bearing on the Earth} = 078 + 12 \cdot 14$$
$$= 090 \cdot 14°$$

On a Lambert with parallel of origin, say, at 58°N, the bearing:

$$\text{Convergence} = \text{Ch long} \times n$$
$$= 17 \cdot 5 \times \sin 58$$
$$= 14 \cdot 84$$

and the bearing measured = 078 + 14·84
$$= 092·84°$$

Rhumb Lines
Rhumb lines cut all meridians at the same angle. Therefore they will appear as curves concave to the Pole, taking on the same curve direction as the parallels which are themselves rhumb lines by definition. Meridians are both GCs and RLs.

Shapes
Shapes are distorted but shapes of small areas may be considered to be correct.

Following diagram shows appearance of Rhumb lines and Great circles in relation to straight lines.

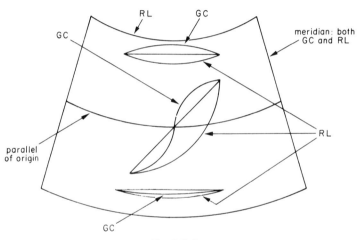

Fig. 6. 3. 4

Plotting on Lambert's Projection
1.   When measuring a track, use the mid-meridian between two points, and use this track angle to calculate the heading. This will be the mean great circle track, and also the rhumb line track as the measurement at the mid-point of a tangent to the curving RL track will almost be the same as straight line GC track.
2.   As always, use the Latitude scale for measuring distance, keeping the habit of measuring in the area where the line is.
3.   When finding W/V, Track and GS method is simpler. This method must be used when finding winds on a track which has a large E—W component (maximum convergency is experienced). If air plot method is used, measure the wind angle from the meridian nearest the Fix.
4.   Bearings given by the station (QTE, QDM, QDR) and VOR bearings are measured at the station and plotted from the station meridian. Therefore, no correction for convergence is called for. Where the work is done at the aircraft (Radio Compass bearings), bearings are measured with reference to the meridian at aircraft's position involving the aircraft's heading. Such bearings must be corrected

for convergence <u>before</u> obtaining the reciprocal to plot from the station. Alternatively, the aircraft's DR meridian may be transferred to the station position, and the bearings plotted from the transferred meridian without correction for convergence.

Examples

Hdg	045		Hdg	045
Rel Brg	100		Rel Brg	100
GC Brg	145(T)		GC Brg	145(T)
Convergence +	2 (Towards Eq)			− 180
	147		Plot	325° from station position
	− 180			with reference to
Plot	327° from station position			the aircraft's transferred
				meridian.

Practice Problems

1. Aircraft in DR position 43°N 81°W obtains QDM 173°, from station A (39°N 84°W) where variation is 36°E. What would you plot?
Answer: 029°

2. Aircraft on heading 270°(T) in DR position 46°N 84°W obtains relative bearing 239° from station 40°N 81°W. What would you plot?
Answer: 331°

3. Aircraft in DR position 69°30'S 65°W obtains QDM 277° from station at 71°S 70°W. Variation at a/c position 19°W; mean variation 22°W, variation at station 25°W. What would you plot?
Answer: 072°

4. Aircraft in DR position 72°S 66°W on heading 359°(T) obtains relative bearing 334°, Q.C. + 1, from station at 68°S 70°W. What would you plot?
Answer: 158°

5. Aircraft on heading 090°(T) in DR position 69°S 68°W
    (i)   obtains relative bearing 090° from station at 72°S 68°W. What would you plot?
    (ii) obtains relative bearings 359° from station 69°S 64°W. What would you plot?
    (iii) obtains QDM 045° from station 69°S 64°W. Variation 20° at the station, 24° at the aircraft, mean variation 22°, all variations are easterly. What would you plot?

Answer: (i)   360°
        (ii) 265°
        (iii) 245°

4: The Polar Stereographic

This is a perspective projection, with a light source at one pole and the plane of projection tangential to the other pole.

Since 360° of the Earth are represented on paper by 360°, the constant of the cone, n, is 1, if you care to consider it that way.

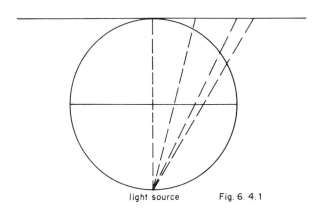

light source   Fig. 6. 4. 1

Construction
Select a convenient point to represent the pole, i.e. the point which is tangential to the model Earth in the basic concept of the projection.

From this point, draw in radial lines representing meridians at an angular spacing equal to the actual ch long.

With the Pole as centre, draw the circles of parallels. The radius of each parallel is calculated from the formula:

$$\text{Radius} = 2R \tan \tfrac{1}{2}\text{co-lat}$$

where R is the radius of the model Earth; this model Earth radius in practice is derived from the Earth's actual radius of 250 000 000 inches divided by the scale required.

Appearance of the Graticule
It will be noticed that a coverage of more than 90° of latitude can be achieved; see the graticule shown overleaf in Fig. 2.

Properties
Scale is correct at the Pole, as this is the point of tangency: with increasing distance from the Pole, scale expands at the rate of $\sec^2 \tfrac{1}{2}$co-lat.

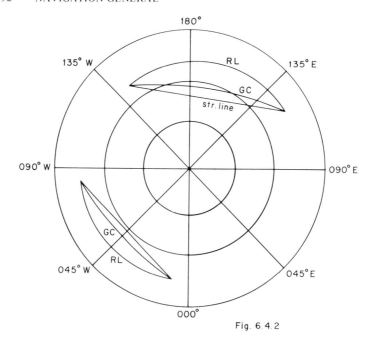

Fig. 6.4.2

Orthomorphism. Since scale varies in the same proportion just noted in all directions from a given point i.e. along the meridians and parallels, and since meridians and parallels cut each other at right angles, the chart is orthomorphic.

Convergency on the chart is the value of ch long, or 1 (one) degree of ch long is shown on the chart by 1° angular difference. On the Earth this difference exists only at the Poles, and only there on the chart is convergency correct. Elsewhere on the Earth, convergency reduces towards the Equator, where it is 0; so chart convergency is constant at 1, correct only at the Poles, too large away from the Pole.

Great Circle cannot be a straight line, since convergency is not correct. However, when plotting in high latitudes not too far away from the Pole where convergency is correct, a GC is taken to be a straight line for practical purposes. As distance from the Pole increases, a GC in fact curves concave to the Pole, and finally the Equator, itself a GC, will appear as a distinct curve. Rather an academic point for a chart used for aviation in the polar regions, perhaps.

Rhumb Line is a curve concave to the Pole. Parallels of latitude are demonstrative.

Equal Area only very nearly for small areas; from the properties of scale and convergency already mentioned, it is clear that the chart cannot be equal area.

Plotting Radio Bearings

Because a straight line approximates a GC, QTEs, QDMs, Consol bearings et alia, may be plotted direct from the meridian of the station, after the usual resolution into the bearing True which the station measured.

Radio compass bearings, though, measured from the aircraft's meridian, must be resolved into an angle to be plotted from the station's meridian. Convergency must be applied before the reciprocal is found, its value being ch long.

Problems

Since convergency is 1, the sums are of no real profundity, only off-putting because the chart is not widely familiar.

1. What is the approximate GC bearing of B(71°N 50°E) which would be found by measuring the direction of A(71°N 90°E) on a straight line joining A to B? See Fig 3

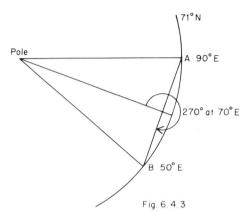

Fig. 6.4.3

The mean approximate GC bearing must be measured at the mid-meridian, as above. Both places are on the same parallel.

$$\text{Convergency between A and B is ch long} \quad = \quad 40°$$
$$\therefore \text{convergency between mean meridian and A} \quad = \quad 20°$$
$$\text{and GC bearing of B from A} = 270 + 20 \quad = \quad 290°$$

2. What is the convergency between A(75°N 60°W) and B(75°N 10°W):

      a. on the Earth?
      b. on the Polar stereographic?

Answer a. 48.29°
     b. 50°

5: Transverse Mercator

This is a cylindrical projection, like a Mercator's but it differs from Mercator in that the cylinder is presumed to be tangential to any chosen meridian and its anti-meridian. Fig. 1. The meridian to which the cylinder is tangential is called the Central Meridian (CM). The point where CM and the Equator intersect is called the point of origin.

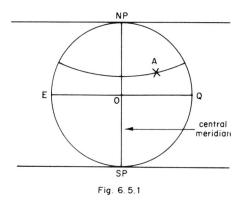

Fig. 6.5.1

Principle of Construction

A cylinder is presumed to be wrapped round the reduced Earth (model globe reduced to the scale), being tangential to a chosen meridian with a light source at the centre of the Earth. The graticule resulting from such arrangement is modified mathematically to give orthomorphism. In practice, the chart is constructed mathematically throughout. A point to be projected on the chart is resolved in terms of N/S (N or S of the Equator) and E/W (E or W of the central meridian) co-ordinates and these co-ordinates (normally in inches) are then plotted on the graticule.

Suppose point A in Fig 1 is to be plotted on transverse mercator graticule. Fig. 2. A GC is drawn up in the first instance from G passing through A, inter-

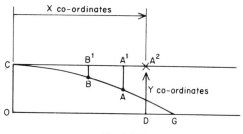

Fig. 6.5.2

secting CM at 90° at C. 0 is the point of origin and G is a point on the Equator, 90° removed from 0. Now, if you think of the curve GAC in terms of a meridian on a Mercator, with pole at G, you will appreciate that when the cylinder is unwrapped A will appear at A^1. Similarly if there was another point B on the same GC it will appear at B^1. If you are wondering why on an ordinary Mercator no such GC are plotted initially, the reason is that point A on an ordinary Mercator would be on a meridian which is already a GC by definition, whereas A on this projection is on a parallel of latitude which only represents rhumb line distances.

The shifting of A on the Earth to position A^1 on the chart causes expansion of the scale in the N/S direction (exactly as the meridians expanded in E/W direction on an ordinary Mercator). This expansion must be compensated by extending the distance CA^1 to CA^2 to obtain orthomorphism. This extension is calculated mathematically. The co-ordinates to be plotted are : CA^2 (called X co-ordinates) and DA^2 (called Y co-ordinates).

Graticule

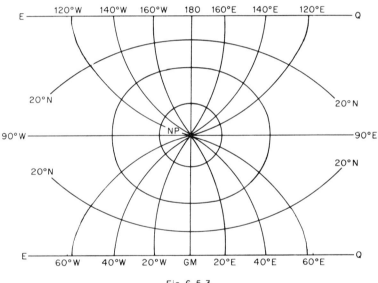

Fig. 6. 5. 3

The appearance of the graticule is shown in Fig 3 above. Note that the central meridian appears as a straight line. It is a GC by definition. The two meridians 90° removed from the CM also appear as straight lines (90° E and W in above figure). They are GC by definition as well as by construction. (In Fig 2 notice that the curve of GC is projected as a straight line perpendicular to the CM). The Equator appears as a straight line – in three places, in between the two Poles and at two extremities where the projection provides full N/S coverage. Other parallels appear as ellipses, almost circles near the Poles. Since on this projection both the meridians and the parallels (with exceptions as shown above) appear as curves perhaps this feature clearly distinguishes this projection from the ones we studied previously. This particular feature, however, may not be discernible on small sheets.

Just as on a Mercator, on this projection a point 90° removed from the point of origin in an E/W direction on the Equator cannot be projected:

Properties

Orthomorphism. Yes, the meridians and the parallels cut each other at 90° and the scale variation from a given point is the same in E/W direction as in N/S direction by construction. This makes the chart orthomorphic.

Scale. The scale is correct along the central meridian. Expands away from the CM at the rate of secant of the great circle distance.

Convergency. Convergency is correct at the Equator and the Poles. Elsewhere it is incorrect. However up to 1 200 miles from the CM the error is very small and may be neglected.

Great Circles. Any straight line which cuts the central meridian at 90° is a great circle by construction. Elsewhere it is a complex curve as shown in Fig 4. For practical purposes any straight line drawn near the CM may be taken to represent a GC.

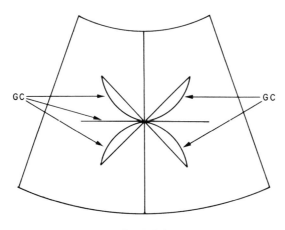

Fig. 6. 5. 4

Rhumb Line. All meridians and parallels are rhumb lines. Examine how they appear in Fig. 3. Elsewhere a rhumb line is a curve concave to the nearer pole.

Shapes. These are correct for small areas.

·Fits. You can attach another chart to your chart if the track goes beyond your chart coverage, but only in the N/S directions and provided both charts have the same central meridian and the same scale. There is a rolling fit in E/W directions for two charts of the same scale.

Uses. The projection is quite accurate up to about 300 nm of the CM. This makes it ideal for use as topographical maps of countries having large N/S extent (Italy, New Zealand, UK.) The projection is not suitable for use as plotting chart due to curving meridians and parallels except in the polar regions where the meridians are still straight lines.

6: Grid Technique

In previous chapters we discussed Mercator, Lambert, Polar Stereographic and Transverse Mercator projections. Each one has certain advantages and disadvantages. Mercator is ideal for flying constant track angles but this involves flying RL distances. Further, radio bearings cannot be plotted directly. These two disadvantages practically disappear on Lambert and Polar Stereographic, but the pilot has to contend with changing tracks due to convergency of the meridians on the chart. Ideally we want a chart on which a straight line is a great circle, scale is considered constant and the meridians do not converge. No projection could provide all these properties together. However, by gridding a Lambert or a Polar Stereographic (and a Transverse Mercator in polar regions) we could combine all these on a single chart.

The first step towards gridding a chart is to select a suitable meridian as the Datum. The grid meridians are then drawn up parallel to and at a constant distance from the datum meridian. We now have two sets of directions on the chart: geographical meridians indicating true north and grid meridians indicating grid north. Fig 1.

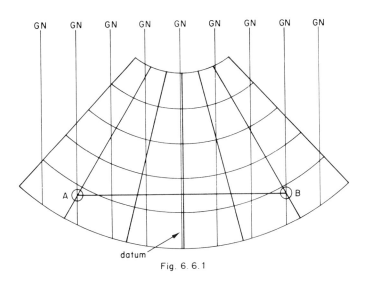

Fig. 6.6.1

Convergence of Meridians

It will be noticed in the above figure that only one grid meridian (i.e. datum) coincides with true meridian; away from the datum there is an angular difference

between the two, the difference increasing with distance from the datum. This angular difference between True North and Grid North is called Convergence.
Relationship between TN and GN.

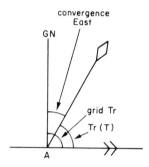 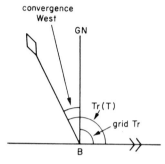

Fig. 6.6.2

Where the track starts at the datum meridian, the Grid track and True track will be the same initially. The grid track, however, will remain the same throughout the flight. Where a flight commences elsewhere e.g. from A to B in Figure 1, it is necessary to establish the relationship between grid and true tracks. Positions A and B are reproduced in Figure 2 above, showing the disposition of directions grid and true north. The grid track in both cases is 090° and if the convergence at A and B is, say, 5°, true track at A is 085° and at B 095°. This relationship may be expressed in the following formula, the convention being,

Where true north lies to East of Grid North, Convergence is East
Where true north lies to West of Grid North, Convergence is West

$$\text{Direction True} \quad \begin{array}{l} + \text{ Convergence } \quad E \\ - \text{ Convergence } \quad W \end{array} = \text{Direction Grid}$$

$$\text{and, Direction Grid} \quad \begin{array}{l} + \text{ Convergence } \quad W \\ - \text{ Convergence } \quad E \end{array} = \text{Direction True}$$

Example

Heading Grid is 150°, Convergence 10°W, What is Heading True?

Hdg(T) = Hdg(G) + Convergence W
        = 150 + 10
        = 160°

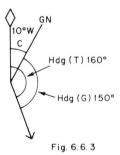

Fig. 6.6.3

Problems

1. Hdg(T) is 258°, Convergence 20°E, What is Hdg(G)?
Ans: 278°

2.   Hdg(G) is 040°, Hdg(T) is 065°, What is the convergence?
Ans: 25°W.

Grivation and Isogrivs

We established the relationship between GN and TN in the above article. However, in mid-latitudes, aircraft still steer by magnetic compass and therefore it is necessary to establish the relationship between GN and MN as well. The angle between TN and MN is variation. The angle between GN and MN is called Grid Variation, abbreviated to <u>Grivation</u>. Its value for any particular place is obtained from the lines of equal grivation, called <u>Isogrivs</u>. Isogrivs might be printed on a gridded chart or they may be added to such chart by plotting co-ordinates from simple calculation. As regards grivation, the convention is:–

   If MN lies to East of Grid North, Grivation is East.

   If MN lies to West of Grid North, Grivation is West.

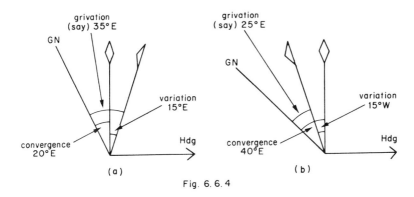

Fig. 6. 6. 4

From Fig. 4 we establish the relatiosnhip in the following formula:

$$\text{Grid Direction} = \text{Magnetic Direction} \begin{array}{ll} + \text{ Grivation} & \text{E} \\ - \text{ Grivation} & \text{W} \end{array}$$

Thus, by measuring the Grid heading and applying local Grivation, magnetic heading to steer is obtained.

<u>Grivation is the algebraic sum of convergence and variation</u>

In Fig 4 (a),

   Grivation   =   20°E + 15°E

               =   35°E

In Fig 4 (b),

   Grivation   =   40°E + 15°W

               =   25°E

When converting one heading to another, from above diagram, we establish the following rule:

$$\text{Hdg(M)} \begin{array}{l} + \text{ E Var} \\ - \text{ W Var} \end{array} = \text{Hdg(T)} \begin{array}{l} + \text{ E Convergence} \\ - \text{ W Convergence} \end{array} = \text{Hdg(G)}$$

In Fig 4 (a) if the magnetic heading is 075°, the grid heading   =

      075° + 15°E(Var) = 090° Hdg(T) + 20°E (Conv) = 110° Hdg(G)

   If you are converting in the opposite direction, that is from Hdg(G) to Hdg(M), reverse the sign. E throughout is minus, W is plus. In 4 (b), given Hdg(G) = 130°, then Hdg(M) =

130 – 40 (E conv) = 090° Hdg(T) + 15°(W Var) = 105° Hdg(M)

Alternatively, Hdg(M) may be converted directly to Hdg(G) and vice versa by application of Grivation. In Fig 4 (a),

Hdg(M) = 075° + 35(E Griv) = 110°Hdg(G)

In 4 (b)

Hdg(G) = 130° – 25(E Griv) = 105°Hdg(M)

Construction of Grid on Lambert's

Two steps are involved in the construction of grid on a plain chart: construction of grid itself and plotting the isogrivs.

Construction of grid is quite simple. Simply choose a convenient meridian as the datum meridian and draw up lines parallel to the datum at a convenient distance (usually 60 or 100 nm). It should be appreciated that only those charts could be gridded which are considered constant scale charts. Grid is completed by drawing up another set of parallel lines, same distance apart but at 90° to datum meridian if necessary for Plotting purposes. The chart will then look like the one in Fig. 5.

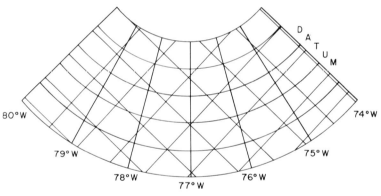

Fig. 6. 6. 5

Isogrivs contain two elements — variation and convergence. Variation lines (isogonals) are already on the chart. Therefore, in order to plot isogrivs, we will first need to draw up lines of convergence at 1° apart.

It will be remembered from the study of Lambert's that the convergence on this projection, (i.e. value of n) is always less than one. That is, one degree ch long on the Earth will appear at a distance less than one degree on the chart. For gridding purposes, we must calculate the distance from datum where one degree convergence will occur. This will invariably occur beyond one degree ch long printed on the chart. The calculation is simply carried out by dividing 1° (that is 60 minutes) by the value of chart convergence, that is, n.

Say, chart convergence was given as n = .7488. Then, 1° convergence on the chart =

$$\frac{60}{0.7488} = 1° 20.1'$$

Plot the first line of convergence on the chart at distance of 1° 20.1′ from the datum. For example, if the datum was Greenwich meridian, one degree convergence occurs at 01° 20.1′W; two degree convergence at 02° 40.2′W and so on. These lines are lightly drawn on the chart so that they can be removed when isogrivs are drawn.

Next step is to calculate the value of grivation individually at every point where the line of convergence intersects isogonals on the chart. Finally, points having the same value of grivation are joined up by a smooth curve to give isogrivs. Fig 6. The square grid is omitted for clarity.

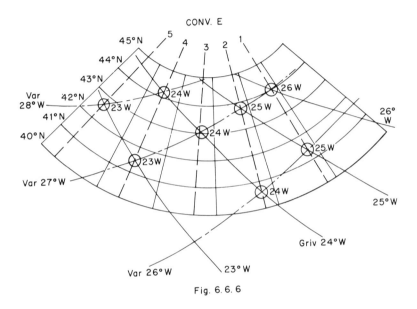

Fig. 6. 6. 6

Grid on Polar Charts

In polar regions, polar stereographic with a grid is generally used. A modified form of Lambert is also available and with its one standard parallel very near the pole it hardly differs from the other. Transverse Mercator may also be gridded in polar regions since meridians appear as straight lines radiating from the pole and curves of latitudes may be considered to be concentric. For all practical purposes near polar regions transverse mercator may be considered to be a constant scale chart.

On these charts, convergence is 1; that is, one degree of ch long on the Earth appears at 1° distance on the chart. This makes construction of the grid easy in that lines of convergence need not be first constructed. Thus, if the datum is Greenwich meridian, then parallels of grid lines will cut 30W at an angle of 30°, 60W at an angle of 60° and so on. (see Fig. 7 overleaf)

On a complete polar grid, the direction from NP along the Greenwich anti-meridian is generally the direction of Grid North. Therefore, at the North pole, instead of having all true directions south only, we have a complete compass rose with reference to grid direction. Study Fig. 8 to appreciate this.

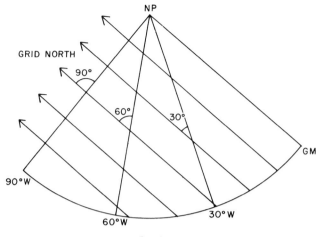

Fig. 6. 6. 7

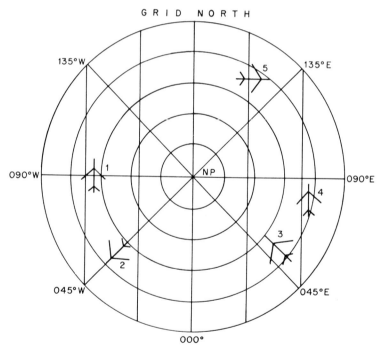

Fig. 6. 6. 8

In Fig 8,
Grid Heading of aircraft 1 is 000
                          2 is 225
                          3 is 315
                          4 is 000
                          5 is 090

As for the conversion of Grid value to True and reverse, since the value of n is 1 the conversion formula becomes

$$\text{Grid direction} = \text{True direction} \begin{matrix} - \text{ Long E} \\ + \text{ Long W} \end{matrix}$$

$$\text{and True Direction} = \text{Grid Direction} \begin{matrix} + \text{ Long E} \\ -- \text{ Long W} \end{matrix}$$

For illustration, the Grid Heading of aircraft 2 in Fig 8 is $225°$

Its true heading $= 225 - 45$ (Long W)

$\qquad\qquad\quad = 180°$

True heading of aircraft 3 (heading along meridian to NP) is $360°$. Therefore its Grid Heading $= 360 - 45$ (Long E)

$\qquad\qquad\quad = 315°$

These signs must be reversed in a South Polar Grid — See typical problem 3 below.

In the lower regions where the magnetic compass may still be used, isogrivs must be first constructed. These are again simpler since in this case the value of grivation is the value of ch long in whole degrees combined with the value of local variation.

Transverse Mercator outside Polar Regions
The task of gridding in such areas becomes difficult due to curving meridians. If it is necessary to grid such chart, convergence should be determined at numerous points all over the projection, before following up the normal steps.

Typical Grid Problems
1.   An aircraft in position $40°N\ 10°E$ has a magnetic heading of $150°$ and a grid heading of $170°$. If variation is $10°W$ and $n = .8$, what is the datum meridian?

a.   Hdg(T) $= 150 - 10°W$ (Variation)

$\qquad\qquad = 140°$

b.   Convergence $=$ Hdg(G) $-$ Hdg(T)

$\qquad\qquad\qquad =$ $170 - 140$

$\qquad\qquad\qquad =$ $30°E$ (See Fig. 9)

c.   Ch long from Datum $= \dfrac{\text{Convergence}}{n}$

$\qquad\qquad\qquad\qquad = \dfrac{30}{.8} = 37\frac{1}{2}°$

d.   Therefore Datum 10E + 37½E

$\qquad\qquad\qquad = 47\frac{1}{2}°E$

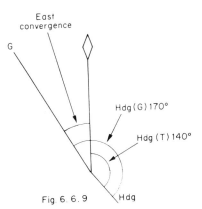

Fig. 6. 6. 9

2.   Using Grid based on $20°W$, what will be the magnetic heading of an aircraft in position $50°E$, given variation 8W and $n = .75$. Grid heading of the aircraft is $224°$.

a.   Convergence $=$ n x ch long

$\qquad\qquad\qquad =$ $.75$ x 70

$\qquad\qquad\qquad =$ $52\frac{1}{2}°W$ (see sketch)

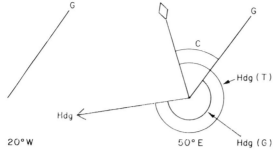

Fig. 6.6.10

b. Hdg(T)   = Hdg(G) + Convergence W
               = 224° + 52½°
               = 276½°
c. Hdg(M)   = 276½° + 8°W (Variation)
               = 284½°

3. An aircraft on south polar grid in position 75°S 20°W has a grid heading of 210°. What is his true heading?

Hdg(T) = Hdg(G) + Long W
        = 210 + 20
        = 230° (see Fig. 11)

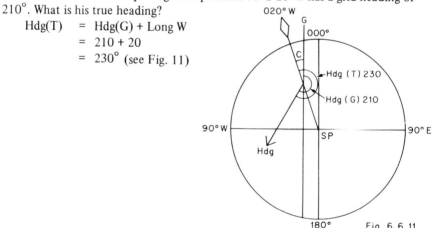

Fig. 6.6.11

4. An aircraft on North polar grid is steering a true heading of 080°(T) and a grid heading of 140(G). What is his longitude?

$$Hdg(G) = Hdg(T) \begin{array}{c} - \text{ E Long} \\ + \text{ W Long} \end{array}$$

$$\therefore Hdg(G) - Hdg(T) = \begin{array}{c} - \text{ Long E} \\ + \text{ Long W} \end{array}$$

140 – 80
= + 060
= 060W (see Fig. 12)

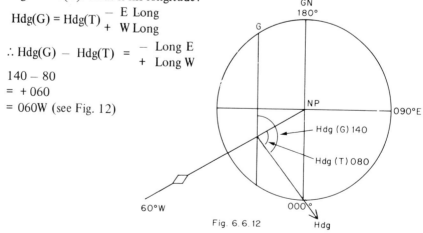

Fig. 6.6.12

Practice Problems
1. Hdg(T) is 258°, Convergence 20°E; what is Hdg(G)?
Answer: 278°
2. Hdg(G) is 040°, Hdg(T) 065°; what is the Convergence?
Answer: 25°W.
3. An aircraft on North Polar grid is steering a true heading of 080° and a grid heading of 140°. What is its longitude?
Answer: 60°W.
4. An aircraft has a grid heading of 310° using a chart based on grid datum of 40°W. If the variation is 10°E, n = .8 and Hdg(M) 340°, what is the aircraft's longitude?
Answer: 10°E.
5. Grid datum meridian is 50°W, n = .7, aircraft's position 50°N 20°W. If the grid heading is 257° what is the magnetic heading, given the variation is 8°W?
Answer: 286°.

7: Relative Motion

Relative Speed

Whenever two aircraft are in motion, each aircraft has a speed which is relative to the other. Two aircraft flying in formation at a given speed, have a relative speed with regard to each other: it is zero speed, because neither aircraft is going ahead or falling behind. If two aircraft are approaching on reciprocal tracks, aircraft A doing a speed of 150 kt and aircraft B speed of 200 kt, then each aircraft has a speed of 350 relative to the other. We call this the closing speed. Again, if an aircraft A with ground speed of 350 kt is overtaking aircraft B having a ground speed of 300 kt, each aircraft's relative speed is 50 kt, whereas aircraft A's closing speed is 50 kt. Therefore, if the two aircraft were initially separated by, say, 100 nm aircraft A will be alongside B in two hours.

Example. Two aircraft A and B are initially separated by 200 nm and are approaching each other. A's ground speed is 300 kt, B's ground speed is 260 kt, How long will they take to meet?

$$
\begin{aligned}
\text{Relative (or closing) speed} \quad &= \quad 300 + 260 \\
&= \quad 560 \text{ kt} \\
\text{Time taken to meet} \quad = \quad &200 \text{ nm at } 560 \text{ kt} \\
= \quad &21\frac{1}{2} \text{ min}
\end{aligned}
$$

How far would each have flown before they meet?
Aircraft A with ground speed of 300 kt will travel 107 nm in 21½ min
Aircraft B with ground speed of 260 kt will travel   93 nm in 21½ min

Practice problems

1. Two planes take off from stations 500 nm apart. They meet in 44 minutes. If the first plane travelled 3/5th of the total distance, find the ground speed of each.
Answer: 410 and 273 kt
2. An aircraft A, flying at ground speed of 390 kt is overtaking aircraft B, flying at ground speed of 310 kt. Two aircraft are initially 50 nm apart.
(a)   In how many minutes will aircraft A be 5 nm behind B?
(b)   When will aircraft A be 3 minutes behind B?
Answer: (a)   33½ minutes; (b)   34½ minutes

Relative Direction

When two aircraft are moving, each will have a relative direction with respect to the other. If two aircraft A and B left a point X at the same time, A on a track due North and B on a track due East, then to an observer in aircraft A, B will appear to be tracking SE. To an observer in aircraft B, A will appear to be tracking NW; this is A's relative direction with respect to aircraft B.

Relative Velocity

When a body has velocity, it has both speed and direction, and problems of relative velocity are essentially solved by accurate scale plotting. The first step is to bring to a stop the aircraft which wishes to observe the other.

In above example, say A's ground speed is 400 kt, B's ground speed is 320 kt. To find B's relative velocity with respect to A, bring A to a stop. This is done by imparting A's negative velocity to B. B, therefore, now has two velocities, its own velocity and A's negative velocity. Fig 1.

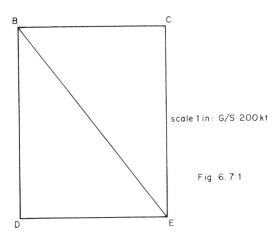

scale 1 in: G/S 200 kt

Fig. 6. 7. 1

In Fig 1 BC is B's own velocity, that is, one hour's ground speed due East. BD is A's negative velocity, 400 nm due <u>south</u>. Complete the parallelogram BCED. BE is the relative velocity of B with respect to A which is 140° at 508 kt (by actual measurement).

If A's relative velocity with respect to B is required, B is brought to rest by imparting its negative velocity to A.

Where two flights do not originate at the same point as above, the relative velocity may still be estimated as in following illustration.

Given: Aircraft A's track is 050(T), G/S 210 kt. Aircraft B which bears 140(T) from A is doing a track if 355(T) at G/S250 kt. B is 200 nm from A. Find the relative bearing of B from A.

In these problems since the distance between two aircraft is generally very small in comparison with aircraft speeds, it is necessary to select two different scales, one for ground speed and one for distance in order to separate the two aircraft for neat plotting. In above illustration the ground speed scale chosen is 1 in to 100 kt, and distance scale is 1 in to 50 nm.

Steps
1. Choose a convenient point A and plot from here A's Track and one hour's ground speed (at ground speed scale) — AC.
2. From A, plot B on given bearing (140° in above illustration) at a given distance (200 nm) at distance scale — AB.

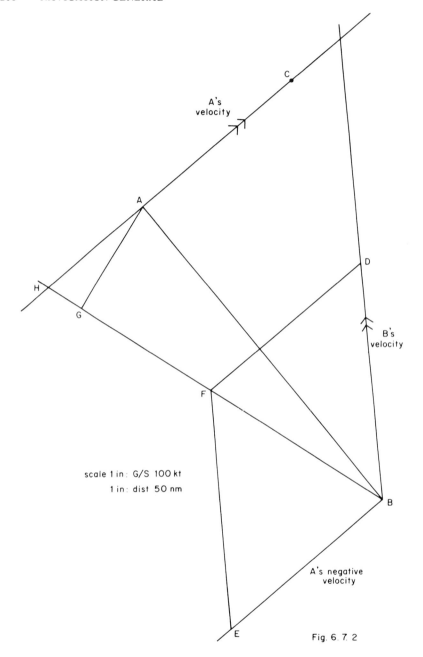

A's
velocity

C

A

D

H

G

B's
velocity

F

scale 1 in : G/S 100 kt
1 in : dist 50 nm

B

A's negative
velocity

E   Fig. 6. 7. 2

3.   From B, plot B's velocity for one hour – BD
4.   From B, draw A's negative velocity for one hour – BE.
5.   Complete parallelogram BDFE.
6.   Join BF
     BF is B's relative velocity with respect to A – 302° at relative speed of 215 kt.
     The above figure tells us more than just the relative velocity.

Produce BF to intersect A's track at H. If this line intersects A's track exactly through A's position, two aircraft are on such headings and speeds that a collision will occur. If BF produced crosses A's track behind A's position, as in above illustration, B will pass behind A. The shortest distance that A and B will be apart is indicated by AG drawn perpendicular from A to BH, measured at distance scale. Similarly, if BF produced crosses A's track ahead of it, B will pass ahead of A.

The above is true even if distance AB initially is not known.

2.   H is the point where B will cross A's track behind A. AH is the distance – use distance scale.

3.   The time that B will be shortest distance from A is calculated from known information of B's relative ground speed and the distance BG.

In Fig 2, it is 188 nm at 215 kt = 52½ min

Interception

Interceptions are carried out on the principle of maintaining a constant relative bearing. Aircraft A sights another aircraft B on a relative bearing of 140°. If A wishes to intercept B, it must maintain such a heading and TAS that would result in B's relative bearing remaining constant throughout. Fig 3.

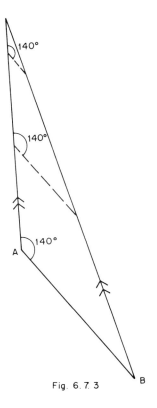

Fig. 6. 7. 3

In the above figure, it will be noticed that if the bearing is not maintained constant, aircraft B is either going to fall ahead or behind of A.

In order to carry out an interception, the first step is to establish the positions of both aircraft and plot them. The line joining the two aircraft at any given instant is the bearing that must remain constant. In Fig 4 this is the line AB, and is known as the Line of Constant Bearing.

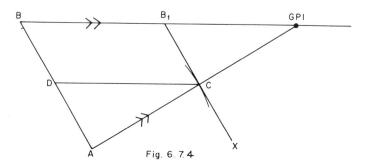

Fig. 6. 7. 4

At B, plot B's Track and mark off B_1 to represent one hour's G/S to vector scale.
At B_1 draw BX parallel to BA; this is the Line of Constant Bearing.
With centre A and radius A's G/S to scale, inscribe an arc of a circle to cut B_1 X at C.
Join AC and produce it to meet B's Track at the Ground Position of Interception (GPI)
From C draw CD parallel to B_1 B. Then AD to scale represents the speed of closing, while AB is the distance to close at closing speed.
All plotting may be done with Headings and TAS, but it must be borne in mind that the end product is an Air Position of Interception; to find the GPI from this is simply a matter of applying the wind effect for the time taken.

To find the latest time to divert to an alternate would be worked out on these lines. An aircraft with 5 hours endurance has an alternate to beam of Track. Join departure point A to the alternate B, measure the distance and derive its hypothetical G/S from the endurance. Along both Tracks, using the same vector scale for both, plot the distance covered in one hour; this is the Line of Constant Bearing GF. Produce GF, Still with same vector scale, at A, plot a W/V vector and from it with radius TAS, strike an arc on GF produced at K. Join AK. AK paralleled from B to cut the outbound Track is the Ground Position of Turning, and the plot contains all the necessary information for the diversion.

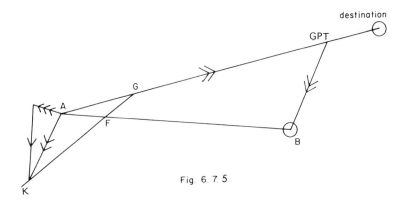

Fig. 6. 7. 5

Problems

1.   An aircraft A in position 55N 02W is making good a track of 180(T) at ground speed of 210 kt. Aircraft B is flying along parallel of 49°10'N and at 1000 hrs, it bears 220° from A. Both aircraft eventually meet.

What is B's bearing from A at 1030 hrs?

Answer: 220°(T)

2.   Aircraft A making good a Tr 030(T) at 300 kt passes over B which is making good a track of 310 at 260 kt, Estimate relative velocity of B from A prior to passing over B.

Answer: 255° – 363 kt

3.   Aircraft A on track of 090 is doing ground speed of 200 kt. It will collide with B in 5 min if no alteration to heading is made. B at present is on bearing of 030 relative from A. If B's ground speed is 250 kt, estimate B's track and relative velocity, assuming zero drift.

Answer: Tr 323; Rel.Vel. 300° – 402 kt

4.   Aircraft A whose TAS is 270 observes aircraft B on relative bearing of 040°. Aircraft B observes A on relative bearing of 330°. If two aircraft are on collision headings, determine

(a)   TAS of aircraft B;

(b)   speed at which the two aircraft are closing.

Answer: (a)   320 kt   (b)   480 kt

5.   An aircraft A is flying due south at ground speed of 170. B is flying East at ground speed of 210 both having left the same point. What is the relative bearing of B with respect to A?

Answer: 050° – 270 kt.

6.   Aircraft A is heading 030(T), TAS 230. Aircraft B which bears 310(T) from A is heading 080(T) at TAS 320 kt. If neither aircraft alters heading or speed, which will pass ahead of the other?

Answer: Aircraft B.

8: Solar System: Time

The Solar System consists of the Sun, nine major planets of which the Earth is one, and about 2 000 minor planets or asteroids. All members of the solar system are controlled by the Sun which is distinguished by its immense size and its radiation of light and heat; for all practical purposes, it may be considered as the stationary centre round which all the planets revolve.

Unlike the Sun, the planets and their satellites are not self-luminous, but reveal their presence by reflecting the Sun's light. The planets revolve about the Sun in elliptical orbits, each one taking a period of time about the job: Mercury takes 88 days, for example, while Pluto which is rather a long way from the parent body, is thought to take about 248 years. The planetary satellites in the meantime are revolving about their own parents.

Certain laws relating to the motion of planets in their orbits were evolved by the astronomer Kepler, who died in abject poverty as a reward:

    (i) each planet moves in an ellipse, with the Sun at one end of its foci;

    (ii) the radius vector of any planet sweeps out equal areas in equal intervals of time.

These are the important laws for our purpose in studying the Earth's motion, as we shall see.

The Earth rotates on its axis in a West to East direction, resulting in day and night. It revolves round the Sun along a path or orbit which is inclined to the Earth's axis at about 66½°, resulting in the seasons of the year. When the Earth is inclined towards the Sun, we get the Summer Solstice (June 21); when the axis is away from the Sun, we get the Winter Soltice (Dec 22). When the Earth's axis is at right angles to the Sun, days and nights are equal, the Spring and Autumn Equinox (March 21 and Sept 23). The point where the planet is nearest to the Sun is called

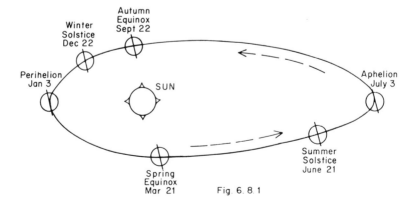

Fig. 6. 8. 1

perihelion, and where farthest aphelion; it is worth noting that in obeying Kepler's second law, the speed of the Earth at perihelion is faster along its orbit than at aphelion; and that the Earth is nearer to the Sun in British winter.

Measurement of Time

The instant at which a heavenly body is directly over a meridian is called a 'transit'. The earth rotates on its axis from West to East and to us on its crust, the heavenly bodies appear to revolve about the Earth from East to West. The period of this apparent revolution is measured by the time elapsing between two successive transits of a heavenly body, called a 'day'. If a star were the heavenly body, since stars are such immense distances away, the 'sidereal' day would be of constant length, for only the Earth's axial movement of rotation would affect the star's apparent movement. The Earth is 8 light minutes from the Sun, but $4\frac{1}{3}$ light years from the nearest star. We measure the day by the Sun, of course, and must needs investigate the problems that result, without involving ourselves with the vast academic matters of the Universe.

An 'apparent solar day' is the time interval between two successive transits of the real or apparent Sun at the same meridian, the word 'apparent' signifying that is how it appears to us as we move with the Earth. Seen from above the North Pole, the Earth rotates on its axis at an even speed in an anti-clockwise direction, and also revolves round the Sun in its orbit in an anti-clockwise direction; since the direction of axial rotation is the same as orbital revolution, West to East, it follows that it must rotate on its axis through more than 360° to produce successive transits.

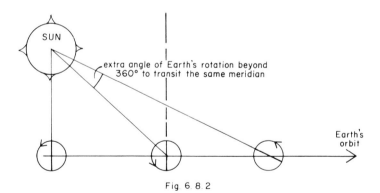

Fig. 6.8.2

Furthermore, since the Earth's orbit is elliptical, the Earth's speed of revolution on its orbit varies continuously and the length of an Apparent Solar Day will not be constant.

The time of transit is called Local Apparent Noon; but these facts and their unequal variations would make human working life difficult.

Mean Solar Time

In order to have a constant measurement of time which will still have the Solar Day as a basis, the average length of an apparent solar day is taken. called the <u>Mean Solar Day</u>, divided into 24 hours of mean solar time. This is arrived at as follows:

The time of orbital revolution of the Earth in one year is constant at 365 days 5 hours 48 minutes 49 seconds. A mean sun is imagined to travel once round a circular path in the same plane as the Equator at a constant speed in the same time as the True Sun travels round its apparent elliptical path at its varying speeds: thus, the time of two successive transits of the Mean Sun over any given meridian is constant, as both the Earth and Mean Sun are rotating in the same plane at constant speeds. In other words, we keep time by an imaginary or Mean Sun which leaves a meridian and returns to it 24 hours later of mean time.

The discrepancy between the transit of the Apparent Sun and the Mean Sun over the Greenwich meridian is not large enough to affect the working day (Mean noon at Greenwich is approximately $16\frac{1}{4}$ minutes later than Apparent noon in November; and $14\frac{1}{3}$ minutes earlier in February).

The year of 365 days 5 hours 48 minutes 49 seconds (again measuring in Mean Solar Time) is itself an inconvenient measure: the Calendar year is 365 days, so to even things up, a leap year of 366 days is inserted every 4 years, and to round things off, 3 leap years are suppressed every 4 centuries.

Time in arc

Time can also be measured in arc since in one day of mean solar time, the Sun is imagined to travel in a complete circle round the Earth, a motion of 360°. The measurement of 24 hours then is the same measurement as 360° of longitude. Really, that is the only thing to remember, for any conversions of one to the other is mental arithmetic; for reference:

24 hours	=	360° of longitude
1 hour	=	15° of longitude
1 minute	=	15′ of longitude
1 second	=	15″ of longitude

Conversely:

360°	=	24 hours of time
1°	=	4 minutes of time
1′	=	4 seconds of time
1″	=	1/15 second of time

Local Mean Time

The beginning of the day at any place is midnight, or 0000 hours LMT, e.g. 0000 hours at a place in longitude 50W will be when the Mean Sun is in transit with the ante meridian 130°E. This means that the LMT of places in different longitudes varies by an amount corresponding to the change in longitude. A standard meridian has to be fixed to which all LMTs can be referred, and the meridian at Greenwich is internationally accepted as this standard. Local Mean Time at Greenwich is called Greenwich Mean Time.

The Greenwich Day commences when the Mean Sun is in transit with the ante meridian of Greenwich and as the Sun appears to travel from East to West, it will be in transit with Easterly meridians before it is in transit with Greenwich. Thus, LMT of places East of Greenwich will be ahead of GMT and places West of Greenwich will be behind GMT.

Consider these diagrams for a Sunrise at 0600 hrs LMT, in order to establish the relationship of LMT to time on the Greenwich meridian.

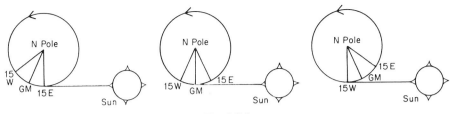

Fig. 6.8.3

The rule is:

Longitude East, Greenwich Time Least

Longitude West, Greenwich Time Best

All flying is done on GMT, no matter whereabouts on the globe a pilot is operating, but the Sun rises and sets at different times on the same meridian, depending on the celestial latitude (declination) of the Sun and the Earthly latitude of the observer; more later on this, but the times of the phenomena are listed in the Air Almanac in LMT, so the conversion from one to the other is very necessary knowledge indeed. A few examples:

(i) GMT 1200 hrs,   then LMT at 60°E = 1600 hrs

and LMT at 80°W = 0640 hrs

(ii) What is the GMT and GD of a place in longitude 46°25′E where LMT is 14h 23m 15s and LD is 2nd June?

46°25′ in time	= 3h 05m 40s	
LMT and LD	= 14h 23m 15s	June 2nd
GMT least	11h 17m 35s	and GD still
		June 2nd

(iii) If GD and GMT are 2nd Dec 21h 02m 24s, give LD and LMT in longitude 96°47′E.

96°47′ in time	= 6h 27m 08s	
GMT least	= 21h 02m 24s	2nd Dec GD
LMT	03h 29m 32s	3rd Dec LD

The Air Almanac, on one of the last odd pages of the book gives a table for the conversion of arc to time from 1° to 360°, so that 341° for example is at once read off as 22h 44m; the end column gives minutes of arc into minutes and seconds of time e.g. 17′ of arc is 1m 08s of time.

Standard Time

Standard Time is the set time used for a particular country or part of a country. In general, it is based on the LMT 7½° on either side of a regular meridian divisible by 15°, but this of course often conflicts with political and national requirements, and has finally become arbitrary. The UK normally kept GMT as its Standard Time, but now has added one hour to GMT. A country like the USA is too longitudinally vast to keep one standard time, and divides itself up, so that the Atlantic Seaboard keeps Eastern Standard Time, 5 hours behind GMT, while Hawaii is 10 hours slow on GMT.

All Standard Times are listed in the Air Almanac, in three tables: (1) Places East of Greenwich, fast on GMT, (2) Places on GMT, (3) Places West of Greenwich, slow on GMT. With many local adjustments and divers boundaries of separation, there is a plenitude of footnotes to be watched: a pleasant note is that the adjustment one to the other of GMT to ST is explained in each table, to the chagrin of Ministry Examiners.

Dateline

When travelling Westward from Greenwich, an observer would eventually arrive at longitude 17959W, where the LMT is about to become 12 hours less than GMT. An observer travelling Eastward from Greenwich would eventually arrive at 17959E where the LMT is about to become 12 hours more than GMT. Thus there is a full day of 24 hours difference between the two travellers, although they are both about to cross the same meridian; When the ante-meridian of Greenwich is crossed, one day is gained or lost, depending on the direction of travel: the Dateline is the actual line where the change is made, and is mainly the 180 meridian, with some slight divergences to accommodate certain groups of South Sea Islands and regions of Eastern Siberia. The problem readily resolves itself in flying – your watch is always on GMT: the place whose Standard Time you want is listed in the Air Almanac: apply the correction to GMT, and the date will take care of itself. Crossing the dateline always seems to excite passengers in aircraft much more than crossing the Equator: you will want to let them know when, on a leg from HONOLULU to TOKYO, the date changes from the 2nd to the 3rd.

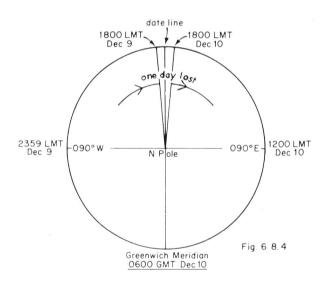

Fig 6.8.4

Sunrise and Sunset

We are only concerned with the visible phenomena, when the centre of the Sun is coincident with the observer's horizon: at the moment of this vision, the centre of the Sun is actually 1° below the horizon, but due to refraction, we see it as higher than it really is. All this is mercifully built into the Tables to let the pilot cope with what he sees, and let the theory look after itself.

The times of S/R and S/S at any place change by only a minute or two each day except in high latitudes; so the time of the occurrences at specified Latitudes on the Greenwich meridian may be taken as the same for all longitudes. A tabulation of 0708 for a certain date and latitude is in fact the LMT of the phenomenon on the Greenwich meridian, it will also be the LMT on any other longitude on the same local date and Latitude: by the time 0708 LMT comes along at 30°W, the time on the Greenwich meridian is by now 0908. And if you are at 30°W in an aeroplane with your watch set to GMT as usual, you will look up the Air Almanac for your Latitude, find 0708 LMT and apply the usual rule to find the GMT at the time of the rising. Check again with Fig. 3.

The tabulation in the Air Almanac covers every band of Latitude for dates three days apart: the bands of Latitude are sometimes 10° apart, sometimes 2°. The times of S/R and S/S vary considerably as the Latitude of the observer increases. The interpolation from the tables for the date required on the observer's Latitude may be done without tedious calculation: take the nearest tabulated day, and interpolate on that day for the Latitude required.

The diagrams which follow will explain the effect of Latitude; and, bearing in mind that the Sun's declination is a maximum 23½°N or 23½°S approximately, how it comes about that the Sun can be above or below the horizon all day in some Latitudes. CH is the observer's horizon.

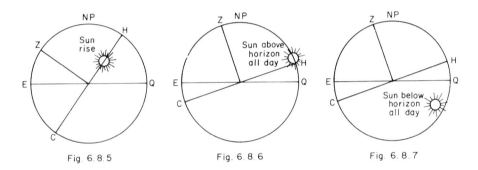

Fig. 6.8.5   Fig. 6.8.6   Fig. 6.8.7

With a midsummer's day N Hemisphere, the length of the day from S/R to S/S from Fig 5 increases with the observer's latitude Z until eventually, in Fig 6, he is Northerly enough to have the Sun above his horizon all day: this particular observer gets his come-uppance as the Sun makes its way South, for then it is continuous Northern night (Fig 7). The symbols in the Tables for such occasions are explained at the beginning of the Air Almanac, after the daily pages.

Sample: What is GMT of S/S in Position 32°00'S 172°15'W on 13th Jan LD?
The extract from the Air Almanac looks like this:

	Jan 11	Jan 14
Lat. S30°	1906	1905
Lat. S35°	1918	1917

and 13th Jan is thus as for 14th Jan. Interpolate for 32°S, 2/5 of 12 minutes
= 5 minutes   Thus

13th Jan at 32°00'S	=	1910 LMT
172°15'W to time		1129
GMT		3039 best
	=	0639 14th Jan GMT & GD

i.e. the time and date on the Greenwich meridian when the sun sets in 32°00'S 172°15'W.

Twilight

When the Sun is below the horizon, an observer will still receive light which has been reflected and scattered by the atmosphere. It is divided into three stages: Astronomical (12° below Horizon, and it's dark); Nautical (6° − 12° below the Horizon, and has something to do with the sea horizon being indistinct, and artificial light being required to box the compass abaft the foc'sle); and Civil Twilight when the Sun's centre is actually between 1° and 6° below the horizon, when work is possible without artificial light, and the stars are not clearly visible. This last is the one we're concerned with.

The Air Almanac tabulates in exactly the same form as S/R and S/S the beginning of morning twilight and the end of evening twilight, all in LMT as before. The duration of morning twilight is then simply the difference between S/R and the twilight tabulation for that place on that day. Just as in high latitudes we had occasions of 24 hours daylight or darkness, so again we shall have occasions where twilight lasts all night. The symbol is explained in the same place as before in the Air Almanac.

The whole period of twilight has particular significance to pilots beyond the obvious transition of light and dark, and the impairment of visual judgments at that time. It is around twilight that the ionosphere starts to move, with the consequent reduction of the effective range of MF radio aids especially, and of HF aids to some extent. The radio compass becomes sluggish; a cathode ray tube presentation in an aircraft working a station well within its normal ground wave range gets thoroughly grassed up; even HF R/T suffers increased noise with the altering properties of the atmosphere for radio transmission as the Sun's powers change. The navigator is meanwhile denied the heavens for astro-navigation. It is worth a thought that in fast aircraft and long range radio aids, a twilight zone can exist between the aircraft and the station for quite a long time, most noticeable on Easterly and Westerly flights.

Effect of Height

The tabulations in the Air Almanac for risings and settings and twilight are all for an observer at sea level; in flight, the visible horizon is extended. and the phenomena will occur earlier in the morning and later in the evening. The rate of movement of the Sun through the angle of depression varies with the latitude of the observer and the time of year as well as with the observer's height, and the calculation of the time difference, though measurable, takes the pilot into matters at present outside his syllabus of study. An explanation and all the necessary figures are in the Air Almanac.

The Moon

The Moon is a perfect sphere which travels round the Earth according to Kepler's Laws 1 and 2, but due to the Earth's own orbit its apparent path is somewhat irregular though calculable. It rotates on its axis West to East in exactly the same time as it takes to get round the Earth, so that we are always presented with the same face (actually, over a period, 59% of the Moon's surface has been seen by the Earthbound observer). One half of the Moon is always illuminated by the Sun, and as the Moon revolves round the Earth, the sunlit half is presented in varying amounts, the phases of the Moon.

When the Moon passes between the Earth and the Sun, it is said to be in conjunction, and its sunlit half is away from the Earth, a new Moon. It is in opposition when the Earth lies between the Sun and Moon, the illuminated face is straight towards us, a full Moon. When the direction of the Moon is 90° to that of the Sun, it is in quadrature, when half of the disc is visible from the Earth, called the first and last quarter; crescent phases are less than half full, gibbous more than half. The age of the Moon is the number of days which have elapsed since it was last new, and even that is recorded in the daily pages of the Air Almanac.

In the diagram which follows to illustrate the phases, it must be borne in mind that the three bodies are not in a straight line; if they were, then an eclipse, total or partial, solar or lunar, would be seen from the Earth. In simple terms, a latitude projected into the celestial sphere is called the declination of a heavenly body, and the declinations of the Sun and Moon must be nearly equal to give a solar eclipse; and there must be a relationship for a lunar eclipse when the Moon passes through the Earth's shadow.

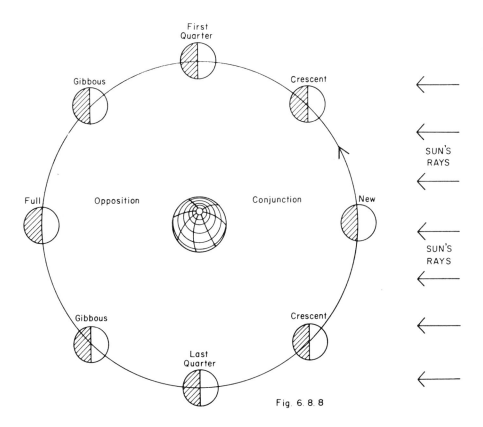

Fig. 6. 8. 8

Moonrise and Moonset

The Moon revolves on its orbit West to East round the Earth once in 29½ days: its average daily movement =

$$\frac{360}{29\frac{1}{2}} = 12\frac{3}{4}° \text{ which is 51 minutes of time.}$$

If the declination of the Moon (i.e. its celestial latitude) were constant, it would rise and set on the average 51 minutes later each day.

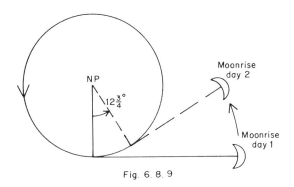

Fig. 6. 8. 9

But the declination changes very rapidly, and the difference between M/R or M/S on successive days is marked and inconstant. The extra amount of revolution required to transit the same meridian successively is known as the DAILY LAG, and it varies with the latitude of the Observer and the declination of the Moon. So the daily changes of the M/R and M/S are great enough to prevent figures tabulated in the Air Almanac for the phenomenon on the Greenwich Meridian to be regarded as LMTs for other meridians.

Precise times of M/R and M/S are seldom required however: and a tabulation of two different daily lags for correction to Easterly or Westerly longitude is avoided in the Almanac by inserting under the term 'Difference' half the daily lag. This 'difference' is found against the observer's latitude, on the daily pages, with the LMT of M/R or M/S. This difference is then taken to the 'Interpolation' of Moonrise/Moonset (on the loose flap usually), and entering with difference and observer's longitude, the correction is read off: this correction is added to LMT M/R or M/S if Longitude W, subtracted if Longitude E. A thumbnail sketch would illustrate why — the lag is progressive, and East of Greenwich the phenomenon will occur at an earlier LMT than at Greenwich, so the correction is subtracted: on Westerly meridians, the correction is additive since the Moon will have moved further on its orbit.

As the time interval between successive phenomena is more than 24 hours, it follows that in each month there will be one day when there will be no M/R and another when there will be no M/S.

This will occur when M/R or M/S is near to local midnight. The tabulations are for the phenomena on the Greenwich meridian; in the illustration above, it is clear that the effect of the lag for M/S on Easterly meridians may not have caused the jump from local Friday to local Sunday, i.e. the M/S could have occurred on late local Saturday. To allow for this, the Air Almanac gives the time as 2400 +, as a basis

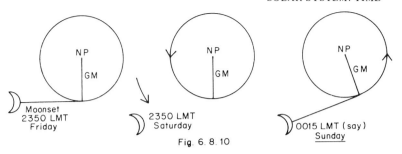

Fig. 6. 8. 10

for calculation of the occurrence in other longitudes; the point to watch is the date. 2431 as the tabulated time on 7th Jan is really 0031 on 8th Jan, the date at Greenwich.

It can happen that the times found are for the day before, or day after, the one required: in which case, it is quite in order to add or subtract twice the difference, watching the date carefully, as:

Required GMT of M/R 8th March 1968, at 52°N, 150°E.

From daily Page M/R 8/3/68	0958	diff. 25
From Flap Table 25 v 150	− 22	
LMT 8/3/68	0936	
Long. 150°E	1000	
GMT	2336	Least 7/3/68
Twice diff.	+ 50	
GMT + one day	0026	9th March

In other words, there was no M/R in this position on 8th March, GD.

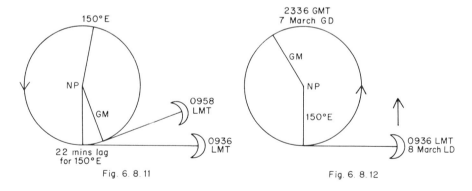

Fig. 6. 8. 11   Fig. 6. 8. 12

Fig 11 is a sketch of the tabulated M/R for the Greenwich meridian with times at the occurrence for Greenwich meridian and 150°E. Knowing then that the M/R takes place (Fig 12), 10 hours (approx.) earlier for 150°E than on the Greenwich meridian, the Greenwich time will be 2336, 7th March 1968 GD and no moonrise will take place at 150°E on the 8th, for the lag (or double the difference) will whip the next occurrence there to the 9th March, *the calculations being all for GD.*

A final touch about the tabulations of M/R and M/S on the daily pages. With this wretched body so near the Earth, there is plenty of parallax and refraction, all allowed for in the Tables, so that the usual rule of visible rising and setting is obeyed: the differences in higher latitudes are often too erratic to be reasonably measured, and an asterisk is inserted to warn you. If the difference is noted as negative the correction duly found from the Interpolation table on the flap is applied in the opposite direction, as the footnote points out. On this table, too, it is accurate enough to take the nearest noted figure for difference v longitude without interpolation.

It's a lot of hard work for very little value when flying. A full moon at night can make for less tedious flying, I suppose, but a navigator would never use the thing if the stars are visible, and it hardly ever interferes with his sights; though by day, in the right position in the celestial globe, it can provide a Sun/Moon Fix, but that's the navigator's problem.

9: PNR Theorems

1. **To prove that if fuel available is just sufficient to reach the destination both CP and PNR are in the same position.**

E x O is the total distance the a/c can travel out within its endurance.

If endurance is only sufficient to reach its destination, then

$$E \times O \quad = \quad D; \quad \text{and CP is } \frac{DH}{O+H}$$

$$\therefore \quad \frac{EOH}{O+H} \quad = \quad \frac{DH}{O+H}$$

2. **To prove that the distance to PNR remains unchanged if the wind component is reversed.**

Let TAS of the aircraft be T knots and the wind component, W kt   Then,

with headwind, the ground speed Out   = $(T - W)$ kt., and

ground speed Home   = $(T + W)$ kt.

Distance to PNR with headwind component

$$= \frac{EOH}{O+H} \quad = \quad \frac{E \times (T-W)\,(T+W)}{(T-W)+(T+W)}$$

$$= \quad \frac{E\,(T^2-W^2)}{2T}$$

Distance to PNR with tailwind component

$$= \frac{EOH}{O+H} \quad = \quad \frac{E \times (T+W)\,(T-W)}{(T+W)+(T-W)}$$

$$= \quad \frac{E\,(T^2-W^2)}{2T}$$

(Note: with tail wind O   =   T + W and

H   =   T–W)

Thus, the distance remains unchanged.

3. **To prove that in zero wind condition the distance to PNR is the maximum distance.**

When wind is zero, the Distance to PNR formula may be rewritten

$$\frac{EOH}{O+H} \quad = \quad \frac{E \times T \times T}{T + T}$$

where T is the TAS and in zero wind conditions O = H = T.

$$= \quad \frac{E \times T^2}{2T}$$

$$= \quad \frac{ET}{2} \quad \ldots \ldots \quad \ldots \ldots \quad \ldots \ldots \quad \ldots \ldots \quad 1.$$

We note, from above theorem (no. 2) that distance to PNR with head or tail component is given in formula

$$\frac{E\,(T^2-W^2)}{2T} \qquad \ldots\ldots \qquad \ldots\ldots \qquad \ldots\ldots \;\; 2.$$

The value of formula 1 is higher than formula 2, or, the distance to PNR is maximum when wind is zero. You check.

4.   To prove that the distance to PNR is reduced to zero distance when wind component equals TAS.

Distance to PNR in terms of TAS

$$= \frac{E\,(T^2-W^2)}{2T} \quad \text{irrespective of whether W is head or tail component.}$$

When W = T, the formula becomes —

$$\frac{E \times zero}{2T}$$

$$= \text{Zero}$$

5.   To prove that with no wind, the CP is midway between departure and destination.

$$\text{Distance to CP} \quad = \quad \frac{DH}{O+H}$$

With no wind, H = O = T and the formula becomes

$$\text{Distance} \qquad = \frac{D \times T}{2T}$$

$$= \frac{D}{2}$$

or, midway.

6.   To prove that the CP is closer to destination (as against departure aerodrome) when there is head wind component.

$$\text{Dist} \;=\; \frac{DH}{O+H}\;; \quad \text{with headwind, H } = T + W. \text{ Rewriting the formula,}$$

$$\text{Dist} \;=\; \frac{D\,(T+W)}{2T}$$

$$= \frac{D}{2} \;\times\; \frac{(T+W)}{T} \quad \text{which is greater than} \frac{D}{2}$$

Therefore, CP is nearer destination.

7.   To prove that with tail wind CP is closer to the departure

$$\text{Dist to CP} \;=\; \frac{D}{2} \times \left(\frac{T-W}{T}\right)$$

$$\text{which is less than} \quad \frac{D}{2}$$

8.   To prove that a reduction in TAS with head wind component results in increase of distance to CP.

Distance to CP at normal TAS with head wind

$$= \frac{D}{2} \times \frac{T+W}{T} \quad \text{or,} \quad \frac{D}{2}\left(1+\frac{W}{T}\right)$$

Let the TAS T be reduced by X knots; then $\dfrac{DH}{O+H}$

$$= \frac{D \times (T-X+W)}{(T-X-W) + (T-X+W)}$$

$$= \frac{D(T-X+W)}{2T-2X}$$

$$= \frac{D}{2}\left(\frac{T-X+W}{T-X}\right)$$

$$= \frac{D}{2}\left(1+\frac{W}{T-X}\right) \quad \text{which is greater than} \quad \frac{D}{2}\left(1+\frac{W}{T}\right)$$

(Note: This is because factor $\dfrac{W}{T-X}$ is greater than factor $\dfrac{W}{T}$ in that in the first

factor you are dividing W by something less than T).

Therefore, the distance to CP is increased.

It can similarly be proved that the distance decreases with tail wind component.

RADIO AIDS

1: Introduction

Theory of Propagation of Radio Waves

Radio waves appear much like an alternating electric current, the electrons of which move about a mean position. An alternating current fed into an aerial will cause radio waves, which are electro-magnetic energy, to be emitted from that aerial, and they will induce a similar alternating current into another aerial placed in their path, though much weaker in strength. All that the receiver does is to convert and amplify these incoming waves so that they are usable for whatever purpose they are originally emitted. The first step in the control of such waves is to know and define various characteristics of these waves and then to study the relationships between various terms as they arise. The following terms are noted in connection with an AC which are also applicable to radio.

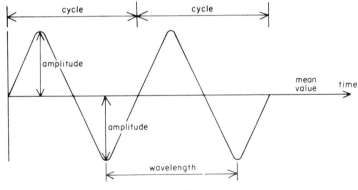

Fig. 7.1.1

Cycle: A cycle is a one complete series of values, or one complete process.

Amplitude: Amplitude of a wave is the maximum displacement or value it attains from its mean position during a cycle.

Frequency: Frequency of a radio wave is the number of cycles occurring in one second.

Wavelength: Wavelength is the distance between successive crests of the wave or distance between two consecutive points at which moving particles have the same displacement from the mean value and are moving in the same direction.

Polarisation: This term arises in radio and you should be generally familiar with it. A radio wave has two components — electrical and magnetic. These two components travel together but their planes of travel are separated by $90°$. In other words, if an electric component is travelling in the vertical plane, its associated magnetic component travels in the horizontal plane. If a radio signal is emitted from a vertical aerial, the electric component travels in the vertical plane and the signal is called vertically polarised. If the signals are emitted from a horizontal aerial, the waveform is horizontally polarised. Its practical importance lies in the orientation of the receiver aerial, in that a vertical aerial will efficiently receive a vertically polarised signal and a horizontal aerial will efficiently receive a horizontally polarised signal. This requirement becomes increasingly critical as transmission frequency increases.

Wavelength — Frequency Relationship

A radio wave travels at a speed of 186 000 statute miles per second, or 162 000 nautical miles per second, or 300 000 000 metres per second.

The relationship is established when it is considered that if a transmission of one cycle per second is made, that one complete cycle will cover a geographical distance of 300 000 000 metres. If two cycles are transmitted in one second, two complete cycles will occupy a space of 300 000 000 metres between them or one cycle will occupy 150 000 000 metres. One complete cycle is also its wavelength. Therefore, this relationship can be put in the formula:

$$\text{Wavelength} = \frac{\text{speed of radio waves}}{\text{frequency}}$$

By use of this simple formula it is possible to convert frequency into wavelength and vice versa. The important thing to keep in mind is to use basic units, metres and cycles per second.

The formula also tells us that the higher the frequency, the shorter the wavelength. As for frequencies, alternating current at a frequency of one and two cycles (as in the above illustration) when fed to transmitter aerial does not leave the aerial as a radio wave. In fact, initial emission takes place only when the frequency is increased to about 3 000 cycles per second. This is the beginning of the radio spectrum. To talk of cycles per second in radio would be too much of a mouthful, so,

1 000 cycles/sec	=	1 kilocycle/sec (kc/s) or 1 Kilo Hertz (kHz)
1 000 kc/s	=	1 Megacycle/sec (Mc/s) or 1 Mega Hertz (MHz)
1 000 Mc/s	=	1 Gigacycle

The abbreviation 'c/s' for cycles per second is now obsolete, and the expression 'Hz' is the replacement. This is short for Hertz, meaning cycles per second; thus, kHz, MHz, and so on.

Examples

1.   If the wavelength is 1.5 kilometres, what is the frequency?

$$F = \frac{\text{Speed in metres per second}}{\text{Wavelength in metres}}$$

$$= \frac{300\ 000\ 000}{1500}$$

= 200 000 cycles per second

= 200 kHz

2.   If transmission frequency is 75 MHz, what is the wavelength?

$$\text{Wavelength in metres} = \frac{\text{Speed in metres}}{\text{Frequency in cycles}}$$

$$= \frac{300\ 000\ 000}{75\ 000\ 000}$$

= 4 metres

3. If wavelength is 3 cm, what is the frequency?

$$\text{Freq. in hertz} = \frac{\text{Speed in metres}}{\text{Wavelength in metres}}$$

$$= \frac{300\ 000\ 000 \times 100}{3}$$

$$= 10\ 000\ 000\ 000\ \text{Hz}$$

$$= 10\ 000\ \text{MHz}$$

Now try these
1. Wavelength is 3 metres, what is the frequency?
Answer: 100 MHz
2. Express 100 kHz in metres
Answer: 3 000 metres
3. Wavelength is 3 520 metres; what is the frequency?
Answer: 85 kHz
4. Frequency 325 kHz, what is the wavelength?
Answer: 923 metres
5. Frequency 117 000 kHz, what is the wavelength?
Answer: 2.564 metres
6. Wavelength 3.41 centimetres, frequency?
Answer: 8797 MHz
7. Express wavelength of 2.515 metres in frequency.
Answer: 119.2 MHz
8. If wavelength is 2.739 metres what is the frequency?
Answer: 109.5 MHz

Phase and Phase difference
Consider a vector, rotating about central axis 0 and producing an AC waveform. As the vector OR, starting from its position of rest, R, completes one revolution, it will produce one complete cycle of AC. This cycle may be plotted on a horizontal axis, representing 360°.

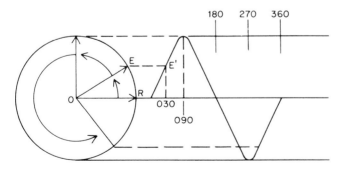

Fig. 7.1.2

If the vector is stopped at some stage of its revolution, say at point E (30° anti-clockwise from OR position), it will have traced the cycle from zero position on the horizontal axis up to point E^1. E^1 is then the instantaneous phase of that cycle. In other words, any stage in the cycle of an alternating current is referred to as its phase.

If two transmissions were taking place on the same frequency, two waveforms would superimpose each other, if the transmissions commenced at the same instant. Then, the two waveforms are said to be "in phase". A fractional delay in sending off the second transmission will cause them to be out of phase. To define the term — if two alternating currents of the same frequency (therefore, their amplitudes need not be the same) do not reach the same value at the same instant of time, they are out of phase. The phase difference is the angular difference between the corresponding points on the waveform and is measurable. This forms a principle of some of the navigational aids. Two waveforms having any number of degrees of phase difference between them can be drawn by considering revolutions of two vectors placed similarly apart and by tracing their instantaneous values. Fig 3 (a) and (b) illustrate the point.

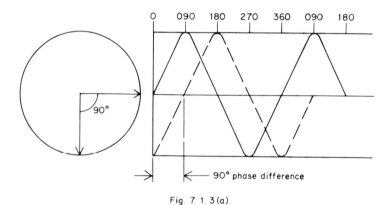

Fig. 7. 1. 3 (a)

Fig. 7. 1. 3 (b)

Modulation

Radio waves as such are inaudible to the human ear because of the high frequency of the transmission. Therefore, if these waves are required to convey audible information they must be modified or varied so that the variation itself is audible.

This process of modification is known as modulation. Modulation may take place in several ways, two primary methods being amplitude modulation and frequency modulation.

Amplitude Modulation

This is a process whereby the amplitude of the radio wave (carrier wave) is varied to conform with the audio signal (a signal which is within range of human ear). Thus, a carrier wave carries an audio signal with it. At the receiver, both signals are picked up when the carrier frequency is tuned in. The carrier wave is then discarded whereas the audio wave is fed to the loudspeaker via various stages of detection, amplification etc. Fig 4 illustrates an amplitude modulated signal.

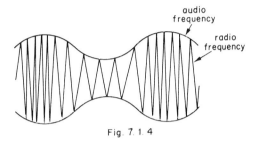

audio frequency

radio frequency

Fig. 7.1.4

Frequency Modulation

As the title suggests, this is the method of conveying information by modifying frequency and not the amplitude – Fig 5. The frequency increases to maximum at audio frequency's positive peak; it reduces to minimum at the negative peak.

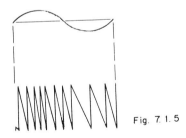

Fig. 7.1.5

In the case of frequency modulation the receiver tuned to a specific frequency accepts varying frequency and a discriminator unit detects the variations. This process makes such receivers more complex but it has advantages:
1. transmitters are simpler;
2. less modulating power required;
3. static due to weather (thunderstorms, Cb clouds, etc) is generally vertically polarised and therefore it has negligible effect on frequency modulated signals (no external 'noise' – hence the popularity of FM broadcast). Generally, if the frequency is low, amplitude modulation technique is used. At higher frequencies, signals are generally frequency modulated (FM broadcast in VHF band).

2: Propagation of Radio Waves

Radio waves are found to have different characteristics which vary according to their frequencies. In order to identify certain groups of frequencies which display similar properties, the full range of radio frequencies has been divided into various bands by international convention.

Designation	Abbreviation	Frequency Band	Wavelength
Very Low	V L F	3 – 30 kHz	100 km – 10 km
Low	L F	30 – 300 kHz	10 km – 1 km
Medium	M F	300 – 3 000 kHz	1 km – 100 m
High	H F	3 – 30 MHz	100 m – 10m
Very High	V H F	30 – 300 MHz	10 m – 1m
Ultra High	U H F	300 – 3 000 MHz	1 m – 10 cm
Super High	S H F	3 000 – 30 000 MHz	10 cm – 1 cm
Extremely High	E H F	Above 30 000 MHz	Less than 1 cm

When the radiation takes place at the open end of the aerial the radio waves propagate in all directions, as shown in Fig 1.

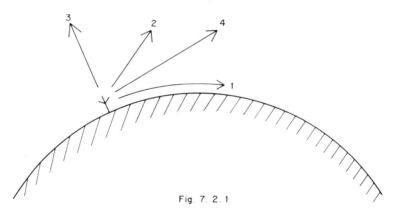

Fig. 7. 2. 1

Ground Wave

That wave which leaves the transmitter tangential to the surface of the Earth is called 'Ground Wave'. The term ground wave is also used to indicate all the waves which are not received having been first reflected from the ionosphere.

If the wave marked 1 in above diagram travelled in a straight line it would start rising (or gaining height) as the Earth's surface curved away from it. In such circumstances the signal would only be available within the line of sight range. Fortunately, however, it does bend with the surface of the Earth to a varying degree. In fact when a wave commences its travel over the surface, two things happen:

1.   It induces currents in the Earth and thereby loses its own energy. Thus, as the signal travels further and further, it gets weaker and weaker until it finally becomes undetectable. Therefore the transmission power is one factor which will determine how far a particular wave will still remain usable. This process of losing power when the wave comes in contact with the Earth's surface is known as Ground Attenuation. The extent of the loss or attenuation depends on two factors:

(a)   The Type of Surface. For given power output, a radio wave travels the greatest ranges over the sea; least over very dry soil. The ideal example is a navigation aid known as Consol. Over the sea the Consol range is nearly double that over the land.

(b)   Frequency in Use. The higher the frequency, the more the contact with the ground surface and therefore the greater the attenuation.

2.   At the same time as attenuation takes place the bottom of a vertically polarised wave front is slowed down, causing the top of the wave to lean forward. This leaning forward causes the signal to curve with the surface, giving ranges well beyond the visible horizon.

To summarise
1.   Radio waves bend round the Earth giving increased range.
2.   The signal strength decreases with range owing to attenuation.
3.   The amount of attenuation depends on the type of the surface and the signal frequency.

From the above, and disregarding the nature of the soil we can generalise the range expectations of ground waves as follows:

1.   L F.   Attenuation is low and the signal will bend with the Earth's surface. Therefore ranges of the order of several thousand miles are obtainable, given sufficient power to counteract low incidence attenuation.

2.   M F.   Signals still bend but attenuation is increased. Ranges obtainable are approximately 300 – 500 miles, maximum 1 000 miles. Again, whether maximum ranges will be achieved or not will depend mainly on the power output. Broadcasters, Consol, Decca and Loran fall within this band.

3.   H F.   Bending is least and attenuation is great. Result – maximum range obtainable is approximately 100 nm only. Once these ranges have been achieved any increase in power will have no further effect in increasing them.

4.   V H F and Above.   Signals in these bands do not curve with the Earth's surface and therefore only line of sight ranges are possible. In practice, ranges obtained are slightly higher than line of sight range.

Sky Wave
Going back to Fig 1 it would appear that waves 2 and 3 would finally be lost to space. Fortunately again, this is not quite so. Waves with vertical incidence from the transmitter may return to the Earth having been refracted and reflected from the ionosphere, given suitable conditions.

Ionosphere.   The ultra-violet rays from the Sun impinging upon the upper atmosphere cause the free electrons to be emitted from gas molecules. These free electrons in unbalanced state form a reflecting layer, known as the ionised layer. Because the absorption of the solar radiation is uneven at different levels in the upper atmosphere, several distinct layers are formed, as shown in Fig. 2.

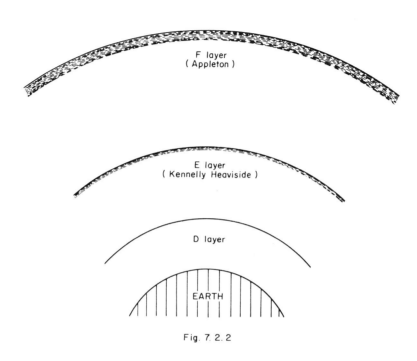

F layer
(Appleton)

E layer
(Kennelly Heaviside)

D layer

EARTH

Fig. 7. 2. 2

The heights of the various layers are:

	Winter Day		Summer Day
D Layer	50 to 100 km, av	75 km.	Same as winter day but less dense.
E Layer	100 to 150 km, av	125 km.	Same as winter day but relatively less dense.
F Layer	175 to 350 km, av	200 km.	400 to 500 km, av 450 km.

Night

D Layer — Disappears
E Layer — 125 to 175 km
F Layer — 300 to 400 km

When a radio signal penetrates the ionosphere, it is not only refracted but also loses some of its energy due to ionospheric attenuation, the extent of which depends on density or intensity of ionisation.

Density.   Higher the altitude lesser the atmosphere and more apart the molecules. Here the solar radiation has greater effect in splitting the molecules than at lower levels. Electron density in E layer is higher than in D layer, in F layer higher than in E layer.

Attenuation.   As pointed out above, radio energy is absorbed in the ionosphere. More and more energy is absorbed as the signal penetrates deeper and deeper.

The amount of energy loss is also related to the frequency in use and the relationship is : lower the frequency, greater the attenuation. Signals in LF and MF are generally absorbed during the day time when the electron density is relatively high.

Reflection.   A radio wave on entering the ionosphere is bent or refracted from its original path. If the refraction is high enough, it will be reflected back to the Earth. Generally the D layer has no significance as a reflecting layer. A signal may be reflected at the E layer. If it manages to get through it, it will still have undergone a certain amount of bending by refraction. Further bending which will occur at the F layer may probably be sufficient to reflect it back. Whether a signal will be reflected and return to the Earth depends on the following factors:

(a)   Critical Angle. The angle at which the signal strikes the ionosphere is one of the factors which decides whether the signal will return or not. In Fig 3 below, signal 1 strikes the reflecting surface at normal to it and no reflection will take place at all.

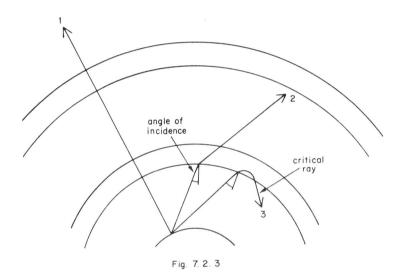

Fig. 7. 2. 3

As the angle of incidence is progressively increased the signals start to bend (signal 2) until an angle is reached (signal 3) for given frequency and ionospheric distribution when the first reflection will occur. This angle when the first return takes place is called Critical Angle for that frequency under those circumstances. At this angle and higher, there will be an uninterrupted return but how far beyond this point signals will be usable will depend on the transmission power, attenuation and the distance the signals have to travel out and back.

(b)   Frequency in Use. Higher frequencies require higher electron density to reflect. Therefore, a signal in MF will be reflected at the E layer whereas one in HF will penetrate into the F layer before reflection occurs. Signals in VHF and above do not bend sufficiently to give a return and we have no sky waves on these frequencies, that is, 30 MHz and above.

(c)   Time of the Day. Ionospheric activity is subject to diurnal and seasonal variation and is also affected by the 11-year solar spot cycle.

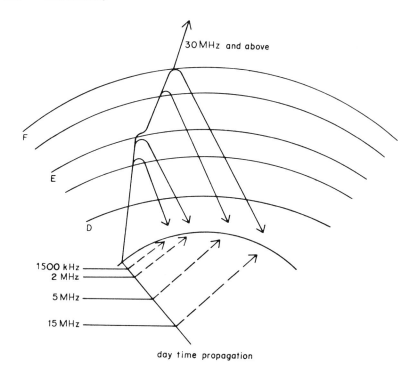

day time propagation

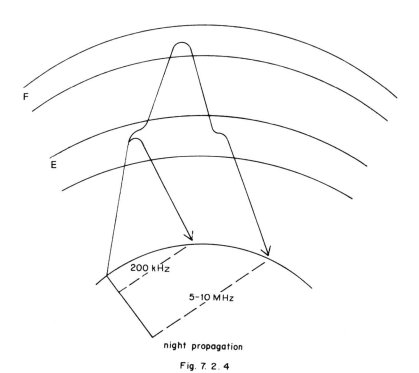

night propagation

Fig. 7. 2. 4

Diurnal. During the day time solar radiation increases the ionic density with the result that the reflection height moves much closer to the ground. As the Sun crosses the meridian the period of maximum density is reached. At this stage the effect due to attenuation is in predominance and considerable loss of communication occurs. At night when the Sun is beyond the horizon the process of recombination begins. D layer completely disappears. In the E layer the intensity decreases and the reflecting height rises. F layer practically remains unaffected (although it does gain some height). Sunrise and sunset produce unstable conditions as the layers start rising or falling. These are the critical periods for the operation of radio compass, and other MF aids.

Seasonal. The amount of intensity depends on where the Sun is with regard to the position under consideration. There is maximum activity when the Sun is closest.

11-Year Cycle. Very marked changes in ionisation occur during this sunspot activity period. Occasionally very large patches of intense ionisation occur in the E layer — intense enough to reflect VHF frequencies up to 50 MHz.

Ranges Obtained

For given ionospheric distribution the ranges obtained depend upon :

1.   The depth the signal penetrates before it is reflected. Since HF signals are reflected at higher altitudes than MF all long distance communication is achieved on HF band frequencies.

2.   Angle of Incidence also decides the range since the angle of reflection approximately equals the angle of incidence. Lower frequencies reflect at lower levels and produce shorter ranges.

Fig 4 illustrates the propagation through the ionosphere at various frequencies.

Summary

Reflection from the ionosphere depends on :

1.   Ionospheric intensity. Higher intensity occurs at higher altitudes.
2.   Attenuation. The lower the frequency the greater the attenuation.
3.   Critical Angle. This is directly related to frequency.
4.   Frequency in use. Lower frequencies reflect at a lower critical angle; higher frequencies at a higher critical angle. Higher frequencies penetrate deeper before being reflected.
5.   Time of the day.

From above we can generalise as shown in the table overleaf

Space Wave

Wave 4 in fig 1 is neither following the ground surface nor is it likely to be returned as a sky wave. Such a wave is termed "ground wave" and recently it has been given the more specific name of "space wave". This wave travelling in a straight line only produces optical range. VHF and higher frequency bands are straight-line propagation. However the actual range is slightly above mere optical range. Distance to the horizon is given in the formula:

$D = 1.05 \sqrt{H}$ where D is the distance to the horizon in nm, H is height in feet.

The practical range formula for VHF and above is $D - 1.2 (\sqrt{H_T} + \sqrt{H_R})$

Freq.	Ground Wave	Sky Wave	
		Day	Night
LF	Several thousand miles	None	Sky waves are present and use is made of them in such navigation aids as Consol and Loran. Nuisance to radio compass operation.
MF	Approximately 300 – 500 miles	To weak to use. Generally absorbed in lower half band.	Sky waves present – Consol Loran utilise them. Radio compass suffers.
HF	100 miles	Sky waves are present. Signals reflect at lower altitudes (E layer) giving shorter ranges. For long range, an increase of frequency is required. The reflection will then occur at F layer.	Sky waves are present and full use is made of them in long range communication. E layer is less intense and relatively lower frequencies penetrate E and reflect from F layer, giving greater ranges at lower frequencies.
VHF	Quasi-optical	None	None

where D is range in nm, H_T is the height of the transmitter in feet and H_R the height height of the receiver in feet. This modification to the range occurs due to atmospheric refraction. Density changes with height. As the signal gains height and meets less dense atmosphere it is refracted towards the medium of high density, that is, towards lower altitudes. This refraction depends upon pressure, temperature and humidity and is independent of frequency. The effect of the refraction is to bend the wave towards the Earth's surface, giving greater than optical range for a given height.

Short waves lose their energy due to atmospheric attenuation. This effect is unimportant for frequencies up to 600 MHz but at frequencies above this it is very important. VOR (VHF band) may be received at range of 200 nm at 20 000 ft; TACAN/DME (UHF 1 000 MHz) at 30 000 ft.

Attenuation in these frequencies also occurs due to rain drops. In fact, at the shorter end of the radio spectrum atmospheric attenuation is the limiting factor.

Now we will consider certain terminology arising through use of ground and sky waves, as well as other miscellaneous items.

Skip Distance is the minimum range at which a sky wave can be received.

Dead Space. If the skip distance is greater than maximum range of the ground wave then there will be an area where neither ground nor sky wave will be received. This area is called 'Dead Space'.

Multi-hop Reflection. Reflection of a sky wave may not be confined to a single "hop" and a signal may be reflected between the Earth and the ionosphere many times.

Other Factors affecting Range

A further factor affecting range is the extent to which atmospheric and other

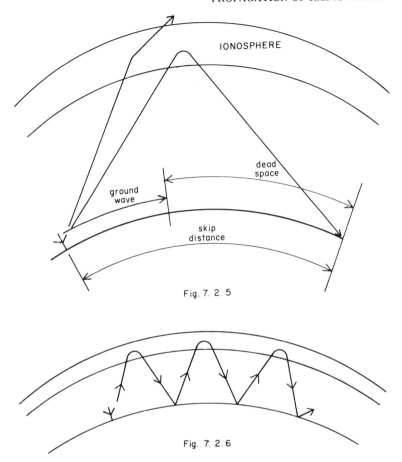

Fig. 7. 2. 5

Fig. 7. 2. 6

interferences are received. The "cracking" noise that is often heard in a receiver is due to:

(a) noises set up by electrical disturbances within the receiver or in nearby electrical equipment;

(b) electrical disturbances in the atmosphere whose radiations are picked up by the receiving aerial.

The former can be reduced by careful receiver design but in the latter case once the radio signal to be detected has become weaker than the atmospheric disturbance it is impossible to amplify it to usable strength without amplifying the accompanying atmospherics.

Duct Propagation

An extension of ground wave range occurs on VHF and higher frequencies when an abnormal reflecting layer appears only a few thousand feet above the Earth's surface, such a layer being associated with meteorological conditions such as :

(a) warm, dry air blowing over cool sea;

(b) subsidence, or

(c) pronounced radiation cooling.

These will be recognised as conditions tending to produce temperature inversions.

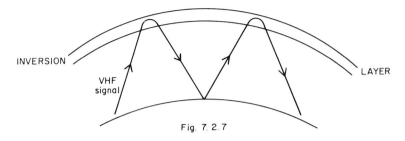

INVERSION

VHF
signal

LAYER

Fig. 7. 2. 7

The amount of ducting depends on differences in density and the amount of water vapour at different levels. Duct propagation is more noticeable in tropical and sub-tropical latitudes than in temperate zones.

3: NDBs and Radio Compass

From navigation plotting you will remember in connection with radio bearings that great care was required in deciding who did the work, you in the aircraft or the chap on the ground. We will now deal with the aircraft getting a bearing on a ground based radio station. Ground radio stations providing such a facility are known as Non Directional Beacons, NDBs for short.

These stations, NDBs, transmit vertically polarised signals in the MF frequency band, and are emitted in all directions from the point of transmission. This is why they are known as non-directional. An aircraft, carrying associated radio equipment known as the Radio Compass, tunes in the station on its frequency and measures the direction of the incoming wave with reference to the nose of the aircraft, the nose representing 000 direction or dead ahead.

Loop Theory
How does it do it? Quite simple. The aircraft carries two aerials, known as loop aerial and sense aerial. The loop aerial measures the direction of the incoming wave (which may be the relative direction, or its reciprocal) and the sense aerial resolves the ambiguity arising from the loop aerial.

The loop aerial is rectangular in shape, made up with a number of strands of wire wound round the frame and is mounted vertically in the most suitable position on the fuselage. The aerial is rotatable round a compass rose, and will pick up signals from the tune-in station in varying strengths according to its position with regard to the incoming wave.

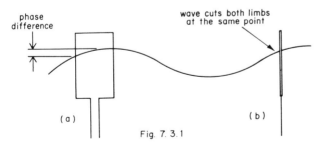

Fig. 7. 3.1

The vertical members of the loop are designed to pick up the signals. In Fig 1 (a), these are in line with the incoming signal, or putting it mathematically, the loop is at 0 degree to the wave. The wave will; (i) intersect the two vertical members of the loop at a different phase and therefore, current will flow in the loop; (ii) the receiving members of the loop are at maximum distance apart with reference to the incoming wave, therefore, maximum phase difference will exist and maximum current will flow.

In Fig 1 (b) the loop is rotated until both the vertical members are facing the incoming wave, or, the loop is at 90° to the wave. The wave strikes the loop at the same phase, and therefore, no current will flow.

This establishes the relationship between the direction of the aircraft's loop aerial and the direction of the incoming wave. If the loop is at 0°, the current induced is maximum, if it is at 90° it is zero current; therefore at any other angle, the current produced will be the value of cosine of the angle between the loop and the station. If a polar diagram is traced out of the signal strength produced by the loop at different angles relative to the station, a figure of eight diagram results.

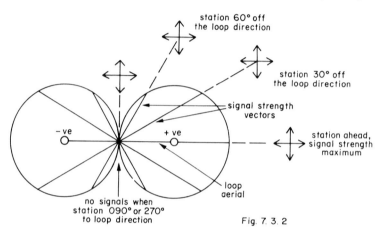

Fig. 7.3.2

Going back to Fig 1 (a) it will be appreciated that if the loop (which carries a compass rose) is rotated through 180° it will again produce maximum signal but the relative direction of the station indicated on the compass rose (radio compass) will be 180° out. The same effect could be observed in respect of Fig 1 (b) or the study of the figure of eight polar diagram. This is known as 180° ambiguity and it is resolved by use of the second aerial, the sense aerial. Sense aerial, being an omni directional aerial, will receive a same strength signal, irrespective of the station direction. Or, its polar diagram is a circle, which is electronically adjusted to fit on top of the figure of eight polar diagram.

To resolve ambiguity, these two fields are mixed together, the result being a heart shaped polar diagram called the cardioid. Compare the cardioid (Fig 3) with the figure of eight diagram above and observe that the cardioid has only one maximum position and one minimum position.

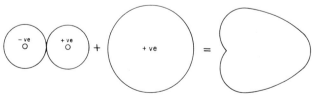

Fig. 7.3.3

Just one more point on the figure of eight polar diagram. When the aerial is lined up with the station, maximum signal is heard. But, near maximum signal persists for 10°−15° either side of it (value of cosines fall very slowly from 0°) and aurally, it will be most difficult to ascertain the exact maximum position (and therefore, correct bearing). On the other hand, when the aerial approaches 090° to the wave, the values of the cosine fall rapidly, and at 90° there ought to be a definite point where no signals whatever are heard. This is called Null position, and because the human ear can identify a null more readily than a maximum signal condition, the station is in practice tuned to null position. This is a more accurate bearing. As far as the indications are concerned, all that is necessary is to offset the compass rose by 90° so that it indicates dead ahead position when the aerial is at 90° to it.

How do you resolve ambiguity in the air? Several ways. If you know your DR position, ambiguity is resolved. Or, observe the changes in bearing with time. The bearing would increase or decrease as flight progresses unless you are homing to or away from the station. This change would tell you which side of the station you are — study Fig 4.

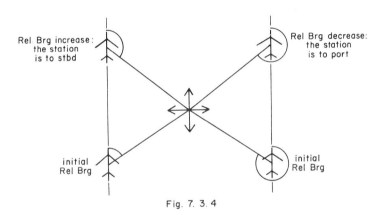

Rel Brg increase: the station is to stbd

Rel Brg decrease: the station is to port

initial Rel Brg

initial Rel Brg

Fig. 7. 3. 4

If your radio compass is automatic — most of them are these days — it resolves the ambiguity for you. This is done by use of a two phase motor. In pilot's language, by adjusting the phasing of the loop and sense aerials, the cardioid and its image are produced in rapid alterations. The image is 180° removed from the cardioid, and whichever one contains station signals, feeds in current to the motor which then turns, turning the pointer with it, in the correct direction. Even if the pointer is indicating exactly 180° out, the aircraft vibrations displace the pointer slightly, the motor taking over and doing the rest.

Most automatic radio compasses also incorporate a facility to check the sense manually. The drill is, change over from automatic to manual, by means of a handle provided, turn the loop scale (indication on the compass) to read less. If the signal strength decreases, the indicated sense is correct.

Types of Emission
Emissions of radio signals are classified according to the characteristics of the signal.

Different types of radio emissions are identified by means of a simple code consisting of one letter of the alphabet and one numeral. The letters used are A, F and P and they describe the type of modulation carried by the carrier, A stands for amplitude modulation, F for frequency modulation and P for pulse modulation. The numbers used are between 0 and 9 and they describe the type of transmission. The full decode is given in Ministry publication CAP 46, and the ones that are used in conjunction with NDBs are as follows :

0   The carrier carries no modulation intended to convey information.

1   Information is conveyed, not by modulation but by causing breaks in the carrier wave (or, in technical language, ON/OFF keying of the carrier) and thus producing morse characters.

2   Information is conveyed by ON/OFF keying of the modulating signal and not the carrier wave.

3   Telephony information, e.g. broadcasters where information is conveyed by speech or music.

Thus, information may be conveyed either by means of breaks in the carrier wave (A1) or by breaks in the modulated wave (A2). This makes it imperative to have a control switch which may be used to receive signals with appropriate coding. This switch is usually found on the radio compass control box and is named either CW/RT switch or BFO (beat frequency oscillator) with ON and OFF positions. The first thing necessary to use an NDB is to ascertain its type of emission, otherwise, with CW/RT switch in wrong place the signal may not be heard, and if heard, may not be identified. This information is found on aerad charts as well as in UKAP.

CW position (BFO ON) is used when tuning or identifying a signal which is AO or A1. In both cases the unmodulated carrier is used; to tune the signal you have to be able to hear it, and you have to be able to hear the signal to identify it by its morse. Now, the carrier wave is inaudible. CW/RT switch placed in CW position makes it audible. This is done by means of an oscillator inside the receiver which produces internally a frequency slightly different from the received frequency (e.g. received frequency 400 kHz, internally generated frequency 399 kHz). It then takes the difference between the two (1 kHz in above example) which is now audible. This difference is called the Beat Note.

If the signal emission type is A2 the question of producing a beat note does not arise, since the signal is audio modulated. A2 signal therefore suggests CW/RT switch in RT position (or BFO OFF). The following is the summary of use of the switch.

Station Type	When Tuning the Station	When Identifying the Station
A1	CW position (BFO ON)	CW Position (BFO ON)
AOA1	" " "	" "
AOA2	" " "	RT position (BFO OFF)
A2	RT position (BFO OFF)	RT position (BFO OFF)
A3	" " "	" "

Types of NDBs

1.   Holding and Let-down NDBs: These are short range NDBs, their main purpose being to serve a location. The type of emission is generally A2 and the range according to the station requirements, usually of the order of some 10 nm.

2.   En-Route Navigation Aid beacons. These are installed along airways to mark reporting points and help en-route navigation. The ranges are controlled by operational requirements, generally between 20 to 50 nm. Usually, the type of emission is A2.

3.   Long Range Beacons. These, subject to requirements radiate up to 200 nm during the day; 70 nm at night. Type of emission will generally be A1, although there are a number of A2 NDBs in Europe giving a range of 200 nm.

Factors Affecting NDB Ranges

1.   Night Effect. The range of a long range beacon was given above as 200 nm by day, 70 nm by night. This serious cut down in the range occurs due to the presence of sky waves in the MF band. In this band during the day time sky waves are not present, but at night they affect the radio compass accuracy when they enter the horizontal members of the loop from above. Fig 5.

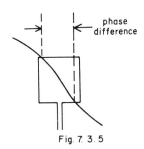

Fig. 7. 3. 5

These waves will start coming from skyward from approximately 70 to 100 nm range upward. If the receiver is also within the range of the ground wave, the two signals will mix and distortion of the null will occur. On an automatic radio compass, this will be indicated by excessive oscillations of the needle. True null is masked and efforts to find a mean over a wavering area can lead to error since the mean is not necessarily the centre of a wavering needle. If the aircraft is only receiving sky waves, there will be a good null but that indication can again be erroneous since there is no guarantee that the reflecting plane is parallel to the earth's surface. In other words, the signal may not arrive from the station direction.

This effect on the radio compass is called Night Effect. It is minimised when using a station in the lower section of the frequency band, thus reducing the incidence of the sky wave. Dusk and dawn are critical periods for radio compass operation — extreme care must be exercised. Also, use a more powerful beacon if you have a choice. Lastly, choose the station nearest to you.

2.   Protection Range. Irrespective of the range that an NDB is capable of producing, the use of an NDB in UK is restricted to ranges promulgated in the UKAP. This is known as "Protection Range" and this restriction is necessary in order to provide reception, free from interference from other NDBs transmitting on the same or similar frequencies.

The main reason for the interference is congestion in the MF band. In Europe (and in America) there is always a heavy demand for channel space in this band, which is already overcrowded with NDBs and broadcasters (not to mention the pirates). In LF and MF (lower end of the frequency spectrum) interference between two similar frequencies can take place quite easily (a common experience while tuning radio stations at night) and the protection is afforded by the Board controlling the allocation of power and frequency to the stations. Protection ranges are based on providing a minimum protection ratio of 3. That is, the ratio of the field strength of the wanted signal to unwanted signal will be at least 3 to 1. Or, when translated in terms of noise, the level of wanted signal will be at least 10 decibels higher than that of unwanted signal within the promulgated range. Some NDBs in UK provide a protection ratio of 5½, that is 15 decibels.

But this protection is guaranteed only during day time. At night:
(a) Sky waves seriously affect the operation of the radio compass due to Night Effect. Further, the E layer gains height at night, increasing the ranges where sky waves could be received. In other words, the sky wave from a distant NDB operating on a similar frequency will extend its range and produce interference within the protection range of your NDB.
(b) Broadcasters and other high powered radio beacons will gain field strength at night. This means that at a given place, where during the day time you would receive wanted signals at a level of at least 10 decibels higher than the unwanted signals, the unwanted signals now increased in field strength will produce higher noise, and the protection minimum will fall.
(c) A forecast of interference free ranges could not be made for night periods since (i) the height of the ionospheric layer is variable; (ii) its density is also variable. Among others, these two factors decide the range of the return of the sky waves.

Therefore, the principle of Protection Ranges breaks down at night and the useful ranges are greatly reduced. Extreme caution should be exercised when using the radio compass at night and it is most important to ensure that correct tuning is done to the exclusion of any unwanted signals.
3.   Night Effect. This is a factor which effectively cuts down your ranges. The topic has already been fully dealt with.
4.   Transmission Power. Increase in power has the direct effect of increasing the ranges produced. However, any ranges produced beyond a range where sky waves will interfere, are limited to day time only. Power increase also results in a better signal to noise ratio, a merit most sought after in conditions of atmospheric static. Finally, for given power output, an unmodulated signal will travel further than an amplitude modulated signal — this explains A2 NDBs are short range and A1 long range NDBs.
5.   Type of Surface.
(a) Attenuation, which is the absorption of radio energy as it travels over the surface of the Earth, varies with differing types of surfaces. Maximum ranges are possible where the propagation is entirely over the sea whereas least ranges are produced on very dry soil.
(b) Mountains and other physical obstructions in the path of the wave between the transmitter and the receiver do not completely black out the reception in MF band. But the peaks and valleys have the effect of reflecting the signals, some of which will arrive at the aerial from entirely wrong directions. Climb to minimise the effect.
(c) Coastal Refraction. A radio wave travels at different speeds over different

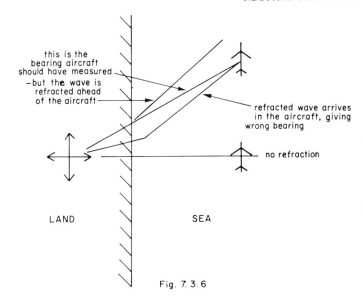

this is the
bearing aircraft
should have measured
–but the wave is
refracted ahead
of the aircraft

refracted wave arrives
in the aircraft, giving
wrong bearing

no refraction

LAND

SEA

Fig. 7. 3. 6

types of surfaces. It speeds up on leaving the coast seaward. If it does not leave the coast at 90°, the wave will bend towards the land mass — a process called Coastal Refraction. See Fig 6.

Errors of the order of 20° will occur when a bearing is taken of any signal which does not leave the coast within approximately 30° to the normal. This factor limits the range of that NDB. To minimise the error, climb or use an NDB which is located right on the coast.

6.   Altitude. NDBs transmit in LF and MF band. In this band the radio waves curve with the surface of the Earth, producing ground waves. Because of this, an aircraft will receive the signals, if otherwise within the range, no matter how low the aircraft is flying. Since the radio waves also propagate in space, aircraft at higher altitudes will also receive signals. Thus, height of an aircraft has no significance as far as ranges are concerned. Height,,however, may become significant, as pointed out above, when flying in mountainous areas or when using coastal NDBs.

7.   Static. This is perhaps the most effective factor in reducing the usable ranges of an NDB. NDB, being an MF aid, will readily pick up any static present in the atmosphere (electrical disturbance, Cb clouds). Static will have the effect of reducing signal to noise ratio, distort the null and if it reaches the level of the signals, the signals will be completely drowned.

Quadrantal Error

This error affects the indication of the compass but does not affect the ranges at which a signal might be received. Incoming signals to an aircraft may be bent by its metallic structure towards the main electric axis — usually the fore and aft line of the aircraft. Greatest errors arise with the wave that strikes across the wing roots, that is 45°, 135° and other points quadrantal, hence the name. A radio compass is usually corrected for this error and any remaining errors are noted in a Q.E. card which should be read together with the radio compass indication. With improved equipment, however, this is an obsolescent problem.

Frequency Band

Frequency band allocated to NDBs (together with broadcasters) is 200 kHz to 1700 kHz. In UK, however, the band generally used is 255 kHz to 455 kHz.

Use of Radio Compass

    (a) En-route navigation aid — position lines
    (b) Fix is obtained when overhead — useful for position reporting on airways.
    (c) Airway flying
    (d) Homing and let-down at destination aerodromes.

Warning

    Radio Compass Equipment (ADF) incorporates no device to give warning of signal failure.

4: Use of Radio Compass

All switches necessary to operate the radio compass are contained in a small control box, installed within easy reach. Having decided on the station to use, switch on the radio compass. This brings in the sense aerial but not the loop aerial. Place CW/RT switch in the appropriate position, and tune in the station frequency. Incoming signal will be audible as the correct frequency is reached. If the control box contains a tuning meter, tune for maximum deflection of the needle. You may need retuning or fine tuning. Identify the signals and place the function switch on to ADF (automatic D/F) position. Now the loop aerial is operative and the indicator needle will swing to indicate relative bearing of the station. From then on the bearing indication will be on a continuous basis, that is, all changes in bearing will be indicated. However, if you are not using the radio compass for homing, you do not require a continuous indication and (in the interest of the equipment) once you have taken a bearing, do not leave it permanently in the ADF position.

Homing

When homing to a station on the radio compass, the point to bear in mind is that the station is directly ahead of you (if not, you want it to be so) and therefore, the radio compass indication is 360° or around 360°. Similarly, if you are leaving a station on the radio compass, the station is directly behind you and the indication you are looking for is 180° or around 180°.

Theoretically, a station may be reached by maintaining 360° on the radio compass, but if there is any wind blowing (and when doesn't it blow?) you will fly a curved path to the station. Further, consequent upon wind, you will be continually

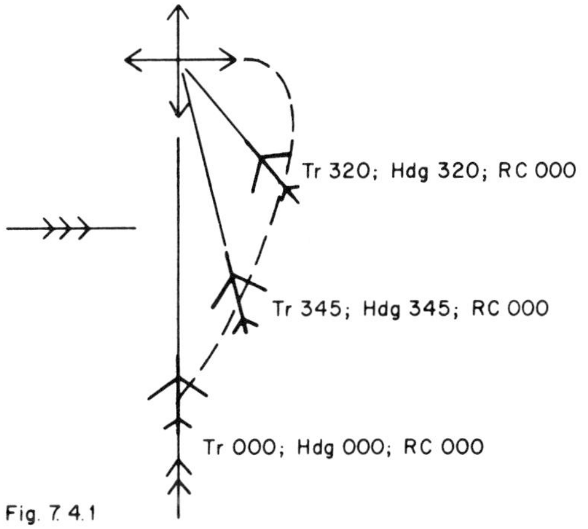

Tr 320; Hdg 320; RC 000

Tr 345; Hdg 345; RC 000

Tr 000; Hdg 000; RC 000

Fig. 7.4.1

altering heading to combat displacement caused by the wind and ultimately you will arrive overhead from a direction facing into the wind. See Fig 1.

The above method of homing, apart from being time-wasting, may not be possible due to track maintenance requirements. In congested areas and on airways, when homing from beacon to beacon you are required to fly notified tracks. This may be done by simply making allowance for the wind velocity right at the start, adjusting as the flight progresses if a wind change is noticed.

In Fig 2, say, the drift is 10°S at the start. Steer 350° to allow for the drift. The radio compass will then read 010° (take away from the nose, add to the indication). As long as 010° remains indicating, you are maintaining the track, and you will arrive overhead. If the indication starts a gradual decrease, you are drifting to starboard, and you must allow for more than 10°S drift.

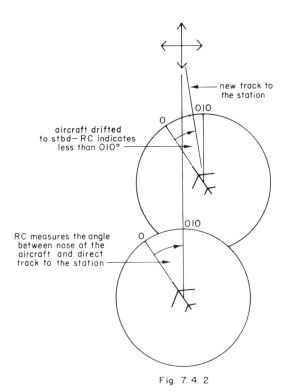

Fig. 7. 4. 2

For the same reasons, if the reading started to increase, you have allowed for too much drift and should alter heading accordingly. After one or two such alterations you will hit on a heading which is right.

If while juggling with headings you managed to get off the track, or if you wish to join a given track, the technique employed is to intercept the desired track at a convenient angle, generally 30° — that is, at an angle of 30° between interception heading and the desired track. To calculate what bearing the radio compass will indicate when you arrive at the track, the rule is:

Add on the nose (i.e. heading), take away from 360;

Take away from the nose, add on 360.

Thus, if you intercept at an angle of 30° and your heading is smaller than your track (that is, you have taken away 30° from the nose) R C indication of 030 will tell you that you are crossing the track.

An aircraft in position 1 in Fig 3 wishes to intercept and follow a track of 070°; drift 5°P. Follow stages 1, 2 and 3 in the diagram.

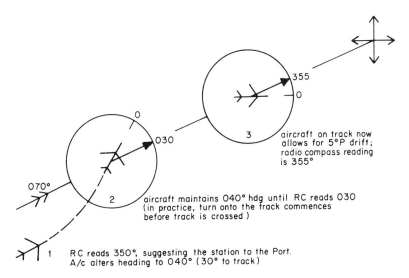

355
0

3   aircraft on track now
allows for 5°P drift;
radio compass reading
is 355°

030

070°

2   aircraft maintains 040° hdg until RC reads 030
(in practice, turn onto the track commences
before track is crossed)

1   RC reads 350°, suggesting the station to the Port.
A/c alters heading to 040° (30° to track)

Fig. 7. 4. 3

Tracking Away from the Station

As the station approaches the radio compass needle starts to oscillate, oscillations increasing as the station gets nearer. As the station is overflown the needle swings through 180° to 6 o'clock position on the indicator and indicates 180° ± drift. Thus, in the illustration in Fig 3, the radio compass will indicate 175 (5° port drift — add on the nose, take away from 180) once the aircraft is past the station. Subsequent handling of the radio compass as regards maintenance and interception of the track is the same as explained above.

Angle of Lead

A turn on to the track must be commenced before the track is reached, otherwise the track will be overshot and a further alteration of heading in the opposite

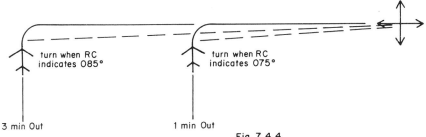

turn when RC
indicates 085°

turn when RC
indicates 075°

3 min Out

1 min Out

Fig. 7. 4. 4

direction will be necessary. This angular allowance that you will make for the turn
is known as the Angle of Lead. It is dependent upon various factors, e.g. aircraft's
TAS which governs its radius of turn, its distance out from the station, wind velocity
and the aircraft's rate of turn. Two points must be noted:

1.   For a given airspeed, the angle of Lead decreases as the distance from the
station increases (Fig 4).

2.   For a given time out from a station, the angle of lead is constant irrespective
of aircraft speed (Fig 5)

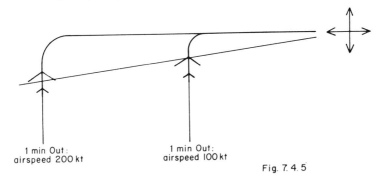

1 min Out:
airspeed 200 kt

1 min Out:
airspeed 100 kt

Fig. 7. 4. 5

5: VHF Omni-directional Radio Range

This equipment, primarily a homing aid but immensely useful as en route navigation aid, is gradually replacing NDBs. Since it operates in the VHF band, it is practically free from static interference and night effect. It utilizes a small aerial, is pleasantly accurate but is restricted broadly to line of sight range. It provides an infinite number of magnetic bearings, called radials.

Principle
The principle of VOR is bearing measurement by phase comparison. The principle is implemented as follows:

Ground transmitters transmit two signals to provide phase comparison between them. One is called the reference signal, the other the variable or directional signal.

Reference Signal
This is an omni-directional carrier wave transmitted on a basic frequency varying between 108 and 118 MHz. Being omni-directional, it produces a constant phase pattern throughout 360°, that is a phase pattern independent of the bearing of the

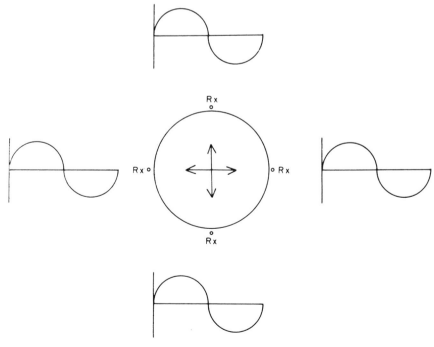

reference signal – same phase in all directions

Fig. 7. 5.1

aircraft from the station. It is frequency modulated at 30 Hz. A frequency de-modulator can detect this 30 Hz signal arriving in the receiver, which could then be utilized as a reference or datum (being a non-directional signal) to measure the phase difference with the directional signal.

Directional Signal

This is again transmitted on basic frequency, but it is so arranged that the resulting polar diagram is a figure of eight. Similarity with Radio Compass? Yes, so far. In the radio compass we had omni-directional polar diagram due to the sense aerial and figure of eight due to the loop aerial. But the similarity ends here. VOR directional signal, that is the figure of eight polar diagram, is a rotating figure, rotating at the rate of 30 Hz. This signal when combined with the reference signal gives us a card-ioid. This cardioid differs from the radio compass cardioid in that this one does not really have a null position. The cardioid, formed of the rotating figure of eight and the omni-directional polar diagram, also rotates at 30 Hz as shown in Fig 2.

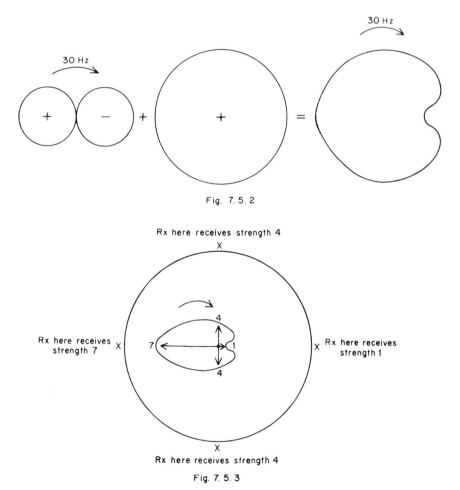

Fig. 7.5.2

Fig. 7.5.3

Now, the power relationship between the reference and the bearing (directional) signal is so adjusted that a different signal strength (amplitude) will be picked up of the same cardioid in different directions, at any given instant. Further, as the cardioid rotates, this amplitude initially picked up will be a fluctuating amplitude, the signal appearing to be a 30 Hz amplitude modulated signal. The effect of this is shown in Fig 3.

Phase Measurement and Bearing Resolution
If the amplitudes in Fig 3 are plotted in graphical form during one complete revolution of the cardioid, the curves plotted will reveal directional characteristics (Fig 4).

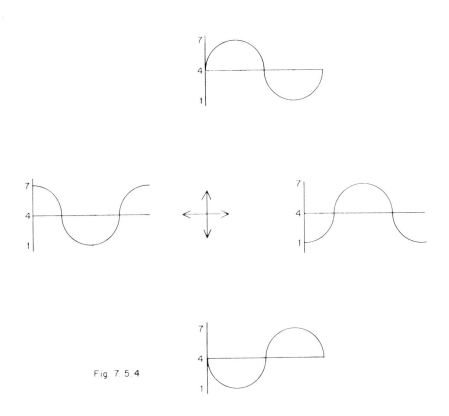

Fig. 7.5.4

Now we have two 30 Hz signals, the reference signal producing a constant phase as shown in Fig 1 and the directional signal producing the directional phase, that is the phase depending on the bearing of the aircraft. It will further be noticed that the receiver north of the station receives the same phase from both signals. We start then from the datum point *Magnetic North of the Station,* where the two signals are in phase (that is, the phase difference is zero). Having established this datum, it follows that a receiver on any other bearing from the station will measure a phase difference between the two signals which will be equal to the magnetic bearing of the aircraft. See Fig 5.

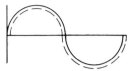

Rx MN: phase difference O

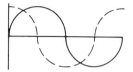

Rx 270(M): phase diff. 270

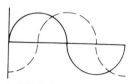

Rx 090 (M): phase diff. 90

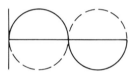

Rx 180 (M): phase diff. 180

Fig. 7. 5. 5

Thus, an aircraft on a bearing of 045(M) will measure a phase difference of 45°; on a bearing of 307(M), it will measure a phase difference of 307° and so on.

A phase comparison meter in the aircraft could display this result in terms of magnetic bearing from the station, or magnetic bearing (track) to the station.

Airborne Equipment

Airborne equipment consists of a special aerial, matched to the frequency band, a receiver which could be used for both VOR and ILS, and an indicator. The indicator consists of three basic components which might all be installed as a single unit or might be installed individually. These components are:

(a) Heading or Bearing Selector;

(b) To-From Indicator and

(c) A left/right deviation indicating needle.

Fig 6 shows the indicator in two separate units.

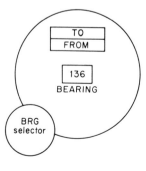

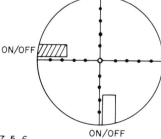

Fig. 7. 5. 6

Omni-Bearing Selector (OBS)

Bearing Selector knob is used to select the VOR radial (magnetic track) on which the pilot wishes to home to the station or home away from the station. When the bearing is selected, the vertical left/right needle is displaced from its central position either to the left·or to the right, unless the aircraft is on that selected radial at that instant.

To/From Indicator

At the same time the TO/FROM indicator will indicate either To or From. This tells you which radial is nearer — the one that is selected (in which case TO will appear) or its reciprocal (FROM will appear). This indication is the result of two factors — the bearing selected and the aircraft's bearing from the station. In the following diagram (Fig 7) all aircraft have selected radial 000.

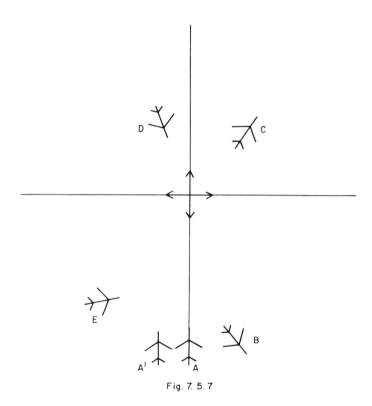

Fig. 7. 5. 7

Aircraft A, B and E will indicate TO, since in all three cases if they wish to reach the station either on magnetic track of 000 or its reciprocal 180, then 000 will take them to the station.

For similar reasoning, aircraft C and D will indicate FROM, suggesting that not the selected bearing 000 but its reciprocal 180 is the nearer radial to the station.

It will be observed that TO/FROM does not mean that with TO indicated an aircraft is heading towards the station (aircraft B and E). It simply indicates which

radial is nearer. TO/FROM display changes when the aircraft either crosses overhead the VOR station or crosses a line 90° to the selected bearing passing
through the station.

Left/Right Indication

The rule is — follow the needle to regain the radial, provided your heading and the
selected bearing are in general agreement.

In Fig 7, aircraft A will have its needle central, since the aircraft is on the
centreline of the radial. If the aircraft was displaced to the A1 position, the needle
will swing to the right, indicating turn right. Aircraft B will have a left turn
indication, since the aircraft's heading is virtually reciprocal of the selected radial,
Aircraft C has 000 selected and its heading is in general agreement, therefore,
its indication will be correct, that is, turn left to intercept the radial. Aircraft D
will have an incorrect indication. Aircraft E will have a turn right indication.
Follow through the following exercise to get a complete picture. (Fig. 8.)

Homing Procedures

1. Select the VOR frequency on the frequency selector box.
2. Switch on.
3. Identify the signal.
4. Select the required radial, using bearing selector control knob.
5. Check TO is indicated. If your heading generally agrees with the selected track,
    follow the needle indication to join the track. In other cases, the question
    whether any alteration of heading is required, and if so whether to the left or
    to the right, is resolved from DR position or with reference to RMI. For
    example, aircraft E in Fig 7 although indicating turn right, will not require any
    alteration of heading to intercept the track. Aircraft B has left turn indicated,
    but in view of its heading and position, a right turn would bring it on the radial
    more quickly.

    If FROM is indicated, the aircraft is more than ± 90° off the required
    track and the pilot either with reference to DR position or the RMI will have
    to manoeuvre the aircraft into a position within ±90° of the track before the
    above procedure is followed.

    Once on the radial, the needle will indicate central position. Now allow for
    the drift. Needle will still indicate central position since the needle is only
    affected by the track and not by the heading.
6. In the final stages the indication will become erratic as the beacon is approached.
    On passing overhead, TO will change to FROM.
7. With FROM indicated and going away from the beacon, needle indications are
    correct so follow the needle.
8. If after passing the station a 180° turn is made, TO/FROM indicator will still
    indicate FROM, but left/right indications must be reversed.

Taking a Bearing

1. Select the frequency of the VOR station.
2. Switch on.
3. Identify the station

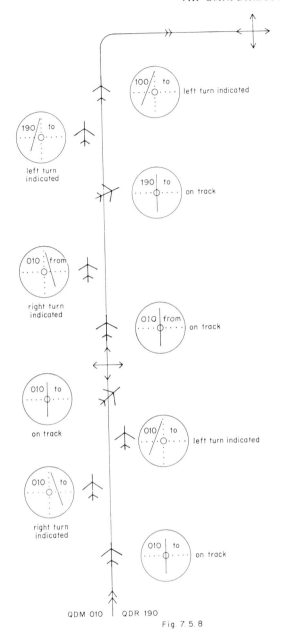

left turn indicated

left turn indicated

on track

right turn indicated

on track

on track

left turn indicated

right turn indicated

on track

QDM 010 | QDR 190

Fig. 7.5.8

4. Turn Bearing Selector control until needle is centralised.
5. Read off the bearing selected. Note TO/FROM indication. If TO is indicated, it is QDM, if FROM is indicated it is QDR.
6. If QDM appears when QDR is required or vice versa, it is just the question of applying 180° to the selected bearing, or alternatively, turning the Bearing Selector knob through 180° until the needle is centralised again. This will have the effect of changing the TO/FROM indication.

Deviation Scale

When the aircraft is not on the selected radial, its angular distance from the radial is estimated by noting the amount of the needle deflection to left or right with reference to a scale marked by dots along the horizontal line on the face of the instrument. A full scale deflection occurs when the aircraft is 10° or more away from the selected radial. The instrument may have a 4 dot scale or 5 dot scale. If it is 4 dot scale, then one dot deflection indicates a deviation of 2½° and so on.

ON/OFF Indicator

An OFF warning signal appears on the face of the instrument in the following circumstances:

1.   Aircraft receiver failure
2.   Indicator failure
3.   When signals received are poor or the aircraft is out of range
4.   Failure of the transmitter.

Frequencies

VOR operates in 108 to 118 MHz band as follows:

Between 108 MHz and 112 MHz, VORs operate on even decimals, that is, 108.2, 110.6, 111.4, etc. Between 112 and 117.9 MHz, it operates on both odd and even decimals, e.g. 112.1, 112.2 and so on. In the near future we may expect to see frequencies spaced at .05 MHz interval, e.g. 112.1, 112.15, 112.2.

Range

Being in the VHF band, the ranges obtainable are optical ranges. In practice, they are slightly better than pure optical ranges, sometimes called quasi-optical ranges. The range obtainable from any VOR for a given aircraft height is calculated from the VHF formula as follows:

$$\text{Range in nm} = 1.20 \left(\sqrt{H_T} + \sqrt{H_R} \right)$$

Where H_T and H_R are respectively height of the transmitter and the height of the receiver in feet. Typical ranges are of the following order:

Aircraft height	1 000 ft	range	30	nm
	5 000		100	
	10 000		120	
	20 000		200	

Satisfactory operation cannot be achieved at distances greater than 200 nm. Care should be exercised when using VOR beyond 100 nm.

Factors Affecting Range

1.   Protection Range and Altitude

VOR operates within a very limited band, and with the number of VORs operating this band is already congested. Therefore, a protection plan similar to NDBs is essential. VORs are protected not only in range but also in altitude. Protection in altitude is required in view of VHF transmission (Fig 9).

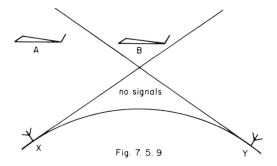

Fig. 7. 5. 9

In the above figure, aircraft A's reception is interference free whereas B, tuned to station X receives signals from both X and Y, transmitting on the same frequency. Frequency allocation to various VOR stations is based on the principle that protection from harmful interference is only afforded for protection ranges and altitudes which are operationally required for each facility. These values are given in the RAC section of the UKAP. No attempt should be made to use VOR outside the prescribed protection altitude and range, or below the line of sight of the facility.

2.   Power of the Transmitter

Power is directly concerned with the range. For example, terminal VORs (TVORs) which operate as a local homing and let-down facility generally transmit at power output of 50 watts and produce ranges of the order of 10–15 nm, whereas more powerful en route VORs produce ranges up to 200 nm. VHF, however, being a line of sight transmission, once maximum operational range has been obtained for a given altitude, any further increase in power output will have no effect in increasing ranges.

3.   Line of Sight Range

This is a factor inherent in VHF transmission and it simply means that larger ranges may be obtained only at higher altitudes. However, as pointed out above, the actual ranges obtained are slightly better than line of sight ranges. This improved performance is due to atmospheric refraction. As the wave gains height and meets decreasing density layers, the wave is refracted towards the medium of high density, i.e. towards lower altitude. In other words, instead of shooting out in a straight-line, it slightly curves with the surface of the earth.

4.   Nature of Terrain

This could be an effective limitation on the ranges received. Intervening high ground, mountains, etc, will block out the transmission. Mountains have the effect of bending and scalloping the waves, giving faulty bearings. Where such effects have been noticed to exist, the details are given the UKAP.

Uses of VOR

1.   Gives visual indication of the aircraft's magnetic track TO and FROM the beacon.
2.   Homing to or away from the beacon.
3.   Let-down
4.   Holding or stacking of aircraft.
5.   Position lines – QDM, QDR.

Accuracy

UK VORs are monitored to an accuracy of 1°. An automatic monitor switches off the facility and switches on a standby facility should the bearing information change by more than one degree. The overall accuracy of indication equals class A bearing, that is ± 2°, for protected altitude and range.

Identification

A morse ident is normally broadcast at least 6 times per minute, that is once every 10 seconds.

In the event of a VOR transmitter developing a fault, an automatic change-over device brings in a reserve transmitter. This changeover may not be complete for several minutes during which period the bearing information radiated might be inaccurate. As a warning to users of these VORs as approach facilities, no ident signal is transmitted until the changeover is complete. Pilots making an approach using VOR should, therefore, monitor the ident signal throughout the approach.

Advantages

1. Visual indication, easy to see.
2. Provides infinite number of tracks.
3. Free from static and night effect.
4. Ranges can be accurately forecasted before the beacons are sited and thus interference can be avoided.
5. Indicator can be used in conjunction with ILS
6. It can be frequency paired with DME to give fixes.
7. Incorporates equipment failure warning device.
8. Channel spacing much better than NDBs.

Disadvantages

1. Left/Right indication does not point to the beacon, thus no continuous bearing information is available unless RMI is used.
2. Only position lines are obtained unless the aircraft is overhead the beacon or the aid is used in conjunction with DME.
3. Irregular terrain in vicinity of the transmitter and mountainous countryside affect accuracy of the bearings.
4. Numerous beacons are required to provide full coverage on airways.

6: Radio Magnetic Indicator (RMI)

It will be remembered that an ADF gives the relative bearing of the station whereas the usual VOR presentation is in terms of Left/Right indication. It would be a great advantage if we had an indicator which would directly read off QDM, the magnetic track to the station. An RMI is just that. It does it by employing a rotatable scale card instead of a fixed one(as in the case of ADF, with its zero datum fixed in line with the nose of the aircraft), and taking advantage of the fact that the needle always points in the direction of the station. In the following illustration an aircraft on heading 030(M) has tuned in to station X which gives a relative bearing of 090° (Fig. 1).

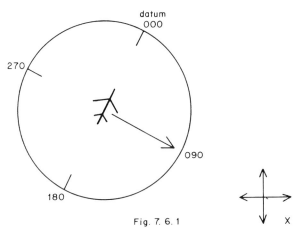

Fig. 7. 6. 1

This reading can be converted to QDM simply by adding aircraft's heading to it:

Rel Brg	090
Plus Hdg(M)	030
QDM	120

Thus, the basic relationship between RB and QDM is the heading. Therefore if we rotated the scale card in the indicator from its present position of 000 against the datum until Hdg(M) appeared against the datum, we would have automatically added heading to the relative bearing and the QDM (120° in above illustration) could be read off (Fig. 2).

In an RMI the scale card is fed with heading information from the aircraft's gyrosyn compass which keeps it in continuous synchronism with the heading being

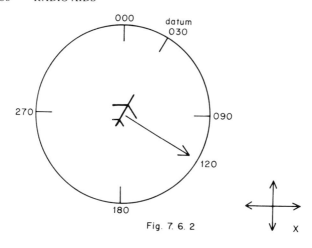

Fig. 7. 6. 2

steered. The pointer, therefore, reads off QDM. Some models of RMI also carry a fixed outer scale against which relative bearing may be read off.

In practice, the RMI does better than giving QDM from just one station. It incorporates two concentric pointers and both these pointers may be energised simultaneously to give QDMs from two different stations – NDBs or VORs. In order to avoid any confusion, the two pointers are of different shapes. The single pointer is coloured red and by convention is called the number one needle. The double pointer is green and is called the number two needle. Thus, if you are tuned to an NDB, you can have presentation either on number one or number two needle by a flick of a switch. Similarly, you can use the indicator to give simultaneously NDB on number one and VOR on number two, or both needles on two NDBs or two VORs. Each has its own control box.

Advantages of RMI
1. QDM/QDR read directly.
2. Using two beacons, instaneous fixes may be obtained.
3. Very useful guide when initially joining a radial for homing on VOR
4. Can be used for homing.

VOR – NDB – RMI Exercises
1. An aircraft bears 220°(T) distance 20 nm from a VOR beacon. Its heading is 055°(M) and variation is 20°W.
    (a) What selected bearing should make the L/R needle central?
    (b) Would the L/R needle indicate turn to left or right if the selected radial was 055?

     (a) Brg Mag = 220°(T) + 20°W (Var)
                 = 240
     ∴ QDM = 240 – 180
                 = 060 which, when selected will make L/R needle central.
Also, its reciprocal, 240 will make the needle central.

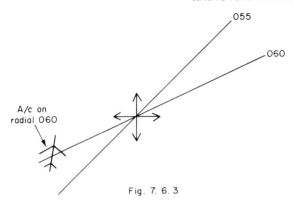

Fig. 7. 6. 3

∴ 060 TO and 240 FROM

(b) If 055 was selected, the indication will be Turn Right – See Fig 3.

2.   An aircraft is heading 060°(T), tracking on a VOR radial 078 TO the station. Variation 10°W. What should ADF read on beacon sited at VOR station?

Hdg(M) = 060°(T) + 10°W

= 070°(M)

A/c's track is 078°(M) ∴ aircraft has 8° starboard drift.

∴ NDB will read 360 + 8

= 008°

3.   An aircraft is heading 060°(T). Variation is 10°E. An NDB bears 200°(R). Show by means of a sketch how this information would appear on the face of RMI.

RB   = 200

Hdg(M) = 050

QDM   250   (See Fig. 4)

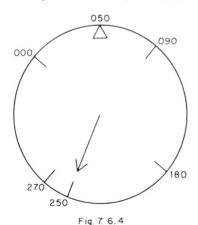

Fig. 7. 6. 4

4.   An aircraft is flying a constant heading with 8°P drift and is making good a track parallel to the centre line of an airway, but 5 nm off to the left of the centre line. Estimate the ADF reading of an NDB sited on the centre line of the airway, but 30 nm ahead.

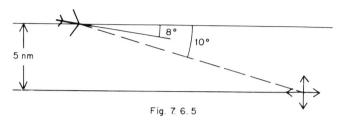

Fig. 7. 6. 5

In Fig. 5, the angle between the aircraft's track and the radio station is worked out using one in sixty rule.

$$\text{Tr Error} = \frac{\text{Dist off x 60}}{\text{dist to go}} = \frac{5 \times 60}{30}$$
$$= 10°$$

The nose of the aircraft is offset to the right (to compensate for port drift) by 8°. Therefore, the angle between the nose of the aircraft and the NDB

$$= 10 - 8$$
$$= 2°$$

The radio compass will read 002°

7: Ground DF; Fan Markers

A ground station can be equipped for taking a bearing of an aircraft on that
aircraft's transmission. In earlier days such service operated in MF, HF and VHF
bands. In UK this service now only operates in the VHF band, that is, the frequency
band of 118 to 136 MHz. Service in other bands still exists in certain parts of the
world and where applicable, relevant information such as frequency in use, range,
accuracy is found in the Aerad Flight Guide.

When the service is required the procedure is to call up the station on
appropriate R/T frequency (found in RAC section of the UKAP) and request
any of the following:
QDM, QUJ, QTE, QDR. If a series of bearings or headings to steer are required, the
appropriate code is QDL.

The station will pass back the information verbally, together with his
classification of the bearing, as follows:

Class A — accurate to $\pm 2^{\circ}$
Class B — accurate to $\pm 5^{\circ}$
Class C — accurate to $\pm 10^{\circ}$

A station can refuse to give bearings if the conditions are poor or the bearings
do not fall within the classified limits of the station but it must give its reason for
the refusal.

There are many automatic VDF stations whose purpose is purely to assist in
radar identification for ATC purposes. As these installations do not provide any
other service, they are not promulgated in the UKAP. Where a station does provide
a "Homer" service, the information is given in the Air Pilot, and generally, the
bearing accuracy is not better than class B. As far as automatic VDF stations are
concerned, they are not to be used as en route navigation aids except in
emergency.

Automatic stations (Homers as well as those established for radar ident
purposes) utilise a cathode ray tube for bearing measurements. These tubes are
calibrated through 360° and a trace of the aircraft's transmission appears on the
face of the tube, the bearing being read off against the scale. The main advantage
here is that only a very short transmission is required — just long enough to read
off the bearing.

Range is limited to the line of sight and may be calculated for a given height
using the VHF formula. Generally, it is 100 nm at 10 000 ft.

Fan Markers

These transmit a narrow vertical fan shaped radio beam from a ground transmitter.
All fan markers operate on one single frequency, 75 MHz. Because of the shape of

the transmission, they cannot be heard unless the aircraft is in the fan and therefore cannot be used as directional aids. They have two main uses — they are used to mark reporting points on airways and they are also used in conjunction with ILS to provide precision approach facility.

On airways, the transmission goes up to 15 000 ft. and is identified by high pitch sound (3 000 cps) giving out identification in morse. Further, the white light in the airborne installation glows to identify it visually while in the fan. Because of its width at 15 000 ft, if accurate navigation is required, time entering and leaving the fan should be noted and the mean time taken for the fix.

Its use in conjunction with ILS is described in the chapter on ILS.

8: Consol

Consol is a long range navigation aid which operates in the MF band. Ground installation consists of a transmitter and three aerials sited in a straight line. Transmitted signals are received in the receiver and heard in the earphones as dots and dashes. The type of emission is A1 and to receive such signals the aircraft only requires a CW receiver, operating in 200 – 400 kHz frequency band. The bearing resultant from dot and dash count is plotted on a special consol chart which has these counts printed on it. There will be more than one position line on the chart representing the same count, but if the aircraft is a reasonable distance away from the transmitter this will cause no ambiguity. Should any ambiguity arise (due to closeness to the station, uncertainty of position, etc) it is resolved by taking a loop bearing on the transmitter. As an alternate to the printed chart, CAP 59 gives several tables from which possible great circle bearings for a given count may be extracted. When using these tables, if the bearings are plotted on a Mercator's projection, conversion angle must be applied.

Principle

Current from a common transmitter is fed to three aerials, installed in a straight line and three wavelengths apart from each other. At the start, with reference to the transmission phase of the centre aerial B (Fig. 1), aerial A

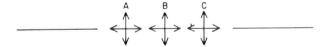

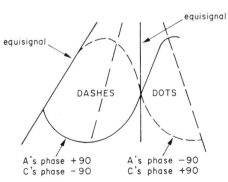

A's phase +90
C's phase – 90

A's phase –90
C's phase +90

Fig. 7. 8. 1

transmits a signal which is +90° in phase, and aerial C −90° in phase. The phases of the outer aerials are then reversed, that is, A transmits at −90° and C at +90° with reference to B. This interchanging of phase between outer aerials and centre aerial produces a transmission lobe pattern as shown in Fig 1.

The resultant pattern of the equisignals produced right round the transmitter is shown in Fig 2.

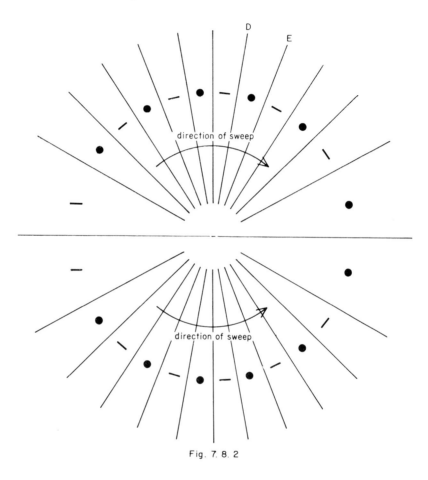

Fig. 7. 8. 2

The pattern is made up of sectors of alternating dots and dashes, separated by lines of equisignals, that is, the bearing where the operator would hear a continuous signal instead of dot or dash. There are eleven such equisignals on either side of the base line. Sectors normal to the base line are approximately 10° wide and they open up to approximately 15° − 20° in direction along the base line. Two sectors on either side of the base line where continuous dots or dashes are received cannot be used.

These equisignal lines lie on known bearings from the station. Therefore, whenever an aircraft passes through one of these equisignals, it can obtain a bearing. It would, however, be most inconvenient if the aircraft had to wait until the next equisignal line is crossed, which in some cases may be as far as 200 miles away.

Therefore, instead of moving the aircraft to an equisignal line, the equisignal lines are made to move to the aircraft. The direction in which the equisignals move is called the direction of sweep and is shown in Fig 2.

As the sweep takes place, all lines of equisignals progressively move in the direction shown until they occupy the position previously occupied by their immediate neighbours. For example, D in Fig 2 will progressively move towards E and will occupy E's position in a given time, usually 30 or 60 seconds. The transmission stops at this stage, and all equisignal lines are brought back to their original positions to start a new cycle.

How does this all help us to get a bearing? Follow this illustration:

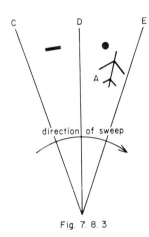

Fig. 7. 8. 3

As the cycle commences, D will progressively move in the direction of E to occupy E's position in say, 60 seconds. During that time, 60 dot characters will be transmitted, DE being a dot sector. If an aircraft A was say two thirds of the way from D, then there are 40 dots between the aircraft and equisignal D, which the operator will count as the sweep progresses. Equisignal will then arrive. As the equisignal goes past the aircraft (to reach E) characters from sector C–D (dashes) will be heard. When the operator has counted 20 such dashes, the equisignal will have reached E and the cycle stops.

Aircraft's count of 40 dots and 20 dashes tells that:
1. It is in dots sectors, since dots were heard first.
2. That it is two thirds of the way (40 : 60) from D to E.

A bearing which is two thirds of the way; thus a bearing of any proportion of 60 is determinable, since the bearings of two equisignals are known. Therefore, the system can be used to provide bearing information.

Taking a Consol Count
1. Tune the receiver to correct frequency. CW/RT switch to CW (BFO on). A narrow band receiver is advantageous from the accuracy and range point of view, since the frequency band occupied by a consol signal is small.
2. Automatic Gain Control – off.
3. Identify the station.

4.   If necessary, take an ADF bearing on a long dash which is transmitted prior to the sweep cycle for this purpose.

5.   Start counting as soon as the signals are heard.

6.   Note time when equisignal is heard. This is the time of the position line.

7.   Add up both the counts (of dots and dashes). These, in normal circumstances will not add up to 60, since some characters are invariably lost in the equisignal. Suppose the count was as follows:

40 dots, equisignal, 16 dashes. 4 symbols were lost in the count during the equisignal. Here we will presume that of these 4, the number of dots lost was 2, and the number of dashes 2. The dot count is then 42 dots, which is plotted.

Example: equisignal, 56 dots.

Here, 4 characters are lost — attribute 2 to dots and 2 to dashes. Therefore, the count to plot is 2 dashes.

Example: 54 dots, equisignal.

Six characters are lost, 3 dots and 3 dashes. Therefore, the count to plot is 54 + 3 = 57 dots.

Usable Sectors

1.   Very close to the station, that is 15 – 20 nm, the consol count is not clearly defined and therefore cannot be used.

2.   Approximately 15 to 20° either side of the base line there is a continuous dot or dash pattern, and consol cannot be used in these areas.

3.   When close to the station – 30 to 40 miles – the pattern is clear but the sector width is very small. Hence an aircraft travelling in direction normal to the equisignal line may race the count.

4.   Between 350 and 450 miles from the station both ground and sky waves are received at night. These give erroneous readings. Beyond that range, sky waves only are received, and the count is correct again.

Range

	Flat Land	Sea	
Day	700	1000	on 90% of occasions
Night	1200	1200	on 95% of occasions

Accuracy

1.   Accuracy depends on the bearing of the aircraft from the station. The error is minimum on the normal to the line of the aerials, twice the minimum value at 60° to normal and 20 times the value of the minimum in the direction of the line of the aerials.

2.   Minimum errors at Normal

Day: Land – 4 characters or 2/3°;

Sea – 2 characters or 1/3°

Night: Land and Sea – between range 350 and 450 miles : 15 characters or 2½°

Beyond 600 miles – 4 to 6 characters or 2/3° to 1°

(Thus, accuracy improves as range increases).

Checking Accuracy
If the total count is more than 59 or less than 52, the accuracy of the count is suspect, and the count should be discarded.

Advantages of the System
1. No special equipment required in the aircraft.
2. Simple to use.
3. Very long ranges available.
4. Ground equipment easy to maintain.

Disadvantages
1. Simultaneous fixes cannot be obtained.
2. Taking a position line is a slow process — takes about a minute to identify and count, and further time wasted if you tuned in in the middle of a sweep when you should wait for a new sweep to start.
3. Counting of signal requires concentrated effort — when you see your navigator tapping his pencil on the table you would know what he is doing.
4. Not suitable as a homing aid.
5. Being an MF aid, it suffers from static.

Extract from Consol Tables — CAP 59
Bushmills Consol station — DOT SECTORS

Count of dots — True Bearing from Station

Count of dots	True Bearing from Station								
21	027·0	053·4	098·5	125·7	151·9	185·0	255·4	288·6	314·7 341·9
	*	*	*	*	*	*	*	*	*
30	—	—	096·2	123·8	149·8	181·8	258·7	290·6	316·6 344·2

Where the bearing is not available, the count is not plottable. In other cases, a bearing nearest to the aircraft's DR bearing (or bearing given by radio compass) is selected and plotted from the station. Appendix III in CAP 59 gives the values of conversion angles for aircraft in different positions, very handy indeed when using a Mercator Chart.

9: Instrument Landing System (ILS)

This aid is tremendously popular as the pilot has a simple instrument in front of him which indicates his position relative to the centre-line of the runway on approach, as well as relative to the glide path or descent angle. Accurately flown, he will arrive over the threshold at the optimum touch down point without any assistance from ground controllers and whatever the weather. Pointer movements are large for small deviations from the centre-line of the glide path, and the information is presented on a continuous basis.

Ground Equipment
Ground transmission system consists of :
1.   the Localiser Transmitter
2.   the Glide Path Transmitter, and
3.   two or three Marker Beacons
All transmitters are permanently installed and serve only one given runway.

The Localiser Transmitter
This transmitter produces a runway centre-line and provides directional inform-ation to an aircraft in terms of left/right deviation of the needle. The aerial is in line with the runway centre-line and is placed about 1 000 feet from the up wind end of the runway it serves. It transmits two lobes of radiations along the runway and beyond in the approach direction. This transmission takes place on the same frequency, the ILS frequency as given in the UKAP and on navigational charts, and the lobes are prevented from intermixing by means of different modulations. That lobe on the right hand side of the runway as seen by the pilot on approach is modulated by an 150 Hz note and the sector it forms is called the Blue sector. See Fig.1

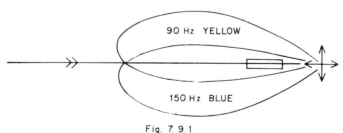

90 Hz   YELLOW

150 Hz   BLUE

Fig. 7. 9. 1

The lobe on the left hand side is modulated by a 90 Hz note and the sector formed by it is called the Yellow sector. An aircraft flying to the left of the centre-line will now receive more of the 90 Hz signal and relatively less of the 150 Hz modulation. This excess of 90 modulation will place the needle to indicate a right hand turn. Similarly, aircraft flying to the right hand side of the centre line will have an excess of 150 Hz modulation the needle indicating left hand turn. At midway between the two modulations there will be one point where the modulation depth due to both 90 Hz and 150 Hz modulations will be equal. This is where there will be no deflection of the needle — indicating that the aircraft is on the centre-line. This centre-line is arranged to be produced in the correct direction. The needle affected is the vertical needle — the same one used for VOR. As far as the deviation scale is concerned, the beam produced is 5° wide; therefore, maximum deflection of the needle occurs when the aircraft is 2½° or more off the centre-line. Thus, in a 4-dot indicator, one dot will represent a deviation of approximately .6°

On the ILS/VOR indicator, blue and yellow sectors are marked, but blue appears on the left hand side and the yellow on the right hand side. Thus, the needle tells you which way to turn (needle to left, go left, i.e. follow the needle) and also which sector you are in when not on the centre-line. Follow the illustrations in Fig 2.

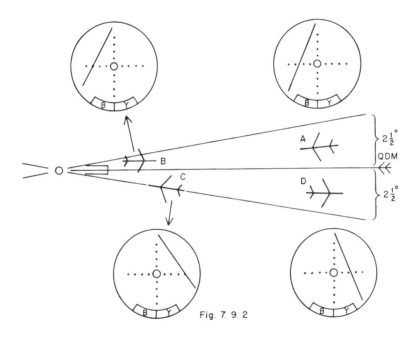

Fig. 7. 9. 2

Aircraft A is in Blue sector, and needle indicates left turn

Aircraft B is in Blue sector, and needle indicates left turn. Thus, the indication is given according to the sector the aircraft is in, not according to its heading. In this case aircraft B is on the right hand side of the centre-line and on reciprocal heading, therefore it will have to <u>reverse</u> the indication. Same applies to aircraft D which is on the left hand side (or yellow sector) with reciprocal heading. Its turn right indication is reversed if it wishes to regain the centre-line. In all cases notice that

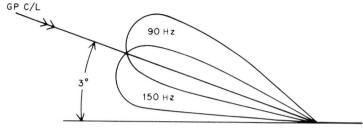

Fig. 7. 9. 3

the needle indicates the sector the aircraft is in and "follow the needle" rule applies when making an approach. Reverse the indication if going away on the QDR.

Glide Path Transmitter
This aerial is situated to one side of the runway, about 350 feet from it near the down wind end and it is beamed in the vertical plane in two similar patterns. The upper lobe has 90 Hz modulation, the lower 150 Hz. The line along which the two modulations are equal in depth defines the centre line of the glide slope. It is generally 3° from the horizontal (Fig 3) but it could be adjusted to suit particular local conditions.

If the aircraft is below the glide path, the horizontal needle moves upwards, indicating that the aircraft should fly up to regain the glide path. This indication will occur irrespective of the heading, that is whether the aircraft is on QDM or QDR. Therefore, a departing aircraft wishing to climb along the centre line will obey the needle, just as much as an approaching aircraft making a descent.

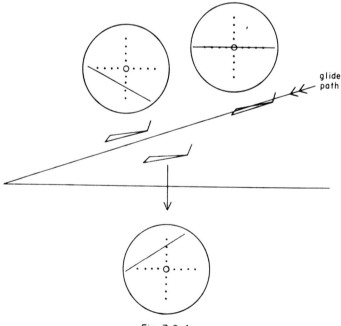

Fig. 7. 9. 4

If the aircraft is above the glide path, the needle will move downward. Full deflection occurs as follows:

Aircraft above the glide path, a 0.7° deviation will cause full deflection. In a 4-dot indication one dot will represent approximately .17 of a degree.

Aircraft below the glide path, a 0.7° deviation will cause full deflection, one in four dots representing a deviation of approximately .17°. For this reason, and also for the fact that an ILS path centre-line could bend, the law says that a 2 dot fly up indication out of 4 dots or 2½ dot fly up indication out of 5 dots (that is, half the full scale deflection) is to be regarded as the maximum safe deviation below the glide path. On any indication beyond this, an immediate climb must|be instituted. Glide path indications are shown in Fig. 4.

Combined Indication

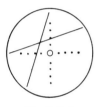

Fig. 7. 9. 5

On QDM the indication is – turn left and climb
On QDR the indication is – turn right and climb.

Marker Beacons

Usually two, sometimes three marker beacons are installed along the extended centre-line to give range indication on approach. This enables the pilot to check his height as he passes each marker. These are the fan markers referred to earlier and all operate on a single frequency of 75 MHz. When operating in conjunction with ILS they radiate a fan pattern up to a height of approximately 3 000 feet. The marker farthest from the touch down point is placed approximately 4 nm from the touch down point and is called the Outer Marker. It transmits a low pitch (400 cycle modulation) signal which identifies in morse as well as visually on the pilot's panel. When crossing the beacon, dashes are heard, the rate being two per second, and simultaneously the Blue marker light will flash dashes at the same rate.

The next marker on the approach path is called the Middle marker, placed approximately 3 500 feet from the touch down point. It transmits a series of alternate dots and dashes at a higher pitch (1 300 Hz) which are heard in the earphones and also seen on the Amber marker light.

The marker nearest to the end of the runway is called the Inner marker. It transmits six high pitched dots (3 000 Hz) per second, and the White marker light flashes. This is the same light which flashes the marker code when passing over a fan marker on airways. This marker is not usually installed in UK in conjunction with ILS.

The UK Air Pilot gives details of the actual distances involved in the case of the above markers for each station having an ILS facility. It also gives the actual glide slope angle, the distance of the localiser from the end of the runway and the glide path transmitter frequency (this is for information only; the pilot is not concerned with this frequency). ILS approach charts for aerodromes concerned give a pictorial presentation of the ILS flight pattern and give a minimum height for aircraft at various markers.

Problems often occur in the examinations requiring calculation of height of an aircraft at various distances from the touch down point. These are solved using one in sixty rule.

Example

What will be approximate height of an aircraft on ILS when at 2 nm range?

$$\text{Track Error (glide path angle)} = \frac{60 \times \text{Distance off (height in feet)}}{\text{Distance to go (in feet)}}$$

In the absence of further information, a 3° glide path angle may be presumed.

$$3 = \frac{60 \times \text{height}}{2 \times 6\,080}$$

$$\frac{3 \times 2 \times 6\,080}{60} = \text{height}$$

$$\text{Height} = 608 \text{ ft}$$

Frequencies

Localiser: 108.1 to 111.9 MHz odd decimals only (even decimals are allotted to VOR). Localiser frequency is the published ILS frequency, therefore to tune for ILS, this frequency is tuned.

Glide Path: glide path operates in frequency band 332.6 MHz to 335.4 MHz. Pilot does not tune this. Localiser and glide path work as matched pair, that is, they are frequency paired so that on selecting the localiser frequency, the appropriate glide path frequency is automatically selected.

Marker: this is standard equipment operating on 75 MHz frequency and must be switched on separately.

Identification

The station identifies in morse once every ten seconds on localiser transmission. In emergency, speech transmission can be made by the air traffic controller on this frequency.

Ranges

The localiser can produce ranges up to 75 nm. However, if this is being used as a navigation aid, it should be noted that the localiser signals are protected from interference only out to a range of 25 nm at an altitude of 6 250 feet along the on-course line. As for accuracy, they are only checked up to 10 nm. Remember these figures for examination purposes even if you do not use it as navigation aid.

Localiser Needle

This needle shows centre position when:
(a) no signals are being received, or
(b) when the aircraft is on the centre-line.

Monitoring

Both localiser and glide path transmissions are continuously monitored and in the following instances the monitor will automatically switch off the equipment and bring in a standby transmitter

(a) when the on-course line shifts by 1/3rd of a degree or the glide path shifts by 1/10th of a degree;

(b) when power is reduced by half of the normal power;

(c) when the course sector width changes by more than 20% or the glide path sector changes by more than 10%.

ILS Reference Point

The ILS reference point is the optimum point of touch down. It is generally not less than 500 feet from the approach end of the runway. It may be beyond 500 ft up to 1 000 ft if the local conditions so require.

ICAO Weather Categories

ILS systems are classified according to performance capability in three categories as follows:

Category 1: Operation down to a decision height of 200 ft (60 m) with a visibility of more than 800 m (2 600 ft).

Category 2: Operations down to decision heights between 200 ft and 100 ft (60 m and 30 m) with visibility between 800 m and 400 m (2 600 ft and 1 300 ft).

Category 3a: Operation down to and along the runway with a minimum external visibility, during the final landing phase, of 200 m (700 ft).

Category 3b: Operation down to and along the runway with a visibility of 50 m (150 ft) which is sufficient only for visual taxying.

Category 3c: Operation down to and along the runway without external visibility.

ON/OFF Warning Signal

ILS indicators normally incorporate two on/off warning windows on the face of the indicator, one in conjunction with the localiser needle and the other with the glide path needle. The OFF flag will appear in the appropriate window in one of the following circumstances:

(a) in case of malfunctioning of the equipment – airborne or ground installation;

(b) when out of range or the received signals are poor.

Back Beam

Usually, there is a certain amount of overspill of radiation behind the localiser aerial, where signals would be received. This beam is not normally used. Where the back beam is strong enough to be used, the colour pattern reverses.

New Equipment

The UK is in the process of introducing new ILS equipment at present which will be used in conjunction with ILS categories II and III. It is more accurate and is less susceptible to bending of on-course beams, thus more reliable. Further, it produces a greater service area where the signals will be received (35° either side of the centre line of the approach runway). Outside this sector, and behind the localiser transmitter, the back beam is still present, where weak transmission of reversed signals can be received. These, again, are not for general use.

10: Basic Radar

The word Radar was coined from the term "RAdio Detection And Ranging". The present day function of radar is not limited to detection and ranging only, neither is the function of detection and ranging achieved only by means of radar. In these fields radio and radar overlap, each being capable of performing the other's task and the only distinguishing feature between the two appears to be the nature of the transmission of the electromagnetic waves. Radio waves are of a continuous nature; radar waves are broken waves, transmitted in short bursts of energy, the bursts so emitted being known as pulses. Fig 1.

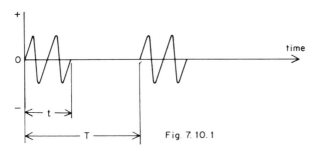

Fig. 7. 10. 1

In Fig 1, the distance 't' is called the "Pulse Width". Distance "T" is the time interval between two pulses. This is known as "Pulse Recurrence Period", abbreviated PRP. Number of pulses transmitted in one second is called the "Pulse Recurrence Frequency" – PRF for short.

To locate an object at a distance, we require information as to the object's distance and its direction from us. Pulse technique radar is ideally suited for this function, as shown below.

Distance Measurement

For distance measurement, radar utilises what is called the Echo Principle. To illustrate this principle, we must have a boy standing in front of a tall cliff, shouting. In due course he will hear his echo – sound waves reflected by the cliff and received in the boy's ears. If the boy had a stop watch and had timed the time interval between the start of the shout and the start of the received echo, he could have calculated the distance of the cliff. Let us say that the time interval was 12 seconds. Sound waves travel at speed of 1 118 feet per second at surface level – call it 1 100 feet. We know that the time of 12 seconds represents the distance to the cliff and back, or, actual distance to the cliff is only 6 seconds. Then, the distance

$$= \quad \frac{1\ 100 \times 12}{2}$$

$$= \quad 6\ 600\ \text{feet}$$

Radar finds the distance of an object by exactly the same principle, except that the time measurements involved are extremely minute indeed. If, for example a pulse is transmitted to an object, 1 500 metres away, the time taken for the pulse to travel to the object and return is:

$$\frac{1\ 500 \times 2}{300\ 000\ 000} \quad \text{or}$$

100 000th of a second. Such timing must essentially be done electronically and later in the chapter we will see how a Cathode Ray Tube could be utilised to do just this. Time units employed are milliseconds (m sec) and microseconds (μ sec) which are one-thousandth of a second and one-millionth of a second respectively.

Going back to the deserted boy, it must be appreciated that he must not shout continuously. Otherwise, his echo will be swamped in his own noise and even if he could distinguish the echo he will not be able to relate a particular part of the echo to a particular part of the shout for timing purposes. This is where pulse technique comes in. A very short pulse is sent out directed towards the object, and the next one is not transmitted until the first one returns. Another way of saying this is that the PRF of transmission determines the maximum range of the equipment. Let us suppose we wish to have an equipment capable of measuring distances up to 185 kilometres. The pulse must travel 185 x 2 kilometres before the next pulse goes out.

$$\text{Time taken to travel} \quad = \quad \frac{185 \times 2 \times 1\ 000 \times 1\ 000\ 000}{300\ 000\ 000}$$

$$= \quad \frac{3\ 700}{3} \quad \text{or} \quad 1\ 233\ \mu\ \text{sec}$$

The second pulse can go out 1 233 μ secs after the first pulse. Thus, the number of pulses that could be transmitted at maximum in one second

$$= \quad \frac{1\ 000\ 000}{1\ 233}$$

$$= \quad 811\cdot0 \quad - \text{Maximum PRF.}$$

In the same way as PRF determines the maximum distance, the pulse width decides the minimum range. The leading edge of the pulse must not arrive back in the receiver while the trailing edge is still in the process of leaving. In fact, the shortest range that could be measured is the distance equivalent to half the pulse width. Pulse width can be kept smaller by the use of a shorter wavelength which explains why some radar works on very high frequencies. There is another reason for keeping pulse width as small as possible: objects reflect those waves which are comparable to their own size. Thus, to reflect very small objects, the wavelength must be very short — GCA uses 3 cm wavelength on precision approach. Further, if two objects are close enough to be covered by one single pulse, both the objects will appear as a single object on the screen. A pulse of smaller width might be able to separate them, giving better definition.

Measurement of Direction

The principle used to measure direction is commonly called the "Searchlight Principle". A narrow rotating radar beam is used. If the beam starts from a known direction (say true north) and rotates at a known speed, then when it produces an echo from a reflecting object, the direction which the beam was facing at that instant can be determined. Under this principle, a 360° azimuth scanning or a limited angular scanning in the elevation plane are possible. The beam must be a narrow one for better definition, otherwise, as with the distance measurements, the beam will hit two objects at the same time and produce one single echo.

Primary and Secondary Radar

The elements outlined above constitute what is known as Primary Radar. A transmitter transmits a train of pulses directed towards an object. The object reflects the pulses back. Some of these reflected pulses will be received back at the point of transmission. These will give an indication of the object's range and bearing. In the process no co-operation whatsoever is required of the reflecting object. In fact, the object need not know that it was reflecting radar energy. This type of radar contrasts with the other type, called "Secondary Radar". This type of radar works only with the co-operation of the object. Both the ground as well as the aircraft equipment, consists of a transmitter and a receiver. The ground transmitter transmits pulses which are received in the aircraft receiver (or it may be the other way round as with DME). The aircraft receiver then instructs its transmitter to reply to the ground. Thus, the reflecting object must co-operate for secondary radar to work. There are certain advantages with this system over primary radar. These are dealt with later in the chapter on DME.

Cathode Ray Tube – CRT

The purpose of the CRT is to display visually the radar signals that are reflected by the objects. Further, by incorporating a time base, distance and bearing (or other data for which the CRT is being used) can be determined. The CRTs are classified according to the way in which focussing and deflection are achieved.

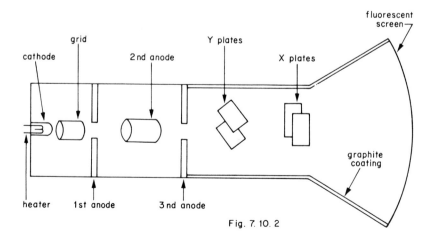

Fig. 7. 10. 2

There are three such classes: Electrostatic CRT having electrostatic focussing and deflection devices, Electromagnetic CRT having electromagnetic focussing and deflection, and lastly a combined CRT which has electrostatic focussing and electromagnetic deflection. For the purpose of the present study the electrostatic CRT is described below.

The main components of a CRT are : a Cathode, a Grid, three anodes and two pairs of deflecting plates. Fig 2.

Cathode

Cathode consists of a small cylinder one end of which is coated with a small quantity of barium or other similar oxide. The cylinder covers a low voltage heater which heats the barium oxide. Barium oxide when heated emits electrons.

Grid

This is a metal cylinder and surrounds the cathode. Its purpose is to catch as many electrons as possible emitting from the cathode and direct them in a narrow beam towards the anodes. This is done by applying a potential which is negative with respect to the potential of the cathode. Electrons are negative charges and when they find that the walls of the grid are more negative than they are, they tend to be repelled from the wall and pass through the grid in a narrow beam at the centre. By varying the grid potential we can control the number of electrons passing through the grid. This is the brilliance control.

Anode System

As soon as the electrons are emitted from the cathode, the cathode becomes positive relative to the electrons and the most natural thing would be for the electrons to return to the cathode. This must be prevented; the electrons are in fact encouraged to travel forward to the screen by means of three anodes. First and third anodes have the shapes of plates while the second anode has the shape of a cylinder. Fig 3.

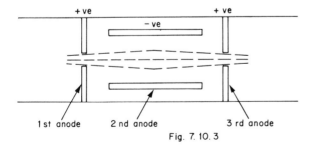

1 st anode   2 nd anode   3 rd anode

Fig. 7. 10. 3

First and third anodes are positive, second anode is negative. The first anode attracts the electrons which pass through its centre and then start diverging. This tendency to diverge is checked at the second anode (being negative) and the electrons deflect back and pass through the third anode under the attraction of positive potential. When they hit the fluorescent coated screen they show up as a glow. How sharp the glow is depends on how much divergence took place at the second anode. The potential of the second anode can be varied to give different sharpness – this is focussing control. As to where on the screen the electrons will hit depends on the potential of X and Y plates.

X and Y plates

The set of plates nearest to the third anode is called the Y plates. As the electrons pass through the pair of Y plates, if, say, the top plate is positive and the bottom plate is negative, the beam will be deflected upward towards the top of the plates. This means that the beam will hit at the top of the tube, the Y axis. If we had the bottom plate positive initially and varied the potential gradually until the top plate became positive, the beam hitting the screen during this time would appear to move from the bottom of the tube towards the top. If the potential was varied quickly enough we would only be able to see a continuous vertical trace.

Similarly, X plates produce a trace in the X axis or horizontally.

These traces are the basis for forming time bases to measure distances. For example, earlier in the chapter we calculated that a radio wave will travel 370 km in 1 233 μ sec. If we move the spot on the CRT so that it takes 1 233 μ sec to travel from one end of the tube to the other, what we have done is to produce a scale along which the distance of the echo could be measured. Fig 4.

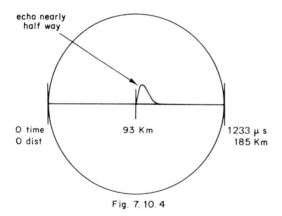

Fig. 7. 10. 4

In Fig 4 the time base is produced by X plates, and the echo is presented through Y plates. The time base so produced may be calibrated to read in terms of micro-seconds or distance, knowing that the distance from one end of the tube to another in this case is 185 km. The time base may then be calibrated by pips at convenient distances. Further, for more accurate reading, a small portion of the time base where the signal appears may be exploded to a larger scale. This is done by "strobing" the signal, a process you will read about later in Loran.

It will be appreciated that in order to produce the time base, the voltage (that is, potential) to the plates must be varied progressively and systematically. The voltage that has this effect is called "Saw-tooth" voltage or waveform. This is shown in Fig 5.

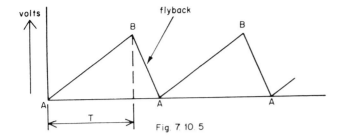

Fig. 7.10.5

In the above figure, the voltage starting at A is increased progressively and steadily to the value of B in time T. In this example, the value of T is 1 233 μ secs. The voltage AB is called the sweep voltage and the trace is visible. Once the beam reaches the opposite end, it must be brought back to the other end to start a new cycle. Certain time is lost as the voltage falls back to the original value. This part of the voltage change is called the "Flyback" voltage, and it is, in general, not visible.

In practice, radar transmitters incorporate a master circuit. As the master instructs the transmitter to transmit, it simultaneously triggers the time base and the cycle commences. So the time base and echo remain in synchronism.

Gain Control
Atmospherics and noises set up by electrical disturbances within the receiver or caused by nearby equipment manage to get on to the radar screen. These tiny signals travel on to the CRT via Y plates and show up on the screen as multitudes of small blips in the vertical axis. These blips are known as 'grass' because of their appearance. Their presence is an essential check that the CRT is serviceable to a stage beyond producing the time base. The size of the grass is controlled by the "Gain Control".

Problems
1.   A particular radar equipment operates on a PRF of 1 000 per second. Two-fifths of the cycle is used in the flyback. What is the maximum range possible in statute miles?
Answer: 55.8 sm
2.   If a radio signal takes 400 μ sec to travel from A to B, what is the distance of B from A in nautical miles?
Answer: 64.8 nm

11: Radio Altimeters

Frequency Modulation Altimeters

Radio altimeters are designed to give indication of actual height above the ground. Those operating on the principle of frequency modulation are mostly used for low level flying where a high degree of accuracy is required. They are otherwise unsuitable for level flight since they indicate the contour of the ground below instead of a constant level. When installed, however, they may be used to check the accuracy of a pressure altimeter if the elevation of the ground below is known. In the past much use was made of them in flying "pressure pattern". In the latest development, they can be used to feed "height" information to an automatic landing system.

Principle

The principle of frequency modulation is utilised to measure time (and thereby, height) taken by a radio wave to travel to the ground directly beneath, and to return.

The frequency band allocated is 1 600 MHz to 1 700 MHz and one complete burst of transmission covers a space of 60 MHz.

The aircraft transmits radio signals vertically downward. The transmission frequency, however, is not constant but it is varied progressively and <u>at a known rate</u> from its start frequency to "start + 60" MHz, and then back to the start frequency. This constitutes one complete cycle of modulation.

Some of these transmitted signals will be reflected and return to the aircraft. The frequency of these returning signals, however, will be different from the frequency actually being transmitted at that instant. Further, the higher the aircraft, the greater the difference between the two. Since the rate of change of frequency is constant, this difference must be proportional to the time taken, that is, the height of the aircraft, since the speed of the radio propagation is known.

$$\text{change of freq} = \text{rate of change of freq} \times \text{time taken}$$

This frequency difference is measured and is registered on the indicator as height.

Equipment

<u>Transmitter/Receiver.</u> These generally work in conjunction with separate transmitter/receiver aerials.

<u>Indicator.</u> Several different types of indicators are available, one of them, shown below in Fig 1, has a pointer on the face of the dial calibrated in hundreds of feet. Thousands of feet indication is given on a counter in the window at the

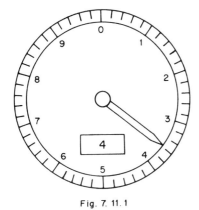

Fig. 7. 11. 1

6 o'clock position. The instrument shown reads 4 350 feet.

The indication is not limited to one single indicator in one position. As many repeater indicators as necessary may be installed to cater for various crew positions.

Limit Height Indicator

This indicator works in conjunction with a Limit Switch and is used when flying below 1 000 feet. The height the pilot wishes to fly is selected on the Limit Switch (which has the facility to select 50 feet, 100 feet and intervals of 100 feet until 1 000 feet) which operates a system of lights on the Height Indicator as follows:

Amber: flight is being made above the height selected.

Green: flight is made ± 15 feet of the selected height.

Red: flight below the selected height.

Uses

Mainly low-level flying. Most instruments cater for height up to 4 000 to 5 000 feet.

Accuracy

Fixed Error. This error arises in the method of transforming frequency difference into height and feeding the current to the indicator. The indicator pointer moves in steps of 5 feet, which means, an error up to 2½ feet may be present any time.

Mushing Error. This occurs where transmitter and receiver aerials are not at the same height. Generally ignored.

Overall accuracy is of the order of 5 feet ± 3% of the indicated height.

Pulse Modulation Altimeters

These altimeters also operate in the frequency band of 1600 MHz and are generally designed for high level operation, the upper limit being 50 000 feet. The height is indicated by a blip on a circular time base, and is read off in terms of its distance from the start of the time base which also appears as a blip.

Principle

Principle utilised is the echo. The time taken by a radio pulse to travel out and back is the direct measure of the distance (height in this case) on assumption that the speed of the radio wave is constant. This assumption is not an unfair one, since the speed of a radio wave is known to a considerable degree of accuracy. The timing, of course, must be done electronically.

The master circuit instructs the transmitter to transmit, and at the same instant, instructs the time base circuits to start timing. The transmission takes place vertically downward in the form of series of pulses. On the CRT the start of the time base is indicated by a blip in approximately the 12 o'clock position and the time base itself is a greenish, circular glow.

Signals reflected from the ground underneath will be picked up by the receiver aerial. These will be fed to the CRT via receiver and other components such as rectifier and video amplifier. On the CRT these will appear in the form of a blip on the time base.

The distance of this received pulse along the time base from the start point of the time base is the measure of the time taken by the pulse to return. This distance is read off against a scale in terms of height of the aircraft.

Formation of the Time Base
If the distance between two blips (start of the·time blip and the echo received) is to represent the height, the total length of the time base must relate directly with the total height it measures. In other words height and time taken by a radio pulse out and back must correspond.

On this equipment, the operator has the choice of selecting 0-50 000 or 0-5 000 feet scale. Say, 0-50 000 feet scale is selected; this means that the pulse tracing out the time base must complete one full circuit in exactly the time the radio wave takes to travel 100 000 feet. Time base is then complete, new pulse goes out and new time base begins. To the naked eye, these breaks are not visible; the time base and both the blips are continuously visible. Now, if the aircraft is flying at 50 000 feet, the time base start blip and the echo will be coincident. If the return blip appears at, say, the 6 o'clock position, it has travelled only half of the time base, that is, 50 000 feet. The aircraft height then is 25 000 feet which is read off against the scale.

Similarly, when 0 − 5 000 feet scale is selected, the length of the time base represents 10 000 feet and the next pulse is timed to go out in the revised time.

Indicator
The indicator consists of a CRT with a radial scale and two circles printed on the face of it. The inner circle defines the radius of the 0 − 50 000 feet time base; outer circle defines the radius of 0 − 5 000 feet time base.

Controls
A simple control on the indicator is used to adjust the radius of the time base so that it coincides with the appropriate circle. This ensures that a correct time base is formed.

Two zero knobs (one for 0 − 5 000 feet time base and the other for 0 − 50 000 feet time base) are used to zero the start of the time base, where the leading edge of the start blip is not at 0 position. If this is not done, wrong heights will be read.

Reading the Indicator

Read the height on the scale at the leading edge of the received blip. As the time base moves clockwise, the leading edge is the edge in anti-clockwise direction, or, it is that edge which is earlier in time. Make sure the leading edge of the start blip is at zero.

When flying below 5 000 feet, use 0 – 5 000 feet scale for accuracy. When flying above 5 000 feet, use 0 – 50 000 feet scale to read off the height within the nearest 5 000 feet and then go over to the 0 – 5 000 scale for readings in hundreds of feet. See Fig. 2 (a) and (b).

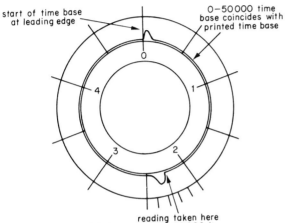

Fig. 7. 11. 2 (a)

On interpretation, the aircraft height indicated is 22 400 feet.

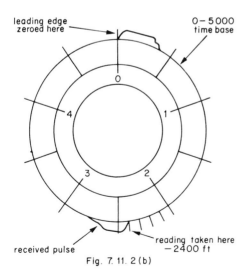

Fig. 7. 11. 2 (b)

Aerials

Two separate aerials are used, one for transmission and one for reception.

Limitations

Minimum range is limited by the pulse width. The equipment is inaccurate below 500 feet.

Accuracy

The main cause of inaccuracy is the instability of the transmitter. Any deviation from correct frequency will result in an incorrect time base. In the worst situation, the time base may not even form a true circle.

Accuracy of the equipment below 10 000 feet is ± 100 feet. Above 10 000 feet, 150 feet or ½% of the height, whichever is the greater.

12: Distance Measuring Equipment (DME)

The purpose of Vortac (VOR and Tacan) or DME is to provide rapid fixing capability when used in conjunction with VOR. VOR provides magnetic bearing information and DME (or the DME part of Tacan) provides slant range information from the DME station. VOR and DME are operated in conjunction with each other by use of the principle of frequency pairing. DME channels are frequency paired with neighbouring VORs; thus, on selecting the appropriate VOR frequency, DME ranges are automatically indicated on DME indicator. With certain types of equipment it is necessary to select the DME channel separately but the principle still remains the same.

Vortac

Initially, in the early 60's when only the military Tacan stations were operational, use was made of the DME part of their transmission when their locations coincided with VOR locations. Sometimes, Tacan transmitters were used even where the VOR station position did not coincide with Tacan but was considered to be close enough to it. Such arrangement came to be known as Vortac and it still exists. To indicate to the pilot what type of Vortac he is using, that is, whether the two transmitters are located together, or they are just close to each other, the CAA have made the following arrangement —

1. Where both VOR and DME transmit the same call sign and in synchronism, the two stations are "associated" and are operating on the principle of frequency pairing. The word "associated" is defined as follows:

the stations which are associated are either co-located or,

(i)   they are a maximum distance of 100 feet apart where the facilities are used in terminal areas for approach purposes or other procedures requiring highest fixing accuracy; or

(ii)   they are at a maximum distance of 2 000 feet apart where their purpose is other than that indicated in (i) above.

To simplify this, when only one call sign is heard, both the stations are either co-located or 100 feet apart or 2 000 feet apart. Where this information is required for en-route navigation, both the range and bearing may be plotted from the same position. Where the pilot is using information in terminal areas, he should be aware of the above limitations.

2. Those VOR and Tacan (DME) stations which are not associated but serve the same station and which may be used in conjunction with each other are also frequency paired. But in this case both VOR and DME identify separately (VOR ident once every 10 seconds; DME once every 37·5 seconds) and one of the two

has a Z as the last letter in the group of the call sign, e.g. DVR, DVZ.

3.   VOR and Tacan (DME) stations located at entirely different locations. These might or might not be frequency paired. Thus, if a pilot selects a VOR frequency and a Tacan happens to be paired to that VOR frequency the pilot will start reading DME ranges, but from a station which has no connection with the VOR he is using. So that the pilot does not use this information inadvertently, both VOR and Tacan (DME) will transmit entirely different identifiers.

DME

Once the importance of the DME part of Tacan transmission was realised, it was decided to install independent DME stations along selected points on airways where VOR alone operated before. More and more of these are now being installed and it is expected that by the early seventies VOR/DME will be the main navigational aid for airway flying in Europe.

Airborne Equipment

This consists of a VOR receiver and a distance measuring equipment (DME interrogator), together with a DME indicator and aerial.

On selecting the appropriate VOR frequency, the interrogator selects the correct ground beacon frequency from within a range of 1 025 MHz to 1 150 MHz and commences the transmission. The equipment at the same time begins to search for a reply, and locks on to the first such reply arriving at the aircraft which is correctly coded. The ground beacon, called the Transponder, identifies itself in morse once every 37·5 seconds. After the identification if it is found that the equipment has locked on to a wrong station (not a common situation) a signal release button on the control box is pressed and a new search commences. Once finally locked on to the correct signal it will remain locked and the indicator will from then on continuously indicate the aircraft's slant range from the station.

Most makers incorporate a memory device which, in case of temporary signal loss, takes over for a limited period (8 to 10 seconds). During this period it computes and feeds in range information to the indicator on the basis of the rate of change of recent ranges. If signals have not returned after this period, a new search will commence.

Indicator

Two types of indicators are shown in Fig. 1 opposite. The pointer type of indicator normally has a mechanical limitation at a maximum range of 197 nm., whereas the digital type will read up to 199 nm.

Poor signal, no signal or out of range conditions are indicated on either type by an OFF flag or a bar falling across the range window.

Principle of Range Measurement

Once the VOR frequency is selected, DME transmitter automatically transmits on the correct frequency, a series of coded pulses in pairs. Some of these pulses will arrive at the ground beacon (transponder). On being interrogated the transponder will reply by means of coded pulses on a frequency which is 63 MHz removed from

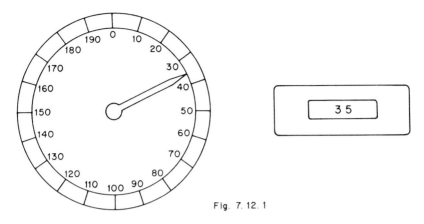

Fig. 7. 12. 1

the received signal frequency. The receiver computes the elapsed time between transmission of interrogating signals and receipt of the reply signals and determines the distance from knowledge of the speed of the radio waves.

One aircraft will not accept a transponder reply meant for another aircraft since all aircraft transmits at random PRF. They will accept replies to their own code only.

Frequency

DME operates in UHF band (1 000 MHz). The frequency allocation is divided in two bands: high and low, as follows:

	A/c Transmits	Ground Replies	Channels
Low	1 025–1 087|MHz	962–1 024 MHz	1– 63
High	1 088–1 150 MHz	1 151–1 213 MHz	64–126

Under the above arrangement 126 DME channels are produced. If an aircraft transmits on 1 100 MHz, the reply will come on 1 163 MHz, 63 MHz different, and this arrangement holds good for any transmission frequency given above.

Ranges

DME is a short range navigation aid. Maximum range of 200 nm is obtained at 30 000 feet (compare with VOR – 200 nm range at 20 000 feet). Range at 10 000 feet is 110 nm.

Ranges obtained are slant ranges. Suppose an aircraft is flying at 24 320 feet (that is, 4 nm) at 30 nm ground range from the station. His DME indication is calculated from Pythagoras as follows:

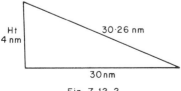

Fig. 7. 12. 2

$$4^2 + 30^2 = (\text{Slant Range})^2$$
$$916 = (\text{Slant Range})^2$$
$$\therefore \text{Slant Range} = \sqrt{916}$$
$$= 30 \cdot 26 \text{ nm.}$$

Similarly, given DME reading, ground distance may be calculated. At 10 nm range the error in indication is less than 1 nm. However, when directly overhead the beacon, the DME will not read zero range — it will in fact read your height in nm.

Use of Secondary Radar
It will be appreciated from the earlier chapter on radar that DME uses the principle of Secondary Radar. The advantages of secondary radar are as follows:
1.   Inteference due to weather is reduced, as seen in Fig. 3 below.

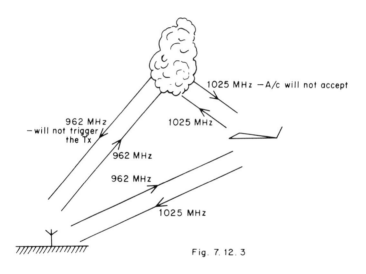

Fig. 7. 12. 3

It will be seen in the above diagram that an active cloud not directly in line between the aircraft and the ground beacon will have little effect in causing interference or clutter.

2.   Transmission power required is only that which is sufficient to carry the signal up to the station. In other words, the signals need not be strong enough to survive a two-way journey.

3.   Ground beacon uses a different frequency from that used by the aircraft. Therefore, self-triggering will not occur.

Accuracy
Slant range accuracy is between 0·25 and 0·50 nm.

Uses
1.   Provides fixes when used with VOR.
2.   Range indications are very useful when carrying out instrument approaches.
3.   Eases the task of the ATC in identifying when an aircraft reports its

position in terms of range and bearing from a VOR/DME station.

4.   When two aircraft using DME are flying on the same track, the positive ranges from these aircraft enables the ATC to maintain accurate separation.

13: Ground Controlled Approach (GCA)

The popularity of this aid is in direct proportion to the reputation of the airfield's controllers. It is a radar search system in the airfield areas; the controller gives instructions on the R/T to the pilot all the way down to visual contact.

There are two separate radar systems:

1. Surveillance Radar Element (SRE). A 10 cm radar unit which finds and identifies the aircraft in the approach zone and vectors it on to the final approach path. This is the responsibility of the Traffic Director.

2. Precision Approach Radar (PAR). A 3 cm radar element which scans the final approach path of the aircraft and talks it down to visual contact. The responsibility is the Precision Controller's.

SRE

It is common, to ensure firm identification, to call on the aircraft to perform a simple manœuvre and follow its blip on the radar screen. It is then guided verbally to join the approach path at 1 500 feet, where the PAR takes over. ICAO lay down a minimum specification of being able to identify a small single engined aircraft at 20 nm at 8 000 ft. The SRE aerials give a 2° beam in azimuth to an elevation of 30° from the horizontal. The scanner rotates at 10, 15 or 20 rpm, and the system is duplicated: the scanner can be sited up to 5 nm from the display screen and in any suitable and safe position on the airfield. The practical range is 25 nm and an accuracy of 500 yd on the same bearing within the 2° azimuth band enables more than one aircraft to be visually separated on the cathode ray tube. The display face though is switchable to scales of 10, 20, 40 or 60 miles range.

Frequency: 2 960 – 2 980 MHz, wavelength approximately 10 cm.

PAR

Precise information must be readily visible for immediate instructions to the aircraft, so two discriminators of 3 cm wavelength are available.

Frequency: 9 080 MHz.

This is a beam sweep in azimuth and elevation along the approach line, and the antennae are therefore sited to one side of the runway, at an angle of 79° to the runway centre-line near the touch down point. The azimuth scans 10° either side of the centre-line, with an elevation of 7°, and ICAO demand an accuracy of 30 feet in azimuth and 20 feet in elevation up to a height of 5 000 feet, and a high data display rate of one per second to allow for immediate correction for any deviation from the on-course approach path, up or down, left or right. These demands are always satisfied at least, and the errors (for example, 100 feet in range at 2 nm) are so small as to be ignored. The precision controller too can separate two aircraft visually on his screen if they are $1\cdot2°$ in azimuth and/or $0\cdot6°$ in elevation of each other.

General notes
It is important that when PAR is on a location also served by ILS that Glide Path and azimuth indications are coincident inbound from the outer marker. Two pilots in CAVOK will practise the two approaches, one monitoring the other.

The advantages are clear: no special gear is required in the aircraft, the pilot has only to obey R/T instructions, the radar beam is narrow and suffers no obstruction reflections, the equipment is ground based and duplicated, and what is more, PAR is movable from runway to runway to be operational within half an hour.

The disadvantages are: several R/T channels are needed at busy airfields, landing rate is limited, ground controllers must be highly skilled (as well as pretty durable), identification of blips can be difficult, and there will be some clutter in rain or snow (remember that a pulse is reflected from objects of comparable wavelength – PAR is 3 cm.)

The procedure is precisely laid down in the Air Pilot, and the pilot doing the GCA is on Airfield QFE, azimuth and elevation information is given absolutely and in relation to the On-Course and Glide Path Line.

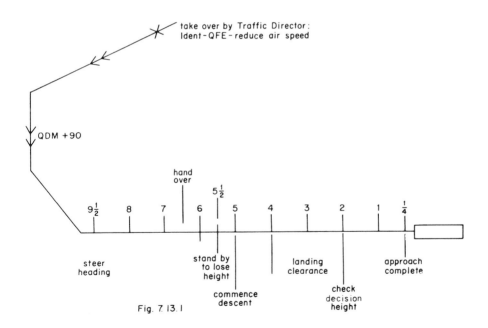

Fig. 7.13.1

At 7–6 miles the Traffic Director hands over to Precision Controller. Satisfactory R/T contact, then do not acknowledge further instructions. Prepare to descend, and commence descent to maintain a $x°$ glide path.

Azimuth instructions and information as to position with regard to centre-line from hand over to completion.

Elevation instructions and information as regards glide path from start of descent to completion.

> 4 miles out — 'clear to land, surface wind so and so'
> 2 miles out — 'check decision height'
> ¼ mile out — 'approach completed'

After landing contact Tower on frequency . . . for taxying instructions.

It is the pilot's obligation to break off if not in visual contact at decision height. The controller throughout gives definite headings(M) to fly, so he has made wind adjustments for the QDM to make good. He usually, too, gives range every mile until 4 miles off, every ½ mile thereafter — sometimes every ¼ mile after 2½ miles off. The last range given is ½ mile, when all the crew are searching for the approach lights.

14: Airborne Search Radar (ASR)

The primary purpose of the Airborne Search Radar is twofold:
1. to provide a radar presentation of the ground features below and ahead of the aircraft, called radar mapping, and
2. to provide a weather warning radar, by locating the presence of cloud ahead.

Besides these two purposes, the nature of the equipment yields two further advantageous uses:
1. pictorial presentation could be interpreted to discriminate between safe clouds and clouds that are turbulent and dangerous.
2. by manipulating the aerial tilt angle, cloud base and cloud top may be estimated.

Principle
In both mapping and weather radar the requirements are to find range and bearing of the objects. Range is found by the echo principle; direction is found by the principle of bearing by DF, the searchlight principle. Both these principles have been explained earlier in the text.

Mapping Radar
With the function switch in "Mapping" position, a narrow beam, $85°$ deep, is thrown downward and scans through a sector of $180°$ ahead. Fig. 1.

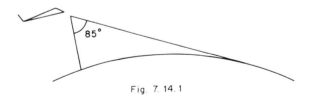

Fig. 7. 14. 1

With this type of beam the problem is that, for a given transmission power, the features nearest to the aircraft produce very strong reflections whereas those farthest away produce very poor reflections, the picture on the CRT fading away outward from the centre of the screen. This situation is remedied by directing maximum power to the farthest point and progressively reducing it in the same ratio as the range reduction. The trigonometrical ratio of cosecant answers this requirement — range varies as the cosecant of the depression angle, so does the power. Thus, the beam actually produced is called a cosecant beam, and it gives a uniform intensity picture.

The other point that arises with employment of this type of beam measurement is that the ranges it reads are slant ranges and not true ranges. This has the effect of distorting the picture on the screen. Fig 2 shows the picture of a straight coast-line, six miles ahead.

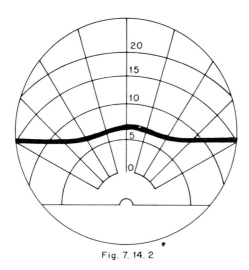

Fig. 7. 14. 2

The amount of distortion will depend on the range of the object and the aircraft height. If a very high degree if accuracy is required, this distortion may be removed by the employment of a non-linear time base. This is not called for in normal operations.

Cloud Warning Radar
For the purpose of cloud detection the type of beam used is a conical beam. It is normally 5° wide and is radiated in the forward direction. Range and bearing are determined on echo and searchlight principles. An aerial tilt control provides a facility for adjusting the beam direction in the vertical plane so that, for example, if high ground is approaching ahead the aerial may be tilted upward to avoid ground returns. Similarly, with sufficient downward tilt the beam may be used for mapping a limited strip of ground ahead.

Clouds at varying distances produce varying strength echoes. This effect produces no great difficulty when clouds are located at long distance, say 100 nm. When at close distance this effect is eliminated by operating the Sensitive Time Control switch.

Iso-Echo Display
Although the operator can see on the screen the complete cloud distribution ahead of him, without sufficient experience he would find it difficult to pick out dangerous cloud from among the less dangerous ones. The iso-echo type of display simplifies this distinction. It is known that strong turbulent clouds produce strong echoes compared with weak, inactive clouds, and this fact is utilised in the production of iso-echo display. All reflections above a pre-determined echo level are cut off from reaching the screen. About the turbulent centre there is usually the

remainder of the cloud whose activity is below the pre-determined level. This will be seen on the screen. This signifies that a cloud on the screen with a hole in the centre is dangerous. The hole or the blacked out portion of the cloud is particularly dangerous; the degree of the danger from the remainder of the cloud depends on the steepness of the contour. Fig 3.

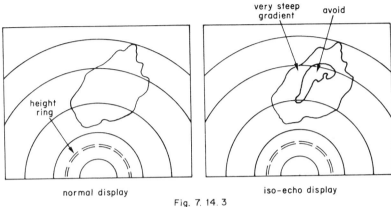

normal display   iso-echo display

Fig. 7. 14. 3

Calculating approximate height of the Cloud

This is done by tilting the beam upward or downward as necessary until the cloud just disappears from the screen. At this time, the base of the cone is directly on top of the cloud. This gives the angular measure of the cloud height above or below the aircraft's level. We also know the range of cloud. Thus, we have sufficient information to apply the 1 in 60 rule to calculate the height above/below the aircraft level Fig 4.

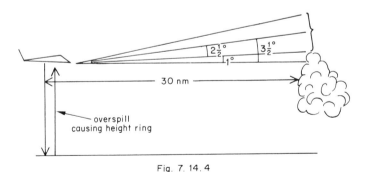

Fig. 7. 14. 4

For example, it is required to estimate the height of the top of an active cloud, 30 nm range.

The first step is to tilt the aerial (Fig 4) until the cloud top just disappears. Say, at this time the tilt angle is 3½°. This 3½° defines the centre line of the beam. Therefore, the base of the beam is 1° above the aircraft's horizontal plane. Now the data is put on computer as follows:

$$\text{Angle above a/c} = \frac{\text{Dist off (Rel Ht) x 60}}{\text{Dist}}$$

$$1° = \frac{Ht \times 60}{30}$$

$$\text{i.e. } Ht = \frac{1 \times 30}{60}$$

$$= ½ \text{ nm or 3 040 feet}$$

This is the height above the aircraft height. Alternatively, the makers provide pre-computer graphs from which the height is read off against tilt angle.

Height Ring

With conical radiation there is an overspill of radiation vertically downwards (Fig 4). This is reflected back to the aircraft and the echo appears like a ring, indicating aircraft height. This is called the "Height Ring".

Mapping on Weather

As pointed out earlier in the chapter, an arc of the Earth's surface could be seen on the CRT by appropriate tilting of the aerial. This technique of map painting is useful when scanning the ground a considerable distance away. The reason is, although the cosecant beam is capable of reaching its maximum distance, the energy is spread out over a very large angle, whereas in conical radiation it is confined to a very small angle, and the power produced by the transmitter is the same for both types of beams.

Controls

These are the typical controls found in conjunction with ASR:

On/Off. If it is required to be switched ON while on the ground, ensure that there are no large hangars or other reflecting objects in the vicinity, otherwise the strong reflections will damage the equipment. And for the very same reason, never select the mapping beam on the ground.

Range. Range switch provides facility for selecting a range of 20, 60 or 120 miles.

Weather/Mapping. The switch controls the type of the beam being radiated.

Aerial Tilt. This switch moves against a scale from 0° up to 5° and down to 15° and is used to estimate cloud top height, to remove ground returns and when on mapping, to get the best ground returns.

Contour On/Off. When in Off position, plain picture is seen. This position is used when operating on 120 nm range. As the clouds get closer, contour is switched on to see the turbulent areas.

Manual Tune. This switch is used to tune the receiver to give the best responses.

Switching off. Equipment takes approximately four minutes to warm up, therefore if the equipment is not required for short periods, put it on the standby position instead of switching off. When finally switching off, select stand by position for 15 seconds before switching off otherwise the screen will be burnt.

Range Considerations

The equipment works on 3 or 10 cm band; therefore, the ranges obtained are essentially line of sight ranges. Further, tall objects, e.g. hills will reflect the energy, and cast a shadow behind. Ranges also depend on transmission power, receiver sensitivity, aerial characteristics and PRF.

The PRF controls the upper range limit. Thus, if the maximum range of say 120 nm is required, time must be allowed for a pulse to travel that distance and return before the next pulse is sent out. Calculating at speed of travel of radio wave at 162 000 nm per second,

$$\text{Time taken to cover 240 nm} = \frac{240}{162\ 000} \text{ sec}$$

$$= 0.00148 \text{ sec}$$

and in one second, the maximum no. of pulses that can be sent out

$$= 675 \text{ PRF}$$

15: Doppler

In 1842 when the Austrian scientist C.J. Doppler heard that a horseless carriage was scheduled to pass through a railway station, he couldn't resist his curiosity. The train thundered past him at 10 mph, the whistle going full bore. Doppler returned home, puzzled at the varying pitch of the whistle that he heard. He noted that the pitch was high as the train approached and it suddenly dropped as it passed.

Let us put this in simple arithmetic. You are standing on a beach with your feet in the water. You note that 15 waves break against your feet every minute and that each wave is 2 feet long. Now you decide to walk against the tide, still counting the number of waves intercepted. Say, after walking for one minute you counted 20 waves. Fig 1.

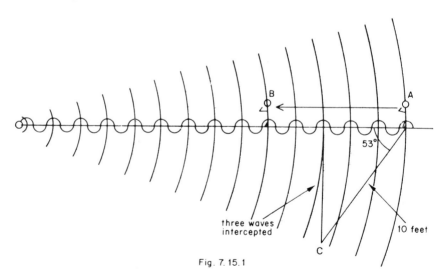

Fig. 7. 15.1

In the above figure you walked from A to B. In doing so, you intercepted 15 waves (which is the normal transmission frequency) which you would have intercepted even if you had been stationary at A. The extra 5 waves you counted were entirely due to your motion in the direction of the source of transmission. Now, since you know that each wave is 2 feet long (wavelength 2 ft) the distance you walked is 5 x 2 = 10 feet. Or, your ground speed is 10 feet per minute. This result may be expressed in a formula as follows:

$$F_R = F_T + \frac{V}{\lambda}$$ Where

F_R = frequency received (20 waves)
F_T = transmission frequency (15 waves)
V = ground speed
λ = wavelength (2 feet)

$$20 = 15 + \frac{V}{2}$$

or, $(20-15) \times 2 = V$

$$V = 10$$

In the above illustration, for similar reasons, if you had walked <u>away</u> from the source of transmission the number of waves (frequency) received would have been less than 15. Relating this to Doppler's experience, higher pitch was heard as the train approached due to increased frequency; lower pitch was due to decreased frequency.

This phenomenon is not limited to sound waves. It applies equally to waves of all types, e.g., light waves, electromagnetic waves.

To put this result in more formal language, we say that any time when there is relative motion between the transmitter and the receiver, a frequency change takes place. This frequency change or shift is not a true change of frequency – only an apparent change – and is called Doppler Shift, Doppler Frequency or simply Doppler Effect. If the frequency increases, it is called Positive Doppler Shift, and if it decreases, it is negative Doppler Shift. Since this frequency shift is directly related to the relative motion of Tx and Rx it enables us to measure an aircraft's ground speed, if a transmission from the aircraft is received back into it.

In order to measure the ground speed the aircraft must transmit electro-magnetic waves directed towards the ground. This means that the radiating aerial is not aligned with the aircraft's horizontal but depressed through a given angle. This will affect the doppler frequency and the formula given above must be modified to make an allowance. Going back to Fig 1, if A, instead of walking in the direction A–B, had walked 10 feet in the direction A–C ($53°$ to A–B) the number of waves he would have intercepted would have been 18. This is a cosine relationship:

Frequency increase when walking in line with the tide (A–B) = 5 waves
∴ Frequency increase when walking at an angle of $53°$ to A–B
= 5 x cosine 53
= 5 x 0.6018
= 3.0090 or number of waves = 18 i.e. 15 + 3

The formula modifies as follows:

$$F_R = F_T + \frac{V \cos \theta}{\lambda}$$ where θ = angle of depression

Lastly, in an aircraft since both transmitter and the receiver are moving, the final formula appears as follows:

$$F_R = F_T + \frac{2 V \cos \theta}{\lambda}$$

The choice of the angle of depression of the aerial is limited between $60°$ and $70°$ for reasons seen in Fig 2.

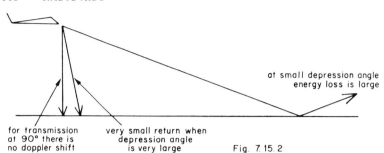

at small depression angle
energy loss is large

for transmission
at 90° there is
no doppler shift

very small return when
depression angle
is very large

Fig. 7.15.2

Principle of Ground Speed Measurement

Aircraft transmits electromagnetic waves from an aerial which is depressed by an angle of approximately $60°$. The signals are either pulse modulated or frequency modulated in order to distinguish the ground returns from reflections caused by the aircraft fuselage. With a single aerial, the radiation is either directed to the ground ahead of the aircraft or behind the aircraft. In either case, some of the energy will be reflected back by the ground and arrive in the aircraft aerial. The frequency of these returned signals will be different from that of transmission frequency. If the transmission was ahead, there will be positive doppler shift; if the transmission was to the aft, there will be negative frequency shift.

The aerial feeds these signals to the receiver where comparison is made between the transmission and received frequency and a beat note is extracted (the difference between the two). This beat note is the direct measure of rate of change of range between the aircraft and the ground-causing echo and the current produced is presented on the indicator via computers in terms of the aircraft's ground speed.

Example: An aircraft transmitting on frequency of 8 000 MHz observes a frequency shift of 8 kHz. Angle of aerial tilt is $60°$. What is its ground speed in Kt?

$$\text{The wavelength of 8 000 MHz} = \frac{300\ 000\ 000 \times 100}{8\ 000\ 000\ 000}$$

$$= \frac{30}{8}$$

$$= 3.7 \text{ cm}$$

Now substituting the known information in the formula –

$$F_R = F_T + \frac{2\ V \cos \theta}{\lambda}$$

$$8\ 000\ 008\ 000 = 8\ 000\ 000\ 000 + \frac{2 \times V \times \cos 60 \times 100}{3.7}$$

$$8\ 000 = \frac{2 \times V \times 0.5 \times 100}{3.7}$$

$$V = \frac{8\ 000 \times 3.7}{2 \times 0.5 \times 100}$$

$$= 80 \times 3.7$$

$$= 296 \text{ metres/sec}$$

$$= 574.9 \text{ kt}$$

Aircraft Aerial Systems

In the above example, we presumed that the aircraft was carrying a single aerial with either fore or aft transmission capability only. Such systems suffer from two disadvantages which make them unsuitable for practical use. First, in order to measure the ground speed accurately it is necessary to have a reasonable quantity of frequency shift. A shift of 10 kHz is considered to be adequate. This calls for a very high transmission frequency. Doppler consequently transmits in 8 000–10 000 and the 13 500 MHz band. The difficulty here is, airborne transmitters operating on such high frequencies are apt to wander off from designed frequency. When the echo comes back the only data available for comparison purposes is the actual transmission being made at that instant. If this is any different from the original transmission, a wrong beat note will be extracted, resulting in a wrong ground speed. In our example, if when 8 000 010 000 cycle signal arrived back, the transmitter at that instant had wandered off and was transmitting 8 000 010 000 cycle signal, it would produce a zero beat note. This disadvantage is overcome by employing aerials capable of transmitting 2, 3 or 4 beams and taking a comparison between fore and aft returns.

Secondly, with the single aerial system when an aircraft attains a pitch attitude, the angle of depression is no longer θ and thus large errors are introduced.

Janus Aerial System

This system consists of four aerials, two looking to the front (right forward and left forward) and two to the rear (right backward and left backward) which illuminate the ground by a conical shaped beam. This, together with the transmission pattern, is shown in Fig 3.

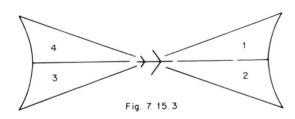

Fig. 7. 15. 3

Beams 1 and 3 transmit together; then after a short delay, beams 2 and 4 transmit together. Reflections are similarly compared, thus bypassing the transmitter. Mathematically:

Front Response: $F_{R_F} = FT + \dfrac{2V\cos\theta}{\lambda}$

Rear Response : $F_{R_R} = FT - \dfrac{2V\cos\theta}{\lambda}$

Difference $F_{R_F} - F_{R_R} = \dfrac{4V\cos\theta}{\lambda}$

Thus, the value of V can still be obtained by comparing forward and rear frequencies, independent of the transmitter. The formula is modified from

$2 V \cos \theta$ to $4 V \cos \theta$. Let us go back to the data in the previous example. We had a doppler shift of 8 kHz. Now, in the same case, we will have + 8 kHz from the front and − 8 kHz from the rear. Thus, the frequencies received are:

From Front (F_{R_F}) = 8 000 008 000 cycles

From Rear (F_{R_R}) = 7 999 992 000 cycles

Subtracting   16 000 = $\dfrac{4 V \cos \theta}{\lambda}$

= $\dfrac{4 \times V \times \cos 60 \times 100}{3.7}$

or V = $\dfrac{16\ 000 \times 3.7}{4 \times .5 \times 100}$

= 80 x 3.7

= 296 metres/sec

= 574.9 Kt

This system reduces but does not quite eliminate pitch errors. When the aerial is pitched up, both forward and backward received frequencies are in error but the errors are in opposite sense tending to cancel each other out. At very high angle of pitch, however, although the errors are in opposite sense they are not equal and the drift and ground speed measurements are affected.

A further advantage of the Janus system is that because of the conical shape beam pattern, the aircraft can roll on the edge of the cone without losing signals during normal turns.

Drift Measurement

Aircraft's drift measurement is achieved by comparing the beat frequency extracted from 1 and 3 aerials with the beat frequency from 2 and 4 aerials. Fig 4.

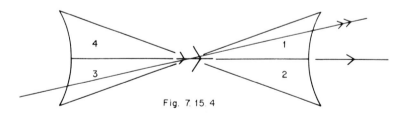

Fig. 7. 15. 4

In the above illustration, the aircraft is experiencing port drift and the aerial is aligned with the fore and aft axis of the aircraft. The frequencies received will be something like this:

From beam 1: it is forward transmission and the return frequency will be higher than the transmission frequency, say +10 kHz. From beam 2, it will still be higher than the transmission frequency, but not as high as the return from no. 1 beam, since the aircraft is drifting away from no. 2 to no. 1 beam. Say, the frequency received is +8 kHz. No. 3 will produce −10 kHz and no. 4 −8 kHz. Beat note from nos 1 and 3 = +10 −(−10) = +20. Beat note from 2 and 4 = +16. This difference between the two is entirely due to the direction of the aircraft aerial and the aircraft's track not being the same. As soon as such a difference arises between the two beat notes, a signal is raised which actuates a motor. The motor turns in the direction of the track, turning the aerials with it and will continue to turn until the difference between the two pairs of aerials is reduced to zero. At this time the aerial is aligned with the aircraft's track (Fig 5) and the motor switches off.

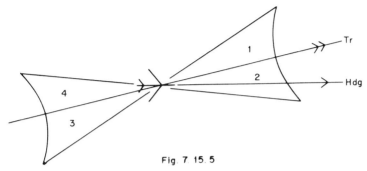

Fig. 7. 15. 5

The angular move of the aerial from the fore and aft axis of the aircraft is the drift which is indicated on a suitable indicator. (It will be noticed in Fig 5 that the aerial is aligned with the track and the doppler spectrum is symmetrical about the track axis). This is a condition for the groundspeed measurement to be correct.

Frequencies

Frequencies used are in one of the two bands:
X band: 8 000 – 10 000 MHz
J band: 13 500 MHz.

These high frequencies are necessary in order to produce measureable doppler frequencies. These have advantages in that they permit the use of small aerials and produce a narrow beam width. The disadvantage is that at very short wavelengths, signals suffer from atmospheric attenuation, thus limiting the maximum altitude for a given transmission power.

Indicator

The basic information produced by Doppler is ground speed and drift. A typical indicator displaying this information is shown in Fig 6.

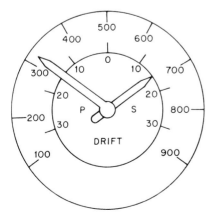

Fig. 7. 15. 6

The accuracy of the basic information is ± 0.1%of the ground speed and ±0.1° of drift.

Drift and ground speed together with heading reference supplied by the aircraft's gyrosyn compass can be utilised to produce such ground position information in digital form as:

1.   distance along and across track;
2.   latitude and longitude;
3.   distance gone or distance to go to next turning point.

In the matter of accuracy of this information the weakest link is the aircraft compass which, in normal circumstances, is only accurate to half a degree. The accuracy falls to approximately 1° track, 1% ground speed.

Setting up

At the beginning of a flight it is necessary (particularly with early generation equipment) to put in approximate or flight plan values of drift and ground speed with manual reset knobs. After this the equipment will lock on to the true measured values. In flight it is possible that the information received will be too feeble to do the work — over a calm sea — and the doppler will unlock. Doppler may also unlock as a result of severe manoeuvres or flight near large cumulonimbus cloud. These conditions may call for new resetting.

If the signal strength is reduced to a level at which it cannot drive the indicators, a memory device takes over and continues to drive the indicators for short periods, calculating on the basis of the latest strong signals received. While the memory is operating the doppler counters, should the winds change, wrong information will be presented. After memory has operated, and on various other occasions, it will be necessary to correct the doppler information from a more reliable fix. This process of correcting doppler counters is called "updating Doppler"

Errors are not introduced while flying over mountainous territory for the reason that Doppler does not measure the time difference between the transmitted and reflected signals. It only depends, as we saw in the formula, on aircraft speed, wavelength and the angle of depression of the aerial. Sufficient irregularities in the surface are required in fact to provide detectable echoes; large land targets will give rise to individual Doppler frequencies, and the spectrum will be coarse, but the mean frequency of the spectrum will give a measure of G/S very effectively. Over a calm sea, however, the spectrum may be too fine to provide anything measurable, causing the Doppler to unlock.

Errors

Basic Doppler suffers from systematic and random errors as follows:
Systematic Errors.

1.   Due to misalignment of the Aerial. If the aerial is not most accurately aligned initially with the fore and aft axis of the aircraft errors will occur in drift measurements.

2.   Altitude and Latitude Errors. We have always assumed that a nautical mile is 6 080 feet. This is only an average value. Actually, it is 6 046 feet at the Equator and 6 108 feet at the poles. The Doppler computer, clocking on one

nautical mile every time 6 080 feet is flown will be correct only when flying in the vicinity of 48° N/S. Elsewhere the information will be slightly in error. Further, 6 080 feet equals one nautical mile only on the surface of the Earth. At altitude, the length of a nautical mile increases, for the distance subtended by 1' of arc at the centre of curvature of the surface increases with altitude. These errors have always been present but they become noticeable with highly accurate equipment such as Doppler. Nothing is done about these in normal circumstances as the error is small; if a very high accuracy of navigation is required, correction charts may be used.

Random Errors

1.   Tidal Movement. If the reflecting surface itself is in motion, an error will be introduced, since the velocity of a moving current of water becomes the basis of Doppler measurement, and not the stationary bed beneath. You are not likely to be flying over a tidal race for long, and the ocean currents are not fast enough to affect the Doppler. Thus, the error is really effective only when flying a coastline with a fast tide and for a considerable time.

2.   Manœuvres, climb or descents will clearly give an error as the slant distance will differ from the ground distance. The angle which the aerials make with the flight path, too, introduces some error which is not entirely eliminated by the Janus set-up.

Pictorial Display

Lat and Long, distance gone, distance to go type of information which is available could be set to actuate a stylus over a suitable map on a roller to give a continuous picture of the aircraft's track and position.

Advantages

1.   High accuracy.
2.   No range limitations – worldwide operation
3.   Operates independent of ground co-operation.

Caution

Ground speed and drift indications are instantaneous values. If these are being used for plotting purposes, an average over a period of 20 – 30 minutes must be calculated and used.

16: Loran

Loran, a hyperbolic navigation system, derives its name from "LOng Range Aid to Navigation". Because of the long ranges obtained, the system is mainly used to cover the vast expanses of the world's oceans.

Hyperbolic Systems
A hyperbola is defined as the locus of a point having a fixed difference in range from two other fixed points. What does that mean? Simply this. The system calls for two fixed points – let M and S be such points in Fig. 1.

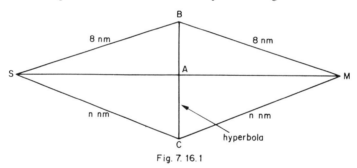

Fig. 7. 16. 1

Join M – S by a straight line. The straight line thus drawn is called the base line between the two fixed points.

Point A is halfway between M and S and, say, the distances A–M and A–S are 5 nm respectively. The difference between the two ranges = 5 – 5 = 0.

Point B is 8 nm from M. Therefore, it must be 8 nm from S, BAC being the perpendicular bisector of MS. Differential range equal to 8 – 8 or 0.

If point C is 'n' nm from M and S, its differential range is also 0.

Draw up a smooth curve (it will be a straight line in this case) BAC which is a hyperbola. The curve BAC may be extended in both directions and any point on that curve will yield zero differential.

Curve BAC need not be the only hyperbola between M and S. Any number of hyperbolae may be constructed to cover the area. Take point P, a distance of 7 nm from M and 3 nm from S, along the base line (Fig. 2).

Point Q is 8 nm from M and 4 from S, giving a differential range of 4.
Point P is 7 nm from M and 3 from S, differential range 4.
Point R is 9 nm from M and 5 from S, differential range 4.
Curve QPR is a hyperbola of differential range of 4 nm.

To utilise the system we want equipment in the aircraft which gives us the differential ranges. Loran is one of them. Then, once we know that the differential is 4, for example, we know that we are on curve QPR, a position line . But to plot ourselves on that curve we also need printed hyperbolic charts. Such charts are available for use in conjunction with Loran or any other existing hyperbolic system.

As for the information, it is not necessarily needed in terms of nautical miles as in the above illustrations. It may well be in terms of phases of the signal received in the aerial (Decca) or in the time in microseconds (μ sec) that the radio wave took to travel to the aircraft (Loran). In either case, the principle still remains the same, that of differential range. For example, if the information is in terms of time, at point R, signal from M will take 55·62 μ sec (6·18 μ sec = 1 nm) and the signal from S will take 30·9 μ-sec to arrive at the aircraft. The differential of 24·72 μ sec will be labelled against the hyperbola QPR instead of 4 nm as in Fig 2.

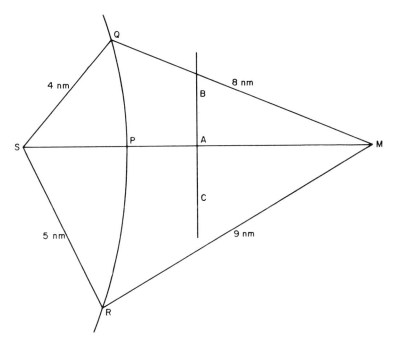

Fig. 7. 16. 2

Loran

Loran works on the principle of differential range by pulse technique. Two stations called Master (M) and Slave (S) operate as a pair to give a single position line. They are generally placed between 200 and 400 nm apart to give a wide coverage and it is usual to have more than one slave operating in conjunction with a common master to provide 2 or 3 position lines. The operator tunes in the chain and measures off the time difference between two signals on the screen. He then enters the Loran chart with this value and plots a position line. Usually there are two or three chains printed on a Loran chart, each in a different colour so that no confusion arises in selecting the correct hyperbola. Hyperbolae are normally shown at 100 μ sec interval and it will be necessary to interpolate for values in between them. Up to about 800 nm from the station the hyperbolae are continuous lines; beyond that range they are shown by pecked lines. Pecked lines suggest an extended reception area during night periods.

Transmission Sequence

If both Master and the Slave transmitted synchronously it will be impossible to determine which is which. Therefore, in Loran, the Master transmits first. It transmits a pulse, 50 μ sec wide (pulse width) in all directions. When this pulse reaches the slave it triggers the slave transmitter. This transmitter, however, does not respond instantly. There is a calibrated delay before the Slave transmission takes place. The transmission again is in the form of pulses radiating in all directions. The Master then transmits again and the sequence repeats. In one second, approximately 25 pulses are transmitted, the transmission PRF. The actual PRF depends on the chain and varies from 25 to 34 as we will see later in the chapter.

Time Base

The time base is the time that the 'spot' on the CRT takes to travel from one end of the tube to the other. This movement of the spot appears to the naked eye as a trace and provides a scale for measuring the time difference. Since the measurement is in time, the length of the time base is calculated in microseconds. It is synchronised with the PRF of transmission so that the signals from other chains operating on the same frequency do not remain stationary on a wrong time base. If these signals do break through they will simply sweep across the screen. Assuming a PRF of 25, the transmission takes place every 1/25th of a second. In microseconds this equals

$$\frac{1\ 000\ 000}{25} = 40\ 000\ \mu \text{ sec}$$

Thus, the length of the time base will be 40 000 μ sec. This length, however, is split up in two traces, as shown in Fig 3, each of approximately 20 000 μ sec.

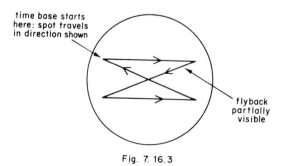

Fig. 7. 16.3

We said "approximately" because some time is lost in the flyback shown in above diagram. The flyback portion is not used.

The purpose of this split up is mainly to enable the operator to identify the master and the slave signals. It is so arranged, by adjusting the delay at the slave transmitter, that the slave signal always appears more than half the time base away from the master. We will come back to the topic of identification later. Presently, it will be appreciated that the delay required to put two signals on different traces must be at least half of the length of the time base. This is 20 000 μ sec. In addition to this, there is a further small delay of approximately 1 000 μ sec called a "Coding" delay, giving a total delay at slave of 21 000 μ sec. However, when taking the actual reading on the indicator you will not need to deal with such large figures. The time delay of 20 000 μ sec is automatically subtracted from all indicator readings, making the task easier. Typical readings that will be obtained at various positions are shown in the following calculations, to be studied with reference to Fig 4.

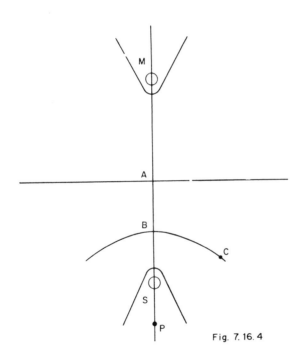

Fig. 7. 16. 4

<u>Observer at S</u>
1. Time taken for the pulse to travel M − S, distance of, say, 200 nm.
    = 200 x 6·18 = 1 236 μ s
        Delay at S = 1 000   (20 000 μ sec delay is not considered here because it will not be read)
    Slave transmits at 2 236 μ s
2. At S, therefore S is seen after 2 236 μ s
                        M   1 236 μ s
    Time difference   1 000 μ s Indicated

Observer at P, 50 nm behind S along extended base line M – S

1. M – P   =   250 x 6·18 = 1545 μ s
2. M – S   =   1 236 μ s
   Delay   =   1 000 μ s
   S – P   =   309 μ s
   ──────────
            2 545 μ s

3. Difference 1 and 2 = 1 000 μ s, the same value as above example.

Therefore, along the extended base line M – S the differential range obtained is a constant figure and thus, an ambiguous area.

Observer at M

1. M signal is received instantaneously.
2. Slave pulse –
   M – S   =   1 236 μ s
   Delay   =   1 000
   S – M   =   1 236
   ──────────
            3 472 μ s

3. Difference 1 and 2 = 3 472 μ s and the same value will be received anywhere along the extended base line S – M, giving an ambiguous area.

Observer at A, half way between M and S

1. M – A   =   618 μ s
2. M – S   =   1 236 μ s
   Delay   =   1 000
   S – A   =   618
   ──────────
            2 854 μ s

3. Difference 1 and 2 = 2 236 μ s. This is the value of the hyperbola of the perpendicular bisector.

Observer at B, 140 nm from M along the base line

1. 'M – B   =   140 x 6·18 = 865 μ s
2. M – S   =   1 236 μ s
   Delay   =   1 000
   S – B   =   371
   ──────────
            2 607 μ s

3. Difference 1 and 2 = 1 742 μ s

Observer at C, 160 nm from M, 80 nm from S

1. M – C   =   160 x 6·18 = 988 μ s (approx)
2. M – S   =   1 236 μ s
   Delay   =   1 000
   S – C   =   494 (approx)
   ──────────
            2 730

3. Difference 1 and 2 = 1 742 μ s, the same value as position B.

Thus, B and C are on the same hyperbola and having located C and a few other points having a similar value, a curve is drawn up joining the points. How did we locate C? It is going back to the basic : differential range. If you notice the ranges of B and C from M and S bear this relationship : MC – SC = MB – SB. Thus, knowing the differential range and one true range, the other one can be calculated.

Frequencies

Loran operates in the upper MF band, and the actual frequencies allocated are four in number, each one being called a "channel". These are :

Channel 1 : 1 950 kHz
Channel 2 : 1 850 kHz
Channel 3 : 1 900 kHz
Channel 4 : 1 750 kHz

It will be appreciated that in this state only four Loran chains could operate and if station A was operating with three slaves its neighbouring station B would only have one remaining frequency to operate one single slave. This severe limitation is removed by Loran operating on 16 different PRF in conjunction with each channel, thus extending its scope of operation to 64 simultaneous master-slave pairs. This is considered quite adequate. Two basic PRF are chosen – 25 and $33\frac{1}{3}$, called Low and High respectively, each having a possibility of 8 variations. These variations are called "rates". Low PRF of 25 increases by $\frac{1}{16}$ and the high increases by $\frac{1}{9}$. The following table is given to clarify the situation.

Rate No.	Low	High
0	25	$33\frac{1}{3}$
1	$25\frac{1}{16}$	$33\frac{4}{9}$
2	$25\frac{1}{8}$	$33\frac{5}{9}$
3	$25\frac{3}{16}$	$33\frac{2}{3}$
4	$25\frac{1}{4}$	$33\frac{7}{9}$
5	$25\frac{5}{16}$	$33\frac{8}{9}$
6	$25\frac{3}{8}$	34
7	$25\frac{7}{16}$	$34\frac{1}{9}$

There are three controls to select a chain. Say you are selecting a chain which is described as "2L7". Figure 2 is the channel number suggesting that the frequency in use is 1 850 kHz. Letter L stands for Low and this is set on Low/High control. Figure 7 stands for the rate number, giving the PRF of $25\frac{7}{16}$. This figure is selected on "Rate Number" control which is marked from 0 to 7. PRF of $25\frac{7}{16}$ gives us the time of the cycle –

$$\frac{1\ 000\ 000 \times 16}{407}$$

$= 39\ 310\ \mu$ sec and this figure governs the length of the time base produced.

Operation

Switch on the set and allow it to warm for a period of 4 to 5 minutes. Select the chain number, L or H position on L/H control and the rate number. If you are within the range you should now see two signals on the screen. Other controls are:

L/R Switch	– this positions signals on trace required
Drift Switch	– controls drift of the signals, or stabilises them on the trace.
Rx Gain	– incorporates ON/OFF and gain control
Coarse Delay	– governs coarse movement of the moveable strobe.
Fine Delay	– governs finer adjustment of the moveable strobe.
Amplitude Bal	– gives differential adjustment of signals on positions 2 and 3 of the Function Switch

Function Switch   — this has 5 positions.

Having seen the signals the next step is to identify which is Master and which is Slave. Remembering the fact that the master signals arrives first and the slave arrives at least half the time base distance away, the signals are identified as shown in Fig 5.

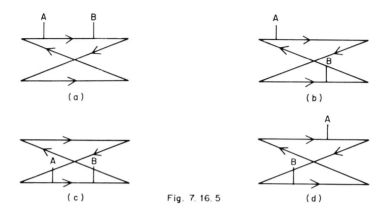

Fig. 7. 16. 5

In Fig 5(a), signal A is clearly not the master because signal B is not more than half the time base away. B is the master and it can be seen that A is more than half the time base away, following the time base in the direction of the arrows.

In Fig 5(b), A is the master, B being placed more than half the time base in the direction of the arrows.

In Fig 5(c), B is the master.

In Fig 5(d), B is the master.

Having identified the signals the next step is to place both the signals on the bottom trace, slave at the extreme left hand edge. This is done by use of the L/R switch. Fig 6.

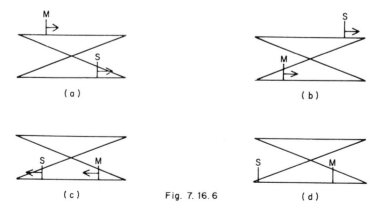

Fig. 7. 16. 6

Starting at position (a) the signals will move as shown until S is at the left hand edge of the lower trace (d). If during this process the signals seem to move, apart from the operation of the left/right switch, this means that the time base is not

quite matched to the PRF and the fine tuning is required. This is done by means of
the drift control, which is moved in a direction opposite to signal drift until the
drift stops. You are on position 1 of the function switch during this operation,
and just one more thing remains to be done before moving on to No. 2 position.
S, as in Fig. 6 (d), is placed on an invisible strobe. It is necessary to similarly strobe
M. This is done by use of the coarse delay control which moves a V shaped visible
strobe along the bottom trace. Place the strobe beneath M. Signals on the bottom
trace will now appear as shown in Fig 7.

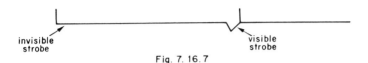

invisible
strobe

visible
strobe

Fig. 7. 16. 7

Position 2. In this position the space occupied by two strobes is presented in
expanded form. Two traces still appear but now the slave is on the top trace,
master on the bottom. The time base generated in this position is an exponential
time base, fast time being towards the left of the centre. The signals as they appear
in this position as shown in Fig 8.

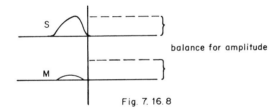

S

balance for amplitude

M

Fig. 7. 16. 8

First, drift the signals slightly to the left of the centre, i.e. in the fast portion
of the time base (this has the effect of opening them up) and then balance them
for amplitude so that the two signals look alike or as close as possible.
Position 3. In this position both signals are superimposed on each other for
accurate matching. Match up the leading edges as close as possible — accuracy
of time measurement depends on it — by means of fine delay control. Fig 9.

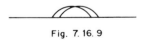

Fig. 7. 16. 9

Note the time and throw the function switch to position 4. This is the
time of the position line.
Positions 4 and 5. Actual count of the time interval is carried out in these two
positions, in position 4 the time being read to nearest thousand microsecond,
hundreds and tens in position 5.

Later models of Loran eliminate use of positions 4 and 5 by presenting veeder
counter reading, counters being placed directly as coarse and fine delay controls
are adjusted.

Range

Loran utilises both ground wave and sky waves and the charts are made out with sky wave corrections printed on the hyperbolae. Normal ranges are given in the table below.

| | Ground Wave | | Sky wave | |
	Land	Sea	Land	Sea
Day	200	850	–	–
Night	very little	500	1300	1300

Sky Wave Utilisation

This navigation aid actually makes use of the sky waves. The first pulse to arrive at the aircraft must be ground wave (if within the range) since it has the shortest distance to travel. Given proper range, the ground signal could be followed by a trail of sky waves at night. Range from the stations is of paramount importance, as is the time of the day. As for the time, from previous studies we are aware that sky waves by day and at twilight are quite unpredictable but at night there is constancy about the height of the E layer and the resulting reflections. In the absence of ground waves, the time difference can be measured between two sky waves, the reading then adjusted to the ground wave measurement on which the charts are based.

The reflections are numerous — one hop E, second hop E, one hop F — and only the first sky wave (one hop E) is used. The others are ignored as they are greatly fallible. The vital problem is to identify the sky waves since on no account must the time difference between one ground wave and one sky wave be taken: measure ground wave with ground wave, sky wave with sky wave. The limit of the sky wave reception is governed by the geometry of the earth's surface together with the height of the E layer. A wave leaving tangential to the surface will produce the maximum range.

Principle of Sky wave Correction

The difference between the distance that the master sky wave arrives after the master ground wave and the distance that the slave sky wave arrives after the slave ground wave is the error in reading and must be corrected before plotting the position line. The error may be positive or negative, depending on which of the two sky waves is closer to the ground wave. These distances may be estimated from visualising the geometry involved. Follow these principles:

(a)   Aircraft is close to the master and at considerable distance from the slave. As the aircraft gets near to one station, the sky waves will get further behind the ground wave : the solution is triangular — the base of the triangle is the ground wave and the difference between it and the sum of the two other sides (representing the distance of travel of the sky wave) will be greater at short ranges — Fig 10.

In Fig 10 the difference between ground waves is shown by (x). This is the correct distance which you would have measured had you been measuring two

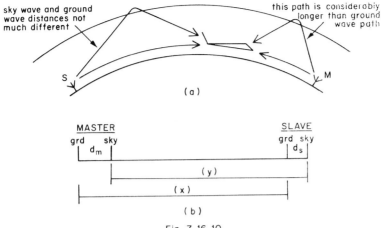

Fig. 7. 16. 10

ground waves. The distance between the two sky waves is shown as (y). This is the distance actually measured using sky waves.

d_m is the distance between master ground and sky waves; d_s is the distance between slave ground and sky waves. From Fig 10(a) we know that the distance d_m is greater than distance d_s. Therefore, distance (x) must be greater than distance (y); or, the measurement taken on the sky waves must be too small and the correction is positive. $(d_m - d_s)$, the value of the correction, is additive.

(b) Aircraft close to the slave and considerable distance from the master.
Fig 11.

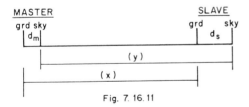

Fig. 7. 16. 11

Here, the distance required is (x); distance measured using sky waves is (y). d_m is smaller than d_s (being nearer the slave), the correction $(d_m - d_s)$ is negative.

(c) Aircraft at equal distance from master and slave.
In this case d_m will equal d_s or (x) will equal (y) and therefore no correction will be required.

Accuracy
Accuracy depends on the type of waves being used. With basic accuracy of $\pm 1 \mu$ sec, the ground wave accuracy is of the order of $\pm 6 \mu$ sec and the sky wave accuracy of $\pm 16 \mu$ sec.

Accuracy also depends on how well the two pulses were matched before taking the count. This matching is necessary because a pulse of 50 μ sec pulse width is being used in Loran. A pulse of this size takes a measurable time in rising and any measurement taken in the meantime will be erroneous. This limitation is overcome by amplitude matching which we discussed earlier in the chapter.

Unserviceability
Should any of the two signals blink or jump along the time base, the chain is unserviceable and must not be used.

Interference
Being an MF aid, Loran is sensitive to weather static.

Problem

1.   The length of the base line M – S is 1 000 μ sec. An observer A, 250 μ sec from master along the base line reads a time difference of 2 100 μ sec. What is the delay at S? (Answer : 600 μ sec).

Decca is another hyperbolic navigation system, operating on the master – slave basis. It differs from Loran in many ways. First of all, the basic principles employed by the two systems to produce differential ranges are different. Decca measures differential ranges by comparison of phases of the master and slave signals arriving in the aircraft. The presentation of information is different – Decca displays information by means of three decometers, on the dial and pointer system. Decca operates on yet lower frequencies, the LF band in fact, and lastly, Decca is a short range navigation aid.

A standard Decca chain consists of a master transmitter and three slave transmitters, the slaves being known as Red, Green and Purple. The slaves are placed around the master, approximately $120°$ apart from each other and at a distance of between 70 and 110 nm from the master. One master–slave pair gives one position line, but unlike Loran, information from all three pairs is continuously presented on the decometers and thus, more than one position line may be obtained without having to select another station, as with Loran.

Principle

The principle of Decca is differential range by phase comparison. Let us see first of all, how it is possible to have a knowledge of range simply by measuring the phases of two signals and comparing them. See Fig. 1 overleaf.

We have a M–S combination, each transmitting at two cycles per second. At any given instant, the signals relationship is as shown in the figure. Master's signal is shown as wave A, slave's as wave B. Both waves are phased locked, that is, their crests and zero values occur at the same instant.

Let us now consider the phases produced by these two waves at different positions in the area MW. Signal A (master) will produce phases of 045, 090 and 135 respectively at positions a, b and c. At these same positions signal B (slave) will produce phases 315, 270 and 225. Both signals will produce O phases at M and 180 at W.

Now, if we had a meter sensitive to phases, at position M it would read O phase from both the signals. Further, if this meter was capable of displaying the result as a difference of the two phases, it would still read O, as shown by a meter in the figure. If we now move to position a, the phase meter will read a phase of 045 from A signal, 315 from B signal, and the result displayed will be $045 + 360 - 315 = 090$.

At b, the phase difference will be $090 + 360 - 270 = 180$
At c, the phase difference will be $135 + 360 - 225 = 270$

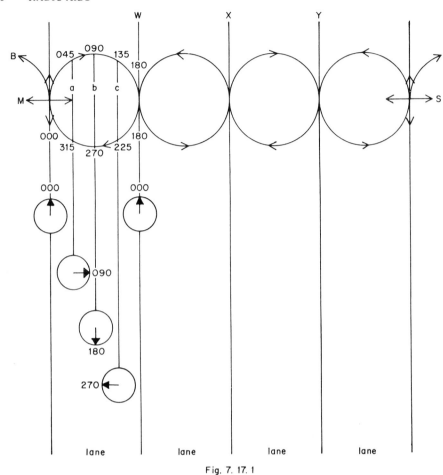

Fig. 7. 17. 1

Lastly, at W, the phase difference will be 180 – 180   = 0.

Thus, as we moved from M to W, we went through an area of complete 360° phase difference, or the needle in Fig 1 completed one full revolution. This is the basis of the principle. We can calculate the distance from M to a point where, for example, a phase difference of 090 or any other given value will occur. We can do this because the distance M–W is the distance of half the wavelength. We know the frequency, therefore, we know the wavelength.

In Fig 2 opposite a hyperbolic lattice is drawn up for a two-wave transmission as illustrated in Fig 1.

In this figure, master and slave waves are shown every 90°, master's transmission being continuous curves, slave's pecked curves. Hyperbolae are determined as follows:

Starting at M, the phase due to master signal at point a is 90, the slave phase is 270. Difference is 090 + 360 −270 = 180.

Now we want to find all other points in the vicinity of M which will give the same phase difference, i.e. 180. Take point b. Master's phase here is 180, slave's phase 360, difference 180. Points c, d and e are similarly found. A smooth curve joining these points gives a hyperbola of 180 phase difference. This means that an aircraft anywhere along that curve will read a phase difference of 180, and a small portion of that hyperbola in the vicinity of the aircraft's position is its position line. (Note: positions a, b and c in this figure are not related to a, b and c in Fig 1).

By a similar process hyperbolae at any convenient interval may be drawn up between master and slave and then the original wave pattern erased. Note that the perpendicular bisector is a straight line curve. Note also that ambiguity exists behind master and slave.

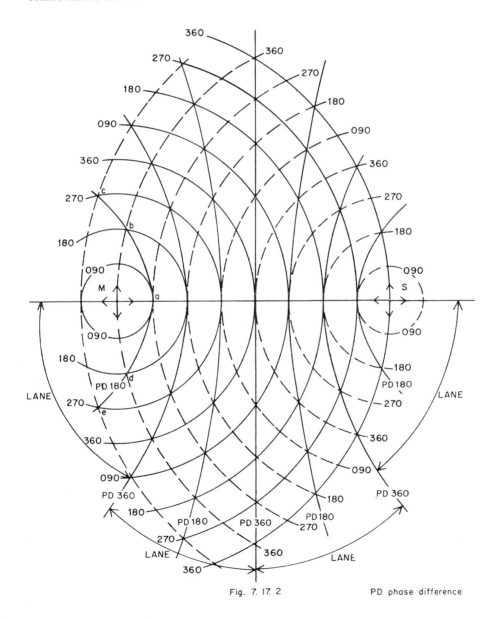

Fig. 7. 17. 2   PD phase difference

We are now ready to see how this principle is implemented in practice. In our illustration in Fig 1, we have both master and slave transmitting on the same frequency. In practice, this is not possible since two signals on the same frequency arriving at the aerial will merge and appear as a single voltage. Unless separate identity is maintained the phase comparison cannot take place. Therefore, a Decca master and the three slaves transmit on different frequencies. Each station (i.e. master and three slaves) has a basic or fundamental frequency called f. The value of f is always in the region of 14 kHz. Master and its slaves then transmit on fixed harmonics of that fundamental frequency. Harmonics are the multiples or divisions of a given frequency and they are easier to produce. These fixed harmonics in respect of the four transmitters are as follows, and they are valid for a Decca chain anywhere in the world.

$$
\begin{array}{lcc}
\text{Master} & - & 6\text{ f} \\
\text{Red} & - & 8\text{ f} \\
\text{Green} & - & 9\text{ f} \\
\text{Purple} & - & 5\text{ f}
\end{array}
$$

Just to repeat for the sake of emphasis, the multiples remain constant throughout, the value of f varies from chain to chain. A typical chain operating on a basic frequency of 14.2 kHz is shown in Fig 3.

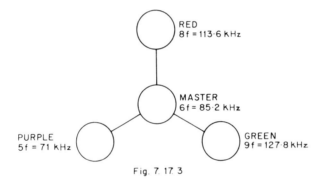

RED
8 f = 113·6 kHz

MASTER
6 f = 85·2 kHz

PURPLE
5 f = 71 kHz

GREEN
9 f = 127·8 kHz

Fig. 7. 17. 3

Comparison Frequency

By staggering the four transmission frequencies we solved the problem of keeping the signals separate. But in doing so, we created a new problem. Phase comparison cannot take place between any two signals which are not on the same frequency for the simple reason that they do not bear phase relationship. Now we have two signals in the receiver but not on the same frequency and we cannot compare their phases. So where do we go from here? The obvious solution is to step them up now to a common frequency and then take the phase difference; Decca has done just that. Each master-slave combination is stepped up in the receiver to the value of their LCM and phase comparison is then taken. These stepped up values are called Comparison Frequencies, and they are as follows:

Master and Red

M transmits at 6 f
R transmits at 8 f   LCM = 24 f which is the comparison frequency

Similarly, the comparison frequency for Master and Green is 18 f and master and purple, 30 f.

Thus, the principle is finally implemented and the result of phase comparison displayed by a pointer on the decometers. The only observation that remains to be made is how the receiver converts the received frequencies into comparison frequencies. This is shown in Fig 4 which is self explanatory.

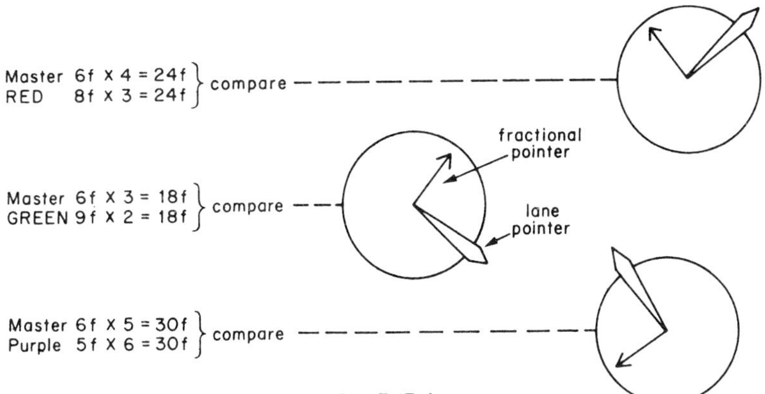

Master 6f X 4 = 24f } compare
RED   8f x 3 = 24f

Master 6f X 3 = 18f } compare
GREEN 9f X 2 = 18f

Master 6f X 5 = 30f } compare
Purple 5f X 6 = 30f

fractional pointer
lane pointer

Fig. 7. 17. 4

Lane Production

The actual distance between a master and its slave, as pointed out earlier, is some thing like a hundred miles. For convenience of taking readings, plotting and so forth, it would be most advisable to sub-divide this distance in smaller units. In Decca, we have natural units of sub-divisions, that is in Fig 1 360° phase difference occuring between M and W, W and X, X and Y and finally between Y and S. Each time the area is crossed the pointer completes one revolution. These areas are adopted by Decca and each one of them is called a lane. A lane, then, is an area which represents 360° phase change starting from zero phase; or, to put it another way, it is the interval between two adjacent position lines having the same phase difference, and a lane's width is determined by the comparison frequency. The pointer which indicates position inside a lane (that is, a phase between 0 and 360°) is called the fractional pointer. This pointer is identified in Fig 4.

The next point for consideration is the number of lanes that will be produced between master and slave. In Fig 1 we notice that there is a direct relationship between the number of waves contained between master and slave and the number of lanes produced. In that illustration we have two waves and four lanes, or, *one wave length = two lanes.*

Therefore, the first thing we need to calculate is the length of the wave in use. Let us work out for frequency f. Say, f = 14 kHz. Then wave length equals:

$$\frac{300\ 000\ 000}{14\ 000} = 21428.57 \text{ m, call it } 12 \text{ nm}$$

Now, if the distance between master and slave is 60 nm there will be five wave lengths between them or 10 lanes. On this basis,

Red compares at 24 f, therefore number of lanes   =   24 x 10 = 240
Green compares at 18 f, therefore number of lanes   =   18 x 10 = 180 and
Purple compares at 30 f, therefore number of lanes   =   30 x 10 = 300

Zones

When we say, for example, that there are 300 lanes between master and the purple slave we mean that the fractional pointer of the decometer will complete 300 revolutions as an aircraft travels from master to slave. This would imply that if the number of lanes is to be read off, we need two pointers, so that every time the fractional pointer completes one revolution the other pointer (called the lane pointer) moves one calibration mark up (or back, depending on the direction of aircraft travel). The lane pointer, however, must move round a dial having, in the case of the purple, 300 calibration marks. This is a large number to accommodate on a small dial besides the fact that such an arrangmeent would necessarily result in loss of accuracy. To avoid this, a number of lanes are grouped into a Zone. A Zone can be defined as the area between two in-phase position lines, the width between them being determined by the *basic* frequency f.

Red: 24 lanes make one zone. Therefore, for 240 lanes in above example there will be 10 zones.

Green: 18 lanes make one zone, ten zones in 180 lanes.

Purple: 30 lanes make one zone, ten zones in 300 lanes.

These ten zones between master and slave are lettered A to J. If there are more than ten zones between the two stations due to the distance between them, the letters will repeat. 24 lane calibrations on the red decometer are numbered from 0 to 23 (inc.). 18 Green lanes on the Green decometer are numbered from 30 to 47 (inc.). This is done to avoid confusion regarding the slave in use. Similarly, 30 purple lanes are numbered from 50 to 79 (inc.). Lane fractions are shown as decimals, from 0 to 99 instead of 0 to 360° phase. A typical decometer is shown in Fig 5, reading shown is D 41.75. It is therefore a Green slave reading.

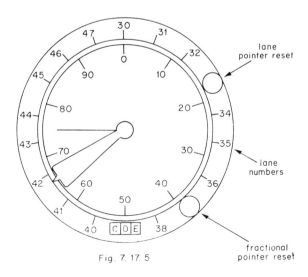

Fig. 7. 17. 5

The aircraft is in D zone, 41st lane and it has gone through threequarters of that lane.

Thus, on a decometer we have a zone indicator, lane indicator and a fraction of the lane indicator. When the fractional pointer completes one full revolution, flight through one lane is complete. The lane pointer which is geared to the fractional pointer will now indicate the next lane. When the lane pointer completes one full revolution, the aircraft will have flown through 24 red lanes or 18 green lanes or 30 purple lanes. The zone indicator which is geared to the lane pointer will now have moved to indicate the next zone.

Lane Identification

It will be appreciated that the length of a Decca lane is a very small distance indeed. For example, for a purple slave, if the master-slave distance is 100 nm, (and we know that there are 300 lanes in that distance) the length of a lane is a mere 1/3rd of a nm. If you are taking off from an aerodrome and planning to use Decca straight away, this causes no problem, since you will have set the base co-ordinates in terms of zone and lane (fractional pointer will pick up correct position automatically) before the start. In that case, Decca will continue to indicate the correct reading throughout the flight. The problem arises in cases where temporary failure of the equipment occurs or when entering a Decca chain from outward or when changing over from one chain to another. In these instances accurate information on lane number is required. On Decca, this information is provided on a Lane Identification Meter, a single indicator calibrated in decimals just like the fractional pointers of the three decometers and which caters for all three slaves. The identification meter consists of two pointers, one is wide and is called the Sector Pointer. The other is a six legged one and is called the Vernier Pointer. Fig 6.

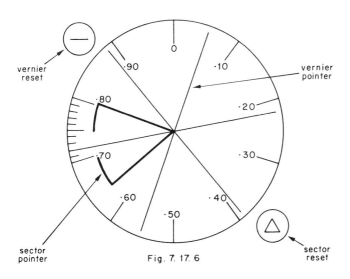

Fig. 7. 17. 6

In the above illustration the reading is .72. If this was a green reading (that is, a reading taken when green light was on) and we wished to set the lane on the decometer in Fig 5., we would move the lane pointer to cover .72 on fractional scale. This would put us in lane 43.

As for zone setting, it is wide enough to be ascertained by DR navigation. On later Decca models (Mk. 10) zone identification also takes place automatically.

We shall now look in the theory and see how lane identification is achieved, and particularly, how does the lane number tie up with decimals on the fractional scale. Let us forget for a minute the LI meter and concentrate on the decometer in Fig 5. As pointed out, the need for LI (lane identification) arises because of the smallness of the lane distances. The obvious answer to this would be to momentarily widen up the lanes. In Decca the lanes are widened momentarily for LI purpose by providing suitable ground transmission to phase-compare the signals at 1 f and 6 f. Figure 7 represents a master and green comparison pattern. 180 lanes are produced which are contained in 10 zones, each zone having 18 lanes in it. This is so during normal transmission. At 1 f, we know from earlier calculations, that there will be 5 waves between master and green (distance 60 nm) or 10 lanes. This 1 f transmission forming 10 lanes between master and green is also shown in Fig 7. Distance X−Y which marks the boundary of D zone (shown exploded for clarity) is now covered by half a wave from master and half from slave. This resembles the wave pattern between M and W in Fig 1. Thus, as the aircraft travels from X to Y, 360° phase change will occur and the fractional pointer will complete one revolution.

Under this arrangement the distance X−Y (or original zone D) is a lane, and the fractional pointer at any time indicates position inside this lane in terms of decimals.

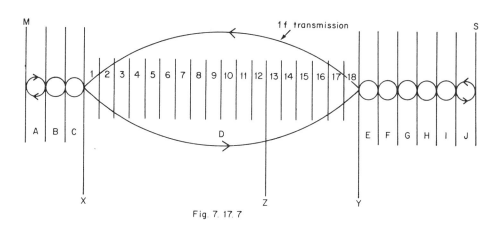

Fig. 7. 17. 7

For example, when the aircraft is at Z, the fractional pointer of the decometer will have gone round 2/3rd of the dial, say, it indicates .72. Now, if against position .72 on the fractional scale, the decometer was calibrated to give lane numbers under normal comparison frequency, the reading would be 43 (30 + 13) from above diagram. If you examine Fig 5, it is calibrated just that way. Fractional value at 1 f indicates lane number at normal comparison frequency. As for the fractional pointer on the decometer, it would be most inconvenient if lane identification readings were fed to it. The needle would jump every minute to indicate a lane.

Hence the use of a separate LI meter. The result of 1 f is displayed on the sector pointer.

Comparison for lane identification also takes place at 6 f simultaneously with 1 f. The reason for 6 f comparison is to improve the accuracy of the L1. If you examine the 1 f curve above you will notice that the curve is very gentle and the phases change very slowly. A comparison on its own would only yield an approximate result, and this accounts for the shape of the sector pointer. 6 f will produce six lanes in the original D zone (6 f = 60 lanes in place of original 180. Therefore, the original 3 lanes will equal one new lane or, there will be six lanes in one original zone). So there will be six positions in distance X—Y where the same phase difference will be measured — hence the shape of vernier pointer. The leg that falls in the area covered by the sector pointer indicates the lane in decimals.

To enable the receiver to carry out phase comparisons at 1 f and 6 f the transmission pattern has to be modified. The transmission sequence together with frequencies transmitted for LI purposes is as follows, and during this period normal transmission stops.

On the minute:	Red Identification
	M transmits at 6 f and 5 f
	Red transmits at 8 f and 9 f
	Purple and Green are switched off
Minute + 15 sec	Green Identification
	Master transmits at 6 f and 5 f
	Green transmits at 8 f and 9 f
	Red and Purple are switched off
Minute + 30 Sec	Purple Identification
	Master transmits at 6 f and 5 f
	Purple transmits at 8 f and 9 f
	Red and Green are switched off.

Each transmission lasts for approximately ½ second during which time the normal flow of data stops. The identification light is kept glowing for approximately 3 seconds to enable the operator to take the reading. The receiver converts the above transmissions to 1 f frequency as follows:

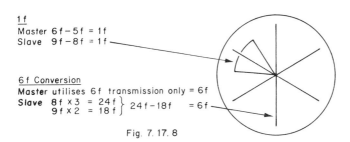

1 f
Master 6 f − 5 f = 1 f
Slave 9 f − 8 f = 1 f

6 f Conversion
Master utilises 6 f transmission only = 6 f
Slave 8 f × 3 = 24 f } 24 f − 18 f = 6 f
       9 f × 2 = 18 f }

Fig. 7. 17. 8

Use of Decca

An On/Off switch is provided to switch on the Decca. Amber light on the control unit glows when the set is switched on. Allow ample time for the set to warm up. The set must be "referenced" when thoroughly warmed up. This is done by throwing the Ref/Op switch on the control unit to Ref position. In this state outside signals are cut off and instead an internally generated 360° phase signal is fed to all three decometers and the LI meter. All three decometer fractional pointers must return to zero phase position (12 o'clock). If they haven't done so, they must be zeroed manually. On the LI meter the sector pointer will be near zero and one of the vernier legs will be at zero. If this is not at zero, it must be zeroed likewise. The purpose of referencing the set is to make allowance for changes in value of electronic components operating in warmed up conditions. Referencing will also be necessary when changing a chain in flight since by selecting a new frequency, new crystals will be brought into operation. Otherwise do not reference the set in flight unless you must, since during the referencing period flow of normal data is stopped and therefore lane identification will be necessary before using the decometers again.

Range
300 nm by day; 200 nm by night

Accuracy
Accuracy of the equipment is very high indeed. If the phase difference is read to the accuracy of 6°, the theoretical accuracy for the red slave would be —

$$\text{Lane width} = 240 \text{ lanes in } 60 \text{ nm}$$
$$= \frac{60}{240}$$
$$= \frac{1}{4} \text{ nm}$$
$$\therefore \text{Accuracy} = \frac{6}{360} \text{ x } 440 \text{ yds}$$
$$= 7\ 1/3\text{rd yard}$$

In practice the accuracy is 1 nm on 95% of occasions at maximum range. The degree of accuracy also depends on the area the aircraft is in in relation to the master and slave stations. See Fig 9.

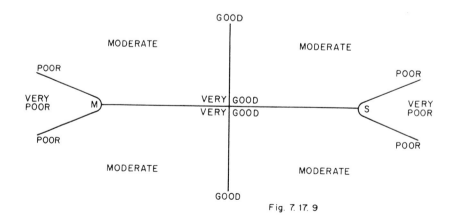

Fig. 7. 17. 9

Errors

1.   Height Error. All decca charts are made up for ground level propagation. Therefore, a slight error occurs, particularly at very high altitudes. There will be no error, however, when the aircraft is along the perpendicular bisector of the base line, and there will be maximum error when overhead the master or slave station. If high accuracy is required correction charts must be used in conjunction with the readings obtained.

2.   Decometer Lag. There is a lag between reception and presentation on the decometer dials. This is greatest when crossing lanes rapidly, along the base line. Purple is the most vulnerable. This error will be rather less than the airman's eye-to-brain agility in reading a decometer, so know about it but don't worry about it.

3.   Night Error. Decca assumes that transmissions to the receiver are the shortest distance and the most direct, the ground wave. Being a low frequency aid there will be sky waves present in the aerial at night, when at distant ranges. At night, therefore one must use caution when 200 nm or so from the master. Dusk and dawn are critical periods.

4.   Lane Slip. Although Lane Identification signals occupy but half a second, the data flow in the receiver is interrupted for about one second and during this time the the decometer concerned will stop. On return of the signal, the decometer starts again quite fast, but if during this time the aircraft has moved through more than ½ lane, the needle will turn the shortest way to the correct position, and a whole lane could be lost. Lane slip will occur at 240 kt and over but the later marks of Decca take care of this error by automatic Lane Identification. Even Mk VIII has been adapted to include a memory device which takes over at the last rate of decometer movement after the signals are interrupted.

5.   Static. Rain static and atmospherics can blot out signals entirely or give incorrect readings through interference.

6.   Interpretation and Interpolation Error. Reading the decometers takes a bit of practice : plotting between wide hyperbolae likewise.

Decca Chart

The lattice is overprinted in the appropriate colours on a Lambert's chart. The AO, A30 and A50 are the base line extensions of Red, Green and Purple respectively, behind the master. Base line extensions behind the slaves have no zone letters allocated. The area immediately behind the master and slave is ambiguous and must not be used in association with that particular slave. Use of particular Master – Slave combination is shown in Fig. 10 overleaf.

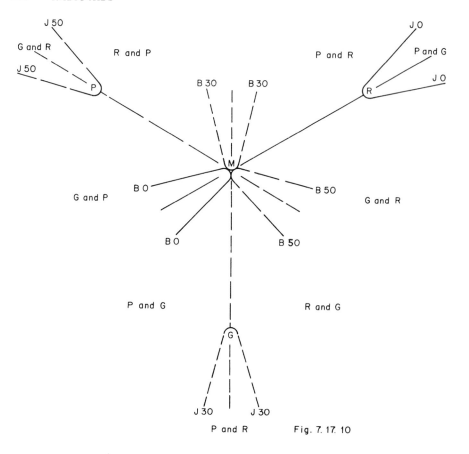

Fig. 7. 17. 10

18: Decca Flight Log

Decca equipment provides zone, lane and fraction of a lane information on 3 decometers. These zones and lanes are geographically fixed areas. This, together with the fact that the decometer information is on a continuous basis makes Decca an ideal system for adaption as a mechanical plotter. That's what a Decca Flight Log is. A moving pen indicates the aircraft's instantaneous position on a chart which also moves, and the pen traces out the aircraft's track made good. The pen and the chart are driven by two Decca slaves, the slaves selected by Decca to give the best result in the area where the flight is taking place.

Charts are specially prepared to meet different flight requirements, e.g. charts for en route navigation, charts for use in congested areas such as Controlled Airspace and approach charts for use in terminal areas. They come in small sections (approximately 2 feet long) and up to 12 charts may be joined up in the right sequence to cover a whole flight. The roll thus made up is loaded on one spool, over the face of the display head and the edge of the start chart fastened down to a spool on the other side.

The chart moves in Y—Y axis, or in a direction up and down this paper. The pen moves in X—X axis, that is, across this paper. Thus, the pen and chart movements are at 90° to each other. This causes a problem since the hyperbolic lattice of any two slaves rarely intersect each other at 90° except in the vicinity of the base lines where they do so approximately. Thus, charts for flights near the base line utilise the lattice pattern as naturally produced but elsewhere the lattice has to be straightened out mathematically, and the flight log charts for these areas have an appearance of a square grid. This adjustment is looked after by the flight log computer but the operator has to remember that with this straightening out process, distortion of geographical features is inevitable. On these charts, therefore, estimations of bearings and ranges are not possible. Ranges along a particular track are marked by the Decca company and where applicable, bearings to reporting points around the Track are shown. Only information shown on the chart may be used.

Another factor that one has to take into consideration is the nature of the hyperbolic lattice. Due to their curvature, distances between 360° phase change lines (that is, lanes) are variable distances : shortest distance along the base line, largest distance at the extremity. Thus, 360° phase change fed by a slave to the pen or roller will have different rate of movement on different charts covering different areas. These variables are summarised as follows :

1.   Scale of the chart
2.   Rate and direction of movement of the chart
3.   Rate and direction of movement of the pen.

These variables for a particular chart are controlled by a Chart Key which is loaded in a turret switch on the control box. The key code in three letters (e.g. BIP) is printed on the side of the chart together with the number of the Decca chain in use for that chart. The turret switch holds a maximum of 12 such keys to cater for 12 charts and the key in the 12 o'clock position is the one which is operative. When one chart is finished and the other is about to start the turret switch must be turned until the next key is in the 12 o'clock position.

Operating Procedures

1.   Switch on Decca and allow it to warm up.
2.   Switch on the Flight Log (no warming up time required).
3.   Select appropriate turret key.
4.   Adjust the pen and the chart so that the pen indicates the point of start. This may be done from known base co-ordinates or from decometer readings. Simple buttons left/right and Up/down permits this setting to be done, with Function switch against correct colour of slave.
5.   Function switch to Standby position for normal operation.

Errors

Normal Decca errors are present plus a small error in flight log due to gear train back lash.

Accuracy

± 1 nm at 120 nm range; ± 2 nm at 200 nm range.

19: Inertial Navigation

This is a technique for determining a vehicle's position and velocity by measuring its acceleration with respect to a known set of axes, and processing that acceleration in a computer. This self-contained navigation is now in reasonably common use by · airlines whose routes justify it and who can afford it, especially after sacking their navigators.

The term *acceleration* means rather more than just increasing speed as it is considered in the loose phraseology of daily life; it is changes in velocity, and velocity is speed measured in a definite direction along a straight line. *Inertia* is the property of matter by which it continues in its existing state of rest or uniform motion in a straight line unless that state is changed by external force. An *accelerometer* is the device that measures the force required to accelerate a mass, i.e., it measures the acceleration of the vehicle containing the accelerometer. The motion of an aircraft in inertial space can be determined therefore from information contained within the aircraft itself, by successively integrating the accelerations of the aircraft along a system of axes to produce its velocities and its displacements within a defined space frame.

In its simplest terms, the system has three accelerometers in an aircraft, each held irrevocably in its chosen reference axis, North/South, East/West and local vertical; each measures the acceleration along its axis, and the integration of this acceleration with respect to time will provide the velocity along this axis, though initial conditions must be known. A computer converts the time integrals along each axis into terms of distance travelled, and still further into latitude and longitude.

The System

The platform consists of a gyro-stabilised cluster of accelerometers whose outputs are fed to a computer. The platform isolates the accelerometers from angular rotations of the aircraft, and maintains them in a fixed orientation relative to the Earth, usually with two of the input axes being locally level. The structure, gimbal mounted, on which the gyros and accelerometers are mounted, is called the *stable element*: the gimbals allow the aircraft to rotate without disturbing the stable element. Keeping the accelerometers exactly in the chosen reference axes, with an immediate reaction to the smallest deviation therefrom, is not regarded as much of a problem, using accurate gyros and high performance servo mechanisms. The gyros act as error detectors to sense inadvertent rotations of the stable element, and apply corrections to gyro torque motors to cause the appropriate precession.

The computer calculates the aircraft's position and velocity from the outputs of the two horizontal accelerometers; it also calculates the gyro-precession signals which maintain the stable element in the desired orientation relative to the Earth, since the Earth itself is rotating and the aircraft is rotating about the Earth, so the platform must rotate at these combined rates to stay aligned with the chosen Earth's axes; it also calculates accelerations other than those caused by changes in the aircraft's motion relative to the Earth.

In each case, the computer initiates the required compensation. When the computer is turned on, it must be set up so that it knows the initial position and ground speed of the aircraft; the stable platform must have the correct initial orientation relative to the Earth; the platform is typically aligned in such a way that its accelerometer input axes are horizontal, often with one of them pointed North. A vertical accelerometer is sometimes added to speed up the indication of altitude on the dial as measured by the barometric altimeter or air-data computer.

The Calculation of Velocity from the Outputs of the Horizontal Accelerometers
This involves some pretty terrifying mathematics, which you might enjoy but won't get here. It is necessary to derive the velocity of the aircraft relative to the ground, a ground which is part of a rotating Earth. The first co-ordinate frame is centred at the Earth's centre, projecting through the essential reference points of the Equator, Greenwich and the Pole, and considered to be motionless with regard to the stars. The second co-ordinate frame is similarly centred, but fixed to the Earth. The axes of both will be aligned only at the instant of alignment, for the Equatorial axis of the latter will move at $15.4°$ per hour relative to the former, and only the Polar axis will remain near-enough coincident. The third set is the actual co-ordinates of the aircraft itself at a given moment, one axis East/West, another North/South, another vertical, all radiating as it were from the aircraft itself.

Furthermore, the platform has its three co-ordinates with respect to the input axes of the accelerometers, at right angles to each other, set North-pointing or in the aircraft's axes lines. Thence, with the time factor since alignment of the system, the output of the accelerometers is solved in the computer to give a speed over the ground from a complex working of the initial angular velocity of the platform, the components of the platform axes proportional to the accelerometer outputs, the angular velocity of the Earth in inertial space, eliminating unwanted accelerations of gravity, of coriolis and centrifugal forces (the tendency to move outwards due to following a curved path in space in order to maintain a Great Circle path on a turning Earth): these will be picked up by the accelerometers, which cannot differentiate, but are processed and rejected by the computer.

In providing information about altitude, the vertical accelerometer does not perform its function with quite the facility of the horizontals. A small error in the early stage, whether of initial altitude, of altitude rate, or of the mechanisation of the vertical gravity component, will increase considerably with time, rendering the indications useless even after a few minutes. A baro-inertial altimeter is used, therefore, a combination of the two, which utilises the basic stability of the barometric altimeter, but avoids the time-lag from measuring altitude to its dial appearance, utilising the accelerometer to do this.

The Calculation of Position from the Velocities
From the sets of co-ordinates already mentioned and the measurement of ground speed, it becomes a simple matter for the computer to solve the position of the

aircraft in terms of latitude and longitude continuously in flight. The resolved components of velocity provide the essential ingredients of position finding, since they are speeds in a given direction, and the direction as a Northing or Easting element is as intrinsic as the speed, all of which are instantly readable in the normal accepted figures.

Alignment
It is vital that the platform is accurately levelled and aligned in azimuth before take-off and is maintained so during flight.
1. *Position co-ordinates* — exactly as known on the ground, or from a Fix when airborne.
2. *Speed co-ordinates* — zero on the ground, and when airborne the best known from Fixes, doppler.
3. *Platform orientation co-ordinates* —
    i. levelling by rotating the inertial platform until the platform-borne accelerometers read zero; as you can imagine, with precession being the principle, this is not so easy as it sounds.
    ii. azimuth alignment consists of rotating the stable element around the vertical until it is aligned with a desired reference direction, which may be True North or a GC track. Again, with automatic rotation, this cannot be hurried.
4. *Orientation Rates* — the values of gyro drifts must be known at the instant of completing the alignment.
   The system may then be switched from 'align' to 'navigate', and position, velocity and azimuth errors begin to increase with time, whether the aircraft is stationary or not.

The Advantages of the Inertial System
1. Indications of position and velocity are instantaneous and continuous.
2. Utterly self-contained, with no need of ground stations or whatever.
3. Navigation information is obtainable at all latitudes and in all weathers.
4. Navigation information is substantially independent of aircraft manoeuvres.
5. Any inaccuracies may be considered minor as far as civil air transport is concerned.

Disadvantages
1. Position and velocity information does degrade with time: and again, this is true stationary or airborne.
2. Equipment is far from cheap, and is difficult to maintain and service.
3. Initial alignment is simple enough in moderate latitudes when stationary, but difficult above 75° Lat and in flight.

20: Secondary Surveillance Radar

The variety of aircraft types with wide differences of speed and altitude in a crowded air demands positive identification of each aircraft for adequate safe control by ATC. Primary radar is insufficiently informative, and has the added disadvantages of clutter on the screen and a necessarily high power output for the two-way journey of the wave. Secondary radar does away with these drawbacks, but does demand the co-operation of the aircraft in that the appropriate equipment must be aboard. When such equipment must be carried in designated UK airspace is firmly and legally laid down.

A ground based transmitter/receiver triggers off a reply from an aircraft's receiver/transmitter when the correct operating procedures are followed: the reply is on a different frequency from the interrogator, this is old stuff to you. The 'interrogator' is the name for the ground equipment, the 'transponder' for that in the aircraft. The aircraft not only identifies itself positively without manoeuvres, but gives its height. On the ground, range and bearing are displayed on the screen, nice and clear, while the aircraft's height is shown either on the screen or on a veeder counter. All signals are coded; the code of the interrogation signal is called the *Mode*.

Frequency
Ground transmits on 1 030 MHz, receives on 1 090 MHz
Aircraft transmits on 1 090 MHz, receives on 1 030 MHz

Process
The method used is the transmission and reception of pulses, and it is essential to eliminate weak or spurious signals, since the coding system depends on the 'presence' or 'non-presence' of pulses. The interrogator transmits two pulses with a known spacing, and there are four Modes, each mode having a different spacing.

Mode A has pulses (always 0.85μ s wide) 8μ s apart
Mode B 17μ s apart
Mode C 21μ s apart
Mode D 25μ s apart.

Modes A and B are used for identification, Mode C for automatic height information, while Mode D is experimental. The aircraft transponder will reply to an interrogation signal provided the pilot has selected the corresponding Mode. The transponder transmits a code in reply to a correct interrogation (correct in that the aircraft equipment recognises the Mode by the time spacing between each pair of interrogation pulses), a code which is obtained by the inclusion or omission of any of up to 12 pulses.

The train of 12 pulses is contained between two framing pulses, 20.3 μ s apart, and these are always sent. Between them, the information is sent by transmitting or leaving out any of the 12. The codes available in a twelve-pulse train then are 2^{12} = 4 096, and the codes are numbered 0000 to 7777, using all numbers except those containing an 8 or 9. Pulses in the transponder are 0.45 μ s wide. A further pulse, the special identification pulse, can be transmitted when the ident button is pressed on the aircraft unit, usually at ATC's request; this pulse is 4.35 μ s after the second frame pulse, and will be automatically and continuously transmitted for about 20 seconds after pushing the button.

The Modes and codes are selected by switches on the aircraft control box: a switch for Mode, a window for code, a button for ident, and a switch for automatic height reporting. The Mode and code are pre-allotted before departure usually, or requested by ATC in flight; there are various routine selections such as Mode A, code 76 to be used in the event of radio failure, to quote an example.

Automatic Altitude Telemetering

On getting Mode C interrogations, the transponder will produce one of 4 096 codes, no matter what code is selected in the window. This code is determined by the output of an altitude digitizer mechanically linked to the altimeter; the sequence of pulses transmitted is thus entirely determined by the aircraft's height. This height is always referenced to 1 013.2 mb, quite independent of altimeter setting; the equipment will provide automatic altitude telemetering up to 128 000 ft, with a change of output every 100 ft. It seems a bit sloppy to be talking about height and altitude when reading a 1 013.2 setting on the altimeter.

Unwanted echoes

The interrogator aerial sends out a wide vertical beam and a narrow one in azimuth: the azimuth beam, though, has side lobes which could produce a transponder response, spreading the echo on the indicator tube and denying the required accuracy of range and bearing. To correct this, an omnidirectional radiation transmission is introduced, whose signal strength is greater than the strongest side lobe but less than the main beam. By fitting a circuit in the transponder for comparing the amplitude of pulses, it can be arranged not to reply to side lobe interrogations; for example, the first pulse of the Mode can be transmitted in the omnidirectional pattern, and the second in the interrogator pattern; the transponder will only reply if the interrogator pulse is equal to, or greater than, the amplitude of the omnidirectional pulse. Or, by a normal transmission of interrogator pulses with an omnidirectional pulse intervening 2 μ s after the first: the transponder will not reply if the omnidirectional pulse is greater in amplitude than the interrogator.

General

The aircraft equipment is kept on 'Standby' until required; this keeps the display on the ground clean. The range of SSR is of the order of 200 nm, and the PRF is about 250 per second. Several aircraft in an area with similar flight plans may have been allotted the same code; identification of one would be demanded by ATC, and the resultant echo on the ground display would show as a 'filling-in' of one of the echoes already showing; or ATC might of course order an aircraft to turn to another code.

Advantages

  i.   Longish range.
 ii.   No clutter, no unwanted echoes from cloud, high buildings, high ground, and so on.
iii.   Reply signals give range, bearing and height positively and automatically.
 iv.   No effort required by the pilot — well, very little anyway.
  v.   All other communication channels are left free.
 vi.   Information to ATC is instantaneous and unambiguous.
vii.   No aircraft manoeuvres required.
viii.   Little power needed.

Disadvantage is that the aircraft must carry the necessary equipment.

In UK airspace, more stringent regulations for the carriage of SSR transponders are being steadily introduced. Mode 3/A with 4 096 codes will become progressively mandatory, it would seem; and Mode C — the automatic height-reporting Mode — looks like following suit if flying above FL 100. There will be reservations, as usual, so keep an eye on those Information Circulars.

There is a standard R/T phraseology for SSR, the operative word being 'Squawk'. For example: Squawk Alpha 3 Code 76 means 'Select Mode A/3 Code 76 on your control box, and switch on transponder'. 'Squawk Ident' means 'Stay on present Mode and code, but press the Identification tit'.

APPENDICES

1: Glossary of Abbreviations

a/c	aircraft
amsl	above mean sea level
ADF	automatic direction finding equipment
ADR	advisory route
agl	above ground level
A/H	alter heading
alt or Alt	altitude
ASI	airspeed indicator
ASR	Altimeter Setting Region
ATA	actual time of arrival
ATCC	Air Traffic Control Centre
ATD	actual time of departure
AUW	all-up weight
BoT	Board of Trade
Brg	Bearing
BS	Broadcasting station
°C	degrees Celsius, hitherto called Centigrade
°(C)	degrees Compass
CA	conversion angle
CAA	Civil Aviation Authority
CAVOK	weather fine and clear
Cb	cumulo-nimbus
ch lat	change of latitude
ch long	change of longitude
CL	chart length
cm	centimetre(s)
CM	Central Meridian
C of G	centre of gravity
Comp	component
C/S or c/s	call sign
CP	critical point
cps	cycles per second
CRT	Cathode Ray Tube
CRV	Centre reading voltmeter
CW	carrier wave
DALR	dry adiabatic lapse rate
Dev	deviation
DF	direction finding
DGI	directional gyro indicator

dist	distance
DME	distance measuring equipment
DR	dead reckoning
EAS	equivalent airspeed
EAT	expected approach time
ED	Earth distance
ELR	environmental lapse rate
EMF	electro-motive force
ETA	estimated time of arrival
ETD	estimated time of departure
ETW	empty tank weight
FIR	Flight Information Region
FIS	Flight Information Service
FL	flight level
FOB	fuel on board
ft	feet
ft/min	feet per minute
°(G)	degrees Grid
gal/hr	gallons per hour
G C	Great circle
GCA	Ground Controlled Approach
GD	Greenwich date
GD	Ground distance
GMT	Greenwich Mean Time
Griv	grivation
G/S	ground speed
Hdg	Heading
HF	High frequency
HHI	horizontal hard iron
h m s	hours minutes seconds
Hmr	Homer
hr	hour(s)
ht	height
Hz	Hertz (or) cycles per second
IAS	indicated airspeed
IFR	instrument flight rules
IMC	instrument meteorological conditions
in	inch
INS	Inertial Navigation System
ISA	International Standard atmosphere
Item A	the fuel from departure point to destination only
kc/s	kilocycles per second (now obsolescent)
kg	kilogram(s)
kg/hr	kilograms per hour
kHz	kilohertz, or kilocycles per hour
km/hr	kilometres per hour
kt	knot(s)
Lat	Latitude

lb/hr	pounds per hour
Ldg wt	landing weight
LD	Local Date; also landing distance
LF	Low frequency
LMT	Local Mean Time
Long	Longitude
LRC	Long Range Cruise
M	Mach
°(M)	degrees Magnetic
Mb/mb	millibar(s)
Mc/s	megacycles per second (now obsolescent)
MF	Medium frequency
MHz	megahertz, or megacycles per second
min	minute(s)
M_{ind}	indicated Mach number
mm	millimetre(s)
MM	Middle marker
MN	Mach number, Magnetic north
mph	statute miles per hour
msl	mean sea level
M/R	Moonrise
M/S	Moonset
NDB	non-directional radio beacon
NH	Northern hemisphere
NM/nm	nautical mile(s)
NP	North Pole
OBS	omni-bearing selector
OM	outer marker
O/R	on request
P	pulse emission
PAR	Precision Approach Radar
PE	pressure error
P/L	position line
PNR	point of no return
posn	position
PP	pinpoint
PPO	prior permission only
Press Alt	pressure altitude
PRF	pulse recurrence frequency
PRP	pulse recurrence period
QDM, QDR, QFE, QFF, QNH, QNE	defined in the text,
RAS	rectified airspeed
Rel	relative
R L	Rhumb line
RMI	radio magnetic indicator
Rpm	Revolutions per minute
RVR	Runway visual range

R/W	Runway
Rx	Receiver
SALR	saturated adiabatic lapse rate
sg	specific gravity
SH	Southern hemisphere
S/H	set heading
sm	statute mile(s)
SP	South Pole
S/R	Sunrise
SRE	surveillance radar element
S/S	Sunset
SSR	Secondary Surveillance Radar
ST	Standard Time
Stn	Station
°(T)	degrees True
TAS	True airspeed
Temp	temperature
TMA	terminal control area
TMG	Track made good
TN	True North
T/O	take-off
TOC	top of climb
TOD	Top of descent, also take-off distance
TOW	take-off weight
Tr	Track
TVOR	terminal VHF omni-directional range
Tx	transmitter
UKAP	United Kingdom Aeronautical Information Publication, known as the UK Air Pilot
UHF	Ultra high frequency
μ sec	microsecond(s)
u/s	unserviceable
Var	variation
VDF	VHF direction finding
VFR	visual flight rules
VHF	very high frequency
vis	visibility
VMC	visual meteorological conditions
V_{NE}	never exceed speed
V_{NO}	normal speed
VOR	VHF omi-directional range
VSI	Vertical Soft Iron, also Vertical Speed Indicator
W/D	wind direction
Wind comp	wind component
W/E	wind effect
W/S	wind speed
wt	weight
W/V	wind velocity

2: Conversion Factors

Imp gal	<u>to</u>	litres	<u>multiply by</u> 4·546
litres		Imp gal	0·22
Imp gal		US gal	1·205
US gal		Imp gal	0·83
gal		cubic ft	0·161
cubic ft		gal	6·25
lb/sq in		kg/cm^2	0·07
lb		kg	0·454
kg		lb	2·205
ft		metres	0·3048
metres		ft	3·2808
sm		nm	0·8684
nm		sm	1·1515
sm		km	1·609
km		sm	0·621
nm		km	1·852
km		nm	0·54
in		mb	33·86
mb		in	0·0295
°C		°F	use formula $(°C \times \frac{9}{5}) + 32$
°F		°C	use formula $(°F - 32) \times \frac{5}{9}$

3: Navigation Equipment, Charts, etc

Plotting gear can be bought at a number of shops providing for draughtsmen, but is best obtained from those specialising in airmen's requirements:
Air Touring Shop, at Elstree Aerodrome, Herts, and
at Oxford Airport, Kidlington, Oxon.
Kay's of Ealing, 8 Bond Street, Ealing, W.5.
Prices are of course only a rough guide.
Dividers: buy the compass-divider type, around £1.50.
Protractor, Douglas: about £1.
Parallel Rules: if you like this sort of thing, £2.50 or so.
Rule: a 20″ one is a good investment, though any form of scale on it should be avoided; inches, especially tenths, is more practical.
Computer: varieties are legion, and prices are from £3 up. Jeppeson are good, robust, expensive. Best value, probably, is CRP5 from Air Touring Shop, plastic, hard-wearing, about £8.
Beware of moveable wind arms on the face; make sure speeds go up to at least 700 kt on the face, and the circular slide rule side includes sg and Mach among its refinements.

Maps and charts: obtainable from
Edward Stanford, Ltd, 12–14 Long Acre, London, W.C.2.
International Aeradio Ltd, Hayes Road, Southall, Mdsx.
International Aeradio (East Africa) Ltd, P.O. Box 3133, Nairobi, Kenya.
Lambert Misc 325 and Mercator GSGS 1938 are essential for the full use of this book, and they are the charts used in CPL examination.
Mercator ICAO GSGS 4943 are used in ATPL examination,
one of following:
LON – GIB – MALTA
SHANNON - KRAKOW – STOCKHOLM
and occasionally
AZORES – SW ENGLAND (PM3 GSGS 4930, NW 36/32)
Aerad charts – the useful one for this book is EUR 1/2.
Aeronautical Information Circulars are obtainable free from
Aeronautical Information Service, Tolcarne Drive, Pinner, Mdsx.
The circular on aviation charts is a handy reference; it also has a list of chart symbols.
Tables, specimen papers from any branch of HMSO, or PO Box 569, London, S.E.1.
Consol Tables, CAP 59, 4/3.
Data Sheets 33 and 34.

Specimen ATPL papers in a bound set of one complete examination.
(CPL papers are not published).

Index